JOHN CALVIN
Student of the Church Fathers

ANTHONY N. S. LANE

 Baker Books

A Division of Baker Book House Co
Grand Rapids, Michigan 49516

Published in Great Britain by T&T Clark Ltd,
59 George Street, Edinburgh EH2 2LQ, Scotland

This edition published 1999 in the USA
under license from T&T Clark Ltd by
Baker Books
a division of Baker Book House Company
PO Box 6287, Grand Rapids, MI 49516–6287

First published 1999

ISBN 0–8010–2229–0

Library of Congress Cataloging-in-Publication Data
is on file at the Library of Congress, Washington, DC

Typeset by Waverley Typesetters, Galashiels
Printed and bound in Great Britain by Bell & Bain Ltd, Glasgow

JOHN CALVIN
Student of the Church Fathers

To Philip and Gwen

Contents

Abbreviations

BAC	A. Ganoczy, *La Bibliothèque de l'Académie de Calvin. Le Catalogue de 1572 et ses Enseignements* (Geneva: Droz, 1969)
Battles	F. L. Battles (tr.), *Institutes of the Christian Religion* (Grand Rapids: H. H. Meeter Center for Calvin Studies / Eerdmans, 1986 – 2nd edition), which is a translation of the 1536 *Institutio*
BBJ	P. L. Janauschek, *Bibliographia Bernardina* (Vienna: Alfred Hölder, 1891)
BO	J. Leclercq *et al.* (eds), *Sancti Bernardi Opera* (Rome: Editiones Cistercienses, 1957–77)
CO	G. Baum, E. Cunitz and E. Reuss (eds), *Ioannis Calvini Opera Quae Supersunt Omnia* (Braunschweig and Berlin: Schwetschke, 1863–1900)
CR	C. G. Bretschneider and H. E. Bindseil (eds), *Corpus Reformatorum. Philippi Melanthonis Opera Quae Supersunt Omnia* (Braunschweig and Halle: Schwetschke, 1834–60)
CRF	A. L. Herminjard, *Correspondance des Reformateurs dans les pays de langue française* (Geneva: H. Georg and Paris: M. Levy, 1866–97)
CT	*Concilium Tridentinum. Diariorum, Actorum, Epistularum, Tractatuum Nova Collectio*, edidit Societas Goerresiana (Freiburg: Herder, 1901–76)
CTS	H. Beveridge (ed.), *Selected Works of John Calvin. Tracts* (Calvin Translation Society edition) (Grand Rapids: Baker, 1983 reprint)
ESB	J. Leclercq, 'Études sur saint Bernard et le texte de ses écrits', *Analecta Sacri Ordinis Cisterciensis* 9 (fasc. 1 & 2) 1953
IA	*Index Aureliensis. Catalogus librorum sedecimo saeculo impressorum* (Baden-Baden: Valentin Koerner *et al.*, 1965ff.)

KDE	R. J. Mooi, *Het Kerk- en Dogmahistorisch Element in de Werken van Johannes Calvijn* (Wageningen: Veenman, 1965)
LCC 20–21	J. T. McNeill and F. L. Battles (eds), *Calvin: Institutes of the Christian Religion* (Library of Christian Classics, vols 20–21) (London: SCM Press and Philadelphia: Westminster Press, 1960)
LCC 22	J. K. S. Reid (ed.), *Calvin: Theological Treatises* (Library of Christian Classics, vol. 22) (London: SCM Press and Philadelphia: Westminster Press, 1954)
OS	P. Barth *et al.* (eds), *Johannis Calvini Opera Selecta* (Munich: Chr. Kaiser, 1926–68 – 1st–3rd editions)
PG	J. P. Migne (ed.), *Patrologia Graeca Cursus Completus* ... (Paris: Migne, 1857–66)
PL	J. P. Migne (ed.), *Patrologia Latina Cursus Completus* ... (Paris: Migne, 1844–55)
RESB	J. Leclercq, *Recueil d'Études sur Saint Bernard et ses Écrits* (Rome: Storia e Letteratura, 1962–92)
SAOJC	L. Smits, *Saint Augustin dans l'oeuvre de Jean Calvin* (Assen: van Gorcum, 1956 and 1958)
WA	*D. Martin Luthers Werke. Kritische Gesamtausgabe* (Weimar: H. Böhlau, 1883–1983)

Works of Bernard[1]

Ann	*Sermo in annuntiatione domini*
Csi	*De consideratione*
Ded	*Sermo in dedicatione ecclesiae*
Div	*Sermo de diversis*
Ep	*Epistola*
Gra	*De gratia et libero arbitrio*
Mor	*Epistola de moribus et officio episcoporum*
OS	*Sermo in festivitate omnium sanctorum*
QH	*Sermo super psalmum* Qui habitat
SC	*Sermo super* Cantica Canticorum
Sent	*Sententiae*
VI p P	*Sermo in dominica sexta post pentecosten*

1 The abbreviations used in BO have been followed.

Works of Calvin[2]

Acta syn. Trid.	*Acta synodi Tridentinae. Cum antidoto*
Art. fac. Par.	*Articuli a facultate Parisiensi determinati. Cum antidoto*
Comm.	*Commentarius super*
Def. adv. calumn. Pighii	*Defensio doctrinae de servitute et liberatione humani arbitrii adversus calumnias Alberti Pighii*
Def. c. err. Serveti	*Defensio orthodoxae fidei de sacra trinitate contra prodigiosos errores Michaelis Serveti Hispani*
Def. pro Farello adv. Carolum	*Pro Farello adversus P. Caroli calumnias*
Def. sec. c. Westph.	*Secunda defensio contra Ioachimi Westphali calumnias*
De praed.	*De aeterna praedestinatione*
Diluc. explic. Heshusii	*Dilucida explicatio doctrinae ad discutiendas Heshusii nebulas*
Disc. Lausanne	*Discours au colloque de Lausanne*
Epist.	*Epistola(e)*
Grat. ad Gabr. de Saconay	*Gratulatio ad Gabrielem de Saconay*
Inst.	*Institutio Christianae Religionis*
Instr. c. Anab.	*Brieve Instruction pour armer tous bons fideles contre les erreurs de la secte commune des Anabaptistes*
Interim	*Interim adultero-germanum, cui adiecta est vera christianae pacificationis ratio*
Psychop.	*Vivere apud Christum non dormire animis sanctos, qui in fide Christi decedunt, assertio*
Psychop.	*Psychopannychia*
Resp. ad epist. Sadoleti	*Iacobi Sadoleti epistola. Ioannis Calvini responsio*
Suppl. exhort.	*Supplex exhortatio ad Caesarem et principes*
Traité Cène	*Petit Traité de la sainte Cène*
Ult. admon. ad Westph.	*Ultima admonitio ad Ioachimum Westphalum*

---

2 The abbreviations used in the new edition of *Ioannis Calvini Opera Omnia denuo recognita* (Geneva: Droz, 1992ff.) have been followed.

Introduction

In 1969 I began research on Calvin. Having majored on patristics in my undergraduate theological studies I was interested in Calvin's use of and relationship to the fathers, an interest which has remained to the present day. Out of this interest have flowed a number of works, most of which appear in the current volume.[1]

It would be quite wrong, however, to imagine that this volume is merely a collection of past papers. One of its aims is certainly to gather together in one place a number of writings on a common theme, but in every case the works have been revised and updated and in most instances the changes are substantial.[2] The different chapters have also been related to one another, with extensive cross-referencing. Finally, over the space of a quarter of a century a particular methodology has been evolved and this is the theme of the eleven theses which make up the first chapter. One aspect of that method should perhaps be mentioned here. The approach of the book might be described as *minimalism*. That is, I adopt a hermeneutic of suspicion, not acknowledging that Calvin used or was influenced by another writer without solid evidence. This approach has been developed in response to the studies of other scholars who have adopted a maximalist approach, claiming use and influence on the basis of little or no evidence. The rigour of the present approach is needed in order to correct these studies, but at the same time it must be remembered that Calvin will certainly have read and have been influenced by more

---

1 For details, cf. chapter 10, below. Those not in this volume are: 'Bernard of Clairvaux: A Forerunner of John Calvin?' in J. R. Sommerfeldt (ed.), *Bernardus Magister* (Kalamazoo (MI): Cistercian Publications, 1992) 533–45; 'Saint Bernard et Calvin' in J. Leclercq, R. Genton and A. N. S. Lane, *Saint Bernard de Clairvaux* (Écublens: Église et Liturgie, 1994) 25–38; *Calvin and Bernard of Clairvaux* (Studies in Reformed Theology and History New Series no. 1) (Princeton: Princeton Theological Seminary, 1996). The publication of this volume should not be interpreted as a promise to cease writing on the theme. A new paper entitled 'Tertullianus totus noster? Calvin's Use of Tertullian' is likely to appear in *Auctoritas Patrum III*.
2 A note at the beginning of each chapter indicates where it originally appeared and the nature of the revision. With two of the chapters significant errors were introduced into the original versions by the editors and the opportunity has been taken to rectify these.

people than the surviving evidence indicates. This reservation should not, however, to be taken as a charter for unwarranted claims based on flimsy or non-existent evidence.

The first chapter, which has never before appeared in print, sets out the methodology adopted in the rest of the book. This is of relevance not just for Calvin studies but also for similar studies of other contemporary figures. The second chapter, on Calvin's use of the fathers and medievals in general, offers a broad and comprehensive study of the topic as a whole. This has been very substantially revised since 1981 and its length has increased by over a third. The third chapter is new to this volume. It focuses on the Greek fathers and, in particular, on the extent of Calvin's *knowledge* of them, a topic on which some extravagant claims have been made and are here examined. The fourth chapter, on Calvin's use of Bernard, is a lightly revised and slightly expanded version of a earlier piece.[3] The fifth chapter, on Calvin's sources of Bernard, is a substantial revision of an article that was written twenty-five years ago. It is almost half as long again as the original and is based upon a significantly wider survey of potential sources. The sixth chapter, on Calvin's use of the fathers in his *Bondage and Liberation of the Will*, and the seventh chapter, on the influence upon Calvin of his debate with Pighius, are lightly revised versions of recent papers. The eighth chapter, examining whether Calvin made use of a particular anthology is a lightly revised version of a recent article. Its detailed conclusions are largely superseded by the following chapter but it has been retained because of its significance for the question of *method*. The ninth chapter, on the sources of the citations in Calvin's Genesis commentary, is the revision of an article that was written little more than a year ago, but the revision is fairly substantial. The tenth chapter is an attempt at an exhaustive bibliography of secondary literature on the topic since 1800. This appeared initially as an Appendix to an article in 1981 and now contains almost three times as many items, both because of the intervening years and because many omissions have been rectified. It will contain some recent items added at the proof stage which therefore will not have received attention in the other chapters. Because the different chapters are on related topics there are rare instances when some sentences or a paragraph are repeated. This happens only where, in my judgment, repetition will be more helpful for the reader than cross-references in a footnote.

One word that recurs throughout the book is 'citation' and it may be helpful to offer a definition at the outset.[4] By a citation is meant a quotation of, a paraphrase of or a clear reference to an author or (a portion of) a work. There must be explicit mention of the author or the work or else some objective proof that Calvin had them in mind.[5] Unacknowledged allusions do not count since identifying these reflects the areas of competence of Calvin's editors (to say nothing of their imaginative powers) more than Calvin's own usage. In this context the reader should be warned

---

3 It is also a convenient summary of much of Lane, *Calvin and Bernard*.
4 Cf. A. N. S. Lane, 'Calvin's Use of the Fathers and the Medievals', *Calvin Theological Journal* 16 (1981) 201.
5 For an example, cf. on c.XXXI in chapter 4, below, section III.

about the indexes to the McNeill / Battles translation of the *Institutes*. These are indexes to the notes of this edition, not to Calvin's text. Thomas Aquinas, for example, occupies almost three columns in the index, but is mentioned by Calvin just twice.[6] Also no distinction is made in the body of the text between Calvin's own biblical and patristic references and those of the editors. The biblical references in the text may or may not go back to Calvin and some of Calvin's own references are dropped. Calvin's marginal patristic references are usually (but not always) found in the footnotes, but these notes make no distinction between the references given by Calvin and those of the editors. In short, this edition is highly misleading as an indicator of which biblical and patristic passages Calvin himself cited.

Scholarship is not a solo activity and over the decades I have benefited immensely from the help and encouragement of others, not all of whom are named here.[7] T. H. L. Parker, my supervisor, has been an ongoing source of encouragement and guidance. During my student years I spent a summer on the Continent when I received hospitality and help from many, especially Heiko Oberman, Rodolphe Peter and Peter Fraenkel. Irena Backus shares similar interests and I have benefited much over the years from her wide learning. I have not needed to travel during the preparation of this book and that is due especially to the three visits that I have paid over the years to the Meeter Center at Grand Rapids, to the long-suffering photocopier there and to the generous assistance of Rick Gamble and the late Peter de Klerk. It is also due to the invaluable proximity of the British Library, the Bodleian Library and the Cambridge University Library (not to mention the college libraries) with their extensive collections of sixteenth-century works. I would especially like to thank the staff of the Rare Books Reading Room in the CUL for their helpful service and their unfailing patience (on this as on other occasions) with my need to consult a number of large, multi-volume sets. Last, but by no means least, I would like to thank David Wright for his friendship and for the very generous way in which he has taken time to answer queries and give advice. Calvin's influences may be elusive but here is one influence upon me that I gladly acknowledge.

This volume would not have been possible without the pioneering studies of Luchesius Smits and R. J. Mooi. The value of their works is seen best from the glaring shortcomings of those writers who have chosen to ignore them. In a number of places in the following pages I question their conclusions on specific points, but this should not mask the fact that in many ways they laid the foundations on which these studies are built. I am grateful to them both for their hospitality on the one occasion that we met in 1971 and for their continuous help through the medium of their writings.

---

6 Cf. LCC 21:1626f.; *Inst.* 2:2:4, 3:22:9.
7 Others are named at the beginning of chapters 9 and 10, below, and in the body of some chapters.

1

❧❧❧

Calvin's Use of the Fathers:
Eleven Theses

The studies collected in the present volume tackle a variety of questions, yet underlying them is a particular methodology, which is summed up in the following theses. The ensuing chapters unfold the theme of the theses while the theses in turn encapsulate the method of the chapters.

THESIS I: *Calvin's citations of the fathers are not to be confused with modern footnotes and must not be used uncritically to establish sources.*

This first thesis might appear too obvious to need stating, but it is foundational for most of what follows. No one would today be so naive as to assert that patristic citations in the sixteenth century correspond precisely to modern footnotes. But there is at times enough similarity between the two to lead the unwary astray. Often Calvin will quote or paraphrase one of the fathers and then give the source. This activity is in some respects not unlike the modern footnote. But there are important differences.

First, sixteenth-century writers, unlike modern scholars, were under no obligation to document their sources. They do so when it suits them, especially when citing authorities such as the Bible or the fathers. But at other times they may totally fail to name major sources. The fact that a sixteenth-century author may very diligently and accurately name some sources does not preclude the likelihood that he may elsewhere be guilty of what *today* would be called gross plagiarism.

Secondly, one cannot assume that they had read, or indeed ever set eyes upon, all of the sources that they name. A sixteenth-century author who came across a useful patristic quotation, complete with reference, in another writer felt free to use the quotation and the reference without verifying either and without acknowledging the intermediate source. So while Calvin's references are very useful for the modern scholar, they must not be taken uncritically to indicate what he had read.

With the fathers Calvin's references must be used with caution and not taken uncritically as an indication of sources. With the late Middle Ages

1

the problem is different. Calvin almost never names late-medieval theologians or theological schools.[1] Instead he uses terms like 'sophists' and 'scholastics'. It is for this reason especially that there has been such uncertainty about the alleged dependence of Calvin upon John Major. The fact that Calvin never names Major is not itself a proof that he was not dependent upon him. As Alister McGrath has put it, 'Why should Calvin wish to, or need to, make any sort of reference to *any* late medieval theologian, let alone one as obscure as Major, in the 1536 edition of the *Institutio?*'[2]

Clearly Calvin must have been influenced at least to some extent by one or more strands of late-medieval tradition. Unfortunately he tells us next to nothing about this, because it did not suit his purposes. 'At no point is it necessary, or even useful, for Calvin to engage in debate with any representatives of late medieval religious thought – and to suggest that this silence reflects an absence of familiarity with such sources, or that it indicates that Calvin has not been influenced by them to any significant extent, is simply a *non sequitur.*'[3]

With Calvin's own contemporaries the problem is similar. These are named more often, especially where Calvin writes treatises against specific people. But he shows next to no concern to indicate which figures have most influenced him. To give one example, the fact that Bucer is very rarely mentioned in no way weakens the argument that Bucer deeply influenced Calvin. Sixteenth-century authors were under no obligation to document their sources or to indicate which figures had most influenced them.

Calvin's Genesis commentary illustrates this. Luther is named five times, but Calvin elsewhere states that he has abstained from naming him more than a hundred times.[4] My own examination of the sources of the commentary confirms the truth of this claim.[5] In the same commentary Calvin refers once, disparagingly, to a contemporary Roman Catholic bishop, Augustinus Eugubinus Steuchus. Tracing the source of this one reference led me to a work of Steuchus that had previously been overlooked by scholars.[6] Further examination of Calvin's other citations revealed that this work is in fact Calvin's second most important source, after Luther.[7]

If Calvin's references are not to be mistaken for footnotes and are an unreliable indicator of his actual sources, how can we trace them? The task is not impossible, but a critical methodology is called for. That is the theme of these theses.

---

1 For details, cf. chapter 2, section XI, below.
2 A. E. McGrath, *The Intellectual Origins of the European Reformation* (Oxford: Blackwell, 1987) 102.
3 McGrath, *Intellectual Origins*, 103.
4 CO 9:54 (*Def. sec. c. Westph.*).
5 Chapter 9, below, especially sections IX and X.
6 A. E. Steuchus, *Recognitio Veteris Testamenti ad Hebraicum Veritatem* (Lyons: S. Gryphius, 1531). Calvin mentions Steuchus just two other times: in his 1545 *Def. pro Farello adv. Carolum* he alludes to Caroli's use of Steuchus (CO 7:322); in *Inst.* 4:11:12 (1559) he refers to Steuchus's defence of the *Donatio Constantini*.
7 Chapter 9, below, especially sections IX and X.

THESIS II: *Calvin's use of the fathers (especially in the* **Institutio** *and in the treatises) is primarily a polemical appeal to authorities.*

If Calvin's patristic citations are not to be viewed as the equivalent of footnotes, what are they? Calvin cites the fathers primarily as witnesses for the defence, as authorities to which to appeal.[8] For this reason, there are vastly more references in Calvin's writings to the fathers than to late-medieval or sixteenth-century figures. But even here it must be remembered that Calvin is not primarily documenting his work (as would a modern scholar) nor declaring influences. He is calling witnesses and he may choose to cite an important authority which he knows only second-hand while ignoring his immediate source. This is seen from the way in which Calvin, when opposing Pighius, expounds patristic writings on the basis either of Pighius's own work or on the basis of Augustine's *Retractationes*. In this work in particular, and doubtless in others as well, Calvin skilfully gives the impression of having consulted a wide range of fathers (sixty-four different works) while probably making use of no more than ten volumes.[9]

The polemical appeal to authorities accounts for most, but not all, of Calvin's use of the fathers. He also, less often, criticizes them – especially where a patristic view has been cited against him and he is unable to interpret the father satisfactorily.[10] He also sometimes cites them for literary reasons, because they have stated something elegantly.[11]

THESIS III: *In his commentaries, by contrast, Calvin is less interested in authorities but instead debates with other interpreters.*

In 1981 I stated, in the context of the *Institutio*, that 'if Calvin had arrived at a profound theological understanding through one of the early fathers we could legitimately expect this to manifest itself in his use of that father'.[12] This has been misunderstood to imply that the same principle should apply to the commentaries.[13] These contain some dogmatic material, where the use of the fathers is likely to be polemical. But on exegetical matters Calvin cites others more often to disagree with them. Where

---

8 Chapter 2, below, section IV; chapter 4, below, section II.b; chapter 6, below, section IV.

9 Chapter 6, below, section II.d.

10 It should also be remembered that he agrees with the fathers less than a study of his citations would lead one to believe. Because of the polemical context Calvin more often than not cites the fathers when they agree with him and ignores them when they do not. In a revealing comment on 1 Corinthians 3:15, Calvin states that fathers such as Cyprian, Ambrose and even Augustine aimed to build on Christ but 'often' turned away from the right way of building. Cf. chapter 4, below, at nn. 88–92.

11 Chapter 2, below, at n. 122; chapter 4, below, at nn. 82f.

12 'Calvin's Use of the Fathers and the Medievals', *Calvin Theological Journal* 16 (1981) 151.

13 In fact the article explicitly denies this, in the discussion of the commentaries some pages later (ibid., 164f.).

exegesis is concerned Calvin is less interested in citing authorities (as in the *Institutio* and the polemical treatises) and more interested in dialogue partners.

In the Genesis commentary, for example, of the forty-five patristic citations, twenty are approving, twenty-two disapproving and three neutral.[14] The exegetical citations are significantly more disapproving than approving (seventeen against eleven), while the theological citations are more approving (nine against five). In particular, the fathers are six times criticized for allegorizing, although Ambrose is once praised for his allegory, when it leads him to teach about justification.

THESIS IV: *In the commentaries a negative comment may be a mark of respect and may serve as a pointer to Calvin's sources.*

What of the works on which we know Calvin to have relied for his Genesis commentary? Luther is mentioned five times: once approvingly, twice disapprovingly and twice with qualified approval. Steuchus is mentioned once only, disapprovingly. Augustine's *Quaestiones in Heptateuchum* is mentioned five times, three times disapprovingly. Jerome's *Hebraicae quaestiones in libro Geneseos* is mentioned three times, each time disapprovingly. The disapproving remarks should be understood as marks of respect, much as a modern commentator may feel the need to justify departure from the stance of a respected precursor.

The patristic citations in Calvin's commentaries must be read with critical discernment. With the Genesis commentary, thirty-five out of forty-five have no significance for Calvin's exegetical sources.[15] Thirteen of these are drawn from his earlier works and a further fourteen probably draw on his memory of earlier reading, even if he may have needed to refer back to the original in some instances. Seven are derived from intermediate sources and one, which is inaccurate, is of uncertain origin. Of the remaining ten, nine were probably read during the preparation of the commentary and one was drawn from Calvin's current reading. It is only by a careful investigation of sources that one can ascertain which citations reflect Calvin's direct reading. It would be easy to interpret the citation of Chrysostom as an indicator that Calvin read him for the commentary, but that is contradicted by the evidence.[16] It would be easy to deduce from Calvin's references to the Septuagint and to Jerome's *Liber de situ et nominibus locorum hebraicorum* that he read these for himself, but he appears to be relying upon Steuchus's *Recognitio* for this material.[17] By contrast the single, negative, comment about Steuchus masks the fact that his *Recognitio* is one of the two major sources for the commentary.

14 For this paragraph cf. chapter 9, at nn. 137f.
15 For this paragraph cf. chapter 9, at nn. 133–36.
16 Cf. chapter 9, at nn. 114–25.
17 Cf. chapter 9, section III.a and at n. 97.

THESIS V: *In seeking to determine which works Calvin actually
read, one must take into account factors like the
availability of texts and the pressures of time.*

Calvin did not always have access to good libraries. Basel and Strassburg
were leading centres of humanist scholarship and while he was in these
cities Calvin would have had access to the fruits of this scholarship. But
even then it does not follow that Calvin possessed many books of his own
and after 1536 he never enjoyed the leisure of a professional scholar. This
means that if he did not have ready access to a particular volume he
was likely not to make any use of it. Geneva was not noted for humanistic
scholarship. For much of his time at Geneva Calvin was probably largely
dependent upon his own personal collection of books. Thus when
examining Calvin's use of the fathers and his knowledge of them one must
not fall into the trap of (subconsciously) assuming that a complete set of
Migne's *Patrologia* was always close at hand.

Availability of texts is a key to understanding Calvin's use of Bernard.
Significant new Bernardine material appears in Calvin's writings in two
stages: in the 1543 *Institutio* and from 1554, especially in the 1559 *Institutio*.[18]
The 1543 citations are clearly the fruit of Calvin's reading of Bernard while
at Strassburg, from 1539 to 1541. The volume that he there used does not
appear to have found a place in his luggage as he returned to Geneva and
there is an interval until 1554 when he begins to cite new Bernardine
material.[19] The appearance of this new material is simply explained by the
publication of a new edition of Bernard in 1552 at Basel.[20] The internal
evidence of Calvin's writings coincides with the external evidence of the
availability of texts.

If lack of resources was a constraint, shortage of time was an even
more important factor. Calvin complained about this in his *Bondage and
Liberation of the Will* and a consideration of his circumstances at the time
bears out his complaint.[21] If anything the situation was worse when he
wrote his Genesis commentary.[22] These two works are mentioned as
special studies have been made of Calvin's use of the fathers there in
particular, but, of course, the time pressures in 1542–43 and 1550–54 were
not markedly different from other times. Time pressure can explain errors
in Calvin's patristic citations.[23]

Another factor to be considered is the 1572 catalogue of the library of
Calvin's Academy in Geneva. Some of the books in this catalogue were
Calvin's. Unfortunately, because he rarely marked his books, very few

---

18 Chapter 4, below, section II.a.
19 From 1543 to 1547 he mainly recycles earlier quotations. *The Bondage and Liberation
    of the Will* contains four brief citations which reflect no more than past reading.
    There are also two new quotations in 1544/45 which are probably dependent upon
    an edition of Bernard's sermons. Cf. chapter 4, below, section II.a; chapter 5, below,
    especially at nn. 34–37; A. N. S. Lane, *Calvin and Bernard of Clairvaux* (Princeton:
    Princeton Theological Seminary, 1996) 16–18.
20 Chapter 4, below, section II.a; chapter 5, below, especially at nn. 83–86.
21 Chapter 6, below, at nn. 5–7.
22 Chapter 9, below, n. 13.
23 For two clear examples, cf. chapter 9, below, at nn. 106–10.

can definitively be identified as his, although some can be traced to Peter Martyr or others. Many of the remainder are potentially Calvin's and if there are reasons for supposing that Calvin might have used a particular edition, its presence in the catalogue is a useful additional piece of evidence. The likelihood that Calvin used the 1552 Basel edition of Bernard is strengthened by the fact that a copy of this edition, which *may* have been Calvin's, is found in the catalogue.[24] On the other hand the presence in the catalogue of the 1534–35 edition of Münster's *Hebraica Biblia* proves nothing as this is a work that would have been owned by many different people and there is no reason to suppose that the library copy was Calvin's.

THESIS VI: *A hermeneutic of suspicion is appropriate in determining which works Calvin actually consulted.*

As a writer Calvin was very skilled at reading the minimum and making the maximum use of it. He could produce works which apparently reflect a wide range of reading while having actually (at least at the time) read relatively little.[25] He could and did cite and discuss works which he had not read. There are various ways in which this happened. Where an opponent cited passages against him Calvin was capable of responding even when he did not have the original to hand or when he did not have the time or inclination to turn to it. This can be seen from his *Bondage and Liberation of the Will* where he discusses passages cited by Pighius without turning to them, either by relying on what Pighius has quoted or by relying on Augustine's own comments on his earlier writings found in his *Retractationes*. Other passages that he cites are taken from the 1539 *Institutio*, with no indication that Calvin has turned to them again. There are at least three further ways in which Calvin can cite works without actually turning to them. He can cite from memory of earlier reading, he can recycle citations from his own earlier works and he can borrow citations from other unnamed works.

Given the limited availability of texts, given Calvin's chronic shortage of time, given the fact that on occasions he is demonstrably citing works with-out turning to them, Calvin's use of the fathers must be approached with a hermeneutic of suspicion. That is, one should not assume from the mere citation of an author or a work that Calvin has first-hand acquaintance of it or that he has consulted the author or work on this particular occasion. He was highly skilled in making the maximum use of minimal resources. He knew how to borrow quotations from others. He knew how to discuss texts without actually consulting them. His memory was such that he could introduce citations on the basis of earlier remembered reading.[26]

A good example of the application of this hermeneutic of suspicion is found in Calvin's Genesis commentary. Twelve times Calvin refers to the Septuagint. This might appear to be clear proof that he used it. It transpires however that all twelve citations are also found in Steuchus's *Recognitio*,

---

24 A. Ganoczy, BAC 188.
25 Cf. chapter 6, below, section II.d; chapter 9, below, section X.
26 For the last two paragraphs, cf. chapter 6, below, section II.a, c. Other examples will be found in chapter 9, below.

which Calvin certainly used. Furthermore, Steuchus has not only the text of the Septuagint but also every comment that Calvin makes about the text. This does not *prove* that Calvin did not use the Septuagint for the commentary, but it is remarkable to say the least that he failed to refer to any passage or express any opinion that was not to be found in Steuchus.[27]

THESIS VII: *Caution must be exercised before claiming that Calvin used any particular intermediate source.*

The previous two theses have warned against an uncritical assumption that Calvin actually consulted all that he cites. But the method of suspicion can itself become uncritical. On what basis can we claim that Calvin used an intermediate source? The fact that a patristic quotation is found in a possible intermediate source, such as an anthology or some other earlier work, does not prove that Calvin found it there.[28] Some passages were very widely quoted in the sixteenth century. A classic example is Bernard's first sermon on the Annunciation, which was one of the most quoted Bernardine passages at that time, if not the most. Calvin quotes two passages from the sermon. He quotes from the same parts of the sermon as others, but his quotation is not fully covered by anyone else's. While his appeal to Bernard here may have been influenced by others, in the last resort it was his own personal interpretation and not a copy of other people's Bernard dossier.[29]

There are instances where one may with some confidence assume the use of an intermediate source. In writing his *Bondage and Liberation of the Will* Calvin had before him both his own 1539 *Institutio* and Pighius's attack on that in his *De libero arbitrio*. Clearly these works are to be seen as sources of Calvin's work. Again, if it is definite that Calvin used a contemporary work at a particular point, this is a clear potential intermediate source.[30] Having established that Calvin used Luther's commentary and Steuchus's *Recognitio* for his Genesis commentary, we can justly assume that citations found in these works are likely to have been derived from them.

Another indication that Calvin might be using an intermediate source is the juxtaposition of citations. Calvin's first Bernardine citation is his definition of *liberum arbitrium*, placed in a list of six definitions. A number of earlier sources link three of these definitions. It is hardly coincidental that Calvin has juxtaposed the same three definitions and it is highly likely that he is dependent upon the tradition,[31] but caution is needed. It would have been easy to locate just one of these earlier sources and to assume that Calvin was dependent upon it. But there is a tradition here and care is needed before claiming that Calvin sampled the tradition at one point

27 Chapter 9, below, section III.a.
28 Cf. chapter 5, below, sections IV and V, for an examination of whether Calvin's Bernardine citations might be drawn either from anthologies or from other authors.
29 Chapter 5, below, at nn. 175–94.
30 Hence the importance of seeking Calvin's contemporary sources *before* going on to consider other sources. Cf. chapter 9, below, section II at the beginning.
31 Cf. chapter 5, below, at nn. 151–53.

rather than another. Maybe there is yet another source that I have yet to find which combines all six of the definitions.

The issues involved in tracing intermediate sources can be seen from the question of Calvin's possible use of Lippoman's *Catena in Genesim*. There was a strong *prima facie* case for thinking that Calvin did use this anthology,[32] but a more careful and critical examination indicates that he almost certainly did not.[33]

THESIS VIII: *A critical approach is necessary to determine which authors influenced Calvin, even where Calvin cites them extensively.*

The mere existence of parallels and similarities between two authors is of itself no proof of the influence of one upon the other. Suppose we can demonstrate very close parallels between the thought of writer A and an earlier writer B. This is not enough even to prove that A knew of the existence of B. There are a number of possibilities. A might be dependent upon B. But, equally, both might be dependent upon an earlier writer, C. Or the points in common might turn out to be the commonplaces of a particular theological tradition, so that no one writer can be singled out as A's source. Alternatively, A might have encountered B's thoughts through an intermediate writer D. Doubtless this does not exhaust the range of possibilities. The existence of very close parallels between two writers does not prove a relationship of dependence, even if one knew the other.

Karl Reuter has argued that Bernard of Clairvaux deeply influenced the early Calvin and also that it was the Scottish theologian John Major who at Paris introduced Calvin to Bernard and to other medieval theologians. Reuter's thesis has been attacked on a number of grounds. It is far from certain that Calvin and Major were even at Paris at the same time. For our present purposes one serious weakness in Reuter's case should be noted. He relies very heavily upon alleged similarities between Calvin and Bernard and all but totally ignores Calvin's explicit citations of Bernard.[34]

T. F. Torrance has also argued that John Major was a formative influence upon Calvin. His case also rests largely on alleged parallels, which turn out not to be particularly distinctive. Arguments like this prove nothing. They certainly do not prove that Calvin had any first-hand knowledge of Major, for which convincing evidence has yet to be found. Even if Calvin was exposed to Major, mere parallels between their thought would not prove that Calvin had derived these particular points from Major rather than some other source. A more measured assessment of the role of Major has come from Alister McGrath, who argues for the influence upon Calvin, while at Montaigu, not of any particular individual but of the *via moderna* and the *schola Augustiniana moderna*. The hypothesis of personal contact

---

32 Cf. A. N. S. Lane, 'Calvin's Sources of St. Bernard', *Archiv für Reformationsgeschichte* 67 (1976) 273.
33 Chapter 8, below.
34 Cf. chapter 2, below, section II; chapter 4, below, section I.

with Major in particular McGrath sees as an unnecessary subsidiary hypothesis.[35]

Another mistaken use of parallels is to use them to demonstrate sources of a commentary. How should one determine the sources of Calvin's Genesis commentary, say? One way would be to look at earlier commentaries and to see whose exegesis Calvin follows. This method is fraught with problems. First, to do it properly one would need to examine at the very least a wide range of substantial passages from Genesis, not just a few isolated passages. Secondly, one would need to examine all of the significant commentators available to Calvin. Otherwise what one might think is a significant parallel might turn out to be a commonplace of the exegetical tradition.[36] For this reason, an examination of Calvin's citations, where by definition he is referring to someone else, is a more reliable point of entry into the subject.[37]

Seeking parallels between Calvin and earlier writers is a precarious way of establishing influence and dependence. This remains true even where Calvin cites an author repeatedly and obviously has a profound knowledge of his writings. In 1926 Joachim Beckmann showed the close parallels between Calvin's and Augustine's teaching on the sacraments and concluded that the latter was the former's prime source.[38] But this was to confuse parallels with influence. Calvin cited Augustine repeatedly because Augustine was an authority acknowledged by his opponents. He had no reason to cite Bucer, say.

There are ways in which influence can be assessed. Where Calvin cites an author frequently it is possible to analyse his citations to see if there is any evidence of influence.[39] Analysis of Calvin's *Bondage and Liberation of the Will* and comparison with earlier and later editions of the *Institutio* reveals the extent of the influence upon Calvin of his debate with Pighius and the writings expounded in that debate.[40]

THESIS IX: *While Calvin's explicit use of a father does not exhaust his knowledge of that father, it does indicate the kind of knowledge that he had and claims about who influenced Calvin should cohere with this evidence.*

One cannot argue that Calvin knows no more of a writer than he quotes. Torrance sounds an important warning here regarding Calvin's knowledge of figures such as Bernard: 'Calvin's indebtedness to their thought cannot be measured simply by the passages where they are mentioned by name, for Calvin's language is often saturated with that of others in such a way that it is clear that they affected him deeply in his early formative years when he was acquiring his primary instruments of thought and speech.'[41] The identification of Calvin's sources by finding

35 Cf. chapter 2, below, section II.
36 Cf. chapter 9, below, at nn. 124f.
37 Cf. chapter 9, below, section I.
38 J. Beckmann, *Vom Sakrament bei Calvin* (Tübingen: J. C. B. Mohr, 1926).
39 This method is pursued with Bernard in Lane, *Calvin and Bernard*, chapter 4.
40 Cf. chapter 7, below.
41 T. F. Torrance, *The Hermeneutics of John Calvin* (Edinburgh: Scottish Academic Press, 1988) 81.

linguistic parallels is if anything even more precarious than the use of alleged parallels of thought.[42] But Torrance is certainly right to maintain that Calvin's knowledge of a writer is not to be *limited* to his use of him.

But without some objective control discussions of influence can degenerate to a subjective search for parallels. The results of such an approach may sometimes be true, but that would be more by luck than by soundness of method. With the fathers we are helped by Calvin's readiness to cite them. With later authors, such as late medievals or Calvin's contemporaries the task is much harder, but must be based on more than the search for parallels.

A good example of this is the claims made by Torrance that Calvin was in important respects influenced much more heavily by the Greek fathers than by Augustine and that he was influenced in particular by Athanasius and Gregory Nazianzen.[43] If one wishes to claim that Calvin was influenced by Athanasius, one should not neglect to study his explicit use of Athanasius. In his citations Calvin betrays a minimal knowledge of Athanasius – so slight in fact that one can plausibly argue that he knew about Athanasius from church histories and the like but that he had not in fact read Athanasius at all. It would be too much dogmatically to affirm that Calvin had never read Athanasius, but one can certainly ask why it is that if Athanasius had significantly influenced him this should have left no mark whatsoever on his citations.[44]

Karl Reuter claimed that Bernard influenced Calvin especially in the 1536 and 1539 editions of his *Institutio*. But Calvin's explicit use of Bernard does not begin until 1539 and in that year it is still minimal and inaccurate. It would be wrong to suggest that Calvin knew no more of Bernard than is indicated by the four citations of that year. But it is not wrong to turn to the citations to see *what sort of* knowledge of Bernard Calvin had in 1539.[45] Those who wish to allege that Calvin was deeply influenced by Bernard in 1536 and 1539 have got to explain why he at that stage manifests a minimal and inaccurate knowledge of Bernard in his writings. The search for Calvin's sources cannot be limited to an examination of his explicit citations, but it should start there and should cohere with the evidence of these explicit citations.

THESIS X: *A critical examination of Calvin's use of the fathers, and especially of his literary citations, can provide pointers to which works he was reading at a particular time.*

In his 1543 *Bondage and Liberation of the Will* Calvin cites many fathers in opposition to Pighius. Most of the works discussed had been introduced into the debate either in the 1539 *Institutio* or in Pighius's *De libero arbitrio* or else came from an intermediary source used by Calvin (such as a work

---

42 Cf. chapter 4, below, n. 50.
43 Cf. chapter 3, below, sections I, III.c, e.
44 Chapter 3, below, section III.c.
45 For a full discussion of this, cf. chapter 4, below, section I; Lane, *Calvin and Bernard*, 8–15.

of Augustine). Others were obvious works (like Augustine's anti-Pelagian works) or appear to reflect Calvin's earlier reading. There are two note-worthy exceptions. Calvin repeatedly cites the decrees of African councils and of the Second Council of Orange. Calvin's citations of these councils are introduced entirely in 1543, apart from three exceptions in 1541, 1544 and 1547. It would appear that Calvin had acquired a copy of Peter Crabbe's 1538 *Concilia omnia* and read it in the next few years. Calvin also introduces two citations from Basil into the debate. One is predictable, from (pseudo-)Basil's *De libero arbitrio*. The other is less predictable, a quotation from Basil's *Homiliae in Psalmos* which contributes little to the argument. Why is this introduced? The answer would appear to be that Calvin had recently acquired the 1540 Cornarius translation and was at that time reading it.[46]

Calvin's Bernardine citations resume after an interval in 1554, probably reflecting his acquisition of the 1552 Basel edition.[47] That Calvin was reading Bernard during these years is confirmed by the fact that from 1554 to 1559, and not before, we have quotations from Bernard which have no discernible apologetic motive but rather reflect an appreciation of his literary style.[48]

Such a critical method can be applied more widely. It is important to look not just at the authors, works and passages cited. One needs to probe more deeply, to look for citations with no obvious polemical motivation, to look for the use of authors or works not previously cited and to correlate this with the availability of new editions. Wider application of such an approach could enable the compilation of a tentative and very partial list of which volumes and works Calvin read and *when*.

THESIS XI: *A careful and critical reading of the evidence can lead to tentative or firm conclusions about which specific editions Calvin used.*

The editions of Chrysostom and of the early church councils used by Calvin have been known for some time. Even the limited range of studies in the present volume has yielded significant further conclusions about which editions Calvin used at specific times.[49] For convenience these are listed here:

Ambrose: for *The Bondage and Liberation of the Will* Calvin used either the 1529 Claude Chevallon or the (identical) 1539 Gervase Chevallon Paris edition of the *Opera omnia*.[50]

46 Chapter 6, below, section III.
47 Cf. n. 20, above.
48 Chapter 4, below, at nn. 82f.
49 Where there is evidence that Calvin used a specific edition at a certain stage after his return to Geneva it is fairly safe to assume that he continued to use that edition. It cannot be assumed that he used a specific edition earlier than the evidence indicates and it certainly cannot be assumed without evidence that he used the same editions in Strassburg as in Geneva.
    For conclusions about non-patristic editions used by Calvin, cf. chapter 9, below, section X.
50 Cf. chapter 6, below, at nn. 94–98.

Augustine: for *The Bondage and Liberation of the Will* Calvin used a Paris edition of the *Opera omnia*, either that of Claude Chevallon (1531/32) or that of Yolande Bonhomme and Charlotte Guillard (1541).[51]

Basil: for *The Bondage and Liberation of the Will* Calvin used Janus Cornarius's translation of the *Opera omnia*, published in 1540 at Basel by Froben. [52]

Bernard: from 1554 or earlier Calvin used Hervagius's 1552 Basel edition of the *Opera omnia*.[53]

Chrysostom: Calvin possessed and marked Claude Chevallon's 1536 Paris edition of the *Opera omnia*.[54]

Pseudo-Clement: Calvin used, for the debates with Servetus, Johann Bebel's 1526 Basel edition. [55]

Councils: Calvin used, in the early 1540s, Peter Crabbe's two-volume *Concilia omnia*, published by Peter Quentel at Cologne in 1538.[56]

Irenaeus: Calvin used, for the debates with Servetus, Froben's 1528 Basel edition.[57]

Justin Martyr: Calvin used, for the debates with Servetus, Robert Stephanus's 1551 Paris edition of the Greek text.[58]

Tertullian: Calvin used, for the debates with Servetus, Froben's 1528 Basel edition of the *Opera omnia*.[59]

These conclusions have been drawn from a wide range of evidence: documentary evidence, specific copies, references to page and line numbers, the dates at which Calvin introduces material, availability of editions, which translation is followed and which editions are found in the 1572 Genevan catalogue. But a careful and critical reading of the evidence is essential as there are pitfalls for the unwary. In particular, it is dangerous to rely upon just one piece of evidence and those results are the most secure which are supported by a number of different indicators.

Four examples will illustrate the dangers.[60] Calvin asked to keep just one volume from Olivétan's library – a Rabbinic Bible. This might appear to be solid evidence that Calvin was competent in rabbinic Hebrew and

---

51 Cf. chapter 6, below, section II.b.
52 Cf. chapter 6, below, at n. 93.
53 Cf. chapter 5, below, especially at nn. 83–86.
54 Ganoczy, BAC 182; A. Ganoczy and K. Müller, *Calvins Handschriftliche Annotationen zu Chrysostomus* (Wiesbaden: Franz Steiner, 1981).
55 Cf. chapter 3, below, section III.a.
56 Cf. chapter 6, below, at nn. 114f.
57 Cf. chapter 3, below, section III.b.
58 R. H. Bainton, *Hunted Heretic. The Life and Death of Michael Servetus, 1511–1553* (Boston: Beacon Press, 1964 – 2nd edition) 187f., based on the page reference in CO 8:759. I have verified that this edition fits the data and there do not appear to be any other potential editions. This edition is found in the 1572 Genevan library catalogue but is, unfortunately, Peter Martyr's copy (A. Ganoczy, BAC 167).
59 Cf. chapter 6, below, at nn. 126–30.
60 For those who have simply asserted which editions Calvin used, without any evidence, cf. chapter 2, below, n. 267; chapter 3, below, at n. 112; Torrance, *Hermeneutics of Calvin*, 184, n. 128.

read the rabbis for himself, but other evidence points in a different direction.[61] François Baudouin wrote to Calvin announcing that he had tried unsuccessfully to send him a copy of the 1544 Greek edition of Eusebius.[62] Maybe he did send it at a later date, but the evidence is that Calvin continued to use the Latin translation.[63] Another volume that Baudouin had failed to send was the 1545 edition of Tertullian's works. As the edition used by Calvin and Servetus in 1553 was the 1528 Froben edition from Basel,[64] not the 1545 Paris edition, it is most likely that Baudouin never sent the volume after all. In both of these instances, against the possibility that Baudouin sent the volumes must be set the internal evidence that Calvin did not use them. Finally, Luchesius Smits claimed that Calvin used the 1528/29 edition of Augustine's works, but a fuller and more careful examination of the evidence indicates that Calvin used either the 1531/32 or the 1541 edition.[65]

Two general features can be noted from Calvin's choice of editions. He opts for reliable editions of the *Opera omnia* of the fathers.[66] But at the same time he chose to read and cite the Greek fathers in Latin translation.[67]

61 Cf. chapter 9, below, at nn. 174f.
62 CO 12:231, J.-F. Gilmont, *Jean Calvin et le livre imprimé* (Geneva: Droz, 1997) 186f. inaccurately claims that Calvin promised to supply three volumes, whereas in fact he announces that he *is* sending (*mittimus*) one volume and that while he *would have* sent (*misissem*) two others this was too much for the messenger. There is no promise to send them at a later date, but he does offer to respond to any further requests at the first opportunity.
63 Cf. I. Backus, 'Calvin's Judgment of Eusebius of Caesarea: An Analysis', *Sixteenth Century Journal* 22 (1991) 435f. for instances where 'Eusebius' must refer to the Latin edition.
64 Cf. chapter 6, below, nn. 126–30.
65 Cf. chapter 6, below, section II.b.
66 An exception would be his 1544–45 anti-Anabaptist Bernardine quotations, if it is true that these derive from reading a fifteenth-century edition of the sermons. Cf. chapter 5, below, especially at nn. 34–37.
67 Cf. chapter 3, below, section IV. The quotation of Gregory Nazianzen in Greek (*Inst.* 1:13:17) is exceptional. Why this exception? The most likely explanation is that Calvin at that stage had access to a Greek but not a Latin edition of Gregory.

2

❧❀❧

Calvin's Use of the Fathers
and the Medievals

I. INTRODUCTION

There are three different types of study of Calvin's relation to his pre-decessors.[1] *First*, some studies set out to compare Calvin's teaching with that of one or more earlier theologians (usually Augustine or Thomas Aquinas). Such studies need not presuppose Calvin's being influenced by, or even acquainted with, the figure concerned. As has been observed, it is possible and profitable to compare Calvin and Thomas Aquinas systematically, even though 'Calvin was not greatly interested in the Thomistic synthesis; at least, Calvin utilized Thomas' thought scarcely at all'.[2] The significance of such studies is usually ecumenical or polemical rather than historical. *Secondly*, other studies examine the use that Calvin made of earlier theologians. Here the emphasis lies not on the similarities or the differences between them, nor on any alleged influence on Calvin by his predecessors but simply on how he viewed them and how he cited them in his writings. *Finally*, there are studies which seek to determine the influence of earlier theologians upon Calvin. Such studies are, historically, the most interesting but they are also the hardest and the least conclusive.

If there are to be reliable conclusions about Calvin's influences it is essential that certain elementary principles be observed. It does not suffice, in seeking to demonstrate influence, merely to draw parallels between Calvin and an earlier figure. There might be the most remarkable parallels with no actual influence. Parallels between Calvin and Thomas Aquinas, say, could arise from their common dependence upon an earlier writer (e.g. Peter Lombard) or from the influence on Calvin of later medieval

This chapter originally appeared as 'Calvin's Use of the Fathers and the Medievals' in *Calvin Theological Journal* 16 (1981) 149–205, which was a revision of a paper first delivered to the Tyndale Fellowship Historical Theology Group in March 1980. Appendix I of that article has been updated in chapter 10, below. The body of the article has been revised to take account of more recent scholarship. Conclusions remain much the same, except that fewer superlatives have been used when assessing Calvin's scholarly standards. Section XI has not appeared before.

---

1 For a full listing of the different types of work, see chapter 10, below.
2 C. B. Partee, 'Predestination in Aquinas and Calvin', *Reformed Review* 32 (1978–79) 17.

theologians following Thomas. In neither instance need Calvin have had any acquaintance with Thomas himself. Unless there is evidence of Calvin's familiarity with a writer, the burden of proof lies heavily upon those who would claim that he influenced Calvin. Even where Calvin was unquestionably familiar with an earlier figure and quoted him freely, mere parallels in thought are not sufficient to demonstrate dependence, without more precise evidence. There are striking parallels in thought between Calvin and Augustine, with whom he was undoubtedly intimately acquainted, but it is hard to prove that Calvin reached his Augustinian positions through the direct influence of Augustine rather than through the Augustinianism of others.[3] There are many writings about the influences upon Calvin which have ignored these basic principles. One important example will be considered here.[4]

II. JOHN MAJOR

There has been much speculation in recent years concerning the influence upon Calvin of John Major (1467/8–1550). Major (or Mair) was a leading Scottish philosopher–theologian who, like his illustrious namesake, argued strongly for a closer link between Scotland and England and died (physically in his case) on the first of May. As well as teaching in Scotland, Major taught at the *Collège de Montaigu* in Paris for some years up to 1518, and again from 1526 to 1531.[5] At St Andrews he taught theology to John Knox[6] who later stated that Major's 'word then was held as an oracle in matters of religion'.[7]

Major taught Knox. Did he also teach Calvin? If so, what did he teach him? There are those who allege that Major was a (if not the) formative influence upon the young Calvin, introducing him to late medieval theology.[8] This theory began in a modest way in 1950 with François

3 Cf. the comments of A. Lang in 'Recent German Books on Calvin', *Evangelical Quarterly* 6 (1934) 73–76, on the works of H. Barnikol and J. Beckmann (1926).
4 Another example, Calvin's alleged dependence upon the Greek fathers, is considered in the following chapter.
5 On Major's life, cf. (in chronological order) A. J. G. Mackay, 'Life of the Author' in J. Major, *A History of Greater Britain* (Edinburgh: T. & A. Constable, 1892) xxix-cxv; R. García Villoslada, *La Universidad de París durante los Estudios de Francisco de Vitoria O.P. (1507–22)* (Rome: Universitas Gregoriana, 1938) 127–37; J. Durkan, 'John Major: After 400 Years', *Innes Review* 1 (1950) 131–39; J. H. Burns, 'New Light on John Major', *Innes Review* 5 (1954) 83–100; J. K. Farge, *Biographical Register for Paris Doctors of Theology. 1500–1536* (Toronto: Pontifical Institute of Medieval Studies, 1980) 304–307; A. Broadie, *George Lokert. Late Scholastic Theologian* (Edinburgh: Edinburgh University Press, 1983) 4–20. Major was also in Paris for part of 1521.
    The date of Major's return to Paris is important. In 1892 Aeneas Mackay stated that this was in 1525, and this date has been followed by many recent scholars. In 1954, however, Burns argued convincingly that the correct date is probably 1526 ('New Light', 93–95). Both dates appear in the literature since 1954, without any further mention of the difference of opinion.
6 T. Beza, *Icones* (Geneva: J. Laonius, 1580) sig. Ee3a.
7 W. C. Dickinson (ed.), *John Knox's History of the Reformation in Scotland*, 2 vols (London, etc.: Thomas Nelson, 1949) 1:15.
8 The role of Major in general is discussed here; the role of Major in introducing Calvin to Bernard in particular is discussed in chapter 4, below, section I.

Wendel's magisterial *Calvin*. Major, he claimed, influenced Calvin while he was a pupil at Montaigu and gave him a direct knowledge of Peter Lombard's *Sentences* and an Occamist interpretation of them.[9] These passing comments were before long to be developed into Karl Reuter's magisterial *Das Grundverständnis der Theologie Calvins*.[10] Reuter's thesis is that Major was a dominant influence on Calvin's theological development.[11] He introduced Calvin to the writings of Augustine, Bernard, John Duns Scotus, Bonaventure, Thomas Aquinas and, 'selbstverständlich', Peter Lombard.[12] Through Major Calvin also came under the spell of Thomas Bradwardine and Gregory of Rimini. No one influenced Calvin more than Bernard, Scotus, Bradwardine and Gregory, although Calvin was not himself aware of the significance of their influence upon him.[13]

Shortly after this, T. F. Torrance produced two studies of the influence of Major on Calvin. In these studies he compares the thought of Major and Calvin and argues in particular for Major's influence on Calvin's epistemology. It was also Major who introduced Calvin to Hilary, Athanasius and Basil.[14] It was through Major that Calvin 'learned of Ockham's rejection of the doctrine of representative perception'.[15] Calvin knew of Richard of St Victor via Major.[16]

The 'Reuter thesis' was initially received with favour. Kilian McDonnell summarized it with approval.[17] The following year, F. W. Snell in his thesis

---

For Major's teaching, cf. A. Broadie, *The Circle of John Mair. Logic and Logicians in Pre-Reformation Scotland* (Oxford: OUP, 1985) via index; idem, *Notion and Object. Aspects of Late Medieval Epistemology* (Oxford: OUP, 1989) via index; idem, *The Shadow of Scotus. Philosophy and Faith in Pre-Reformation Scotland* (Edinburgh: T&T Clark, 1995) via index; J. Durkan and J. Kirk, *The University of Glasgow. 1451–1577* (Glasgow: University of Glasgow Press, 1977) 155–65; García Villoslada, *La Universidad de París*, 139–63; T. F. Torrance, '1469–1969. La Philosophie et la Théologie de Jean Mair ou Major, de Haddington (1469–1550)', *Archives de Philosophie* 32 (1969) 531–47, 33 (1970) 261–93; idem, *The Hermeneutics of John Calvin* (Edinburgh: Scottish Academic Press, 1988) 80–95.

9 F. Wendel, *Calvin* (London: Collins, 1963) 19, cf. 126f. (In his later *Calvin et l'Humanisme* (Paris: Presses Universitaires de France, 1976) 16, Wendel reaffirms this claim as 'certain', noting the works of Reuter and Ganoczy cited below (nn. 10, 25)). He is followed by L. Smits, SAOJC 1:14; A. M. Hugo, *Calvijn en Seneca* (Groningen and Jakarta: J. B. Wolters, 1957) 2; W. F. Dankbaar, *Calvijn: Zijn Weg en Werk* (Nijkerk: G. F. Callenbach, [1957]) 4f. Smits subsequently, in a private conversation in 1971, rejected these views. Earlier A. Hyma, *The Christian Renaissance* (New York and London: Century, 1925) 283f., had claimed that Calvin came to know the fathers and leading medievals at Montaigu, but without mentioning Major.

10 Neukirchen-Vluyn: Neukirchener Verlag, 1963.

11 Ibid., 20–28 and *passim*.

12 Ibid., 32.

13 Ibid., 34, 154.

14 T. F. Torrance, *Theology in Reconstruction* (London: SCM Press, 1965) 84.

15 Ibid., 89.

16 T. F. Torrance, 'Intuitive and Abstractive Knowledge: from Duns Scotus to Calvin' in C. Balic (ed.), *De Doctrina Ioannis Duns Scoti*, vol. 4 (Rome: Congressus Scotisticus Internationalis, 1968) 304.

17 K. McDonnell, *John Calvin, the Church, and the Eucharist* (Princeton: Princeton University Press, 1967) 7–27. In 'Calvin's Use of the Fathers and the Medievals', 152f., I quote examples. Note his reference on p. 13 to 'Karl Reuter, to whom these pages are heavily indebted'.

also followed Reuter's conclusions and based his own upon them.[18] Others accepted the 'Reuter thesis', but more cautiously. T. Stadtland claimed only that Calvin *probably* studied under Major and that Major *could* have given him a knowledge of Scotus, Bradwardine and Gregory.[19] He thought that Reuter had exaggerated their influence upon Calvin.[20] He acknowledged some of the opposition to the 'Reuter thesis' but appealed to a private letter from Torrance which referred to stylistic peculiarities of Major found also in Calvin.[21] He concluded that Major influenced Calvin considerably.[22] L. Richard set out the arguments on both sides in this debate.[23] His studies led him to the conclusion that Calvin was influenced by Major's epistemology.[24]

The 'Reuter thesis' also came under heavy attack. Ganoczy argued that Calvin's studies at Montaigu did not go beyond the field of arts and that it was most unlikely that he attended theology lectures at that stage.[25] He points out that Reuter relies primarily on a study of the 1559 *Institutio*, not the first edition. His thesis 's'appuie principalement sur des comparaisons d'idées relevées presque exclusivement dans les oeuvres calviniennes *postérieures* à la première *Institution*, et assez peu sur des documents proprement historiques'.[26] This charge is especially damning as any influence of Major at Montaigu would appear most markedly in the first edition. Yet of the principal authorities cited in the published versions of Major's commentary on the *Sentences* of Peter Lombard, only one is even mentioned in the 1536 *Institutio*.[27] Ganoczy concedes that Reuter has shown the possibility that Calvin may have read certain theological and exegetical works of Major in the years 1540 to 1559. But the 1536 *Institutio* shows no trace of any theological influence by Major and there are no grounds for claiming that Calvin while at Montaigu, and no more than eighteen years old, attended any of Major's *theological* courses.[28]

Aussi ne pouvons-nous pas accepter l'hypothèse d'une initiation proprement théologique de Calvin par Montaigu. Cette conjecture n'est confirmée par aucun document historique; en outre, elle semble

---

18 F. W. Snell, *The Place of Augustine in Calvin's Concept of Righteousness* (New York: Union Theological Seminary ThD thesis, 1968). Pp. 140–45 summarize the 'Reuter thesis': the conclusions of pp. 203f., 219–22 are based on independent research but are clearly influenced by his acceptance of the 'Reuter thesis'.
19 T. Stadtland, *Rechtfertigung und Heiligung bei Calvin* (Neukirchen-Vluyn: Neukirchener Verlag, 1972) 48, 51.
20 Ibid., 51.
21 Ibid., 55. These are presumably the parallels later set out in Torrance, *Hermeneutics of Calvin*, 80–95.
22 Ibid., 54–57, cf. 28.
23 L. J. Richard, *The Spirituality of John Calvin* (Atlanta: John Knox, 1974) 1–4.
24 Ibid., 181, cf. 144–46.
25 A. Ganoczy, *Le jeune Calvin* (Wiesbaden: Franz Steiner, 1966) 39, 186; ET: *The Young Calvin* (Philadelphia: Westminster, 1987) 61, 173f.
26 Ibid., 188 (his emphasis); ET: 175.
27 Ibid., 189; ET: 175.
28 Ibid., 190; ET: 176. The burden of proof on any theory of influence after 1540 must be much greater. The strength of the 'Reuter thesis' is the Montaigu link with Major. As a proposed (literary) influence on Calvin after 1540 Major competes on equal terms with other theologians whose works were available.

difficilement conciliable avec ce que nous savons du programme des élèves artiens de ce collège. Pour qu'elle devienne acceptable, il faudrait prouver que Calvin, entre 14 et 17 ans, se serait soustrait au règlement scolaire ordinaire de la plus stricte des écoles parisiennes, pour suivre, au lieu ou en plus des leçons de grammaire, de philosophie et de sciences, les cours réservés aux élèves plus âgés de la Faculté de théologie.[29]

The following year, A. A. LaVallee in his thesis also attacked the 'Reuter thesis'.[30] He points out that Calvin studied philosophy at Montaigu and is unlikely to have studied theology under Major. He notes that Major is never mentioned in the *Opera Calvini*. He questions some of the parallels that Reuter detects between the thought of Major and Calvin.[31] In 1975 T. H. L. Parker reiterated these points. He allows that Calvin *may* have attended Major's philosophy lectures but argues that, as an arts student, Calvin would not have attended theology lectures.[32] He adds significantly to the case by a fresh examination of the dates of Calvin's early education.[33] The traditional view is that Calvin studied at Paris from 1523 to 1527/28. Parker questions these dates and proposes instead the years 1520/21 to 1525/26. He argues that Calvin probably left Montaigu for Orléans in 1525 or 1526. Parker states that Major returned to Paris in 1525, but if we accept that he did not return until the following year this effectively eliminates the possibility of his having taught Calvin.[34]

The 'Reuter thesis' came under heavy fire, but there was a counter-attack. In 1981 Reuter responded with the publication of a further book, *Vom Scholaren bis zum jungen Reformator*, in which he responded to the criticisms of Ganoczy in particular.[35] He accepts the point that Calvin's studies were in the arts faculty and that he did not attend Major's lectures in the theology faculty.[36] But he leans heavily upon Calvin's reference in 1539 to his instruction in the *rudimenta* of the faith,[37] which he sees as a reference to the instruction that he received at Montaigu. This teaching was in the tradition of the *Devotio moderna* and the anti-Pelagian branch of the *Via moderna*. Calvin was instructed in terminist philosophy.[38] Reuter also responds to the charge that his evidence is derived from later editions of the *Institutio*. Running through this book like a liturgical refrain are phrases like 'schon 1536', 'in der Erstausgabe', etc.

On the basis of this more rigorously presented case Reuter argues for the influence upon Calvin of his time at Montaigu. He argues that Calvin's

---

29 Ibid., 191f.; ET: 177. Ganoczy also mentions the alternative, unlikely, possibility that Major departed from the established programme.
30 A. A. LaVallee, *Calvin's Criticism of Scholastic Theology* (Cambridge (MA): Harvard University PhD thesis, 1967) 241–47.
31 H. Schützeichel, *Die Glaubenstheologie Calvins* (Munich: Max Hueber, 1972) 68 summarizes with approval the arguments of Ganoczy and LaVallee.
32 T. H. L. Parker, *John Calvin* (London: J. M. Dent, 1975) 11.
33 Ibid., 156–61.
34 Ibid., 11. For the date of Major's return, cf. n. 5, above.
35 Neukirchen-Vluyn: Neukirchener Verlag, 1981.
36 Ibid., 1 *et al.*
37 Ibid., 4 *et al.*, citing the *Responsio ad Sadoletum* (CO 5:411; OS 1.484).
38 Reuter, *Vom Scholaren*, 4–12, *et al.*

encounter with the Augustinian anti-Pelagianism of the late Middle Ages must have been through Montaigu rather than through his later legal or humanist studies.[39] Indeed, he goes on the offensive against Ganoczy by questioning whether Calvin's time at Montaigu was confined totally to the *arts* faculty. What is the meaning of Calvin's statement that his father made him turn from the study of *philosophy* to law? This could not refer to his arts studies since these were completed. Reuter suggests that Calvin may have *commenced* at Montaigu the study of scholastic theology, which he later disparagingly compares to the philosophy condemned by Paul.[40]

Reuter's thesis is summarized with Teutonic succinctness in the following sentence:

> Anfängliche und beibehaltene, später aber mit aufkommender nachhaltiger Kraftentfaltung sich durchsetzende erste Berührungen mit dem Antipelagionismus [*sic*] der Augustin-Renaissance unter dem so weit reichenden Einfluß Majors, des doch von 1525 bis 1532 in Montaigu wieder, aller Wahrscheinlichkeit nach auch an der Artistenfakultät, wirkenden Lehrers, dann das Studium des römischen Rechtes und der den jungen Calvin beschäftigenden Anschauungen einer menschheitlichen Lebensphilosophie und Gesellschaftslehre, weiter die starken Einflüsse und Auseinandersetzungen, die durch sein tiefes Eindringen in den biblizistischen Humanismus Frankreichs herbeigeführt wurden, und die dies alles in sich hineinziehende Umwälzung der geistlichen Existenz des jungen Calvin durch die ihn schließlich überwindende Macht der 'Lehrgestalt' der Reformation Luthers: dieser Werdegang, unter der Vorbedeutung der Vielzahl dieser Auspizien, hat auch das Bild christlich-frommer Lebensauffassung beim werdenden Reformator entscheidend mitgeprägt.[41]

The following year Patrick Le Gal discusses at length the influence upon Calvin at Montaigu of Nominalism in general and Major in particular.[42] Apart from the statement that Major returned to Montaigu in 1526, his case is argued entirely on the grounds of parallels of thought.[43] The points at which he detects Major's influence are both philosophical and theological.

In 1988 Torrance reasserted his claim that Major influenced Calvin.[44] He affirms that Calvin studied under Major, who returned to 'Montaigu in 1525 during Calvin's second year at the College',[45] and perceives his influence in a number of areas. 'There cannot be any doubt that the

---

39 Ibid., 23f.
40 Ibid., 37.
41 Ibid., 149f.
42 P. Le Gal, *La Droit Canonique dans la Pensée Dialectique de Jean Calvin* (Fribourg: Éditions Universitaires Fribourg Suisse, 1984) 30–59.
43 There is a single mention of Reuter, cited via Wendel. Amazingly, there is no mention of Ganoczy's *Le jeune Calvin*.
44 Torrance, *Hermeneutics of Calvin*, 80–95, where much of the material is taken verbatim from his earlier *Theology in Reconstruction*.
45 Ibid., 80. In *Theology in Reconstruction*, 81, he states that Major taught Calvin from 1526 to 1528.

teaching Calvin had received from Major left an indelible imprint upon his thinking and his way of using traditional philosophical and theological language.' This is argued on the basis of 'the connection between Calvin's language and Major's' which appears 'most obviously' in Calvin's famous expressions *experientia docet* and *per accidens*, 'which one finds like liturgical refrains in Major's works'.[46] There is also influence in 'questions of substance even at some of the points where Calvin's thought is so distinctive', such as his rejection of soul-sleep 'and even his peculiar interpretation of 1 Timothy 2:4', which Calvin shares with Major.[47] It is also 'undoubtedly from Major that Calvin received his initiation into patristic studies, for Major's lectures on theology reveal great patristic learning and his biblical exposition shows considerable knowledge of the commentaries of the Fathers'.[48] Major's influence upon Calvin lay in directing him to important patristic and medieval thinkers, including Thomas Aquinas, Duns Scotus and Gregory of Rimini.

> Calvin's indebtedness to their thought cannot be measured simply by the passages where they are mentioned by name, for Calvin's language is often saturated with that of others in such a way that it is clear that they affected him deeply in his early formative years when he was acquiring his primary instruments of thought and speech.[49]

It is also on this principle that Torrance can claim that, despite the fact that Calvin never named Major, nonetheless 'it is clearly his teaching that [Calvin] has in mind'.[50]

There are problems with these arguments. Torrance argues for Calvin's dependence upon Major on the grounds that he studied under him and the impressive range of alleged parallels between them.[51] We have already seen that Calvin may not have overlapped with Major at Montaigu and that if he did it would have been for no more than one year and he would then have been studying philosophy, not theology. As for the alleged parallels, many of them are so general as to be worthless. Calvin and Major both studied the fathers and disliked allegory, but these traits were so widespread that there is no need to postulate Major as Calvin's source. Major was hardly unique either in his patristic learning and knowledge or in his dislike of allegory.

The argument from linguistic parallels to linguistic dependence is also precarious. *Experientia docet* and *per accidens* were established phrases.[52] The most impressive linguistic parallels between two writers are no proof

46 *Hermeneutics of Calvin*, 80.
47 Ibid., 80f.
48 Ibid., 81.
49 Ibid., 81.
50 Ibid., 94, cf. viii.
51 I have listed some only of the parallels of language and substance cited by Torrance on pp. 80f. I am not aware that any of the others are genuinely peculiar to Calvin and Major.
52 In addition, 'experientia docet' is hardly a liturgical refrain for Calvin. In the 1559 *Institutio* it appears just four times with *experientia* and the verb *docere* being linked a further three times. We also have 'experientia ostendit' (3x), 'declarat' (2x), 'testatur', 'demonstrat', 'convincit' and 'loquitur' (all 1x). For this I am indebted to Rick Wevers' concordance of the 1559 *Institutio*.

of dependence unless they are peculiar to those two writers. Torrance makes no attempt to demonstrate such peculiarity. Major is also alleged to be Calvin's source at points where his thought is 'so distinctive'. The rejection of soul-sleep was hardly 'distinctive', soul-sleep itself being the novel, 'heretical' idea. The allegedly peculiar interpretation of 1 Timothy 2:4 in fact goes back to Augustine, a source with which Calvin was most certainly familiar.[53] Finally, it is striking that the passages cited which allegedly show Major's influence are taken almost without exception from the second, 1539, edition of the *Institutio*.[54] If Major had influenced Calvin so deeply in the mid-1520s, would one not have expected to find the evidence in the first, 1536, edition?

The case against the Reuter thesis is reiterated and further developed by Marius Lange van Ravenswaay, who emphasizes the point that university rules did not permit arts students to attend theology lectures.[55] But qualified support for Reuter's case has come from Alister McGrath.[56] He shows how, given the 'near-total absence of primary sources for the period 1523–34 in Calvin's career', we are left only with circumstantial evidence. We can either say nothing about this period or draw tentative conclusions based on this evidence.[57] Adopting the latter course, he argues for the influence upon Calvin, while at Montaigu, of the *via moderna* and the *schola Augustiniana moderna*. He does not wish to tie this influence to any one individual.[58] He suggests that Reuter's thesis 'may be restated in terms of the influence of a general late medieval theological current, rather than of a *specific individual* (i.e. John Major)'.[59] What Reuter and Torrance see as proof of Calvin's indebtedness to Major, McGrath sees as evidence for the influence upon him of the *schola Augustiniana moderna*.

> It is certainly therefore a remarkable coincidence, to say the least, that Calvin should reproduce the leading features of an academic Augustinianism which developed at the same university as that which he himself attended, if he had not himself been familiar with such theological currents.

But he goes on to show that Calvin might have encountered these ideas in books as well as lectures. The hypothesis of personal contact with Major

---

53 E.g. *Enchiridion* 103:27; *De correptione et gratia* 14:44. For Calvin's awareness of Augustine's interpretation during the Bolsec controversy, cf. CO 8:167, 212.

54 Torrance, *Hermeneutics of Calvin*, 183f., nn. 93–126.

55 J. M. J. Lange van Ravenswaay, *Augustinus totus noster. Das Augustinverständnis bei Johannes Calvin* (Göttingen: Vandenhoeck & Ruprecht, 1990) 155–63, being the publication of his 1985 Tübingen thesis of the same title. The same material is also found in idem, 'Initia Augustiniana Calvini. Neues zur Genese von Calvins Augustinverständnis' in *Congresso Internazionale su S. Agostino nel XVI Centenario della Conversione*, vol. 3 (Rome: Institutum Patristicum 'Augustinianum', 1987) 260–69.

56 A. E. McGrath, 'John Calvin and Late Mediaeval Thought. A Study in Late Mediaeval Influences upon Calvin's Theological Development', *Archiv für Reformationsgeschichte* 77 (1986) 58–78; idem, *The Intellectual Origins of the European Reformation* (Oxford: Basil Blackwell, 1987) 94–106; idem, *A Life of John Calvin* (Oxford: Basil Blackwell, 1990) 36–47.

57 *Intellectual Origins*, 94–97; 'John Calvin', 60–63.

58 *Intellectual Origins*, 101–106; 'John Calvin', 63–78; *Life of Calvin*, 39–45.

59 *Intellectual Origins*, 104 (his emphasis). Cf. idem, *Life of Calvin*, 45f.

in particular McGrath sees as an unnecessary subsidiary hypothesis.[60] The strength of McGrath's case is that he builds upon the strong points of both the pro- and anti-Reuter theses.[61]

Heiko Oberman reaffirms the case against Reuter.[62]

The little we know about the young Calvin during his 'student years', from 1523 to 1528 at the Collège de la Marche and the Collège Montaigu in Paris, has had to be squeezed for more information than it could yield. This has led to a history of speculation no less fascinating than fallacious.[63]

He also questions the parallels that McGrath draws between Calvin and the *schola Augustiniana moderna*.

Nowhere is the test-question raised whether or to what extent Calvin's avid reading of St. Paul and St. Augustine can sufficiently – and hence convincingly – explain convictions reemerging (in a markedly different form and context) in the *via Gregorii*.

Calvin's own wide reading in Augustine meant that he could 'bypass the circuitous road of scholastic reception' and found his own 'schola augustiniana'.[64] This argument is not completely convincing. If Calvin reproduces a particular late-medieval intepretation of Augustine (and especially if that interpretation in places adopts a more extreme 'Augustinianism' than Augustine himself), is it likely that Calvin just happened to reach the same conclusions independently? Would one then go on to say that he simply read his Bible and just happened to reach the same conclusions as Augustine?

What conclusions can be drawn from this discussion of the 'Reuter thesis'? The prime need is for rigour in historical method, in three areas especially. *First* of all the historical circumstances must be ascertained. Did Calvin overlap with Major at Montaigu and what was he studying at the time? *Secondly*, appeals to parallels alone do not suffice. If parallels are to be alleged between the writings of Calvin and Major we must ask when they appear in Calvin's writings and how specific they are to Major. *Thirdly*, Calvin's explicit citations must be given due weight, paying attention both to the *extent* (or otherwise) of Calvin's citations of particular figures and to the *nature* of his citation of them. These points can be illustrated from Reuter.

60 *Intellectual Origins*, 105f. Cf. idem, *Life of Calvin*, 45–47.
61 B. Cottret, *Calvin. Biographie* (Paris: J. C. Lattès, 1995) 32f. attempts a delicate balancing act. The parallels between Calvin and Major (drawn from Torrance) are precise enough that one cannot deny the possibility that Major influenced him; but they are general enough to prevent the least positive conclusion! O. Millet, *Calvin et la Dynamique de la Parole. Étude de rhétorique réformée* (Paris: Honoré Champion, 1992) 33, doubts whether Calvin studied scholastic dialectic and philosophy under Major, but points to the importance of Major's publications in the 1520s.
62 'Initia Calvini: The Matrix of Calvin's Reformation' in W. H. Neuser (ed.), *Calvinus Sacrae Scripturae Professor* (Grand Rapids: Eerdmans, 1994) 117–27.
63 Oberman, '*Initia Calvini*', 116f. He does not mention Parker's revision of Calvin's Paris dates (at nn. 33f., above).
64 Oberman, '*Initia Calvini*', 121f., referring to Lange van Ravenswaay, *Augustinus totus noster*, 180.

A major weakness of Reuter's thesis is his neglect of Calvin's citations. He asserts that Scotus, Bradwardine and Gregory were among the greatest influences on Calvin. Yet Bradwardine and Gregory are never cited by Calvin and Scotus receives only two hostile references to his teaching on the real presence.[65] Reuter claims that Calvin 'hat die Tragweite eines gewissen Einflusses der scotistisch-nominalistischen Denkweise auf seine reformatorische nicht erkannt'.[66] It is true that we are not always aware of the things that have influenced us, but there is a heavy burden of proof on a theory which claims as the *major* influences on Calvin thinkers of whom he shows scarcely any awareness.

But how significant is it that Calvin does not name a particular writer? Ganoczy criticizes Reuter's first book in part on the grounds that most of the alleged late-medieval influences upon Calvin are not named in the 1536 *Institutio*.[67] He has rightly been criticized for this. When Calvin cites earlier writers he is not declaring which writers have influenced him nor even necessarily stating his sources in the way of the modern footnote. With the fathers and with a medieval like Bernard he is above all appealing to authorities.[68] McGrath argues that for Calvin, unlike the young Luther, there was no point in naming late-medieval scholastic authors.

> At no point is it necessary, or even useful, for Calvin to engage in debate with any representatives of late medieval religious thought – and to suggest that this silence reflects an absence of familiarity with such sources, or that it indicates that Calvin has not been influenced by them to any significant extent, is simply a *non sequitur*. The question of the significance of Calvin's *use* of theological sources is secondary to a discussion of Calvin's religious concerns, literary and polemical techniques and potential audiences.[69]

Where does that leave us? It would be wrong to suggest that because Calvin rarely names any late medieval authors he was almost entirely ignorant of them. On the other hand, claims of substantial influence by specific individuals require more than parallels in thought to be substantiated. If Calvin never mentions a particular late-medieval writer, or mentions him only rarely and disparagingly, clear proof is needed before one can talk of major influence. Oberman's warning is salutary:

> There cannot be any doubt that it is essential to be committed to the close scrutiny of Calvin's late medieval *resources*. But without clear evidence these resources cannot be transformed into *sources*.[70]

---

65 CO 9:177, 436 (*Ult. admon. ad Westph.*; *Grat. ad Gabr. de Saconay*, both from Calvin's late years). Mooi gives references for the 1536 and 1539 *Institutio* (KDE 21, 47, 369f.), but these refer only to the OS footnotes – Calvin does not name Scotus.

66 Reuter, *Grundverständnis*, 154. Snell also argues that Calvin does not name his sources because he was not fully aware of them (*Place of Augustine*, 204f.).

67 Ganoczy, *Le jeune Calvin*, 189; ET: 175.

68 Cf. section IV, below.

69 McGrath, *Intellectual Origins*, 102–104. Cf. idem, *Life of Calvin*, 37–39; Torrance, *Hermeneutics*, 81.

70 Oberman, '*Initia Calvini*', 124.

It is much safer to confine oneself, as does McGrath, to claiming 'the influence of a general late medieval theological current, rather than of a *specific individual'*.[71]

The greatest weakness in Reuter's book is that he largely ignores Calvin's *citation* of the figures alleged to have influenced him. He claims that Bernard was an important influence on Calvin in his early years, yet this is contradicted by Calvin's citation of Bernard.[72] Bernard is a major alleged influence on Calvin, and yet Reuter almost never refers to the way in which Calvin uses him.[73] Where Calvin never names a potential source (like Gregory of Rimini) one has to resort to other evidence, but where he repeatedly cites an author there is abundant evidence at hand. Studies of Calvin's use of the fathers are less spectacular and less momentous than studies of the influences that might have shaped his theology. But it is only as his explicit usage is studied and as these studies are heeded that there will be any solid and enduring results in the search for influences.

So was Calvin influenced by John Major? In the light of all the uncertainties, there is no room for dogmatism. It is by no means certain that Calvin and Major even overlapped at Montaigu. It is most unlikely that Major taught Calvin *theology*. Any case built on the hypothesis that Major taught Calvin theology is precarious in the extreme, as Ganoczy notes.

> K. Reuter fait de cette hypothèse une véritable thèse, en affirmant que l'enseignement théologique reçu de Major détermina chez Calvin toute une série de positions doctrinales.[74]

The case for Major's philosophical influence upon Calvin is stronger, but for it to be established we need evidence in the *earliest* writings of Calvin of positions that are *distinctive* of Major. Since there has so far been no study which seeks rigorously to establish these two points a definite verdict is not yet possible.

Finally, the case for the influence upon Calvin of a specific *school* of late-medieval thought is much stronger. It is much easier to show that an idea is distinctive of a school of thought than of a single individual. Questions of who was where when lose their urgency. If there are to be any lasting results from this controversy they are likely to concern the school(s) of thought that influenced Calvin rather than specific theologians.

III. LAUSANNE DISPUTATION

During the month of October, 1536, a disputation took place at Lausanne at which a number of Protestant and Roman Catholic theologians competed for the allegiance of the Canton of Vaud.[75] The young Calvin

---

71 McGrath, *Intellectual Origins*, 104.
72 Cf. chapter 4, below, section I.
73 For details cf. chapter 4, below, nn. 37f.
74 Ganoczy, *Le jeune Calvin*, 187; ET: 174.
75 Cf. G. Bavaud, *La dispute de Lausanne (1536)* (Fribourg: Éditions universitaires, 1956); E. Junod (ed.), *La dispute de Lausanne (1536)* (Lausanne: Bibliothèque Historique Vaudoise, 1988). E.-M. Braekman, 'Les interventions de Calvin' in Junod (ed.), *La dispute de Lausanne*, 170–77, stresses the importance of the occasion for Calvin's

was a junior partner to Farel and Viret on the evangelical side. He had intended to keep silent but was stung into action by the charge of Jean Mimard that the Protestants despised antiquity:

> Mais vous faictez bien, et ce pour vostre advantaige, de n'en point admectre ne recepvoir ung seul du si grand college des sainctz docteurs.... Davantaige vous les rejectez tant comme infructueux, imbecilles, asnes, et rien entendans au sainct evangille, dessoubz une umbre couverte, disans ainsi: Nous suyvons l'evangille de Jesuchrist et de sa saincte foy, et ne voulons point de ses traditions et constitutions d'hommes.[76]

In his response, delivered on 5 October, Calvin revealed himself as one who had diligently studied the early fathers.[77] In this brief discourse he manifested in embryo all the major features of his later use of the fathers.

Calvin's use of the fathers in this discourse is unashamedly polemical. What is true of pseudo-Chrysostom is true of the fathers in general: 'reversing all your doctrine, he simply establishes ours'.[78] Calvin indignantly repudiates the charge that the Protestant theologians are guilty of 'condemning and wholly rejecting' the fathers, 'because we feel them to be contrary and hostile to our cause'.[79]

> As for condemning, we should not at all refuse to be judged by the whole world as not only audacious but beyond measure arrogant, if we held such servants of God in so great contempt, as you allege, as to deem them fools. If it be so, we should not at all take the trouble to read them and to use the help of their teaching when it serves and as occasion offers.[80]

The last sentence was to receive abundant confirmation from Calvin's own practice, both at Lausanne and throughout his life. But behind it lay the truth that the fathers did not have the same authority for the Reformers as (theoretically) for the Roman Catholics.

> We have always held them to belong to the number of those to whom such obedience is not due, and whose authority we will not so exalt, as in any way to debase the dignity of the Word of our Lord, to

---

own development. He criticizes Ganoczy for failing to mention the event in a brief survey of Calvin's life, while in fact Ganoczy had already pointed out its significance for Calvin in his *Le jeune Calvin*, 106–108; ET: 109f.

76 A. Piaget (ed.), *Les actes de la dispute de Lausanne 1536* (Neuchâtel: Secrétariat de l'Université, 1928) 204f.

77 The text of this speech will be found in CO 9:877–84, LCC 22:38–45. In 'Calvin's Use of the Fathers and Medievals', 156, I added that he 'was to become one of the greatest patristic scholars of the sixteenth century'. Much more accurate is the observation of Irena Backus that while Calvin was 'never a patristic scholar', he 'was nonetheless a keen reader and user' of the Greek fathers (from an as yet unpublished paper on 'Calvin and the Greek Fathers' given at the Seventh International Congress on Calvin Research (Seoul, 1998)).

78 LCC 22:40, CO 9:880.

79 LCC 22:38, CO 9:877.

80 Ibid.

which alone is due complete obedience in the Church of Jesus Christ.[81]

In fact, we do them such honour as may according to God be accorded to them, while we attend to them and to their ministry, to search the Word of God, in order that, having found it, we should with them listen to and observe it with all humility and reverence, reserving this honour for the Lord alone, who has opened his mouth in the Church only to speak with authority, and in order that every ear be ready to listen to it and every soul to obey it.[82]

Characteristically, Calvin supports this last point with a quotation from Cyprian. But while Calvin admits that the Reformers subordinate the fathers to Scripture, he is not prepared to concede that they therefore respect them less than in practice do the Roman Catholics.

Those who make parade of according them great reverence often do not hold them in such great honour as we; nor do they deign to occupy their time reading their writings as we willingly do.[83]

For Calvin, the fathers are subsidiary authorities to be cited, supporting his own doctrine and refuting Roman doctrine. He demonstrates this in the present context by a series of lengthy quotations from various fathers, taken from memory.[84] Here we see many of the hallmarks of Calvin's use of the fathers throughout his life. He does not simply make remarks about them or make sweeping claims about their teaching but he quotes them at length.[85] The power of his memory is evidenced by the detail that he is able to include. As far as he is able from memory,[86] he gives the source of his quotations, including such details as 'in the 11th Homily about the middle' and 'in Epistle 23 very near the end'.[87] He endeavours to distinguish genuine from pseudonymous writings, a concern by no means universal among his contemporaries: 'whoever be the author of the unfinished commentaries on Matthew which are attributed to John Chrysostom and are included with his works'; 'in the book *De fide ad Petrum Diaconum* (though it is uncertain whether it belongs to him [Augustine] or to some other Father)'.[88] He takes care to set each passage in its context in the writing from which it is taken and the circumstances of that writing.[89] Calvin's scholarly standards would not satisfy twentieth-

---

81 LCC 22:38, CO 9:877f.
82 LCC 22:39, CO 9:879.
83 LCC 22:38, cf. 43, CO 9:877, cf. 9:882.
84 W. N. Todd, *The Function of the Patristic Writings in the Thought of John Calvin* (New York: Union Theological Seminary ThD thesis, 1964) 98f., argues that Calvin had prepared the speech in advance but the opening makes it clear that while it may not have been totally impromptu it was certainly delivered at short notice. While it may be conceded that Calvin had probably earlier prepared his patristic dossier, it seems clear that he had to present it unexpectedly and from memory.
85 CO 9:879–81, LCC 22:40–42.
86 'About the 8th or 9th section (I cannot exactly recall which)' (LCC 22:41, CO 9:880).
87 LCC 22:40f., CO 9:880.
88 LCC 22:40f., CO 9:879–81.
89 CO 9:879–81, LCC 22:40f.

century criteria but by the standards of sixteenth-century polemics they were thorough.[90]

In this discourse Calvin already manifested the emphasis on Augustine characteristic of his use of the fathers throughout his life. There are more quotations from Augustine, 'whom you have made your advocate',[91] than from all the other fathers put together. This reflects both the authority accorded to Augustine in the sixteenth century and also the affinity that Calvin genuinely felt for his teaching.

Calvin cited the fathers because he genuinely believed them to support his cause. The refusal to accord them authority on a par with Scripture does not spring from a fear that the fathers would contradict Reformed teaching. On the contrary, 'we are able in reality to take them as defenders of our opinion'.[92] Thus, 'the whole world is easily able to understand with what audacity you reproach us with being contrary to the ancient doctors'.[93] Calvin could conclude by thus exhorting his opponents:

> I advise and beseech you to charge us no longer with contradicting the ancient doctors in this matter with whom we are in fact in such accord.[94]

After Calvin had spoken, the Franciscan brother Jean Tandy stood up to announce his conversion to the gospel.[95]

IV. PURPOSE

Calvin's use of the fathers is primarily, but not exclusively, polemical. R. J. Mooi, in his comprehensive tables of Calvin's citations,[96] finds more than 40 per cent of them in the treatises, which are predominantly polemical. Here the great majority of citations are polemical. More than 30 per cent

90 Ganoczy, *Le jeune Calvin*, 107; ET: 110, offers a different assessment: 'Les citations patristiques y sont des phrases détachées de leur contexte, privées de la contrepartie qu'on pourrait leur trouver chez le même auteur et choisies assez arbitrairement, plus en fonction de la thèse donnée que d'une solution à rechercher.' To assess Calvin as a twentieth-century research student rather than a sixteenth-century polemicist is surely to be guilty of anachronism.
91 LCC 22:40, CO 9:880.
92 LCC 22:40, CO 9:879.
93 LCC 22:43, CO 9:882.
94 LCC 22:45, CO 9:884.
95 Piaget (ed.), *Les actes de la dispute de Lausanne*, 231f. F. Higman, 'La dispute de Lausanne, carrefour de la Réformation française' in Junod (ed.), *La dispute de Lausanne*, 23–35 shows how Calvin's intervention was the turning point of the disputation.
96 Mooi, KDE 365–97. These tables contain minor inaccuracies but suffice for broad comparisons. They are used here and a number of other times in this chapter as they eliminate the danger of the present writer introducing his own bias through the way that he calculates the totals. But one modification has been made in these present figures. In Mooi's tables material added into the *Institutio* from 1539 to 1550 and retained in 1559 is counted twice. This has been reduced to once so as not to prejudice the figures in favour of the *Institutio* (which would have further strengthened my case). The resulting totals are: Treatises: 1326; *Institutio*: 981; Commentaries: 790; Letters: 63; Forewords, etc.: 33; Commentary on Seneca: 15; Sermons: 9.

are found in the *Institutio* and here again the primary aim is polemical. This can best be seen by an examination of their distribution throughout the work. Of the 866 citations in the 1559 *Institutio,* only one is found in the five chapters on the Christian life, which is one of the least polemical sections of the work. Nearly half (423) of the citations are found in Book IV, which is fiercely anti-Roman, and within this book they are concentrated mainly in the most polemical chapters, those on the rise of the papacy (129), the Lord's Supper (55) and the five falsely-so-called sacraments (55). By contrast, in the first six chapters of Book I, which are less overtly polemical, there are only three citations. Even allowing for variations in chapter length, it can be seen that Calvin's material is concentrated in the most polemical sections. It also predominates in the anti-papal sections, since the Roman Catholics recognized the authority of the fathers. The anti-Anabaptist sections contain less patristic material, since the Anabaptists did not acknowledge the authority of the fathers. The fiercely polemical chapter on infant baptism contains only two citations, while the chapter on 'fanaticism' contains none. The defence of the Trinity, on the other hand, is well supported by patristic citations, since the anti-Trinitarians had themselves sought support from the ante-Nicene fathers. The fathers also feature prominently in Calvin's polemics against Lutherans over the real presence.[97]

To say that Calvin's use of the fathers is primarily polemical is not to accuse him of mere proof-texting. Unlike some of the Elizabethan divines,[98] he did not read the fathers simply in order to find 'juicy' anti-papal quotations. There is no doubt that he read widely in the fathers[99] and that this was for his own benefit, not just for polemical ammunition. There is equally little doubt that the fathers exerted some genuine influence upon Calvin, though that influence is hard to measure precisely and is certainly less than some have suggested.[100] But there is also no doubt that Calvin's *citation* of the fathers is primarily polemical.

It is important to distinguish between Calvin's attitude to and use of four different groups of writings. *First,* the Scriptures are for Calvin normative and the touchstone by which other writings are to be tested. *Secondly,* the fathers are seen as lesser authorities: they have an authority as those who lived in the 'primitive and purer Church' but their teaching is subject to that of Scripture.[101] Calvin treats them as authorities, possibly reflecting his legal background, certainly following the established pattern of medieval theology.[102] As authorities they are to be named and cited.

---

97 In addition to the chapter on the Lord's Supper, this is also true of the treatises against Westphal and Heshusius.
98 For this observation I am indebted to Richard Bauckham, who was thinking especially, but not exclusively, of William Fulke.
99 Cf. section VIIIa, below.
100 Cf. section I, above.
101 Cf. sections VI.a and VII.a, below.
102 Which is not to say that his method is *identical* to the medieval *auctoritas* method as described, e.g. by J.-G. Bougerol, 'The Church Fathers and *Auctoritates* in Scholastic Theology to Bonaventure' in I. Backus (ed.), *The Reception of the Church Fathers in the West,* vol. 1 (Leiden, etc.: E. J. Brill, 1997) 289–335. I am indebted for this observation to Backus, 'Calvin and the Greek Fathers'.

They are witnesses to be called to give evidence for the Reformed cause. Calvin's *Prefatory Address to King Francis* reads like a speech for the defence in which the fathers are called as witnesses.

> Augustine was the undisputed master theologian of the Western world. If mediaeval Roman theology was to be overthrown how could it be done better than through appeal to the authority of Augustine? That had been the line taken by Luther, and Calvin followed him, equipping himself with a great armoury of weapons taken from the works of Augustine.[103]

The scholastics, however, fall into a *third* and very different group. They are primarily opponents, not authorities. As such they can be referred to without being named. There is no need to name them as they are not, for Calvin, authorities and they are not being called upon to testify to the truth. They are being cited as examples of errors to be refuted; they are being set up as targets and as such they are best consigned to the anonymity of *sophistae, scholastici,* etc.[104] The result is that the *Opera Selecta* footnotes give many references to specific passages in the scholastics where Calvin has only a general term like *sophistae.* LaVallee concludes from this that Calvin did not necessarily have a direct knowledge of these writers but that he did know more about scholastic theology in general than his direct references would imply.[105] It is possible to go further than this and to suggest that Calvin may have had more *direct* knowledge of individual scholastics than his references imply. It must always be borne in mind that when Calvin gives references he is not (as we would be) documenting his work, nor (as many would wish) declaring who has influenced him. He is citing authorities. There is, therefore, no need to name the scholastics or to give references, since they are not authorities. The burden of proof rests heavily upon any alleged dependence on the fathers which Calvin does not declare; the burden is far lighter with the scholastics, because Calvin had little reason to name them.[106]

Calvin's contemporaries form the *fourth* group. These again do not need to be named. Calvin can show awareness of contemporary debates without explicitly referring to them, since his references do not have that function.[107] His dependence upon Luther and Bucer is undoubted and yet they are rarely named by Calvin, since his references are not acknowledgements of indebtedness. 'Although Erasmus's name nowhere appears in the *Institutes,* it has been possible to show that numerous passages ... present striking analogies with parallel texts from the great humanist.'[108] He can attack contemporary Roman Catholics without naming them,[109]

---

103 Torrance, *Theology in Reconstruction,* 76.
104 Cf. LaVallee, *Calvin's Criticism,* 26–28.
105 Ibid., 28.
106 This statement does not support the 'Reuter thesis' as it is based on the assumption that the scholastics are Calvin's opponents. Scholastic theologians who supported Calvin's position could be cited as medieval witnesses to the truth, making use of the fact that for the Roman Catholics they were authorities.
107 'Calvin here, as usual, does not name either Luther or his assailants, but shows familiarity with the controversy' (LCC 20:18, n. 12).
108 Wendel, *Calvin,* 130.
109 Cf. OS 3.12–15 footnotes, together with many other places in the OS footnotes.

although when a whole work is devoted to attacking a single opponent, as with many of the polemical treatises, the opponent is normally named.

W. N. Todd, in his comprehensive thesis on Calvin's use of the fathers, offers a somewhat different interpretation. He opposes Imbart de la Tour's statement that the Reformers used the fathers polemically as a defence against Roman Catholic claims to the support of the ancient tradition.[110] He argues that this was a later development. Initially the aim was non-polemical: the Reformers sought to renovate Christian doctrine and so, in accord with the humanist principle of *ad fontes*, they returned to the classical period of Christian theology in the ancient church.[111] The polemical use of the fathers against Rome was a later outcome of this non-polemical use. The *Psychopannychia* is cited as Calvin's first real use of the fathers after his conversion, and it is noted that this was written against other (Anabaptist) Protestants, not against Roman Catholics.[112] No mention is made of any polemical content in the 1535 prefaces.[113] The polemical content in the 1536 *Institutio* is mentioned but minimized. It is argued that Calvin introduced patristic sources in a positive attempt to develop his own doctrine and in the debate with other Reformers. The patristic polemic in the 1536 *Institutio* is anti-Protestant (Anabaptist, Zwinglian and Lutheran) more than anti-Roman. The most heavily anti-Roman chapter, chapter five on the five sacraments falsely so-called, contains little patristic argument but concentrates on attacking the scholastics.[114] Calvin's use of the fathers did not originate with anti-Roman polemics.

There are a number of weaknesses in this argument. It is true that the polemic in the *Psychopannychia* is anti-Anabaptist rather than anti-Roman, but this is because Calvin's first theological work was anti-Anabaptist, not because there are earlier anti-Roman works without patristic polemic. There is another problem too. The text of the 1534 *Psychopannychia* is uncertain, as it was revised in 1536 and not finally published until 1542.[115] Todd claims that the patristic material was probably complete in 1534, but this is far from certain.[116] The patristic citations in the preface to the

---

110 Todd, *Function of the Patristic Writings*, 57f., 85f.
111 Ibid., 133–37, which refer to the Reformers in general but clearly include Calvin.
112 Ibid., 57f.
113 Ibid., 72–77. These are the prefaces to the Neuchâtel Bible of Olivétan and to the Homilies of Chrysostom. Todd dates the latter from 1535 but J. R. Walchenbach, *John Calvin as Biblical Commentator* (Pittsburgh: University of Pittsburgh PhD thesis, 1974) 201–206, argues that it was written in 1559, while W. I. P. Hazlett, 'Calvin's Latin Preface to his Proposed French Edition of Chrysostom's Homilies: Translation and Commentary' in J. Kirk (ed.), *Humanism and Reform: The Church in Europe, England and Scotland, 1400–1643* (Oxford: Basil Blackwell, 1991) 132f. argues persuasively for a date between 1538 and 1540.
114 Todd, *Function of the Patristic Writings*, 82–85.
115 C. Dardier, 'Un problème bibliographique. Quelle est la date de la première édition de la *Psychopannychia* de Calvin?', *Société de l'histoire du protestantisme français. Bulletin historique et littéraire* 19/20 (1870–71) 371–82. This treatise did not of course receive the name *Psychopannychia* until the 1545 edition. For further information on it, cf. J.-U. Hwang, *Der junge Calvin und seine Psychopannychia* (Frankfurt, etc.: Peter Lang, 1991).
116 Todd, *Function of the Patristic Writings*, 61. He does not inspire confidence in his judgment when he fails to detect that the references to Bernard were not introduced until the 1545 edition (p. 63). In a 1535 letter to Fabri Calvin referred to his revision of the 1534 version as a 'new book' (CO 10b:51f.; CRF 3:349f.).

Neuchâtel Bible are polemically anti-Roman, urging Bible reading for all.[117] The patristic material in the 1536 *Institutio* is in fact primarily anti-Roman. The fifth chapter, which supposedly contains little patristic material, contains more references to the fathers than any other chapter.[118] These are all polemical and anti-Roman. In the fourth chapter, the only other chapter with a considerable number of patristic citations, the use of the fathers is overwhelmingly anti-Roman and not anti-Zwinglian as Todd claims.[119] Thus the use of the fathers in the 1536 *Institutio* is predominantly polemical and anti-Roman. This conclusion is reinforced when the *Prefatory Address* is also taken into account.[120] The claim that Calvin's earliest use of the fathers is non-polemical is unfounded, and the chronological priority of anti-Anabaptist polemics reflects the character of Calvin's first theological writing, not the nature of his earliest use of the fathers. While Calvin as a humanist undoubtedly studied the fathers with the *ad fontes* principle in mind, his *citation* of the fathers in his writings starts and remains unashamedly and primarily polemical.

Calvin's polemical use of the fathers usually consists of citing them for his own teaching and against Roman teaching. But sometimes he cites them in order to criticize them along with the Roman view. This is rare but it shows that he was not bound to their teaching and that he did not try to pretend that he never differed from them.[121] Sometimes Calvin also quotes from the fathers to illustrate a (non-controversial) point. If an ancient writer has succinctly expressed what Calvin wants to say, he will quote him. Calvin appreciated style and was, for example, fond of quoting Bernard's word plays.[122]

Calvin's major non-polemical use of the fathers lies in his commentaries, where almost a quarter of his patristic citations are to be found, although much of this material is drawn from earlier works.[123] The historical material in the commentaries falls into two groups. There are citations relating to dogmatic issues, which are primarily polemical, and there are citations on exegetical issues. With the latter the primary aim is to establish the meaning of the text. In expounding Scripture Calvin repeatedly cites the opinions of the fathers, as often as not to disagree with them. Here he is not so much appealing to them as authorities as debating with them.[124] He treats them much as a modern commentator would treat his distinguished predecessors. Citation, even in disagreement, is a mark of respect. This probably explains the frequency of the references to Augustine, most of which are critical. Augustine was so worthy of respect that his judgment had to be considered, even when wrong.

---

117   CO 7:787–90; Mooi, KDE 12; Ganoczy, *Le jeune Calvin*, 88–90; ET: 94–96.
118   Nineteen, compared with seventeen in chapter 4. It is true that the historical material is heavily medieval (fifty citations) (Mooi, KDE 367f.).
119   There are three medieval citations. Of the seventeen patristic citations, only two are anti-Zwinglian and at least eleven are anti-Roman. All the other chapters have only seven citations between them (Mooi, KDE 367).
120   Cf. section V, below.
121   Cf. section VI.a, below.
122   Chapter 4, below, at nn. 82f.
123   Mooi, KDE 134.
124   Mooi, KDE 98f. For further support cf. chapter 9, below, at nn. 137f.

V. PREFATORY ADDRESS TO KING FRANCIS

Calvin's polemical use of the fathers is perhaps best illustrated from the *Prefatory Address to King Francis* at the beginning of the 1536 *Institutio*. Calvin complains that evangelical teaching is called 'new' and 'of recent birth',[125] but he rejects this charge:

> First, by calling it 'new' they do great wrong to God, whose Sacred Word does not deserve to be accused of novelty. Indeed, I do not at all doubt that it is new to them, since to them both Christ himself and his gospel are new. But they who know that this preaching of Paul is ancient, that 'Jesus Christ died for our sins and rose again for our justification', will find nothing new among us.[126]

This essentially amounts to an appeal from tradition to Scripture, to the claim that evangelical doctrine is ancient because scriptural. 'Now, if our interpretation be measured by this rule of faith, victory is in our hands.'[127] While formally sufficient for one professing the final authority of Scripture, this defence is vulnerable to the following charge of Cardinal Sadolet:

> The point in dispute is, Whether [it is] more expedient for your salvation, and whether you think you will do what is more pleasing to God, by believing and following what the Catholic Church throughout the whole world, now for more than fifteen hundred years, or (if we require clear and certain recorded notice of the facts) for more than thirteen hundred years, approves with general consent; or innovations introduced within these twenty-five years, by crafty, or, as they think themselves, acute men; but men certainly who are not themselves the Catholic Church?[128]

Such a charge could not lightly be brushed aside, especially in an age for which, unlike ours, authority lay with antiquity rather than modernity. Calvin meets it with his appeal to the fathers. While this was not formally necessary since the fathers can all err and Scripture alone is normative, it was practically and apologetically essential in that a theology contrary to the unanimous interpretation of the Christian church since apostolic times would seriously lack credibility. Furthermore, the Reformers were not Anabaptists who saw themselves as founding a new church. They believed that they were reforming the old church and that they therefore stood in continuity with the church of the early fathers and even, to a

---

125 Battles 5, OS 1:25. For the source of these accusations, cf. OS 3:12–17; LCC 20:15, n. 8 and, especially, the notes in Battles 231–38, which are based on J. Bohatec, *Budé und Calvin* (Graz: Hermann Böhlaus, 1950) 127–41.
126 Battles 5, OS 1:25.
127 Battles 3, OS 1:24.
128 CTS 1:14, OS 1:450 from his 1539 letter to the Genevans. These words were of course written some four years later than Calvin's *Prefatory Address*, but they have been quoted here because they express most succinctly the charge that Calvin then had to face. For Calvin's response to these words of Sadolet, cf. his *Resp. ad epist. Sadoleti* (OS 1:466f., LCC 22:231–33). Cf. also CO 6:240, where Calvin discusses the same charge in his *Def. adv. calumn. Pighii*.

lesser extent, with the church of the Middle Ages. This claim needed to be substantiated.

Calvin's opponents appealed to the fathers against him 'as if in them they had supporters of their own impiety'. Calvin rejected this claim. 'If the contest were to be determined by patristic authority, the tide of victory would turn to our side.'[129] Calvin's counterclaim reduces to two essential points: the fathers do not support the heresies of Rome, which are contrary to the teaching of the Early Church; the teaching of Calvin and the Reformers is very close to that of the sounder teachers in the Early Church, especially Augustine.

Calvin does not deny that the fathers made mistakes. This is only to be expected. But the Roman Catholics seize only on these errors, ignoring the good teaching of the fathers.

> Now, these fathers have written many wise and excellent things. Still, what commonly happens to men has befallen them too, in some instances. For these so-called pious children of theirs, with all their sharpness of wit and judgment and spirit, worship only the faults and errors of the fathers. The good things that these fathers have written they either do not notice, or misrepresent or pervert. You might say that their only care is to gather dung amid gold.[130]

We are not under any obligation to follow the fathers when they go astray. Their writings are given to us to serve us, not to lord it over us. It is Christ alone whom we obey.[131] It is God's Word that we are bound to, not to that of human beings. Also, it is not only the Reformers who reject parts of the teaching of the fathers. The Roman Catholics 'transgress them so willfully as often as it suits them'.[132] Calvin then gives a list of patristic passages which contradict Roman teaching.[133]

> Why, if the fathers were now brought back to life, and heard such brawling art as these persons call speculative theology, there is nothing they would less suppose than that these folks were disputing about God! But my discourse would overflow if I chose to review how wantonly they reject the yoke of the fathers, whose obedient children they wish to seem.[134]

Roman teaching is contrary to the teaching of the fathers. On the other hand, Calvin's teaching is supported by the fathers, especially Augustine. 'We do not despise the fathers; in fact, if it were to our present purpose, I could with no trouble at all prove that the greater part of what we are saying today meets their approval.'[135]

---

129 Battles 6, OS 1:27. Later editions add an extra phrase (OS 3:17 n. f.).
130 Battles 6, OS 1:27. The last point occurs again in CO 7:644, CTS 3:307 *(Interim)*.
131 OS 1:27, Battles 6.
132 Battles 7, OS 1:27.
133 OS 1:27–29, Battles 7f.
134 Battles 8, OS 1:29. There are minor textual variations in later editions (OS 3:22, nn. c&d). For a well-known later use of this illustration against Protestantism, cf. J. H. Newman, *An Essay on the Development of Christian Doctrine* (Harmondsworth: Penguin, 1974) 185.
135 Battles 6, OS 1:27.

VI. STATUS

(a) The Fathers

Calvin's respect for the fathers was great, but not unqualified.

> We are so versed in their writings as to remember always that all things are ours, to serve us, not to lord it over us, and that we all belong to the one Christ, whom we must obey in all things without exception. He who does not observe this distinction will have nothing certain in religion, inasmuch as these holy men were ignorant of many things, often disagreed among themselves, and sometimes even contradicted themselves.[136]

> The Spirit goes before the Church to enlighten her in understanding the Word, while the Word itself is like the Lydian stone by which she tests all doctrines.[137]

The Scriptures are the only infallible norm and the teaching of the fathers is to be judged in the light of Scripture. After citing Augustine against Origen and Jerome, Calvin adds that 'what these hold makes no difference to us, provided we understand what Paul means'.[138] Some of the fathers made a distinction between *latria* and *dulia*, but 'what, then, if all perceive that it is not only inept but entirely worthless?'[139] The fathers distinguished between John's baptism and Christian baptism, but 'we ought not so to value their authority as to let it shake the certainty of Scripture'.[140] 'Holy Scripture contains a perfect doctrine, to which one can add nothing.'[141] This did not prevent Calvin from adding his not in-substantial *Institutio* as a guide to its meaning, but this, like the fathers, is to be seen as subject to Scripture and open to correction in the light of it. Calvin's approach to the fathers is similar to that which he advocates towards magistrates, pastors and parents: they are worthy of respect but their authority is subordinated to God's.[142] This is seen in a letter where Calvin criticizes Bucer for deferring to the authority of the fathers to the extent of tolerating the unscriptural superstition of the invocation of the saints. It is not that Calvin is against the citation of the fathers as authorities, but they must always be subject to correction by Scripture, a line which Bucer has overstepped.[143]

---

136 Battles 6f., OS 1:27 (*Prefatory Address*).
137 LCC 22:230f., OS 1:465f. (*Resp. ad epist. Sadoleti*).
138 *Inst.* 2:5:17.
139 *Inst.* 1:12:2.
140 *Inst.* 4:15:7.
141 From the *Argument du Present Livre* which took the place of the *Epistola ad Lectorem* in the French translations (OS 3:7).
142 *Comm.* Acts 5:29, cf. 4:17.
143 *Epist.* 87 (12 January 1538) (CO 10b:142f.; CRF 4:347). This point is obscured by C. Augustijn, 'Calvin in Strasbourg' in Neuser (ed.), *Calvinus Sacrae Scripturae Professor*, 175; W. van 't Spijker, 'Reformatie tussen Patristiek en Scholastiek: Bucers theologische Positie' in J. van Oort (ed.), *De Kerkvaders in Reformatie en Nadere Reformatie* (Zoetermeer: Uitgeverij Boekencentrum, 1997) 45–47. There is no conflict here with Calvin's normal attitude.

Todd misunderstands Calvin at this point. He contrasts Luther's appeal to the Word of God with that of Calvin. He argues that Calvin's appeal to Scripture should be seen in humanist terms as a return to historical origins, to Christ and the apostles. The implication is that Scripture is normative because it is primitive.[144] This is not so. Scripture is normative because it is God's Word whereas patristic teaching, however pure and however primitive, is merely human teaching.[145] This is a theological, not merely a humanist, principle. Todd is likewise mistaken in his claim that Calvin could not believe anything that was without historical precedent.[146]

Calvin is prepared if necessary to stand alone against the consensus of the fathers,[147] though he never lightly departed from antiquity. While he has a great respect for the teaching of the fathers, and especially for their consensus, this is because they are, on the whole, scriptural. While he appeals repeatedly to the Early Church, he firmly refuses to give any absolute authority to antiquity:

> And thus the foolishness of the papists is detected, who think that they lie safely concealed under the shield of Ajax, when they boast to us of the examples of their fathers, and the value of antiquity: we clearly see how plainly God's Spirit refutes them when he pronounces that they must obey his statutes and precepts, and not listen to open wickedness only, but not even to good intentions, as they say, and devotions, and the traditions of the fathers.... But since antiquity deserves some reverence, it would be gross and barbarous promiscuously to reject all the examples of the fathers: hence we need prudence and selection here, and God's Spirit suggests this to us when he adds *pollutions* or idols. Hence the traditions of the fathers must be examined; and it is a mark of prudent discretion to observe what they contain, and whence they proceed. If we discover that they have no other tendency than to the pure worship of God, we may embrace them; but if they draw us away from the pure and simple worship of God, if they infect true and sincere religion by their own mixtures, we must utterly reject them.[148]

---

144 Todd, *Function of the Patristic Writings*, 135–37. J. R. Payton, 'History as Rhetorical Weapon: Christian Humanism in Calvin's Reply to Sadoleto, 1539' in E. J. Furcha (ed.), *In Honor of John Calvin, 1509–64* (Montreal: Faculty of Religious Studies McGill University, 1987) 110–21, shows how Calvin in his *Reply to Sadolet* presents his historical material so as to identify Protestantism with antiquity and Roman Catholicism with medieval superstition, while affirming the normative role of Scripture. This is a skilful appeal aimed at Christian humanists.

145 CO 7:645, CTS 3:308f. (*Interim*); *Comm.* Ephesians 2:20. Cf. *Inst.* 4:17:43, 4:19:12 for the fallibility of primitive antiquity. D. Fischer, 'L'Histoire de l'Eglise dans la Pensée de Calvin', *Archiv für Reformationsgeschichte* 77 (1986) 108 also makes the point that for Calvin authority is given to Scripture alone and not to antiquity.

146 Todd, *Function of the Patristic Writings*, 145f., where he appeals to CO 7:498, CTS 3:179 (*Acta syn. Trid.*). But this passage does not at all support his contention. He has been misled by a mistranslation in CTS.

147 In addition to the passages quoted at the beginning of this section, cf. *Inst.* 1:13:5, 3:5:10; CO 7:621, CTS 3:278 (*Interim*).

148 *Comm.* Ezekiel 20:18f. (J. Calvin, *Commentaries on the First Twenty Chapters of the Book of the Prophet Ezekiel*, 2 vols (Grand Rapids: Eerdmans, 1948 reprint) 2:310) (emphasis in original); cf. *Comm.* Psalms 95:9.

The Roman appeal to church teaching as authoritative in its own right Calvin compares with the error of the Anabaptists (thinking in particular of those known today as 'spiritual Anabaptists'). Both alike fall into the same error of separating the Spirit from the Word, of appealing to the Holy Spirit outside of and independently of the word of Scripture.[149] Scripture alone is normative, although antiquity deserves respect.

> For, although we hold that the Word of God alone lies beyond the sphere of our judgment, and that Fathers and Councils are of authority only in so far as they agree with the rule of the Word, we still give to Councils and Fathers such rank and honour as it is proper for them under Christ to hold.[150]

Pontien Polman questions whether Calvin actually follows the theory here outlined. He argues that the Reformers were aware that free enquiry and private judgment would lead to chaos and anarchy and that they therefore recognized the need for an authority beyond Scripture. Calvin, he argues, gave such authority to the Early Church.[151] Smits flirts with this interpretation when he claims that the appeal to the fathers was used not only against Rome but also to maintain Protestant unity and to check free enquiry.[152] But he recognizes that for Calvin Scripture remains the sole criterion by which to judge tradition and that even the unanimous consent of the fathers remains human.[153] Polman's theory has rightly been rejected by more recent writers.[154]

Calvin was aware that the Bible could be interpreted in a variety of ways and that his (Roman) opponents likened Scripture to a nose of wax. He did not accept their solution: the infallible interpretation of the church.[155] Calvin's cure for the evils of private judgment was not the infallible teaching authority of the church, nor the consensus of the fathers, but the balancing of private with public trial of doctrine:

> But a difficult question arises here. If everyone has the right and liberty to judge, nothing will ever be settled as certain and the whole of religion will waver. I reply: There is a twofold trial of doctrine, private and public. The private is that by which each one settles his own faith and safely rests in that doctrine which he knows has come from God.... The public trial relates to the common consent and ολιτεία of the Church. For since there is the danger of fanatical men arising and presumptuously claiming that they are endued with the

---

149 OS 1:465f., LCC 22:230f. (*Resp. ad epist. Sadoleti*); *Comm*. John 14:26.
150 LCC 22:255, OS 1:488 (*Resp. ad epist. Sadoleti*).
151 P. Polman, *L'élément historique dans la controverse religieuse du XVIe siècle* (Gembloux: L. Duculot, 1932) 73f.
152 Smits, SAOJC 1:255.
153 Ibid., 1:255–59.
154 A. D. R. Polman, 'Calvijn en de Oude Kerk', *Vox Theologica* 30 (1959–60) 75f.; Mooi, KDE 351, who cites W. F. Dankbaar.
155 CO 6:268–70 (*Def. adv. calumn. Pighii*); CO 7:411f., 416–18, CTS 3:67–69, 74–77 (*Acta syn. Trid.*).

Spirit of God, it is a necessary remedy that believers shall meet together and seek a way of godly and pure agreement.[156]

Calvin, like the other Reformers, believed strongly in the perspicuity of Scripture, which explains his confidence concerning the prospects for common agreement.

(b) Augustine

Calvin had a great respect for the teaching of the fathers. He did not lightly depart from their teaching. He believed that their teaching largely supported his own. All of this applies *a fortiori* to Augustine. Calvin held Augustine in the highest regard. He was very reluctant to depart from Augustine in doctrinal matters, or at least to admit to it. He made sweeping claims to the support of Augustine.

Augustinus ... totus noster est.[157]

If I wanted to weave a whole volume from Augustine, I could readily show my readers that I need no other language than his.[158]

Calvin clearly believed that, on a wide range of issues, he was simply restoring the teaching of Augustine. Augustine was fallible and subordinate to Scripture, but Calvin was nonetheless reluctant to *admit* that he was departing from him.[159] Sometimes he opposed Augustine's teaching but without naming him.[160] When he did openly dissent from him, he always remained respectful, a favour not granted to all of the fathers.[161] Calvin held Augustine in such high regard that his judgment was sufficient to counterbalance all the other fathers.[162] Why did Calvin give such authority to Augustine?

First it is probable that some, at least, of Augustine's authority derived from the close affinity between his teaching and Calvin's. Calvin's teaching was to a considerable extent, if not to the extent that he actually claimed, a revival of Augustinianism, and it is natural therefore that he should have felt inclined to give considerable authority to Augustine.[163] *Secondly*, it was not just Calvin who gave him such authority. Augustine was accepted in the sixteenth-century Western church as the father *par excellence*. Calvin's Roman Catholic and Lutheran opponents themselves accorded him such

---

156 *Comm.* 1 John 4:1 (T. H. L. Parker (tr.), *Calvin's Commentaries*, vol. 5 (Edinburgh: Saint Andrew Press, 1961) 285).
157 CO 8:266 (*De praed.*). Cf. *Inst.* 3:4,33, 4:17:28. Cf. Mooi, KDE 231–63; Lange van Ravenswaay, *Augustinus totus noster.*
158 *Inst.* 3:22:8. Cf. *Inst.* 4:17:21; CO 6:325 (*Def. adv. calumn. Pighii*) for the volume of material available; *Inst.* 3:22:10, 3:24:1, 4:19:16; CO 6:483, LCC 22:198 (*Suppl. exhort.*); CO 8:265f., 282, 312f., *Predestination*, 62f., 83, 120; CO 9:880, LCC 22:41 (*Disc. Lausanne*) for the sufficiency of Augustine's own words.
159 Smits, SAOJC 1:263f.; Todd, *Function of the Patristic Writings*, 183–88.
160 Smits, SAOJC 1:265.
161 Smits, SAOJC 1:264.
162 Smits, SAOJC 1:260.
163 Smits, SAOJC 1:259.

authority.[164] *Thirdly*, Calvin saw Augustine as the best witness to antiquity and as the guardian of the teaching of the Early Church.[165] *Finally*, Smits has suggested that Augustine was himself responsible for Calvin's conversion and that this to some extent accounts for Calvin's respect for him.[166] This interpretation of Calvin's conversion has not been well received and the evidence does not seem to warrant such a conclusion.[167]

Calvin's almost unqualified respect for Augustine's authority in dogmatic matters is not paralleled in the exegetical realm.[168] Here it is Chrysostom who was Calvin's hero, at least for the New Testament.[169] Augustine's exegesis is severely criticized. He was too subtle, passing over the plain sense of Scripture and indulging in vain speculations. He was too free with the letter of Scripture, indulging in allegory, of which Calvin did not approve. But Calvin could on occasions praise Augustine's exegesis and he often followed him.[170] In exegesis as in theology Calvin always remained courteous when disagreeing with Augustine.

(c) Councils[171]

Calvin respected the first four general councils: Nicea, Constantinople, Ephesus and Chalcedon: 'I venerate them from my heart, and desire that they be honored by all.'[172] Councils are a good way to settle doctrinal disputes, but they are not given any automatic infallibility.[173] It is true that Christ has promised his presence where two or three are gathered in his name, but only where they are gathered in *his name*. The promise applies to a council (or to any other gathering) only when Christ presides, when he rules the council by his Word and Spirit.[174] The church does not err when she is taught by the Holy Spirit through the Word, but it is wrong to talk of the authority of the church in isolation from the Word.[175] If a council

---

164 CO 9:880, LCC 22:40 (*Disc. Lausanne*), for Rome; *Inst.* 4:17:6, for Lutherans. Cf. Torrance, *Theology in Reconstruction*, 76, quoted at n. 103, above.
165 Smits, SAOJC 1:260.
166 Smits, SAOJC 17–24, 261.
167 E. A. Dowey, *Church History* 29 (1960) 103 (in his review of Smits); Snell, *Place of Augustine*, 137, 222f.; Todd, *Function of the Patristic Writings*, 67–71.
168 Smits, SAOJC 1:265–70; G. Besse, 'Saint Augustin dans les oeuvres exégétiques de Jean Calvin', *Revue des études augustiniennes* 6 (1960) 161–72.
169 Cf. Walchenbach, *Calvin as Biblical Commentator*. Chrysostom is cited only three times in the Old Testament commentaries (Mooi, KDE 381, 394). In his *Preface to Chrysostom's Homilies* Calvin notes that the Old Testament homilies suffered from his lack of Hebrew (CO 9:834).
170 Augustine is a 'fidus interpres' of Scripture (*Inst.* 3:2:35), but this comes in a doctrinal context.
171 The Caroli incident is not here considered as it is somewhat enigmatic and does not affect Calvin's mature position. Cf. K. Barth, *The Theology of John Calvin* (Grand Rapids and Cambridge: Eerdmans, 1995) 323–31; E. Doumergue, *Jean Calvin. Les hommes et les choses de son temps*, vol. 2 (Lausanne: J. Bridel, 1902) 252–68; W. Nijenhuis, 'Calvin's attitude towards the symbols of the Early Church during the conflict with Caroli' in his *Ecclesia Reformata. Studies on the Reformation* (Leiden: E. J. Brill, 1972) 73–96; S. M. Reynolds, 'Calvin's view of the Athanasian and Nicene Creeds', *Westminster Theological Journal* 23 (1960–61) 33–37.
172 *Inst.* 4:9:1, cf. 4:9:8, 13.
173 *Inst.* 4:9:13, 4:8:10–12.
174 *Inst.* 4:9:1f.
175 *Inst.* 4:8:13.

is not subject to Scripture, the promise of Christ does not apply.[176] The church has no authority to add to the teaching of Scripture.[177]

In defence of his claim that councils can err, Calvin appeals both to Scripture and to history. The strictures of the Old Testament prophets show that a true church can exist without a faithful ministry.[178] A false council is to be found in the four hundred prophets that Ahab summoned (1 Kings 22).[179] This danger is not limited to Old Testament times. The New Testament contains many warnings about false teachers, even within the church.[180] It was a council that condemned Christ (John 11:47–53).[181] Church history shows how councils have condemned one another, as in the Iconoclastic controversy.[182] Even the purest councils were not perfect: there was internal dissent at Nicea;[183] Leo implied that Chalcedon could have erred.[184] Some councils have strayed from the truth, as at Ephesus in AD 449 and at Nicea in AD 787.[185] The moral is not to follow Gregory of Nazianzus into cynicism about all councils but rather to exercise discernment.[186] A council is to be judged by examining 'at what time it was held, on what issue, and with what intention, what sort of men were present'. Above all, it is to be tested by Scripture, as Augustine himself urged.[187] It is true that Scripture teaches us to be subject to our rulers, but it also warns us to beware of false prophets. All must be tested by God's Word.[188]

VII. PERIODS

(a) 'The Primitive and Purer Church'

Calvin followed the tradition, common to humanists and Reformers alike, of viewing the Early Church as a golden classical period. The fathers are 'the ancient writers of a better age of the church'.[189] He notes that 'for about five hundred years ... religion was still flourishing, and a purer

---

176 *Inst.* 4:9:2, cf. 4:8:11f.
177 *Inst.* 4:8:14–16, 4:9:14.
178 *Inst.* 4:9:3.
179 *Inst.* 4:9:6.
180 *Inst.* 4:9:4.
181 *Inst.* 4:9:7.
182 *Inst.* 4:9:9.
183 *Inst.* 4:9:10.
184 *Inst.* 4:9:11. It was, of course, not the doctrinal definition but canon 28 (on the status of Constantinople) that Leo questioned. A study of Calvin's use of councils in the *Institutio* reveals an overriding interest in disciplinary matters.
185 *Inst.* 4:9:13, 1:11:14–16. Cf. D. J. C. Cooper, 'The Theology of Image in Eastern Orthodoxy and John Calvin', *Scottish Journal of Theology* 35 (1982) 219–41; J. R. Payton, 'Calvin and the Legitimation of Icons: His Treatment of the Seventh Ecumenical Council', *Archiv für Reformationsgeschichte* 84 (1993) 222–41.
186 *Inst.* 4:9:11.
187 *Inst.* 4:9:8. Calvin does not give due weight to the fact that Augustine is here using an *ad hominem* argument.
188 *Inst.* 4:9:12.
189 Battles 6, OS 1:27 (*Prefatory Address*). Cf. 'the writers of a purer age' (LCC 22:190, CO 6:476 (*Suppl. exhort.*)); 'in the better ages, when Religion flourished' (CTS 3:257, CO 7:605 (*Interim*)). Cf. Todd, *Function of the Patristic Writings*, 137–39.

doctrine thriving'.[190] The duration of this period is approximate and it is not to be seen in purely numerical terms. It is not that there is something special about the number 500. The limits of the period are defined in terms of the figures to whom Calvin appeals. Against Sadolet he appeals to 'the ancient form of the Church as their writings prove it to have been in the ages of Chrysostom and Basil among the Greeks, and of Cyprian, Ambrose and Augustine among the Latins'.[191] The significant figures to whom Calvin appealed had all died by the middle of the fifth century. This was 'the primitive and purer Church'.[192] Calvin similarly singles out the first four general councils for special approval, referring to 'the purity of that golden age'.[193]

Todd argues that there is a lower as well as an upper limit to the golden age. He argues that in *practice* the emphasis for Calvin lies on the period from AD 325 to AD 451 the great dogma-defining period of church history.[194] There is much truth in this claim. Almost three-quarters of the citations noted by Mooi fall within this period.[195] But the claim must not be exaggerated. It is not true that 'Calvin was not interested in any figure Latin or Greek after Gregory the Great'.[196] Bernard of Clairvaux clearly refutes that claim. Nor was Calvin as uninterested in the ante-Nicene period as Todd implies. Irenaeus, Tertullian, Cyprian and Origen all receive at least fifty citations,[197] and Irenaeus, Tertullian and Cyprian all appear in Calvin's 'top ten' according to frequency of citation.[198] They are cited consistently throughout Calvin's life and on a wide range of topics: Christology, anthropology, ecclesiology, eucharist, penance, ministry, allegory, tradition.[199] The apostolic fathers and the apologists are only sparsely represented,[200] but the period before Irenaeus was not well known in Calvin's time.

As has frequently been noted, Calvin's interest lies predominantly in the Western fathers.[201] Chrysostom is the favourite Greek father, especially in the realm of *New* Testament exegesis.[202] Irenaeus, Origen and Cyril of Alexandria are the only other Greek fathers receiving fifty or more

---

190 *Inst.* 1:11:13.
191 LCC 22:231, OS 1:466.
192 LCC 22:215, CO 6:498 *(Suppl. exhort.)*.
193 *Inst.* 4:9:8.
194 Todd, *Function of the Patristic Writings*, 170–76.
195 71½ per cent. This figure and those which follow are taken from the totals given by Mooi, KDE 396f. For percentages the (72) citations of Josephus are excluded as he fits into none of the groups here considered.
196 Todd, *Function of the Patristic Writings*, 171. Medievals (post-AD 451) claim 15½ per cent of citations. It is not true that Calvin never mentions John of Damascus (ibid., 175): cf. CO 7:657, CTS 3:322 *(Interim)*; CO 9:490f., LCC 22:292f. *(Diluc. explic. Heshusii)*.
197 84, 122, 121 and 52, respectively. The Ante-Nicenes claim an eighth of the citations.
198 These are Augustine (1708), Jerome (332), Chrysostom (259), Gregory the Great (179), Gratian (138), Ambrose (133), Tertullian (122), Cyprian (121), Peter Lombard (89), and Irenaeus (84).
199 Mooi, KDE 194–212.
200 Ignatius (7), Justin Martyr (10).
201 The Eastern Church claims only some 18 per cent of citations.
202 Cf. Walchenbach, *John Calvin as Biblical Commentator*; Mooi, KDE 273–80.

citations.[203] Calvin cites Basil and Gregory Nazianzen a number of times, but especially on points of interest to Western theology.[204] Irena Backus correctly notes that Calvin's portrayal of the early Greek Church 'was thus a very partial Church, strangely reminiscent of his own conception of theology and Church organisation' and ignoring important elements like spirituality, asceticism and monasticism.[205] As she also notes, 'Calvin's main point of reference was the Bible which he attempted to harmonise first and foremost with the pronouncements of Augustine and only secondly with the Greek post-Nicene Fathers'.[206] The evidence does not support the theory that Calvin was heavily influenced by the Greek fathers. Even less likely is any theory of Athanasius's influence on Calvin.[207]

Some 60 per cent of Calvin's citations are taken from the Western fathers between Nicea and Chalcedon. The bulk of these citations come from Augustine, who alone accounts for almost 45 per cent of the total.[208] Jerome comes a poor second, though ahead of any other father, followed by Ambrose, Hilary and Leo.[209] These fathers are cited for a wide range of topics.[210]

(b) The Corrupt Church

After the golden age the church fell into decline. This took place gradually and there is no one date given when the church 'fell'. Calvin gives different dates for different stages of the decline: belief in the carnal presence of Christ had prevailed for more than 600 years;[211] the heights of papal power were reached only 400 years previously;[212] compulsory confession is less than 300 years old;[213] other errors and darkness have been around for 'some centuries'.[214] For Calvin there was no one fall

---

203 Cyril of Alexandria receives fifty-two citations. E. Doumergue, *Jean Calvin*, vol. 4 (Lausanne: J. Bridel, 1910) 4, started a fruitful legend when he asserted that of the Greek fathers Calvin cites 'surtout Origène'. Cf. Polman, *L'Élément historique*, 67; Wendel, *Calvin*, 115; Todd, *Function of the Patristic Writings*, 175. There are no grounds for singling Origen out from among the Greek fathers.
204 Mooi, KDE 273. Cf. chapter 3, below, section III.d, e, f.
205 Backus, 'Calvin and the Greek Fathers'.
206 Ibid.
207 Cf. chapter 3, below, section III.c.
208 If Augustine is excluded, the citations are distributed as follows: Ante-Nicenes, 23 per cent; AD 325–451, 49 per cent (of which 28 per cent are Western); Post-Chalcedon, 28 per cent; Eastern total, 32 per cent. L. Smits, SAOJC vol. 2 finds many more Augustinian references, but these include allusions and not just explicit citations.
209 The totals are: Jerome, 332; Ambrose, 133; Hilary, 54; Leo, 53.
210 Mooi, KDE 213–69.
211 OS 1:527, LCC 22:164 (*Traité Cène*). Cf. CO 7:621, CTS 3:278 (*Interim*): the belief in the destruction of the bread and the wine in the Supper was unknown for more than 600 years and then suddenly emerged.
212 CO 6:523, CTS 1:218 (*Suppl. exhort.*).
213 *Inst.* 3:4:7. Calvin was clearly ill-informed (or careless) about the dates of Innocent III and the Fourth Lateran Council. Cf. CO 7:605, CTS 3:257 (*Interim*): for more than 1000 years confession was not compulsory.
214 Battles 11, OS 1:33 (*Prefatory Address*); *Inst.* 4:17:19; CO 6:240 (*Def. adv. calumn. Pighii*).

of the church but rather a progressive decline from primitive purity to contemporary darkness.[215]

Calvin draws a contrast between the 'primitive and purer Church' of the fathers and the later corrupt church, but this contrast is not total. Calvin acknowledges at least a measure of continuity between the Early Church and the errors of the Middle Ages and even of contemporary Rome.[216]

> For though we admit that in ancient times some seeds of superstition were sown, which rather detracted from the purity of the gospel, still you know that it is not so long ago that those monsters of impiety with which we do battle were born, or at least grew to such a size.[217]

While he continues that 'in attacking, breaking down, and destroying your kingdom, we are armed not only with the virtue of the divine Word, but also with the aid of the holy Fathers',[218] the confession is significant. Often, when attacking Roman teaching, e.g. on freewill or merit, he has to admit that the fathers were not without fault.[219] While the early fathers do not support the doctrine of purgatory, Calvin has to admit that they erred in praying for the dead.[220] The seeds of Roman error go back to the Early Church.

The decline of the church is linked to the rise of the papacy. The medieval councils which supported the papacy were held 'after the light of sound doctrine was extinguished, and discipline had decayed, and when the merest dolts were present'.[221] Calvin was aware that some of the earliest popes, such as Leo, had made great claims for Rome. But these were not generally accepted.[222] By the time of Gregory I the fall of the Roman Empire in the West had greatly increased the power of Rome. Gregory is portrayed as one who sought to resist this process, though he was imbued with many errors as the age was corrupt.[223] After him the situation became worse until Bernard of Clairvaux protested against it in the twelfth century.[224] For Calvin, Gregory and Bernard are the two great champions of the truth in the Middle Ages.[225] After the time of Bernard things became even worse.[226]

---

215 There is a 'middle period', the period from Leo to Gregory, between the early church and later darkness (*Inst.* 4:7:22, cf. LaVallee, *Calvin's Criticism of Scholastic Theology*, 17–19).
216 Cf. section VII.c, below.
217 LCC 22:240, OS 1:474 (*Resp. ad epist. Sadoleti*).
218 Ibid.
219 *Inst.* 2:2:4, 3:15:2.
220 *Inst.* 3:5:10.
221 CTS 3:89, CO 7:427 (*Acta syn. Trid.*).
222 *Inst.* 4:7:11, cf. 4:7:1–10 for earlier claims.
223 *Inst.* 4:7:4, 12f., 16; *Comm.* Habakkuk 2:19. Cf. L. K. Little, 'Calvin's Appreciation of Gregory the Great', *Harvard Theological Review* 56 (1963) 145–57.
224 *Inst.* 4:7:17f.
225 Note their juxtaposition in *Comm.* 1 Corinthians 3:15. Cf. Mooi, KDE 297–305, 320–27. Cf. B. Jacqueline. 'Saint Gregoire le Grand et l'ecclésiologie de saint Bernard de Clairvaux', *Recherches de théologie ancienne et médiévale* 41 (1974) 200–204, on the affinity between them. Luther also linked together Gregory and Bernard (R. Schwarz, 'Luther's Inalienable Inheritance of Monastic Theology', *American Benedictine Review* 39 (1988) 433).
226 *Inst.* 4:7:19–30.

If the root cause of the decline of the church lies in the papacy, its theological fruit is to be found in scholasticism. Peter Lombard and Gratian both appear in Calvin's 'top ten',[227] but this does not mean that he had any admiration for them. Peter Lombard's *Sentences* was the standard textbook for theology and Gratian's *Concordia discordantium canonum* played a similar role in canon law. Both were cited for evidence of the Roman teaching. Lombard was 'eorum coryphaeus', 'eorum Pythagoras'.[228] He is repeatedly attacked as the spokesman for scholasticism. But Calvin was also aware of the contrast between Peter Lombard and later scholasticism and noted occasions where Lombard was sounder than his successors.[229]

The relative absence of explicit references to the scholastics (apart from Peter Lombard) in Calvin's works has already been noted.[230] Calvin almost totally fails to name them[231] and even naming them is no proof of first-hand acquaintance. Anselm is named and quoted but there is strong evidence that the quotation comes from a secondary source.[232] On the other hand, Calvin had less reason to cite the scholastics by name and his *sophistae* and *scholastici* may conceal a real first-hand knowledge of their writings. The library of the Genevan Academy in 1572 contained works by Thomas Aquinas, Duns Scotus, Gregory of Rimini and Dionysius the Carthusian.[233] But these need not have come from Calvin's personal library and, on the other hand, the Genevan library lacks works with which Calvin was certainly familiar.[234] Not all of Calvin's books went into the library.[235]

One scholastic theologian that Calvin does name is Thomas Aquinas. A glance at the final chapter of this book will show that there are many more studies of Calvin and Thomas than any other figure, except for Augustine. Most of these do not go beyond comparing them, but a few talk of Calvin's use of Thomas and of the latter's influence upon Calvin. Some scholars have been misled by the 145 entries in the index to the Battles/McNeill translation of the *Institutio*, not realizing that Thomas is named just twice in that work. Helge Stadtland-Neumann claims that Thomas exerted 'einen nicht geringen Einfluß' on Calvin's thought on Matthew 5–7, 10, on the basis of shared positions but without considering other possible sources.[236] She is rightly chided for this by Oberman.[237]

227 Cf. Ganoczy, *Le jeune Calvin*, 179–86; ET: 168–73; M. Reulos, 'Le Décret de Gratien chez les humanistes, les gallicans et les réformés français du XVIème siècle', *Studium Gratianum* 2 (1954) 692–96. Mooi, KDE 306–20.
228 *Inst.* 3:4:39, 3:15:7.
229 Lombard is among the *saniores Scholastici* as opposed to the *recentiores Sophistae* (*Inst.* 2:2:6); in comparison with the *posteriores Sophistae* Lombard is *sanus et sobrius* (*Inst.* 3:15:7). Cf. *Inst.* 2:3:5, 3:11:15.
230 Cf. at nn. 104–106, above.
231 Names (with number of citations): Anselm (1), William of Paris/Auvergne (1), Thomas Aquinas (4), Bonaventure (1), Duns Scotus (2), William of Occam (2). Cf. section XI, below, for details.
232 *Inst.* 2:2:4. For the evidence cf. chapter 5, below, at nn. 151–53.
233 Ganoczy, BAC 102–105.
234 Ibid., 106–108.
235 Ibid., 17–19.
236 H. Stadtland-Neumann, *Evangelische Radikalismus in der Sicht Calvins. Sein Verständnis der Bergpredigt und der Aussendungsrede (Matth. 10)* (Neukirchen: Neukirchener Verlag, 1966) 64–69.
237 Oberman, 'Initia Calvini', 118f.

Calvin cites Thomas a mere four times. In the 1539 *Institutio* he cites his definition of *liberum arbitrium*, at the conclusion of a list of six definitions. Three of these definitions probably come from an intermediary source.[238] It is not unlikely that the other three may also come from some such source. The other citation is a criticism of Thomas's doctrine of predestination, accusing him of a subtle quibble.[239] His position is presented accurately, but in such a way that Thomas could himself respond to the criticism. This might mean that Calvin was unaware of the wider context in Thomas, but might simply reflect that he was not impressed by Thomas's answer. Apart from these two citations in the *Institutio* Calvin twice in his polemical treatises unfavourably mentions his opponent's use of Thomas.[240] In addition to these four citations, Thomas is also named in the Sorbonne articles, which Calvin quotes before refuting.[241] He himself makes no reference to Thomas here. What conclusion may be drawn from this? It is possible that Calvin never read Thomas for himself and that the two citations in the *Institutio* are derived from intermediate sources. But it is also possible that he had some knowledge of Thomas but refrained from naming him more often for the same reason that he rarely names scholastics other than Peter Lombard.[242]

One surprising omission should be noted. In 1541 the *De Corpore et Sanguine Domini* of Ratramnus was published *at Geneva*. This work can, at the very least, be made to appear to support Calvin's doctrine of the Lord's Supper and a number of modern writers have felt that 'Ratramnus was the precursor of Calvin'.[243] It is therefore remarkable both that Calvin never once refers to Ratramnus and that this work was not to be found in the Genevan library.[244] A. Barclay notes that 'we have not been able to find any reference to it in Calvin's works, but such a reader as he could not be ignorant of it'.[245] This argument appears to be sound – but so does the argument that had he known it he could not have failed to quote it.

There are three possible reasons why Calvin could have known the work but not used it. First, some sixteenth-century Roman Catholics questioned its authenticity,[246] but this does not suffice to explain Calvin's

---

238 Cf. n. 232, above.

239 *Inst.* 3:22:9.

240 CO 7:668 (*Interim*); CO 9:436 (*Grat. ad Gabr. de Saconay*). In the latter Calvin criticizes Thomas for obscure subtleties, echoing the criticism found in *Inst.* 3:22:9.

241 CO 7:41 (*Art. fac. Par.*). There is also a reference to 'Thomistis' in CO 12:484 (*Epist.* 880).

242 Arvin Vos has written a very useful but unfortunately as yet unpublished paper on 'Calvin's Knowledge of Aquinas' which carefully analyses the citations in the *Institutio*. He concludes that 'it appears that Calvin knew Aquinas only second hand'. He also examines the references to Thomas in the footnotes of LCC 20–21 and finds there no evidence of a direct link between Calvin and Aquinas.

243 J. Martin, cited by A. Barclay, *The Protestant Doctrine of the Lord's Supper* (Glasgow: Jackson, Wylie & Co., 1927) 292 where other similar claims are found.

244 The library did contain John Herold's *Orthodoxographa theologiae sacrosanctae ...* (Basel: H. Petri, 1555) which contained Ratramnus's work (Ganoczy, BAC 229). The library failed to acquire a number of books published in Geneva in the 1540s (B. Gagnebin, 'Les Origines de la Bibliothèque de Genève', *Archives, Bibliothèques et Musées de Belgique* 30 (1959) 229–32.

245 Barclay, *Protestant Doctrine*, 287.

246 Ratramnus, *De Corpore et Sanguine Domini*, ed. by J. N. Bakhuizen van den Brink (Amsterdam: North-Holland Publishing Co., 1974 – 2nd edition) 71–74.

silence. Secondly, while Augustine's authority was unassailable, Ratramnus could be written off as a heretic.[247] But this would not alter the fact that his teaching was considered orthodox in its own time, which presents a powerful argument against the antiquity of the Roman position. Thirdly, Calvin was not too concerned to find medieval support for his doctrine. Augustine suffices to establish the antiquity of Calvin's teaching since 'he is wholly and incontrovertibly on our side'.[248] This leaves only the question of when the Roman heresy was introduced. Calvin cites Berengar not as a witness to the truth but as the one whose recantation marks the introduction of a superstitious carnal view of the Supper.[249] Since Augustine, with other fathers, establishes the antiquity of Calvin's doctrine and the Berengar incident marks the introduction of Roman error, Ratramnus is dispensable. It is possible that Calvin knew Ratramnus but did not use him for this reason. It should also be noted that in his polemical appeal to the fathers Calvin was concerned for rhetorical effect rather than piling up evidence for its own sake. In his use of Bernard he on occasions selects passages as much for their rhetorical effect as for their polemical value and also leaves unused passages that could have supported his argument.[250] It is also possible that he did not have any significant knowledge of Ratramnus.

(c) The True Church

Did the true church cease to exist during the time of medieval darkness? Calvin would not admit that the church had ever ceased to exist. Christ has promised to be with his people to the end (Matthew 28:20) and this guarantees the perpetuity of the church.[251] But for Calvin this does not mean that the church must always be visible and observable. The church can exist without visible appearance, as in the time of Elijah (1 Kings 19:10, 14). The 7000 who had not bowed the knee before Baal had no visible form and yet the Lord was preserving his own people.[252] The mark of the true church is not communion with the pope and his bishops.[253] To those who see withdrawal from the apostolic see as apostasy he retorts that to fall

---

247 Ibid., 79f.

248 *Inst.* 4:17:28.

249 Calvin mentions Berengar briefly in his second Lausanne discourse in 1536 (CO 9:886, LCC 22:45) but does not return to him until 1556 in response to Westphal's charge that he is reintroducing Berengar's heresy (CO 9:57f., CTS 2:260f.). Calvin's interest here and hereafter is not in Berengar's teaching (of which he betrays no knowledge) but in the recantation that he signed (*Inst.* 4:17:12; CO 9:154, 222, 436, 469 20:75).

250 Cf. chapter 4, below, final paragraph, and A. N. S. Lane, *Calvin and Bernard of Clairvaux* (Princeton: Princeton Theological Seminary, 1996) 89f.

251 OS 1:31, Battles 9 (*Prefatory Address*).

252 OS 1:31f., Battles 9f. (*Prefatory Address*).

253 OS 1:31–33, Battles 9–11 (*Prefatory Address*); CO 7:610–12, 632–34, CTS 3:264–66, 291–94 (*Interim*). J. J. von Allmen, 'The Continuity of the Church according to Reformed Teaching', *Journal of Ecumenical Studies* 1 (1964) 428–31, argues that Calvin sees the continuity of the church in the existence of a ministry (cf. 433–36, 441–44). This is rightly rejected by A. C. Cochrane, 'The Mystery of the Continuity of the Church: A Study in Reformed Symbolics', *Journal of Ecumenical Studies* 2 (1965) 90–95.

away from Christ is far worse.[254] To the charge of schism he retorts that 'it is enough for me that it behooved us to withdraw from them that we might come to Christ'.[255]

The fact that the papacy is Antichrist shows that the medieval Catholic Church was the church since Paul taught that Antichrist would have his seat in the midst of God's temple (2 Thessalonians 2:4).[256] Even in Calvin's own time the Roman Church contained churches of Christ, though horribly deformed.[257] They are churches in that a remnant of God's people remains in them and some symbols of the church still survive. But the vital marks of the church ('the pure preaching of God's Word and the lawful administration of the sacraments')[258] have been erased and there is not the lawful form of the church.[259]

Calvin traced his ancestry through the medieval Catholic Church. Gregory and Bernard are the evidence that God's truth had not disappeared. It is significant that Calvin did not trace the true church through medieval dissent. This would have been dangerous in that it would have weakened his claim to continuity with antiquity, weakened his case against the Anabaptists and strengthened the argument that the evangelicals were a seditious sect. Calvin supported the Waldensees of his day but never sought to trace his ancestry via their movement.

VIII. METHODS

(a) Calvin's Sources

How did Calvin find his patristic quotations? The sheer bulk and variety of his quotations amply confirm the judgment of J. Köstlin that 'mann sieht, daß sie [die Citate] der Verfasser nicht blos da und dort aufgelesen, sondern einem reichen Material, das ihm frei zu Gebot stand, entnommen hat'.[260] In keeping with the humanist principle of *ad fontes* Calvin read widely in the works of the fathers themselves. Examination of his quotations at Lausanne makes it clear that this was already his practice by that stage.[261] They are placed in context and their position within specific homilies is given, clearly indicating that Calvin had read the originals. There is no serious doubt that Calvin's knowledge of the fathers came overwhelmingly from his own reading of their writings.[262] But this does

---

254 *Inst.* 4:2:2.
255 *Inst.* 4:2:6.
256 *Inst.* 4:2:12; OS 1:476, LCC 22:242 (*Resp. ad epist. Sadoleti*); *Comm.* 2 Thessalonians 2:4.
257 OS 1:476, LCC 22:241f. (*Resp. ad epist. Sadoleti*).
258 Battles 9, OS 1:31 (*Prefatory Address*). Cf. *Inst.* 4:1:9.
259 *Inst.* 4:2:12.
260 J. Köstlin, 'Calvin's Institutio nach Form und Inhalt in ihrer geschichtlichen Entwicklung', *Theologische Studien und Kritiken* 41 (1868) 35. Cf. Mooi, KDE 354.
261 Todd, *Function of the Patristic Writings*, 128–30, concludes from a study of possible sources that these quotations are drawn from Calvin's own reading of the primary sources. Cf. ibid., 66 for a similar judgment on the *Psychopannychia* and H. O. Old, *The Patristic Roots of Reformed Worship* (Zurich: Theologischer Verlag, 1975) 153, for a similar judgment on the Romans commentary.
262 For Chrysostom in particular cf. Walchenbach, *John Calvin as Biblical Commentator*, 135–54.

not preclude the supplementary use of other sources. Intermediate sources are especially likely for the scholastics, Calvin's knowledge of whom was hazy except for Peter Lombard.[263]

In his early years Calvin made use of two compendia: the *Decretum Gratiani* and Lombard's *Sententiae*. The patristic citations in his Commentary on *De clementia* are drawn heavily from the former.[264] Many of the patristic citations in the 1536 *Institutio* were drawn from these two works.[265] This is not simply evidence for Calvin's use of secondary sources. He had a specific reason for using these two works. They were the standard Roman textbooks for canon law and theology and by combating Rome out of these works he was showing how not simply Augustine but even the Roman textbooks gave him support.[266] After the 1543 *Institutio* Calvin relied less upon these two works.

Detailed studies of Calvin's use of Augustine and Bernard in particular confirm this general picture. Calvin's prime sources were the *Opera omnia* of Augustine and Bernard.[267] But he also made use of other sources for both writers. For Augustine he was sometimes dependent upon Gratian and Lombard and some of the passages that he discussed had first been raised by his opponents. On occasions he drew upon the Augustinian citations of his predecessors and colleagues, but without following them blindly.[268] With Bernard he probably drew on a later medieval source at one stage.[269] Some of his other Bernardine citations may be drawn from an intermediary source while none must be and the majority of his citations cannot be. A number of passages that he cites had already been used by his predecessors, but the length and the text of Calvin's quotations show that he was himself using the *Opera omnia Bernardi* even if others may have first pointed him to specific passages.[270]

Todd concedes that Calvin was a competent scholar of New Testament Greek but argues that there is little evidence for his familiarity with patristic Greek. He claims that the evidence (all of which is negative) implies that Calvin read the Greek fathers in a Latin translation.[271] Subsequent studies have confirmed this last point. Ganoczy has discovered Calvin's own annotated copy of Chrysostom's *Opera omnia* in Latin

---

263 LaVallee, *Calvin's Criticism of Scholastic Theology*, 239–49. Cf. section VII.b. above.
264 F. L. Battles, 'The Sources of Calvin's Seneca Commentary' in G. E. Duffield (ed.), *John Calvin* (Appleford: Sutton Courtenay, 1966) 56.
265 Smits, SAOJC 1:206–11.
266 Ganoczy, *Le jeune Calvin*, 181; ET: 169f.; Smits, SAOJC 1:207.
267 Chapter 6, below, section IIb; chapter 5, below. Caution should be exercised over claims made in this realm. Todd, *Function of the Patristic Writings*, 108–109, asserts that Calvin used the Erasmus editions of the fathers without adequately considering other possibilities; Walchenbach, *John Calvin as Biblical Commentator*, 150–54, concludes from an examination of the Basel: Froben, 1530 Erasmus edition of Chrysostom that Calvin 'undoubtedly' used it. The Geneva library contains Calvin's copy of a 1536 edition with his own annotations (Ganoczy, BAC 182). There are other writers who have made dogmatic, but unsubstantiated, claims about which editions Calvin used.
268 Smits, SAOJC 1:211–13.
269 Chapter 5, below, at nn. 151–57.
270 Chapter 5, below, sections IV-VI.
271 Todd, *Function of the Patristic Writings*, 75–77, 252–57.

translation, Irena Backus has shown that he read Eusebius's church history in Latin and the following chapter argues the same for the church histories of Socrates, Sozomen and Theodoret as well as identifying the editions that he used of some other Greek fathers.[272] But while it may be conceded that Calvin normally read the Greek fathers in Latin, it does not follow that he *could* not read them in Greek or that he never did so.

(b) Spuria

The Middle Ages saw the growth of a vast body of patristic pseudepigrapha. By Calvin's time considerable progress had been made in distinguishing the genuine from the false, but the use of apocryphal writings was still the norm. Calvin accused his opponents of making use of such writings.[273] He was not himself without fault in this matter but his record compares well with his contemporaries. He was diligent in seeking to establish authorship, even if he failed to achieve total success. With Augustine his success rate was more than 95 per cent[274] while he completely avoided the wealth of apocryphal Bernardine material.[275] His diligence can already be seen in his Lausanne discourse. Todd argues that at this stage his judgments were dependent upon Erasmus. He concludes that throughout his career Calvin continued to follow the critical judgments of Erasmus, both his insights and his errors.[276] While Erasmus was no doubt a major source, the dependence is not as total as Todd suggests. With Augustine he could dissent from Erasmus.[277] With a writer like Bernard there was no judgment of Erasmus upon which to rely. Here Calvin probably followed the judgment of the editors of the *Opera omnia* which was in the small print for the diligent reader to discover.[278] Calvin's achievement in this area is not dependent upon his making independent judgments: simply to follow the best critical opinions[279] was to rise above the sixteenth-century norm. In his response to Pighius Calvin amasses arguments against the authenticity of the pseudo-Clementine *Recognitions*.[280] Here the best humanist critical methods are used, but to a polemical end. By contrast, Backus shows that Calvin could refer 'globally to Eusebius while meaning either the Rufinus continuation of the *H.e.* or Jerome's version of the *Chronicon* or Haymo of Halberstadt's *Epitome*'.[281] What explains this discrepancy? Several different factors are at

---

272 Ganoczy, BAC 182; A. Ganoczy and K. Müller, *Calvins handschriftliche Annotationen zu Chrysostomus* (Wiesbaden: Franz Steiner, 1981); I. Backus, 'Calvin's Judgment of Eusebius of Caesarea: An Analysis', *Sixteenth Century Journal* 22 (1991) 435f; chapter 3, below, sections II.a, III.a, b, d.
273 *Inst.* 1:13:29, 3:4:23, cited by Smits, SAOJC 1:248.
274 Smits, SAOJC 1:186, 195.
275 Chapter 4, below, section IIc; Lane, *Calvin and Bernard of Clairvaux*, 25f.
276 Todd, *Function of the Patristic Writings*, 107–109, where allowance is made for 'one or two exceptions'.
277 Smits, SAOJC 1:183–96, especially 187–89, 191, 193, 195. Todd, *Function of the Patristic Writings*, 163f. makes some allowance for Smits' results. Cf. chapter 6, below, at n. 68.
278 Lane, *Calvin and Bernard*, 25f.
279 Todd, *Function of the Patristic Writings*, 158–64.
280 CO 6:261f. (*Def. adv. calumn. Pighii*).
281 Backus, 'Calvin's Judgment of Eusebius of Caesarea', 435–37.

work. Clearly Calvin is capable of careful scholarship and could exercise it on occasions, especially with his favourite fathers (such as Augustine or Bernard) or where the polemical situation required it (as with pseudo-Clement). There are two reasons why his scholarship was less thorough on other occasions. One reason is undoubtedly that he pays especial attention to such issues where it is important for his argument. The more important reason is that after his early years Calvin was always short of time and needing to take short cuts. He simply did not have time to check all of the details unless there was some strong motivation to do so.[282]

(c) Principles of Interpretation

Calvin's interpretation of the fathers followed the humanist principles of his day. His aim was to be faithful to the intention of the author and he criticized his opponents for failing to do this.[283] Smits lists six principles of interpretation followed by Calvin.[284] Four are internal: the importance of individual words is stressed as is the need to give them the meaning that they had when first used, not later meanings;[285] the literary genre must be taken into account;[286] passages must be interpreted in their contexts;[287] light can be shed on obscure passages by other clearer passages in the same writer.[288] Two are external: the person of the author must be remembered, such as the fact that Augustine later revised some of his earlier views;[289] each writing must be set in the context of the age in which it was written.[290] Smits detects these principles in Calvin's interpretation of Augustine in particular. Similar results follow from a study of his interpretation of Bernard.[291] Most of the principles are already manifest in his 1536 Lausanne discourse.[292] Todd, in his study of the use of the fathers in the *Psychopannychia* notes that Calvin studied them, where possible, in their historical context and that he was concerned with grammatical and linguistic questions.[293]

While these were Calvin's principles of interpretation it by no means follows that he was always faithful to them. At least two factors worked against them. First, Calvin nearly always wrote under great pressure of time. This led him to take short cuts and at times to violate his own better principles. Secondly, he was not a detached impartial humanist scholar or

---

282 A simple example can illustrate this point. In the Argument to his Genesis commentary Calvin attributes an Augustinian citation to the *Historia tripartita* (CO 23:7f.; cf. chapter 9, below, Appendix 3). There was no conceivable advantage to Calvin in what was clearly a slip due to haste.
283 *Inst.* 1:13:27, 2:3:7, cited by Smits, SAOJC 1:248–49, 252.
284 Smits, SAOJC 1:249–52.
285 *Inst.* 4:6:4, 4:17:28.
286 *Inst.* 2:5:19, 3:4:4–5.
287 *Inst.* 2:3:7, 3:3:12, 4:19:12.
288 *Inst.* 2:2:9, 3:3:13.
289 *Inst.* 3:22:8; CO 20:450 (*Epist.* 4181 *bis*.).
290 *Inst.* 3:4:23.
291 Lane, *Calvin and Bernard*, 35f. Calvin shows little interest in Bernard's biography.
292 The first, third, fourth and sixth (cf. section III, above).
293 Todd, *Function of the Patristic Writings*, 66f.

a twentieth-century research student. The tools of humanist scholarship are used for a polemical end. This is seen clearly in his interpretation of Bernard.[294]

Calvin did not just offer his own interpretation of the fathers. He also gave a detailed refutation of patristic arguments posed against his own view.[295] Many of the Augustinian passages that he cited were originally cited against him by his opponents.[296] His exposition of the ante-Nicene doctrine of the Trinity was in response to the anti-Trinitarian use of these fathers.[297] Some works cited against him he rejected as forgeries.[298] Sometimes, especially with Augustine, he offered a different interpretation of a passage to that given by his opponents.[299] He was prepared to admit that the fathers were careless in their use of language, as with free will and merit.[300] But even when he admitted that the fathers had erred, as with their teaching on satisfaction and purgatory, he was at pains to point out that their teaching was not that of contemporary Rome.[301]

Calvin did not simply attack Roman errors. He also sought to trace their rise in historical terms.[302] He saw the pope as Antichrist and the minister of Satan,[303] but this did not prevent him from devoting a whole chapter of the *Institutio* to a historical account of the rise of the papacy.[304] He also traced the rise of image worship, prayer for the dead and transubstantiation.[305]

The level of Calvin's scholarship was high by the standards of his day.[306] He did not confine himself merely to commenting on the fathers or to giving brief quotations, as did most of his fellow Reformers. His quotations are long and plentiful and reflect a deep knowledge of the fathers. He was not, however, always concerned to quote with verbal accuracy. Sometimes this may be because he is citing from memory, but sometimes this is simply because he does not regard such accuracy as important.[307] While such an attitude would be unacceptable today it was not frowned upon in Calvin's time. The accuracy of the references that he gives is generally very high, by contrast with many of his contemporaries.[308] But it should be

---

294 Lane, *Calvin and Bernard*, 35f.
295 Polman, *L'élément historique*, 87f.; Todd, *Function of the Patristic Writings*, 65.
296 Smits, SAOJC 1:211f. Almost half of Calvin's citations of Athanasius are in response to his opponents' citations (cf. chapter 3, below, section III.c).
297 *Inst.* 1:13.
298 Smits, SAOJC 1:248; cf. at n. 280, above.
299 Smits, SAOJC 1:211f.
300 *Inst.* 2:2:4–8, 3:12:3.
301 *Inst.* 3:4:38–39, 3:5:10.
302 Polman, *L'élément historique*, 81f.
303 *Inst.* 4:7:25.
304 *Inst.* 4:7.
305 *Inst.* 1:11:8–16, 3:5:10, 4:17:12–15.
306 Todd, *Function of the Patristic Writings*, 171f., lists some of Calvin's shortcomings and then observes that these are all *modern* criticisms.
307 Cf. chapter 4, below, at nn. 94f.; Lane, *Calvin and Bernard*, 21–25. On the related question of the accuracy of Calvin's quotations from the Bible, cf. M. Engammare, 'Calvin connaissait-il la Bible? Les citations de l'Écriture dans les sermons sur la Genèse', *Bulletin de la Société de l'Histoire du Protestantisme Français* 141 (1995) 163–84.
308 Smits, SAOJC 1:237.

remembered that he was no detached historical critic seeking to give an impartial account of the Early Church. He was an apologist and a polemicist, an advocate arguing a case. Humanist scholarship of a high standard is used, but in a carefully controlled way as a means to an end.

IX. ASSESSMENT

How fair was Calvin in his use of the fathers? In recent years a number of studies have sought to answer this question. Mooi gives a list of Calvin's historical errors and Fischer lists tendentious interpretations.[309] There have been assessments of his interpretation of Eusebius,[310] of the second council of Nicea,[311] of Lombard and Gratian,[312] and of Bernard.[313] These are all critical of Calvin's interpretation at specific points,[314] although in some instances the criticisms involve judging Calvin by twentieth- rather than sixteenth-century criteria and some tend to accuse Calvin of bad faith where time pressure and lack of resources may be equally important as factors.

Why did Calvin on occasions misinterpret the fathers? There are a number of factors to be considered. First, Calvin usually wrote in extreme haste without the (relative) leisure normally available for scholarship. His need to work from memory and to cut corners account for some of his errors.[315] Jean-François Gilmont lists some of the distractions that Calvin faced as he sought to write and shows how he was inclined to write in haste and at the last minute.[316] He didn't normally correct his proofs and was careless in revising texts.[317] Such a practice would be reprehensible today but was more acceptable in his own time. Another important factor is that Calvin wrote not as a detached scholar but as a polemicist in the

---

309 KDE 339–43; D. Fischer, *Jean Calvin, historien de l'eglise. Sources et aspects de la pensée historique, et de l'historiographie du réformateur*, 3 vols (Strasbourg: Strasbourg University Doctorat d'Etat en Théologie thesis, 1980) 242–48. Cf. Todd, *Function of the Patristic Writings*, 181–227, for a broad examination of the accuracy of Calvin's understanding of the fathers.

310 Backus, 'Calvin's Judgment of Eusebius', 419–37: Calvin could analyse historical evidence with some finesse but he could also juggle it for doctrinal ends.

311 Payton, 'Calvin and the Legitimation of Icons', 222–41: 'Calvin significantly misread and perhaps purposely misrepresented both the council and its legitimation of icons.' His account is totally derived from the *Libri Carolini*, a hostile source (p. 240).

312 Ganoczy, *Le jeune Calvin*, 181–86; ET: 170–73.

313 Chapter 4, below, section IIc; Lane, *Calvin and Bernard*, 33–90, especially 86–90.

314 J. van Oort, 'John Calvin and the Church Fathers' in Backus (ed.), *Reception of the Church Fathers*, 687, also finds Calvin guilty on occasions of 'a certain manipulation of historical evidence for his own doctrinal ends'. This article is more dependent on earlier works (such as Mooi, KDE and Lane, 'Calvin's Use of the Fathers and the Medievals') than the notes might lead one to suppose, sometimes even regarding wording.

315 This can be seen especially in chapters 6, 9, below. Cf. Fischer, 'L'histoire de l'eglise', 122: 'S'il y a des erreurs, chez Calvin, c'est parce qu'il n'avait pas toujours sous les yeux les ouvrages qu'il citait'.

316 J.-F. Gilmont, *Jean Calvin et le livre imprimé* (Geneva: Droz, 1997) 353–55.

317 Ibid., 280–83. This can be illustrated from Calvin's use of Bernard. His second citation accuses Bernard of Semi-Pelagianism (*Inst.* 2:2:6). Calvin soon came to a different opinion and cited Bernard for support but the second citation, which contradicts this later use of Bernard, was never removed. Cf. Lane, *Calvin and Bernard*, 36f.

heat of battle. His concern was not to present a balanced and objective account of the fathers but to cite them in his support. This may distinguish Calvin from present-day scholarship; it did not distinguish him from his contemporaries.

While Calvin can be faulted on a number of individual points, the extent of these should not be exaggerated. The overwhelming majority of citations accurately represent the father cited and inaccurate interpretation is found more often with writers with whom Calvin had less sympathy (such as Lombard or Gratian) rather than with 'his own' authors (such as Augustine or Bernard). Calvin is generally fair in what he claims. Does it follow that the early fathers were proto-Calvinists who clearly refute Roman Catholic doctrine? Not necessarily. Calvin's use of the fathers is open not so much to the charge of inaccuracy as to the charge of selectivity.[318] He was not seeking to give a balanced detached assessment of the fathers, but was appealing to them for support. This means that he was, not unreasonably, selective in his use of them. He quotes whom he will and those passages which support his case at that moment. On the whole he is fair in what he claims from the fathers, though there are exceptions, such as his claim that Augustine supports his view of reprobation.[319] But what the father is saying does not always establish Calvin's case. For instance, Calvin quotes Bernard for specific objections to current papal claims.[320] He is quite correct in that Bernard does support him at these specific points, but the main thrust of Bernard's teaching was that of Roman Catholicism. Bernard was an orthodox Roman Catholic protesting about details, not a Calvinist reformer. Calvin does not claim the latter: indeed he includes in one of his quotations the assertion that the pope has *plenitudo potestatis*.[321] Calvin does not claim from Bernard more than Bernard gives, but neither does he admit that Bernard's position on the papacy was far removed from his own.

Sometimes the teaching of the father is not as close to Calvin as is suggested. Calvin makes much of Augustine's distinction between the sacrament itself and the use or benefit of the sacrament.[322] It is possible (for a Donatist) to receive valid baptism but not to receive the benefit of baptism. This parallels Calvin's own distinction between the sacrament itself, in which grace is promised, and the receipt of this grace, which may occur later. But there is a major difference between Calvin and Augustine. For Augustine the norm is for baptism to bestow grace immediately. It is only in exceptional circumstances, such as schism or hypocrisy, that baptism and its benefit are separated. For Calvin the two are much more firmly distinguished so that baptism has efficacy only when faith is exercised. Augustine's infidel friend was converted through being baptized while unconscious.[323] To Calvin this tale would have smacked of

318 Todd, *Function of the Patristic Writings*, 164–68; Walchenbach, *John Calvin as Biblical Commentator*, 172–90; chapter 4, below, section IIc; Lane, *Calvin and Bernard*, 33f., 88–90.
319 *Inst.* 3:23:5, 7–8; CO 8:315 (*De praed.*).
320 *Inst.* 4:7:18, 22, 4:11:11.
321 *Inst.* 4:7:18. Cf. Lane, *Calvin and Bernard*, 77–81.
322 *Inst.* 4:14:15. Cf. J. de Blic, *Revue d'histoire ecclésiastique* 23 (1927) 328–30 (a book review).
323 Augustine, *Confessiones* 4:4.

superstition. Augustine believed that infants dying unbaptized were damned; Calvin strenuously opposed this view.[324]

Calvin was accurate but highly selective in his use of the fathers. He showed real discrepancies between his Roman contemporaries and the fathers and he established many valid precedents for his own teaching. But he did not allow for the extent to which the thrust of the patristic teaching might point in the direction of later Roman Catholicism nor does he acknowledge the extent to which the Reformation was a movement of theological revolution as well as restoration.

Calvin's use of the fathers was a masterly sixteenth-century attempt to relate Protestantism to historic Christianity: to trace many of its doctrines to the Early Church and to show how Roman error had arisen. His case, as it stands, is not adequate for today. In the first place, modern historical study of the Early Church has made us more aware of the differences between the sixteenth-century Reformers and the fathers, even between Calvin and his beloved Augustine. Secondly, Calvin operated with an essentially static concept of doctrine where we, living in a post-Newmanian age, see doctrine more in terms of development and other such dynamic concepts. Calvin's case, as it stands, does not suffice for today but the task remains important. Newman stated that 'whatever be historical Christianity, it is not Protestantism. If ever there were a safe truth, it is this'.[325] If Protestantism is to deny this charge, it must seek to relate its doctrine to the continuity of Christian belief over the ages. Calvin, as (one of) the greatest of the earliest Protestants to attempt this task, remains a source of inspiration if not an adequate guide for today.

X. WORKS CITED IN THE 1559 *INSTITUTIO*

The reader can see at a glance from this table which works Calvin cited in his *Institutio*.[326] It is here that most of his serious citations are to be found and important quotations in his other works usually found their way into a later edition of the *Institutio*.[327] By a citation is meant a quotation of, a paraphrase of or a clear reference to (a portion of) a work. There must be explicit mention of the author or the work. Unacknowledged quotations and allusions are not counted since their total would reflect the areas of competence of Calvin's editors (to say nothing of their imaginative powers) rather than Calvin's own usage. The number of citations where Calvin does not himself name the specific work is given in brackets after the total number. Usually it is only a small proportion of the total. So as not to give excessive weight to multiple citations separate lists are given of the number of citations and the number of sections of the *Institutio* within which a work is cited. Thus the quotation of Bernard's *Epistola* 107 in 3.22.10 counts as two citations but only one section.

---

324 *Inst.* 4:16:26.
325 Newman, *Development of Christian Doctrine*, 72.
326 This has not hitherto been possible. Mooi (KDE) gives full tables of the authors cited in each of Calvin's works, but not of the works cited. The index of LCC 20–21 is full but is an index to its own footnotes rather than to Calvin's citations.
327 Mooi, KDE 132f., 178.

Author and Work	Citations	Sections
ALCUIN (pseudo-Augustine)		
De fide sanctae trinitatis	1	1
AMBROSE		
De Abraham	1	1
De Isaac vel anima	2(1)	2
De Jacob et vita beata	3	3
De obitu Theodosii oratio	1	1
De officiis ministrorum	2	2
De sacramento regenerationis sive de philosophia	1	1
Epistolae	8(2)	4
Expositio evangelii secundum Lucam	4(4)	3
Expositio in psalmum 118	1	1
Hexaemeron	1(1)	1
Sermo contra Auxentium de basilicis tradendis	5(2)	3
PSEUDO-AMBROSE		
Sermones	2(2)	1
AMBROSIASTER		
Commentarius in epistolas Pauli	3(2)	3
ANSELM		
De libertate arbitrii	1(1)	1
AUGUSTINE		
Acta seu disputatio contra Fortunatum Manichaeum	1(1)	1
Breviculus collationis cum Donatistis	1	1
Confessiones	4(1)	3
Contra Adimantum	2	2
Contra adversarium legis et prophetarum	2	2
Contra Cresconium grammaticum	1	1
Contra duas epistolas Pelagianorum	22(3)	18
Contra epistolam Parmeniani	15(1)	8
Contra epistolam quam vocant fundamenti	2	1
Contra Faustum tum Manichaeum	10(1)	9
Contra Gaudentium Donatistarum episcopum	1	1
Contra Julianum	14(1)	9
Contra litteras Petiliani	2(1)	2
Contra Maximinum	1	1
Contra secundam Juliani responsionem imperfectum opus	3(3)	3
De baptismo contra Donatistas	7	5
De bono coniugali	1	1
De catechizandis rudibus	2(2)	2
De civitate Dei	15(3)	13
De correptione et gratia	18(8)	13
De cura gerenda pro mortuis	1	1

Author and Work	Citations	Sections
AUGUSTINE (*continued*)		
De diversis quaestionibus LXXXIII	6(1)	3
De doctrina christiana	9	9
De dono perseverantiae	14(1)	8
De fide et symbolo	4(1)	4
De Genesi ad litteram	5(1)	5
De Genesi contra Manichaeos	5	3
De gratia Christi et de peccato originali	4(1)	4
De gratia et libero arbitrio	10(6)	9
De libero arbitrio	1(1)	1
De moribus ecclesiae catholicae et de		
moribus Manichaeorum	7	4
De natura et gratia	7(5)	7
De opere monachorum	5	5
De peccatorum meritis et remissione et		
de baptismo parvulorum	13(3)	12
De perfectione iustitiae hominis	6(4)	4
De praedestinatione sanctorum	7	6
De spiritu et littera	8(4)	7
De trinitate	10(2)	7
De utilitate credendi	2	2
Enarrationes in Psalmos	46(12)	32
Enchiridion ad Laurentium	17(6)	14
Epistolae	60(9)	47
Expositio quarundam propositionum		
ex epistola ad Romanos	1(1)	1
Inchoata expositio epistolae ad Romanos	1(1)	1
Quaestiones evangeliorum	5(4)	5
Quaestiones in Heptateuchum	5	5
Retractationes	5	5
Sermones	27(13)	21
Tractatus in epistolam Johannis I	1(1)	1
Tractatus in Johannis evangelium	62(10)	37
PSEUDO-AUGUSTINE		
De dogmatibus ecclesiasticis	1	1
De praedestinatione et gratia	3	3
De vera et falsa poenitentia	3(1)	3
Hypognosticon (Hypomnesticon)	1(1)	1
Sermones	1(1)	1
BASIL		
Constitutiones (asceticae) monasticae	1(1)	1
Homiliae in Hexaemeron	1(1)	1
Homiliae in Psalmos	1(1)	1
BERNARD OF CLAIRVAUX		
De consideratione ad Eugenium III	10(2)	4
De gratia et libero arbitrio	3(3)	3

Author and Work	Citations	Sections
BERNARD OF CLAIRVAUX (*continued*)		
Epistolae	2	1
Sermones	7	4
Sermones in Cantica	21(3)	12
CASSIODORE		
Historia ecclesiastica tripartita	14	10
PSEUDO-CHARLEMAGNE		
Libri Carolini	24	3
CHRYSOSTOM		
Adversus oppugnatores vitae monasticae	1(1)	1
De compunctione cordis	1	1
Epistolae	1(1)	1
Homiliae	14(5)	12
Homiliae in novum testamentum	11(4)	10
Homiliae in vetus testamentum	9(2)	7
PSEUDO-CHRYSOSTOM		
De fide et lege naturae	1	1
Homiliae	12	11
Opus imperfectum in Matthaeum	2	2
PSEUDO-CLEMENT OF ROME		
Epistola ad Jacobum fratrem Domini	1(1)	1
CLEMENT V		
Clementinae (Liber septimus)	1	1
CYPRIAN		
De ecclesiae unitate	7	3
De lapsis	3(1)	3
De mortalitate	1	1
Epistolae	25(3)	15
Sententiae episcoporum de haereticis baptizandis	1(1)	1
Testimonia	1(1)	1
CYRIL OF ALEXANDRIA		
Commentarius in evangelium Johannis	2(1)	2
De recta fidei ad reginas	1	1
De sancta et consubstantiali trinitate	2	1
PSEUDO-DIONYSIUS		
De caelesti hierarchia	1(1)	1
EPIPHANIUS		
Adversus haereses panarion	2	1
Epistolae	3(1)	3

Author and Work	Citations	Sections
PSEUDO-EUCHERIUS OF LYONS		
(?Claudius of Turin)		
Commentarius in Genesim	1	1
EUSEBIUS OF CAESAREA		
Chronici canones	2(2)	1
Historia ecclesiastica	2	2
Praeparatio evangelica	1	1
EUTYCHES		
Epistola ad Leonem	1	1
FULGENTIUS OF RUSPE (pseudo-Augustine)		
De fide ad Petrum diaconum	2	2
GELASIUS I		
De duabus naturis in Christo	1	1
Epistolae	2(2)	2
JOHN GERSON		
Sermo in festo paschae	1	1
GRATIAN		
Concordantia discordantium canonum	51	29
GREGORY THE GREAT		
Dialogi de vita et miraculis patrum Italicorum	1(1)	1
Epistolae	71(9)	22
Homiliae	9(3)	6
GREGORY NAZIANZEN		
Epistolae	1(1)	1
Orationes	2(1)	2
GREGORY IX		
Decretales epistolae (Extravagantes)	1	1
HILARY OF POITIERS		
Contra Arianos vel Auxentium Mediolanensem	1	1
De synodis seu de fide Orientalium	1	1
De trinitate	5	3
INNOCENT I		
Epistolae	2(2)	2
IRENAEUS		
Adversus haereses	11(2)	3
ISIDORE OF SEVILLE		
Etymologiae	1	1

Author and Work	Citations	Sections
JEROME		
Altercatio Luciferiani et orthodoxi	1	1
Commentarii	4(1)	4
Dialogi contra Pelagianos	4(1)	4
Epistolae	15(4)	12
Praefationes	2(2)	2
JOHN XXII		
Extravagantes	1	1
PSEUDO-JUSTIN		
De monarchia	1	1
LACTANTIUS		
Divinae institutiones	2(2)	2
LEO I		
Epistolae	18(8)	10
ORIGEN		
Commentarii	3(1)	3
De principiis	2(1)	2
PELAGIUS		
Expositiones XIII epistolarum Pauli	1(1)	1
PETER LOMBARD		
Sententiae	39(6)	32
BARTHOLOMEW PLATINA		
De vita Christi ac de vitis summorum pontificum omnium	1	1
PROSPER OF AQUITAINE		
De vocatione omnium gentium	5(1)	5
RUFINUS OF AQUILEIA (pseudo-Cyprian)		
Commentarius in symbolum apostolorum	2	2
SIGEBERT OF GEMBLOUX		
Chronica	1	1
SIRICIUS I		
Epistolae	1	1
SOCRATES		
Historia ecclesiastica	6(6)	6
SOZOMEN		
Historia ecclesiastica	1(1)	1

Author and Work	*Citations*	*Sections*
TERTULLIAN		
Adversus Marcionem	1(1)	1
Adversus Praxean	3(1)	2
De carnis resurrectione	4(3)	3
De fuga in persecutione	1	1
De testimonio animae	1(1)	1
De virginibus velandis	1(1)	1
THEODORET OF CYRUS		
Historia ecclesiastica	7	4
THOMAS AQUINAS		
Scriptum super libros sententiarum	1	1
Summa theologiae	1	1
LAURENTIUS VALLA		
De falso credita et ementita Constantini		
Donatione declamatio	1(1)	1
De libero arbitrio	1(1)	1
ANONYMOUS		
Canones apostolorum	2	2
Statuta ecclesiae antiqua	3	2
Symbolum apostolorum	15	13
CANONS, ETC. FROM COUNCILS		
Council of Carthage (256): Canones	1	1
Elvira (305): Canones	2	2
Nicea (325): Canones	5	5
Symbolum	1	1
Antioch (341): Canones	3	3
Sardica (342/3): Canones	1	1
Laodicea (?360): Canones	1	1
Aquileia (381): Canones	2	2
Constantinople (381): Canones	1	1
Symbolum Constantinopolitanum	2	2
Constantinople (382): Epistola synodica	1	1
Carthage (390): Canones	1	1
Carthage (397): Canones	4	4
Toledo (400): Canones	1	1
Turin (401): Canones	1	1
Milevis (416) [= Carthage (418)]: Canones	3	2
Orange (441): Canones	1	1
Chalcedon (451): Canones	2	2
Orange (529): Canones	1	1
Constantinople (754): Definitio	1	1
Nicea (787): Definitio de sacris imaginibus	2	2
Lateran (1215): Canones	2	2
Constance (1415):		
Decretum de communione sub pani		
tantum specie	1	1

Author and Work	Citations	Sections
ADDENDUM[328]		
PSEUSO-ISIDORE		
Decretales	7	6
SOCRATES		
Historia ecclesiastica	3	3
SOZOMEN		
Historia ecclesiastica	5	3

XI. CALVIN'S MEDIEVAL CITATIONS

Where possible citations are listed by the names of individuals though where the author of a work cited is not known or is more than one person the work is listed by its title. Individuals are listed in order of date of death, the years 500 and 1500 being taken as the limits. The one exception is Cassiodore's *Historia tripartita* which is not listed because its component parts were written in the fifth century. Only the works of Calvin are included, not works edited by him such as the Regensburg *Acta* or the *Interim*, nor those incorporated into his own works, such as the Sorbonne articles or the Tridentine decrees.[329] Works where he is a joint author or signatory (such as letters from the Genevan pastors) are included. Only works found in the *Calvini Opera* are included.

Citations in the *Institutio* and in other works are listed separately. The number recorded for the *Institutio* is the number of sections in which the person or work is named; for the *Prefatory Address* it is the number of pages of the *Opera Selecta*; for other works it is the number of columns of the *Calvini Opera*. It is the total extent of the citation which is considered, not just the places where the name is found. All methods of counting citations have drawbacks but this one at least has the merit of being objective. The source of all citations outside the *Institutio* is given, those within being relatively easy to trace.

Citations are listed separately according to whether or not the author or work is named. This 'naming' may be indirect, as when Peter Lombard is called *magister sententiarum*. A citation is 'unnamed' when Calvin gives the wrong name or the author or work is found in a source that is cited. There must be clear proof of Calvin's intent, a mere editor's parallel not sufficing. The list could no doubt be extended further, e.g. by checking every reference to Gratian and Lombard to see what names are found

---

328 For the reasons given, the above figures do not include unacknowledged citations, but there are three important works cited in this way which deserve mention The pseudo-Isidorian *False Decretals* are the ultimate origin of a number of Calvin's citations from Gratian, and Socrates' and Sozomen's church histories are cited via Cassiodore's *Historia tripartita*.

329 I have also accepted the verdict of C. Augustijn, 'Die Autorschaft des *Consilium admodum paternum*' in W. van 't Spijker (ed.), *Calvin: Erbe und Auftrag* (Kampen: Kok Pharos, 1991) 255–69, that this work (CO 5:461–508) is not by Calvin.

there. Apart from writers and works incorrectly named by Calvin no entries are included which are nowhere named by him.

Many people are named as the recipient of letters, especially of Gregory the Great. These names are included only if the person named appears elsewhere in his own right or if Calvin named him because he was significant in his own right.[330] Two things may confidently be claimed for this list: that it is the most comprehensive to date and that it is still far from exhaustive.

Name	Date	Institutio		Other Works	
		Named	Not	Named	Not
Pseudo-Dionysius	c.500	1		11[331]	
Pope Symmachus	514	1			
Emperor Anastasius I	518			1[332]	
Pope Hormisdas	523			1[333]	
Council of Orange	529	1		5[334]	1[335]
Pope Boniface II	532		1		
Fulgentius of Ruspe[336]	533		2	1[337]	1[338]
Mennas of Constantinople	552	1			
Council of Constantinople	553	1			
Pope Vigilius	555		1		
Emperor Justinian	565			2[339]	
Laurence of Milan	592	1			
John of Constantinople	595	4		1[340]	
Council of Rome	595	1			
Constantius of Milan	600	2	1		
Serenus of Marseilles	599–600[341]		1	3[342]	3[343]
Emperor Maurice	602	4	4	4[344]	
Pope Gregory I	604	29		30[345]	1[346]
Kyriakos of Constantinople	606	2			
Severus of Aquileia	606/7		1		

330 Anastasius of Antioch is only named as the recipient of letters from Gregory but unlike other such names he is mentioned three times in the text, not just in marginal notes.
331 CO 6:444; 7:656f.; 10b:389; 12:16f.; 40:295; 41:296; 48:423; 50:138; 52:73.
332 CO 7:272.
333 CO 7:272.
334 CO 6:289, 305, 363f.; 7:648.
335 CO 6:319.
336 Calvin three times cites pseudo-Augustine, *De fide ad Petrum*, which is by Fulgentius.
337 CO 7:15.
338 CO 9:881.
339 CO 7:272f.
340 CO 7:273.
341 As the date of Serenus's death is not known, the date of his correspondence with Gregory is given instead.
342 CO 38:68f.; 43:559.
343 CO 23:18; 26:153; 39:457.
344 CO 7:38, 273, 403; 32:418.
345 CO 5:37f., 187; 6:416, 491–93, 516; 7:34, 38, 273, 277, 395, 403, 505, 618, 628, 634; 23:18; 24:433; 26:153; 34:684; 38:68f.; 39:457; 43:559; 44:438f.; 49:357; 52:87.
346 CO 7:276.

Name	Date	Institutio		Other Works	
		Named	Not	Named	Not
Eulogius of Alexandria	607	3			
Pope Boniface III	607	1			
Anastasius of Antioch	609	4			
Emperor Phocas	610	1		2[347]	
Pope Boniface IV[348]	615	1			
Muhammad	629			33[349]	
Isidore of Seville	636	2	1		1[350]
Monothelites	624–80	1		1[351]	
Emperor Constans II (Pogonatos)	668			1[352]	
Trullan Synod II	692		1		
Emperor Leo III	740			1[353]	
John of Damascus	749			3[354]	
Pope Zachary	752	1			
Council of Constantinople	754	1			
Emperor Pepin	768	1			
Donatio Constantini	750–800	2		2[355]	
Council of Nicea II	787	4		5[356]	
Nicene bishops[357]	787	6	11		
Libri Carolini	790–92	3			
Empress Irene II	803	1		1[358]	
Alcuin[359]	804		1		3[360]
Emperor Charlemagne	814	4		1[361]	
Pseudo-Isidore	c.850		6	1[362]	
'Pope Joan'	c.857[363]			1[364]	
Pope Nicholas I	867	1			

347 CO 7:273; 32:418.
348 Calvin refers to 'illa decreta . . . Bonifacii' and appears to have *Decretum Gratiani* II, C. 16, q. 1, c. 25 in mind (OS 5:80, n. 3). Gratian's ascription of the decree to Boniface appears to be an error for the Council of Nemaeus (1096).
349 CO 7:533; 9:536; 27:113, 217, 233, 238, 260f., 502f.; 28:519; 33:204; 35:64; 41:270, 441, 599; 42:171; 46:4; 47:91, 335, 363; 48:495; 52:197; 53:60, 165f., 340; 54:25, 37, 50, 138, 449; 55:351.
350 CO 5:37.
351 CO 45:723.
352 CO 7:273.
353 CO 7:417.
354 CO 7:657; 9:490f.
355 CO 7:271f.
356 CO 7:417; 8:591; 31:477; 32:52, 345.
357 Calvin names five bishops at the council and quotes six others without naming them. Rather than list each bishop separately the numbers of references have been added up. Cf. *Inst.* 1:11:14–16.
358 CO 8:591.
359 Calvin cites pseudo-Augustine, *Sermo de tempore* 38, which is by Alcuin.
360 CO 7:323f.; 11:561.
361 CO 7:272.
362 CO 7:668.
363 A later date of *c*.1100 is also sometimes given.
364 CO 7:633.

Name	Date	Institutio		Other Works	
		Named	Not	Named	Not
'Council of Orleans'[365]	867–71	1		4[366]	
Pope Silvester II	1003			1[367]	
Council of Vercelli	1050			3[368]	
Council of Rome	1059		2	4[369]	6[370]
Pope Nicholas II	1061	2		7[371]	
Council of Rome	1079				4[372]
Rudolf of Swabia	1080			1[373]	
Pope Gregory VII	1085	2		9[374]	
Berengar	1086	1		8[375]	
Council of Nemaeus[376]	1096		1		
Cardinal Beno	c.1098			1[377]	
Godfrey of Boulogne	1100			1[378]	
Emperor Henry IV	1106	1		3[379]	
Theophylact	c.1108	1		2[380]	
Anselm	1109	1			
Ivo of Chartres	1116			1[381]	1[382]
Sigeburt of Gembloux	1122	1			
Hugh of St Victor	1141	2	1		
Pope Innocent II[383]	1143	1			
Decretum Gratiani	1140–50	33	9	17[384]	9[385]
Pope Eugenius III	1153	2		2[386]	
Bernard of Clairvaux	1153	23	1	16[387]	
Arnold of Bonnevaux[388]	1156		1		

365 Calvin repeats the error of the *Decretum Gratiani* (Mooi, KDE 125, n. 7).
366 CO 7:493, 501, 629f.
367 CO 52:317.
368 CO 9:152, 436, 885. Calvin has confused this council with the 1079 Council of Rome (Mooi, KDE 340).
369 CO 9:57f., 152, 154.
370 CO 9:222, 225, 436, 469, 769 (Tours should be Rome); 20:75.
371 CO 7:634, 668; 9:57f., 152, 154, 225.
372 CO 9:152, 225, 436, 885.
373 CO 7:274.
374 CO 7:273f., 633; 9:152, 210, 225, 884–86.
375 CO 9:57f., 154, 222, 436, 469, 886; 20:75.
376 See under Pope Boniface IV, above.
377 CO 9:885.
378 CO 6:428.
379 CO 7:273f., 633.
380 CO 9:490, 834.
381 CO 7:667.
382 Calvin's Augustine citation appears to be pseudo-Augustine, *Sermo* 247, which is by Ivo (CO 51:187).
383 Calvin refers to 'illa decreti Innocentii' and appears to have *Decretum Gratiani* II, C. 16, q. 1, c. 22 in mind (OS 5:80, n. 3).
384 CO 6:488, 516; 7:18, 501, 625, 628, 634; 9:57f., 154, 436, 469; 11:706f.; 47:32; 48:IX; 52:317.
385 CO 5:37, 306, 454; 7:493, 629f.; 9:210; 20:75; 47:42.
386 CO 5:403; 7:506.
387 CO 5:215, 403; 6:291, 333–35, 378; 7:13, 126, 457, 479, 506; 23:63; 28:713; 31:540; 49:357
388 Calvin cites pseudo-Cyprian *De coena Domini*, which is by Arnold.

Name	Date	Institutio Named	Not	Other Works Named	Not
Peter Lombard	1160	34	9	5[389]	
Alcher of Clairvaux	1162				3[390]
Emperor Frederick I	1190			1[391]	
Council of Lateran IV	1215	2	1	8[392]	3[393]
Pope Innocent III	1216	2		8[394]	
Glossa ordinaria in Decretum Gratiani	1215+	1	1	1[395]	
Decretales Gregorii IX	1230–34	1	3		
Council of Arles[396]	1234	1			
David Kimchi	1235			2[397]	
William of Paris/Auvergne	1249	1			
King Louis	1270			2[398]	
Moses ben Nahman (Gerundensis)	1270			1[399]	
Thomas Aquinas	1274	2		2[400]	
Bonaventure	1274			1[401]	
William Durandus (Speculator)	1296			1[402]	
Pope Boniface VIII	1303			1[403]	
Duns Scotus	1308			2[404]	
Clementinae	1317	1			
Extravagantes Johannis XXII	1325	1			
Pope John XXII	1334	1		2[405]	
Nicholas of Lyra	1340			2[406]	
William of Occam	1349	1		1[407]	
Theologica Germanica	c.1350			2[408]	
John Wyclif	1384			1[409]	
Jan Hus	1415			1[410]	
Council of Constance	1414–18	1	2	1[411]	

389 CO 6:252; 9:194f., 246; 20:75.
390 Calvin cites pseudo-Augustine, *De spiritu et anima*, which is by Alcher (CO 5:181, 206f.).
391 CO 7:274.
392 CO 6:498; 7:11, 427; 8:69; 9:131, 538; 10b:383; 31:205.
393 CO 5:400; 7:467f.
394 CO 5:400; 6:498; 7:11, 467f.; 8:69; 9:538; 10b:383.
395 CO 9:436.
396 This is a faulty ascription.
397 CO 23:57; 32:174.
398 CO 6:428f.
399 CO 23:511.
400 CO 7:668; 9:436. In CO 12:484 there is a reference to 'Thomistis'.
401 CO 12:483.
402 CO 7:667.
403 CO 7:668 (just mentioned as Boniface, without number).
404 CO 9:177, 436.
405 CO 5:171/2; 7:127.
406 CO 8:498; 41:175.
407 CO 6:397. Both citations of Occam seem to be erroneous.
408 CO 17:441f.
409 CO 6:350.
410 CO 7:287.
411 CO 7:287.

Name	Date	Institutio		Other Works	
		Named	Not	Named	Not
Extravagantes Martini[412]	1425	1			
Jean Gerson	1429	1		1[413]	
Pope Martin V	1431		1		
Council of Basel	1431–49	1		3[414]	
Emperor Sigismund	1437			1[415]	
Nicholas Tudescus (abbas Panormitanus)	1445			1[416]	
Pope Eugenius IV	1447	1		1[417]	
Pope Felix V (Amadeus)	1451	1			
Laurentius Valla	1457	2		11[418]	
Pope Pius II	1464			2[419]	1[420]
Nicholas Perottus	1480			1[421]	
Platina	1481		1		
De vera et falsa poenitentia	n.d.		7		
William and Walter	n.d.			2[422]	

412 According to LCC 21:1620 the *Extravagantes Martini* of *Inst.* 4:7:20 come from Martin V. There are also *Extravagantes* of Martin IV.
413 CO 5:171/2.
414 CO 7:403, 633; 9:885.
415 CO 7:287.
416 CO 7:667.
417 CO 7:633.
418 CO 5:31f., 66, 83, 92; 6:350; 7:416; 8:186, 206; 9:448; 48:548.
419 CO 7:385; 9:885.
420 CO 9:885 (as Enio Sylvio Piccolomini).
421 CO 5:121.
422 CO 5:450; 41:557.

3

⚜

Calvin's Knowledge
of the Greek Fathers

I. INTRODUCTION

Calvin's knowledge and use of Augustine is well-known and much studied.[1] Less well known is his use of the Greek fathers. How well did he know them? How much did they influence his theology? Could it be, as some have claimed, that the Greek fathers were a greater influence upon Calvin than Augustine?

It is the alleged influence of the Greek fathers upon Calvin that has stimulated the present study, but this question will not be tackled directly. There is a prior question to be settled first: how much *knowledge* did Calvin have of the Greek fathers? How can one answer this question? Doubtless there is more than one way to approach it, but the method to be adopted here is that of examining Calvin's *citations* of the Greek fathers. Obviously Calvin did not mention the Greek fathers by name every time that he thought of them, but two, more modest, claims can be made. First, an examination of Calvin's citations of a particular father will demonstrate the *kind* of knowledge of him possessed by Calvin. If Calvin's citations of a church father betray no precise knowledge of his writings, or betray a contempt for him, he is unlikely to have influenced Calvin significantly – at least not in a positive direction! The second claim is that if Calvin did have a good knowledge of one of the Greek fathers, and even more if he was influenced by that father, that knowledge would leave some evidence in the form of explicit mention.

The last claim needs justification. Calvin was undoubtedly influenced in some way by some form of late medieval theology. But in what way and by what form? This question has been much debated in recent Calvin scholarship.[2] Answering it is made much harder by the fact that Calvin

An earlier version of this chapter was presented to the third international colloquium on the reception of the church fathers in the fifteenth and sixteenth centuries, at Bad Homburg in 1997. I am grateful to the other participants for useful suggestions that have left their mark on the final version.

---

1 L. Smits, SAOJC remains the most comprehensive study.
2 Cf. chapter 2, above, section II.

doesn't name his late medieval sources. The alleged influence upon Calvin of John Major, for instance, is not disproved by Calvin's failure to name him. Calvin was under no obligation to document his sources and often (but not always)[3] leaves us in the dark about them. But with the fathers we are in a different situation as he cited them thousands of times: as authorities and witnesses to the truth of his own teaching and to the error of his opponents' teaching; (less often) in order to disagree with them, especially if they have put forward a view that has become the Roman Catholic view; (occasionally) for an apt saying, with a literary rather than theological motivation.[4] He does not cite the fathers every time that they have influenced him, but one can expect serious patristic reading to lead to some explicit citation. His renewed reading of Basil and Bernard in the 1540s and 1550s led him to introduce new illustrative material into his works.[5] It is unlikely that he would have been seriously influenced by any of the fathers without going on to cite them.

T. F. Torrance, in a paper delivered in 1964, makes claims about Calvin's relation to the Greek fathers which he reaffirms a quarter of a century later.

> That explains why Calvin relied so heavily upon Augustine in his attack upon all forms of Pelagianism and in his defence of the Reformation against Roman counter-attack, yet in some of the most important aspects of Calvin's thought he was much more indebted to the Greek fathers.[6]
>
> As soon as he wrote the *Institute* we find that he had already returned very decidedly to the teaching of Athanasius and Hilary.[7]

Torrance is aware that such claims must be related to the availability at that time of the writings of the fathers,[8] but he is not equally cautious about relating them to Calvin's citations of the fathers. It is true that influence cannot be measured simply by volume of citations, but it is equally true that if Calvin had arrived at a profound theological understanding through one of the early fathers we could legitimately expect this to manifest itself in his use of that father. The study of Calvin's citation of the Greek fathers does not support Torrance's assertions. In the 1536 *Institutio* there is no reference to either Athanasius or Hilary and there are

---

3 One of Calvin's major sources for his Genesis commentary was Augustinus Eugubinus Steuchus's *Recognitio Veteris Testamenti ad Hebraicam Veritatem*. This dependence is almost unacknowledged, but Calvin was considerate enough to include a single derogatory reference to Steuchus as a clue for the future researcher (CO 23:15). Calvin also made use of the notes on Genesis by Vatable, to whom he *never* refers in his extant writings. Cf. chapter 9, below.

4 Cf. chapter 2, above, section IV. In his commentaries, however, Calvin more often cites other points of view in order to debate with them, seeking sparring partners as much as authorities.

5 Cf. section III.d, below and chapter 4, below, section II.a.

6 T. F. Torrance, *Theology in Reconstruction* (London: SCM Press, 1965) 76f. This passage is repeated, with minor verbal changes, in his *The Hermeneutics of John Calvin* (Edinburgh: Scottish Academic Press, 1988) 82.

7 Torrance, *Theology in Reconstruction*, 88. Cf. a further claim for Hilary on 92.

8 Ibid., 77.

few citations of any of the Greek fathers.[9] It may be true that there are remarkable and significant parallels in thought between Calvin and the Greek fathers. This is interesting, but it leaves us in the realm of comparison, not of influence. Mere parallels do not suffice to prove influence. It has to be shown that the parallels concerned come from direct influence, not from independently reached conclusions or mediated influence. If Calvin was aware of the influence of the Greek fathers at crucial points in his theology, he would surely have cited them as authorities.[10] If he was not aware of their influence, the burden of proof on those who would affirm such influence is that much greater.

In a more recent article on Calvin's doctrine of the Trinity Torrance argues that 'in spite of his judicious deployment of citations from Augustine, the recognized *magister theologiae* in the West, Calvin's trinitarian convictions were actually rather closer to those of the Greek Fathers Athanasius, Gregory Nazianzen, and Cyril of Alexandria'.[11] Much of the time he is cautious in his claims, stating only that Calvin's teaching is 'like' or 'similar to that of' the Greeks or that it 'reminds us of', 'reflects the views of' or 'recalls the teaching of' the Eastern fathers.[12] But he also includes some unjustified claims to influence: it is a statement of Gregory Nazianzen 'which Calvin evidently has in mind'; 'Calvin evidently has in mind Basil's account ... but also the teaching of Athanasius ...'; 'it is on the teaching of Athanasius that he relies here'; 'actually he takes his chief cue from Gregory Nazianzen'.[13] These claims about Athanasius and Gregory will be examined below.

The basic resource that has been used to trace Calvin's citations is the tables in R. J. Mooi's magisterial *Het Kerk- en Dogmahistorisch Element in de Werken van Johannes Calvijn*.[14] Other resources have also been used and citations are discussed which are not listed by Mooi, but I have not read through every volume of Calvin's works just in order to pick up the odd citation that may have been missed. The citations considered in this chapter will at least be thoroughly comprehensive even if they may not be totally exhaustive. Also, whereas Mooi's task was to catalogue Calvin's citations, the present chapter seeks to go behind the citations to ascertain the extent of Calvin's *knowledge* of the Greek fathers.

This chapter will not attempt to explore the topic exhaustively.[15] Instead we will ask how much knowledge of the Greek fathers Calvin betrays in his earliest years (up to and including the first edition of his *Institutio*) and in the work which contains the most patristic citations after the *Institutio*, his *Bondage and Liberation of the Will*. We will also ask how much knowledge

---

9 For details, cf. section II.a, below.
10 Cf. chapter 2, section IV, above.
11 T. F. Torrance, 'Calvin's Doctrine of the Trinity', *Calvin Theological Journal* 25 (1990) 179. (This article is also found in his *Trinitarian Perspectives. Toward Doctrinal Agreement* (Edinburgh: T&T Clark, 1994) 41–76.)
12 'Calvin's Doctrine of the Trinity', 165–93 *passim*.
13 Ibid., 170, 177, 178, 179. There are similar claims relating to Western fathers.
14 R. J. Mooi, KDE 365–97.
15 In particular, I have sought to avoid unnecessary overlap with the (as yet unpublished) paper on 'Calvin and the Greek Fathers' given by Irena Backus at the Seventh International Congress on Calvin Research (Seoul, 1998). Her paper was given between the original and the final versions of this chapter.

he had of some specific Greek fathers: pseudo-Clement, Irenaeus, Athanasius and the three Cappadocian fathers.

II. CALVIN'S KNOWLEDGE AT DIFFERENT STAGES

(a) Up to the 1536 Institutio

Before tackling this question we need to clarify which works were written before the 1536 *Institutio*. Mooi includes two works whose date is uncertain. Calvin's preface to his proposed edition of Chrysostom's homilies he dates (without argument) as 1535. But this work was never printed and the manuscript is undated. Ian Hazlett argues persuasively that it was written in the period 1538 to 1540[16] and his dating will be followed here. Mooi also, with greater justification, includes the *Psychopannychia*. There are two problems with this work. First, it was not published until 1542 (entitled *Vivere apud Christum non dormire animis sanctis*), although the two prefaces indicate that it was written in 1534 and then revised in 1536. There is no certainty that Calvin added no further material in the 1542 published edition. Patristic citations are precisely the sort of material that can easily be added at a later date to strengthen an argument. This is what Calvin does in successive editions of the *Institutio*. We cannot be sure, therefore, that all of the patristic material from 1542 dates from 1536 or earlier, though that is a real possibility. That material will, therefore, be considered in this section, but separately from the more certain material. The second problem is that there was a second, enlarged edition in 1545, the first to use the actual title *Psychopannychia*. Mooi is aware of this, but his table for the 1542 *Psychopannychia* includes citations which do not appear until 1545.[17]

Which Greek fathers does Calvin cite in this period? Not many. In his 1535 preface to Olivétan's Bible translation Calvin cites Eusebius (once) and Chrysostom (three times) in support of Bible reading by ordinary folk.[18]

Seven Greek fathers are mentioned in the 1536 *Institutio*.[19] Pseudo-Chrysostom's *Opus imperfectum in Matthaeum* is a Latin work.[20] Two more are of little significance. Epiphanius's abhorrence of images in churches is cited, with Jerome being named as the immediate source.[21] This reflects Calvin's knowledge of the Latin, not Greek, fathers. Later Calvin quotes 2 Thessalonians 3:11 (against monks) and then adds a marginal note: 'vide

---

16 W. I. P. Hazlett, 'Calvin's Latin Preface to his Proposed French Edition of Chrysostom's Homilies: Translation and Commentary' in J. Kirk (ed.), *Humanism and Reform: The Church in Europe, England and Scotland, 1400–1643* (Oxford: Blackwell, 1991) 132f.

17 On 11, n. 2, the Bernard citation is correctly attributed to the 1545 edition; in the table on 365 the same citation is attributed to the 1542 edition and therefore dated as 1534.

18 CO 9:788f.

19 For this purpose the Western translator Cassiodore is counted as a single Greek father.

20 OS 1:28, 49.

21 OS 1:28.

in eum locum Theophylactum'.[22] This citation is dropped in the 1539 edition.[23] At around this time Calvin dismisses Theophylact with the comment that there is nothing praiseworthy in his writings that is not taken from Chrysostom.[24] The only other time that Calvin mentions Theophylact is in a polemical work of 1561 where in passing he mentions Heshusius's treatment of Theophylact,[25] without indicating that he himself has any knowledge of Theophylact. In the light of Calvin's subsequent lack of interest in Theophylact, it is most likely that his 1536 citation is simply drawn from Erasmus's *Annotationes*.[26]

The 1536 *Institutio* contains two citations of Eusebius's church history and six of Cassiodore's *Historia tripartita*.[27] Calvin throughout his career makes use of Eusebius's *Historia ecclesiastica* and of the church histories of Socrates, Sozomen and Theodoret via Cassiodore's Latin compilation. Irena Backus has presented evidence which indicates that Calvin read Eusebius in Rufinus's translation.[28] Until 1539 Calvin mentions only Cassiodore; thereafter he often mentions Socrates, Sozomen and Theodoret by name. In many of these instances, however, he also states his source in the *Historia tripartita* and it may reasonably be assumed that on those occasions where he does not name him, Cassiodore is also the source. Two points emerge from this. First, that Calvin makes full use of these church histories and certainly read them for himself. Secondly, that he did not go to the Greek originals but relied upon the Latin editions of Rufinus and Cassiodore. These works were not available in Greek until well into Calvin's career and by that stage he had better things to do with his time than to go back to the Greek originals.

In the chapter on the law Calvin cites Origen's *Homilies on Exodus* in defence of the Reformed division of the Ten Commandments.[29] Later, in the chapter on the sacraments, Chrysostom's letter to Innocent is cited as one of a number of texts (including Eusebius and Cassiodore) demonstrating that in the first millennium the laity partook of the eucharistic cup.[30] Finally, in the chapter on the false sacraments Calvin attacks Peter Lombard's teaching on satisfaction and and accuses him of using delirious monastic writings falsely circulating under the names of Chrysostom and others.[31] This is in effect a citation of pseudo-Chrysostom rather than Chrysostom himself.

22 OS 1:211.
23 OS 5:59, n. c.
24 CO 9:834 (*Preface to Chrysostom*).
25 CO 9:490.
26 A. Reeve (ed.), *Erasmus' Annotations on the New Testament vol. 2: Galatians to the Apocalypse* (Leiden, etc.: E. J. Brill, 1993) 652.
27 Eusebius: OS 1:18, 131; Cassiodore: OS 1:27, 28 (twice), 29, 131, 155.
28 I. Backus, 'Calvin's Judgment of Eusebius of Caesarea: An Analysis', *Sixteenth Century Journal* 22 (1991) 435f. for instances where 'Eusebius' must refer to the Latin edition. Eusebius was published in Greek for the first time in 1544 and François Baudouin in 1545 discussed sending Calvin a copy (CO 12:231. Cf. chapter 1, n. 62, above) but Backus notes instances of Calvin continuing to use the Latin version in 1553 and 1555 (435f.).
29 OS 1:49. This citation continues in a modified form in later editions (OS 3:354).
30 OS 1:151f.
31 OS 1:199.

In the 1536 *Institutio* there are fifteen citations of Greek fathers. This compares with fifty-two citations from Latin fathers of the first millennium, of which twenty-four are from Augustine. Of the fifteen, eight are of Eusebius and the *Historia tripartita*, reflecting Calvin's interest in early church history rather than in the Greek fathers. Two from the pseudo-Chrysostom *Opus imperfectum in Matthaeum* are Latin, not Greek and another is also to pseudo-Chrysostom. The citations of Epiphanius and Theophylact are of little relevance. That leaves just two significant citations, one each from Origen and Chrysostom.

So far we have found evidence for Calvin's knowledge of Eusebius and Cassiodore, cited three and six times respectively. Given his ongoing use of these writers it is likely that this reflects his study of them early in his career. The four citations of Chrysostom are also likely to reflect early study of one who was to become Calvin's most cited Greek father, exceeded only by Augustine and Jerome.[32]

What about the 1542 *Vivere apud Christum non dormire animis sanctis*? Do the citations from that edition substantially alter the picture? Eight Greek fathers are mentioned, together with the heretic Apollinaris. Of these, citations of Polycarp and Melito are based on Eusebius's *Historia ecclesiastica*.[33] Calvin's opponent is mockingly urged to join Apollinaris' camp,[34] which implies no more than Calvin's knowledge of the nature of the Apollinarian heresy. Origen is once named in a list of fathers with a marginal reference to a Homily on Ezekiel.[35] This might reflect a knowledge of the original but it is also possible that Calvin is here dependent upon some predecessor who has written on this topic. Basil's *Hexaemeron* is once named in a marginal reference which includes Hilary and Augustine.[36] So far there is possible, but certainly not definite, evidence for reading from Origen and Basil. Since there will be evidence below both that Calvin acquired a copy of a 1540 edition of Basil and that he was reading it in 1542, it is not improbable that this merely marginal reference was added between 1540 and 1542.

Four fathers remain to be considered. Eusebius is three times cited, one reference being in the earlier, 1534, preface.[37] Since we have already decided that Calvin studied Eusebius in the early years, there is no reason why these citations should not go back to the earliest edition. The same applies to the three citations of Chrysostom,[38] which name five different works and include quotation. But since we also know that Calvin acquired the 1536 edition of Chrysostom and that he studied it for the 1539 and

---

32 Mooi's figures for the three (396f.) are Augustine: 1708; Jerome: 332; Chrysostom: 259. Gregory I comes next with 179. This early reading would not, however, be from the 1536 edition which he subsequently annotated. Cf. A. Ganoczy and K. Müller, *Calvins handschriftliche Annotationen zu Chrysostomus* (Wiesbaden: Franz Steiner, 1981).

33 CO 5:183.

34 CO 5:193.

35 CO 5:187.

36 OC 5:181.

37 CO 5:170, 183.

38 CO 5:180f., 188, 215. None of the passages cited is marked in Calvin's copy of Chrysostom (Ganoczy and Müller, *Calvins handschriftliche Annotationen*, 50–161).

1543 editions of his *Institutio*,[39] we cannot exclude the possibility that some or all of these references have been added between 1536 and 1542 as a result of that reading. Cyril is twice cited, both times referring to his commentary on John.[40] Irenaeus's *Adversus haereses* is cited three times, including two substantial quotations.[41] There is no reason to doubt that the citations of Cyril and Irenaeus reflect Calvin's own reading, though the timing of that reading is uncertain. The only other citation of Irenaeus prior to 1542 is the 1539 addition of a marginal reference to an existing passage from the 1536 *Institutio*.[42] Irenaeus is twice mentioned in the 1543 *Institutio*, which was largely completed at Strassburg, but Calvin refers there not to the writings of Irenaeus but to his opponents' appeal to the church father[43] and to an account from Eusebius's *Historia ecclesiastica*.[44] Given the indication below that Calvin started to read Irenaeus after his return from Strassburg, it may be that the citations in the *Vivere apud Christum non dormire animis sanctis* were also added as a result of that reading.

The citations in the 1542 treatise provide evidence for Calvin's early reading of Irenaeus and Cyril, but not the certainty that this reading goes back to 1534 or 1536.

(b) *In* The Bondage and Liberation of the Will

In 1543 Calvin published his *Defensio sanae et orthodoxae doctrinae de servitute et liberatione humani arbitrii adversus calumnias Alberti Pighii Campensis*.[45] Calvin cites sixteen different works by nine different Eastern fathers – by twelve different writers if we distinguish between Basil and pseudo-Basil, etc. But the knowledge of the Greek fathers displayed is considerably less than these statistics might suggest. In this work Calvin is responding to Pighius who in turn had attacked Calvin's 1539 *Institutio*. Some of the citations here discussed were in fact introduced either in 1539 or by Pighius. We need to ask whether Calvin's discussion reflects any *further* knowledge than that implied by the 1539 *Institutio* or by a reading of Pighius.[46] Applying this method leads to the conclusion that Calvin certainly consulted five of the sixteen works and possibly another three.

Calvin cites three works of Chrysostom and one of pseudo-Chrysostom.[47] But his discussion of them points to no greater knowledge

---

39 Calvin cites the Genesis homilies seven times in the 1539 *Institutio*, explicitly naming them five times (*Inst.* 2:2:4 (3x), 2:5:3, 3:4:38, 3:15:2, 3:16:3). The passages marked by Calvin appear especially in the 1543 *Institutio* (Ganoczy and Müller, *Calvins handschriftliche Annotationen*, 24–27, 162).
40 CO 5:187, 192.
41 CO 5:187, 215, 222.
42 *Inst.* 4:17:32.
43 *Inst.* 4:2:2.
44 *Inst.* 4:7:7.
45 For the source of each citation in this work, cf. the notes in A. N. S. Lane (ed.), G. I. Davies (tr.), *The Bondage and Liberation of the Will* (Grand Rapids: Baker and Carlisle: Paternoster, 1996). As CO column numbers are included in this edition, references below will be to CO. For the question of the works used by Calvin, cf. chapter 6, below.
46 The verdict for each individual work is listed in chapter 6, below, section VI.
47 CO 6:252, 287, 336, 391f., 395f.

than that displayed in 1539, with the one exception where Calvin refers to a passage quoted by Pighius.[48] Why is this so? Calvin's own copy of the 1536 edition is heavily annotated and he seems to have used it for the 1539 and 1543 *Institutio*. Why then did he not make more use of it for this work, especially if he had just been reading it for the 1543 *Institutio*? The answer is simple. Calvin was aware that no amount of interpretation would bring Chrysostom into line on this issue. There was no point in spending more time on Chrysostom, whom he had already conceded to the opposition in the 1539 *Institutio*.

There are four other works of which Calvin displays no further knowledge beyond the 1539 *Institutio* and Pighius's response to it, works of Basil, Cyril, Origen and Pamphilus.[49] There are a further three works to which Calvin is unlikely to have turned while preparing his reply to Pighius. Calvin cites Eusebius's mention of the letters of Clement of Rome.[50] He had not himself seen these letters which were not at that time available in the West. As he had already been making use of Eusebius since 1535 this reference is probably drawn from memory. Calvin also has a brief and loose quotation from Theodoret's *Historia ecclesiastica*, drawn from a passage which he had already cited in the 1543 *Institutio*.[51] Calvin is here drawing upon his memory of that reading.

This leaves five works of the Greek fathers which Calvin seems to have used directly. Pighius made appeal to the pseudo-Clementine *Recognitiones*. Calvin, who had never before referred to this work, shows some knowledge of the *Recognitiones* in his response. The clear implication is that Calvin turned to it in order to combat Pighius's claims. He also repeatedly cites Irenaeus, including two quotations. One of these is significantly long and accurate, suggesting that Calvin has the text to hand.

The remaining three works are all by Basil. Pighius quoted from two works by Basil.[52] Calvin responds to Pighius's quotations, adds some more material from one of the works and quotes from a further two works.[53] We can be more precise about what happened since with Basil there are different translations. Pighius was using the Latin translation by Raphael Maffei Volaterranus, which appeared in five editions of Basil's *Opera* between 1515 and 1531.[54] Calvin, by contrast, in the passages that he cites, used the translation by Janus Cornarius in the edition of the *Opera omnia* published in 1540 by Froben at Basel.[55] This supports the idea that Calvin built up his patristic library on his return to Geneva. How better to start than by purchasing a fresh translation of Basil recently published by Froben at Basel?

48 Cf. chapter 6, below, section VI.
49 Cf. chapter 6, below, section VI.
50 CO 6:262.
51 CO 6:276; *Inst.* 4:8:16.
52 Pighius, *De libero hominis arbitrio et divina gratia* (Cologne: M. Novesian, 1542), f. 33a-b.
53 In CO 6:284–86.
54 IA 114.428,440,448f.,486. Cf. I. Backus, *Lectures Humanistes de Basile de Césarée* (Paris: Institut d'Études Augustiniennes, 1990) 15–27.
55 *Omnia D. Basilii Magni . . . Opera* (Basel: H. Froben and N. Episcopius, 1540) (IA 114:485). On this edition, cf. Backus, *Lectures Humanistes*, 43–48, 232–38. Knowledge of which editions were used is quite important as they vary considerably (Backus, *Lectures Humanistes*, 9, 27, 48).

III. CALVIN'S KNOWLEDGE OF SPECIFIC GREEK FATHERS

Competent studies of Calvin's use of Eusebius and Chrysostom already exist and no attempt will be made to duplicate these.[56] Also not to be considered here are Cyril of Alexandria and Origen, both of whom Calvin often cited. This section will focus on some other Greek fathers, exploring how much Calvin knew of them and when he first began to study them.

(a) Pseudo-Clement

Calvin first mentions the pseudo-Clementine writings in his 1543 *Bondage and Liberation of the Will*.[57] He is disparaging about the contents of the *Recognitiones* and presents arguments for its inauthenticity, showing some knowledge of its contents.[58] Since he had never before referred to this work the most likely scenario is that he now turned to it in order to combat Pighius's claims. He mentions it again in two works of the 1550s. In the first part (1552) of his Commentary on Acts he twice refers to the fictitious debate between Peter and Simon Magus, mentioning the Clementine *Recognitiones* and *Homiliae*.[59] Clement appears again in Calvin's 1553 debates with Servetus over the Trinity. Servetus, after his arrest, was required to respond to thirty-eight statements drawn from his writings by Calvin and the other ministers. In his response Servetus cites 'Loci ex Petro apostolo et Clemente discipulo'.[60] Calvin and the ministers responded with a brief refutation which rejects the authenticity of 'Clement' and proceeds to cite letters bound with it.[61] The following year Calvin published his *Defensio orthodoxae fidei de sacra trinitate*, incorporating material from the debates and developing the 1553 refutation.[62] In 1561 there is a further brief reference to the apocryphal writings circulating in Clement's name in Calvin's response to François Baudouin.[63] It would seem that Calvin read pseudo-Clement for his response to Pighius and thereafter drew upon the memory of this reading.

It may be possible to identify the edition of pseudo-Clement used by Calvin, if not the actual copy. In the debates with Servetus, recorded in the 1554 *Defensio orthodoxae fidei de sacra trinitate*. Servetus five times cites from the *Recognitiones* and Calvin four times cites alleged early papal letters, which were found in the editions of Clement. Both authors give page numbers. There are four potential editions prior to 1553, of which

---

56 For Eusebius, cf. Backus, 'Calvin's Judgment of Eusebius of Caesarea'; for Chrysostom, cf. chapter 10, below, via the index.
57 CO 6:261f., 281, 290, 332, 339.
58 CO 6:261f.
59 CO 48:VIII (*argumentum*), 188 (8:24).
60 CO 8:514.
61 CO 8:534. The letters of Sixtus, Hyginus, Soter and Eutychian are found in the second volume of the two-volume 1526 edition.
62 CO 8:584–86.
63 CO 9:536.

only the 1526 edition fits the page numbers.[64] The likelihood that Calvin used this edition of pseudo-Clement is enhanced by the fact that it is found in the 1572 Genevan Library catalogue, bound together with the 1528 edition of Irenaeus that Calvin also used.[65]

Calvin also mentioned the genuine Clement, but had not seen his writings, which were not then available in the West. Eusebius mentions his letters[66] and he is cited by those maintaining that Philippians 4:3 refers to Paul's wife.[67] Eusebius and others mention him as a possible author of Hebrews.[68]

(b) Irenaeus

There is no question but that Calvin studied Irenaeus for himself. In the latter part of his career he cited him extensively, especially in response to Servetus's attempt to claim him.[69] But two questions remain to be answered: when did Calvin first begin to read Irenaeus and which edition did he use? We have seen above that prior to the 1542 *Vivere apud Christum non dormire animis sanctis* there is just one place where Calvin cites Irenaeus directly – in a marginal note added to the *Institutio* in 1539.[70] While Irenaeus is twice mentioned in the 1543 *Institutio* (largely completed in Strasbourg), this is only via other authors.[71] By contrast, in the 1542 treatise he cites Irenaeus three times, including substantial quotations.[72] Again in the 1543 *Bondage and Liberation of the Will* he repeatedly cites him, quoting him twice.[73] He is quoted a two further times in 1544.[74] There is no reason to doubt that Calvin was reading Irenaeus for himself by 1542. Was this his first reading of Irenaeus? There is no way to answer this with certainty and it is possible that the citations in the 1542 treatise were already included in the 1534 or 1536 redactions. But it is also possible that they were added in 1542 and that Calvin had little or no direct knowledge of Irenaeus until that year.

It is possible to identify the edition of Irenaeus used by Calvin, if not the actual copy. In the debates with Servetus, recorded in the 1554 *Defensio orthodoxae fidei de sacra trinitate*, Calvin and Servetus refer

---

64 CO 8:514 (Servetus); 8:534 (Calvin). The potential editions are Basel: J. Bebel, 1526 (IA 140.921); Basel: [J. Bebel], 1536 (IA 140.923); Lyons: Hugues and heirs of Aimon de La Port, 1544 (IA 140.924); Paris: J. Roigny, 1544 (IA 140.925). I have checked all of these except IA 140.924, but it is clear from the pagination of that edition that it could not be the source. There is one place where Calvin gives the wrong page number, 76 instead of 56. This is clearly a typographical error as the next reference, to page 60, comes 'paulo post'.
65 Ganoczy, BAC 168. For Irenaeus, cf. section III.b, below.
66 CO 6:262 (*Def. adv. calumn. Pighii*).
67 CO 52:58 (*Comm.* Phil. 4:3).
68 CO 55:5 (*Comm.* Heb. *argument*).
69 Mooi lists Irenaeus as Calvin's seventh most frequently cited father. Of his eighty-four citations, sixty-three come in the period after 1550, fifteen from his second period in Geneva to 1550 and just six from the earlier stages of his life (KDE 396). Thirty-seven are found in the Trinitarian writings of 1554–63 (KDE 382f.).
70 *Inst.* 4:17:32. Cf. at n. 42, above.
71 Cf. at nn. 43f., above.
72 CO 5:187, 215, 222.
73 CO 6:260f., 274f., 278, 281f., 288, 290, 339. Quotations at CO 6:275, 282.
74 CO 7:15 (*Art. fac. Par.*); 7:125 (*Instr. c. Anab.*).

repeatedly to Irenaeus, giving page numbers and even, twice, line numbers. The five potential editions prior to 1553 have been examined and the page and line numbers in the Servetus debate fit both the 1528 and the 1534 Froben editions.[75] Can we decide which of these two editions Calvin used? The list of volumes that were sent to the Swiss churches together with the documents of the Servetus trial includes 'ung aultre livre intitule Opus D. Irenaei episcopi Lugdunensis, imprime a Basle par Froben lan 1528'.[76] Also, the 1528 edition is found in the 1572 Genevan Library catalogue, bound together with the 1526 edition of pseudo-Clement that Calvin used.[77] It is unlikely that there were many copies of pseudo-Clement in Geneva, which increases the likelihood that the library copy was Calvin's, which in turn increases the likelihood that the Irenaeus edition was also his. It is possible, to put it no stronger, that he used the copies of Irenaeus and pseudo-Clement that found their way into the Genevan Library.

The edition of Irenaeus used by Calvin was obviously in Latin. Erasmus in his preface stated that it was not sufficiently clear whether Irenaeus wrote in Greek or Latin and ventured the opinion that he wrote in Latin although he was more proficient in Greek. In his second edition (the one that Calvin used) he added a comment revising this opinion and stating, on the basis of Jerome's statements, that Irenaeus probably wrote *Adversus haereses* in Greek.[78] Calvin shows no interest in this question.

(c) Athanasius

How much did Calvin know of Athanasius? Apparently quite a lot. Mooi notes thirty citations,[79] which makes him the sixth most cited Greek father, after Irenaeus, Origen, Eusebius, Cyril and Chrysostom. But how much actual knowledge of Athanasius does this reflect?

---

75 CO 8:510–14, 530, 532, 542 (Servetus); 8:530, 533 (Calvin). The potential editions are Basel: J. Froben, 1526 and 1528; Basel: H. Froben and N. Episcopius, 1534 and 1548; Paris: V. Gaultherot, 1545 and three other 1545 Paris editions (Petit, Regnault and Dupuys). (Cf. O. Reimherr with F. E. Cranz, 'Irenaeus Lugdunensis' in V. Brown with P. O. Kristeller and F. E. Cranz (eds), *Catalogus Translationum et Commentariorum*, vol. 7 (Washington (DC): Catholic University of America Press, 1992) 31.) I have checked all of these except the last three Paris editions which, according to ibid., 37, form 'four issues' together with the other 1545 edition and which, according to the catalogue of the Bibliothèque Nationale in Paris, have the same number of pages as it. The 1526, 1545 and 1548 editions do not fit the page numbers. The 1528 and 1534 editions both fit exactly except for one place (CO 8:513) where p. 20 should read pp. 19f. (a slip that Servetus could easily have made).
76 CO 8:804. I am grateful to David Wright for drawing my attention to this passage.
77 Ganoczy, BAC 168. The Genevan library also had Peter Martyr's copy of the 1548 edition of Irenaeus (BAC 180). On pseudo-Clement, cf. section III.a, above. Were the passages cited by Servetus and Calvin marked in the volume? Irena Backus has kindly checked the Irenaeus/pseudo-Clement volume at Geneva and reports that while she saw no underlinings in pseudo-Clement there were some (very few) in Irenaeus. There were, apparently, no marginal notes.
78 Sigs. a2b, C2a (p. 291) in the 1528 edition. Cf. Reimherr and Cranz, 'Irenaeus Lugdunensis', 35f., 50, where Erasmus's text is quoted in full, though with an error in the second line of the second passage (*scripserit* should be *scripsisset*).
79 Mooi's total is 30, but this is not exact. References to the 'Athanasian Creed' are not here considered, but cf. n. 88, below.

When does Calvin first cite Athanasius?[80] He is mentioned in Calvin's *Preface to Chrysostom* which is probably to be dated between 1538 and 1540, but not in such a way as to imply a significant knowledge of him.[81] Calvin notes that there are no complete commentaries of Athanasius, Basil or Gregory extant. Calvin names six Greek fathers, in addition to Chrysostom, and comments on the exegesis of every one of these save only Athanasius. This at least suggests that Calvin's knowledge of Athanasius may not have extended far beyond the fact that there were no commentaries by him.

Calvin starts to cite Athanasius in 1543. Mostly his citations are allusions to the life of Athanasius drawn from the writings of others. In his 1543 *Traité des Reliques* Calvin states that Athanasius interred a portion of John the Baptist's remains in a wall.[82] In the 1543 *Institutio* there are further biographical references. Augustine's report on Athanasius's attitude to singing is cited.[83] Theodoret's account of how Athanasius named Peter as his successor is cited.[84] Later Calvin states, erroneously, that Athanasius presided over the Council of Nicea.[85] More accurately he describes Athanasius's reception in Rome during his exile to the West, drawing upon Socrates' *Church History*.[86] Finally, there is brief mention of Athanasius where Calvin states that not every age has men of the calibre of Athanasius, Basil, Cyril and the like.[87] So far Calvin has manifested only a modest indirect knowledge of Athanasius's biography.

There are further references to Athanasius in the following ten years. In 1545 Calvin wrote a work responding to Peter Caroli's accusations, including the latter's demand that the Reformers assent to the Athanasian Creed.[88] He mentions that Caroli had cited Athanasius and other fathers against him and responds that these fathers had warned that nothing should be believed save what is scriptural. He then proceeds to discuss Hilary, but not Athanasius.[89] Later Calvin mentions, and rebuts, the claim made by Caroli at Bern that 'Ego hic sum ut Athanasius'.[90] Calvin's reply shows a knowledge of Athanasius's life and character, not of his writings. Also that year, Calvin in a letter notes Athanasius's teaching that Christ is

---

80 The works of Athanasius were often published in Latin. From 1519 to 1556: IA 109:388, 389, 392, 396, 397, 399, 401 , 403.
81 CO 9:834. For the date, cf. n. 16, above.
82 CO 6:436f., supposedly based on Eusebius, actually Rufinus, *Historia ecclesiastica* 2:28 (PL 21:536).
83 *Confessiones* 10:30:50 in *Inst.* 3:20:32.
84 *Inst.* 4:4:11, where Calvin's reference to Theodoret should be 4:17, not 4:20.
85 *Inst.* 4:7:1.
86 *Inst.* 4:7:5.
87 *Inst.* 4:9:13.
88 CO 7:311, 315, especially. For the controversy over the Athanasian Creed, cf. S. M. Reynolds, 'Calvin's View of the Athanasian and Nicene Creeds', *Westminster Theological Journal* 23 (1960–61) 33–37; W. Nijenhuis, 'Calvijns houding ten aanzien van de oudkerkelijke symbolen tijdens het conflict met Caroli', *Nederlands Theologisch Tijdschrift* 15 (1960–61) 24–47. English translation: 'Calvin's attitude towards the symbols of the Early Church during the conflict with Caroli' in his *Ecclesia Reformata. Studies on the Reformation* (Leiden: E. J. Brill, 1972) 73–96. For contemporary correspondence, cf. CRF 4:183–91; CO 10b:82–87. Cf. also n. 109, below.
89 CO 7:318.
90 CO 7:335.

begotten of the substance of the Father.[91] This appears to be a reference to the Creed of Nicea. In 1549 Calvin responds to the Augsburg *Interim*. In the latter Athanasius is cited to the effect that 'quotidie offertur per ministros Dei oblatio'. Calvin, in response, incorrectly lists Athanasius among those cited by the *Interim* in support of the idea that the sacrifice of the mass is prefigured by Melchizedek's offering of bread and wine.[92] Here, far from revealing any knowledge of Athanasius's theology, Calvin (presumably because of time pressure) does not manage even to refer to his opponents' citation accurately. Finally, in his 1551 Commentary on Isaiah 14:16 Calvin mentions that Athanasius referred to the Emperor Julian the Apostate as a mere passing cloud, information that derives from Theodoret.[93]

Not surprisingly, Calvin repeatedly cites Athanasius in his works in defence of the doctrine of the Trinity. In 1554 he published his response to Servetus. This work contains a number of references to Athanasius. Servetus claimed that 'nomen trinitatis ab Athanasio, et patribus Niceni consilii fuisse inventum'.[94] Later on Athanasius is included in a list of eight fathers 'et alii' whose views are described in general terms.[95] Shortly after, Calvin criticizes Servetus's exegesis of Ignatius, claiming that if Athanasius had spoken the same way Servetus would have interpreted the passage very differently.[96] Finally, Calvin notes that Servetus, having heard that Athanasius presided at the Council of Nicea, misses no opportunity to criticize him and also blames him for the iconodule edicts of the *second* Council of Nicea.[97] In this work Calvin is responding to Servetus's use of Athanasius and in so doing reveals no significant knowledge of Athanasius's theology.

After the Servetus controversy Calvin became engaged in debate with other anti-Trinitarians. In 1558 he responded to some questions of Giorgio Blandrata, a work which was published after his death. He notes in passing that when Athanasius 'et reliqui veteres' said that the Son was coessential with the Father, 'non aliud senserunt, quam eiusdem esse essentiae, quia unica sit et individua'.[98] A few years later, in 1561, Calvin published a work in response to the 'impiety' of Giovanni Valentino Gentilis. In his preface Calvin refers repeatedly to Athanasius. Arius was condemned at the Council of Nicea, over which Athanasius 'praefuit' and at which Athanasius 'dictavit' the phrase 'God from God'.[99] Athanasius also presided at the Alexandrian synod.[100] The cause of Gentilis' rage against Athanasius is his teaching that the Son is αὐτόθεος.[101] Calvin also seizes

---

91 CO 12:17. There are two references to Athanasius in CO 10b-20 in letters not by Calvin (18:375f., 19:542f.).
92 CO 7:579, 644.
93 CO 36:280; Theodoret, *Historia ecclesiastica* 3:5. In addition, twice where Calvin cites Theodoret, the latter was drawing on Athanasius (*Inst.* 4:8:16, 4:9:14).
94 CO 8:519.
95 CO 8:574.
96 CO 8:586f.
97 CO 8:591f.
98 CO 9:331.
99 CO 9:367f.
100 CO 9:368.
101 Ibid.

upon Gentilis' statement that Arius and Sabellius had long since been condemned by the church, noting that this conceded the name of 'church' to Athanasius and his colleagues at Nicea.[102] In all of this Calvin is simply responding to Gentilis' material and introduces no new information about Athanasius's teaching.

Two years later Calvin was writing against Polish anti-Trinitarianism. In his *Brevis Admonitio* Calvin again repeats his claim that Athanasius presided at Nicea and 'totam actionem moderatus est'.[103] In his *Epistola* to the Poles he asks why Servetus, Gentilis and others bring forward Basil, Athanasius and others, whose testimonies a thousand times refute their detestable impieties.[104] In all of his controversy with the anti-Trinitarians Calvin does little more than respond to the use of Athanasius by his opponents. His own use of Athanasius is to all intents and purposes an appeal to the Council of Nicea, which he saw as the work of Athanasius. If the knowledge of Athanasius displayed in these writings is a reliable indicator, Calvin knew very little indeed about Athanasius. And where would he have a greater incentive to make use of his knowledge of Athanasius than in controversy over the doctrine of the Trinity, responding to opponents who themselves were bringing Athanasius into the controversy?

Athanasius is also mentioned twice in the eucharistic controversies. In his *Secunda defensio* Calvin comments that having nothing in common with Athanasius but scarcity of support, Westphal seizes upon this as evidence of his orthodoxy.[105] In his *Dilucida explicatio* Calvin responds to a passage from Athanasius that Heshusius has quoted against him.[106] Calvin's reply betrays no knowledge of Athanasius beyond the passage quoted by Heshusius.

In 1561 Calvin in his *Gratulatio ad Gabrielem* responds to Gabriel's appeal to Athanasius with the comment that the latter would reject the idea of giving Nicea an authority higher than that of Scripture.[107] This goes no further than the claim made in response to Caroli in 1545. In an undated letter Calvin responds to Menno Simons' teaching at a number of points. Menno had criticized Athanasius for comparing the two natures of Christ to soul and body in human nature. Calvin's response demonstrates knowledge of Menno, but not of Athanasius.[108]

Mention should also be made of the 1559 *Confessio Gallicana*, which was based upon a draft sent by Calvin. Apart from an affirmation of the Athanasian Creed found in one version of the text,[109] there is a single reference to Athanasius who is listed among those who have rejected trinitarian heresy.[110]

102 Ibid.
103 CO 9:637.
104 CO 9:649.
105 CO 9:56.
106 CO 9:497f.
107 CO 9:430.
108 CO 10a:172.
109 OS 2:311; CO 9:741.
110 OS 2:312; CO 9:742.

What is the extent of Calvin's declared knowledge of Athanasius? He knows a few basic details about Athanasius's life, derived especially from the *Historia tripartita*. He knows that Athanasius gave supreme authority to Scripture. He knows a few elementary points about Athanasius's trinitarian teaching, based mainly on the teaching of the Creed of Nicea. It would be rash, of course, to claim that Calvin knew no more about Athanasius than is revealed by these citations. But is it rash to assume that these citations indicate the depth of Calvin's knowledge of Athanasius? Is it rash to draw conclusions from the fact that in responding to the citations of Athanasius by his opponents, be they anti-Trinitarians, Lutherans or Roman Catholics, Calvin forbears from revealing any significant knowledge of Athanasius beyond the passages cited against him?[111] If Calvin did indeed have a good knowledge of Athanasius he was remarkably uninterested in making any use of it in controversy. In these same controversies he does engage in debate about the teaching of other fathers. It is hard not to conclude that he forbore from doing so with Athanasius because of the paucity of his knowledge of him. It is unlikely that Calvin had more than a superficial knowledge of Athanasius and extremely unlikely that Athanasius significantly influenced his thought.

It is noteworthy that Calvin never quotes from Athanasius and never refers to any of his works. He betrays only a broad knowledge of his life and an elementary knowledge of his teaching. The former is adequately explained by Calvin's thorough knowledge of the church histories of Socrates, Sozomen and Theodoret. The latter reflects little more than a knowledge of the Creed of Nicea and certainly does not demand a first-hand knowledge of Athanasius's writings. From his use of Athanasius it is uncertain whether Calvin had ever read him, and it is very unlikely that he read him widely or was significantly influenced by him. If there are striking parallels in thought between Calvin and Athanasius, these are unlikely to be due to any *direct* influence.

(d) Basil

F. L. Battles makes some bold claims for the influence of Basil upon Calvin. He suggests Basil as the source of Calvin's famous comment about our twofold knowledge in the opening sentence of the *Institutio*. Calvin 'clearly' used the 1532 Erasmus edition of Basil. He rightly notes that the use of Basil in the *Psychopannychia* need not imply that Calvin knew him before 1542. But his own guess is that Basil was among the authors that Calvin read at Strassburg for his exegetical work. 'Yet the strong reference to *duplex cognitio* in *Institutio* 1536 leads to the conclusion that Basil was at hand when, in 1535, Calvin was framing the first edition of the *Institutio*.'[112]

---

111 Calvin's dependence upon the writings of his opponents has been considered, but there has been no consideration of other possible intermediary sources. Such consideration might weaken yet further the case for Calvin's direct knowledge of Athanasius.

112 F. L. Battles, *Interpreting John Calvin*, ed. R. Benedetto (Grand Rapids: Baker, 1996) 245f.

There is a great deal of speculation in this. In the first place, there are other possible sources for the idea of our twofold knowledge[113] and Battles gives no reason for preferring Basil other than the fact that Calvin (in 1543!) cites Basil for the *theatrum mundi* idea. Regarding the edition that Calvin used, there is solid evidence from his quotations that Calvin used the 1540 Cornarius translation.[114]

When did Calvin first read Basil? Prior to his *Bondage and Liberation of the Will* Calvin's citations of Basil are rare and extremely brief. In the 1539 *Institutio* there is a brief quotation from his homilies on the Psalms.[115] In the 1539 *Responsio ad Sadoletum* there is a brief mention of the purer form of the church as seen in the time of Chrysostom and Basil among the Greeks.[116] In his *Preface to Chrysostom* Calvin mentions Basil, but only to state that we have no continuous expositions of his to compare with those of Chrysostom, though he does add that it appears from the surviving fragments ('pauculis') of Basil and Gregory that their prime gift was oratorical.[117]

The next references to Basil need not predate Calvin's return to Geneva. There is a marginal reference to the *Hexaemeron* in the 1542 *Vivere apud Christum non dormire animis sanctis* which may well have been added as a result of his reading of the 1540 Cornarius translation.[118] Basil is mentioned three times in the 1543 *Institutio*, probably in part at least the fruit of Calvin's reading of the 1540 edition.[119]

In his *Bondage and Liberation of the Will*, Calvin quotes from two works of Basil which had not previously entered the debate.[120] Why did he quote these two works? The choice of one is not surprising since it was entitled *De libero arbitrio*. A perfunctory glance at the Basil volume could have led Calvin to this work. But the other work is less obvious. Calvin quotes from Basil's *Homiliae in Psalmos*. Why this work? The quotation is not especially relevant and contributes little to the argument. The natural interpretation is that Calvin was at this time reading Basil and so introduced a quotation from a passage that he remembered.[121] This is entirely consistent with the hypothesis that Calvin's first serious reading of Basil began at this time with the purchase of the 1540 Cornarius translation. His earlier references are consistent with a slight knowledge of Basil either

---

113 Cf. G. Ebeling, 'Cognitio Dei et Hominis' in *Geist und Geschichte der Reformation. Festgabe Hanns Rückert zum 65. Geburtstag* (Berlin: Walter de Gruyter, 1966) 271–322, especially 281–89.

114 Cf. at n. 55, above. In opting for the Cornarius translation rather than the alternative Protestant translation by Musculus (also Basel, 1540), whether by design or by chance, Calvin chose the more reliable and less theologically tendentious edition (Backus, *Lectures Humanistes*, 48).

115 *Inst.* 1:16:8.

116 CO 5:394; OS 1:466.

117 CO 9:834.

118 CO 5:181.

119 *Inst.* 1:14:20 (passing reference to *Hexaemeron*); 4:9:13 (mentioned as defender of true doctrine); 4:13:8 (witness to nature of primitive monasticism).

120 Cf. at nn. 52f., above.

121 This is paralleled by the way in which Calvin acquired the 1552 Basel edition of Bernard's works and two years later began to introduce new Bernardine material (chapter 5, below).

from limited reading or from secondary sources. After 1543 Calvin cites Basil relatively rarely,[122] which might also indicate that he read his works just the once, around 1542, in Latin.

(e) Gregory Nazianzen

In an article about Gregory T. F. Torrance claims that Calvin was influenced not just by Athanasius but also by Gregory Nazianzen.[123] He is more cautious about claims to *direct* influence, suggesting rather that it reached Calvin via Augustine, whose *De trinitate* is steeped in the teaching of the Greek fathers. This article is devoted almost entirely to a comparison of Calvin and Gregory with only the most muted claims about influence.[124] But if we assume that there *are* striking parallels between Calvin and Gregory, the question of possible influence becomes interesting.

Mooi lists fifteen citations of Gregory by Calvin, which looks promising, but these vanish almost to disappearing point. Gregory is quoted three times in the *Institutio*. In 1539 he is quoted in Greek, followed by a Latin translation, to the effect that one cannot think about the unity of God without thinking of his trinity, nor vice versa.[125] In the 1543 *Institutio* he is named as one of the witnesses to the nature of early monasticism (without any source being given) and his famous comment is quoted to the effect that he had never seen a church council with a good outcome.[126] Apart from this Calvin has very little to say about Gregory. In his preface to Chrysostom he acknowledges that Gregory is distinguished, but also implies that he knows only fragments ('pauculis') of his works.[127] Two of the citations in the *Institutio* are four times recycled.[128] Apart from these citations, Calvin four times responds to quotations of Gregory by Westphal and Heshusius, without giving any indication that he himself turned to Gregory.[129]

All we have to suggest that Calvin read Gregory is three citations in the *Institutio*. What is his source for these? The Greek citation from 1539 may well be taken from the 1516 edition of Gregory's *Orations* or from some other printing of them.[130] One of the two 1543 citations derives from

---

122 CO 7:13 (1544), 49:554 (1546), 52:415 (1549), 8:19 (1550), 8:574 (1554), 9:435, 439, 499 (1561), 9:649 (1563).
123 T. F. Torrance, 'The Doctrine of the Holy Trinity in Gregory Nazianzen and Calvin' in his *Trinitarian Perspectives*, 21–40. Cf. at nn. 11–13, above.
124 E.g. Calvin is 'here taking his cue from both Athanasius and Gregory Nazianzen, who had been followed in this argument by Augustine' (24) although Calvin mentions none of these.
125 *Inst.* 1:13:17.
126 *Inst.*, 4:13:8, 4:9:11.
127 CO 9:834.
128 The first part only of the first quotation appears three times, in different Latin translations, in *Epist.* 607 (21 January 1545) (CO 12:19), in *Comm.* John 1:1 (1553) (CO 47:3) and in *Def. c. err. Serveti* (1554) (CO 8:572). The quotation about councils reappears in *Comm.* Acts 15:2 (1554) (CO 48:341).
129 CO 9:112, 146, 500 (twice). Mooi's figure of fifteen citations is reached by counting the three citations in the *Institutio* a second time for the 1559 edition.
130 *Orationes Lectissimae XVI* (Venice: Aldus and A. Socerus, 1516) f. 199a. I am grateful to Irena Backus for pointing me to this edition.

Calvin's reading of the 1540 Cornarius translation of Basil. It is there that he would have found the passage that he cites from a letter of Gregory, which was not in print before that year.[131] In the second 1543 citation Gregory, Basil and Chrysostom are named as eyewitnesses of the rigours of primitive monasticism.[132] There are a number of possible sources for Gregory. The *Opera Selecta* footnotes propose an oration which is found in the 1516 Greek edition mentioned above, which greatly strengthens the likelihood that Calvin read this or a similar Greek edition of Gregory.[133] Alternatively, as this oration was translated by Willibald Pirckheimer and published in 1522 Calvin might have read it in Latin.[134] It is also possible that Calvin derived both this and the 1539 citation from an intermediate source, but the fact that they are both found in the same Greek edition makes it more likely that Calvin was dependent upon such an edition. Finally, there are references to monasticism in the letters of Gregory in the 1540 Basil edition,[135] but these are not nearly as specific to Calvin's citation as the passage in the orations. The most likely scenario is that Calvin read a Greek edition of the orations in time for the 1539 *Institutio* and remembered this reading when preparing the 1543 revision.

At this stage another factor should be mentioned. The complete works of Gregory were printed for the first time in 1550, initially in Greek followed shortly after in the same year by a Latin translation.[136] Did Calvin obtain a copy of either of these new editions and study it, as happened with the 1540 Cornarius translation of Basil and the 1552 Basel edition of Bernard? The evidence is revealing. Calvin *did* turn to Gregory in the light of the trinitarian controversy with Servetus – but by recycling an old quotation not by introducing new material.[137] Thereafter he did no more than respond to other people's material. This is in marked contrast to the manner in which his renewed reading of Basil and Bernard led him to introduce new illustrative material into his works.[138] His citations of Gregory point strongly to the conclusion that Calvin knew a little of him prior to 1550 and did not thereafter study either of the new editions

---

131 Gregory, *Epistola* 130, cited in *Inst.* 4:9:11, is found as *Epistola* 102 on p. 699 of the Cornarius translation. It was printed for the first time here and in the 1540 Musculus translation of Basil (A. C. Way, 'Gregory Nazianzen' in P. O. Kristeller and F. E. Cranz (eds), *Catalogus translationum et commentariorum*, vol. 2 (Washington (DC): Catholic University of America Press, 1971) 115–18).

132 *Inst.* 4:13:8.

133 Gregory, *Orationes* 4:71, found in *Orationes Lectissimae XVI*, f. 99b–100b. Cf. also n. 139, below.

134 Way, 'Gregory Nazianzen', 151, 191. E.g. *D. Gregorii Nazianzeni Orationes XXX* (Basel: H. Froben and N. Episcopius, 1536) 87f. Calvin's trinitarian citation is found on p. 37 but the Latin is so totally different to Calvin's three translations (cf. n. 128, above) that he is unlikely to have used it.

135 E.g. pp. 636f.

136 Both published at Basel by J. Hervagius. The Latin edition (edited by Wolfgang Musculus) was the first to be called an *Opera omnia* but was not complete and contained only five items that had not previously appeared in translation (Way, 'Gregory Nazianzen', 48). Despite this, its appearance is significant in that Calvin clearly preferred to use editions of the fathers calling themselves *Opera omnia* and was unaware of how later scholarship might judge this claim.

137 Cf. nn. 125, 128 above.

138 Cf. section III.d, above and chapter 4, below, section II.a.

of his works. Maybe Calvin considered Gregory less important than Basil and had less time for bedtime reading in the 1550s than in the 1540s.

Torrance has provided us with another simple test of Calvin's knowledge of Gregory. Calvin's doctrine of the Trinity developed in the 1550s in response to the debates with Servetus and other anti-Trinitarians. If he had studied one of the new Gregory editions one would expect this to have left some mark upon this development. Torrance outlines at length the parallels that he discerns between Calvin and Gregory and documents these carefully in Calvin, mainly in the *Institutio*. The test is very simple. Does this material enter the *Institutio* before or after the publication of the two 1550 editions? If the answer is before, it militates strongly against the suggestion that Calvin used the edition and increases the likelihood that, as Torrance suggests, the 'Gregorian' elements in Calvin's doctrine of the Trinity are in fact derived via Augustine. Of Torrance's twenty-seven footnotes identifying passages in Calvin where his teaching on the Trinity shares points in common between Calvin and Gregory, at least nineteen refer to points found before 1550 in the passages cited. Of the remaining eight it may well be that some of these too refer to points found in Calvin before 1550, in places other than the passages from the *Institutio* referred to in Torrance's notes. This is a very crude test but it does confirm the verdict that Calvin did not study either 1550 edition of Gregory in his struggle against the anti-Trinitarians.

(f) Gregory of Nyssa

Calvin never mentioned Gregory of Nyssa. The *Opera Selecta* footnotes once cite him as a possible source, but this is unlikely in the light of Calvin's failure ever to name him.[139] Knowledge of Gregory was confused in Calvin's lifetime with some works of Nemesius being attributed to him, some of his own works being attributed to Basil and a few genuine works being rightly attributed.[140] The explanation for Calvin's neglect probably lies in his interests. Mooi perceptively notes that he cited the Cappadocians especially on those points that were of importance for Western theology: creation, free will, Trinity, Lord's Supper and monasticism.[141] Mooi is probably also right in suggesting that Gregory's Neo-Platonism did not endear him to the Reformer. Basil, the most 'western' of the Cappadocians, is cited the most; Gregory of Nyssa, the most Platonist, is ignored.

IV. CONCLUSION

This limited survey has not encouraged the view that the Greek fathers greatly influenced Calvin. In the period to the 1536 *Institutio*, apart from his knowledge of the church historians, there are just three significant

---

139 OS 5:287, n. 3 (*Inst.* 4:15:3). The other suggested source is the very sermon of Gregory Nazianzen that Calvin had already quoted in the same (1539) edition (1:13:17). This was available in the 1516 Greek edition or in the Pirckheimer translations.
140 H. B. Wicher, 'Gregorius Nyssenus' in F. E. Cranz and P. O. Kristeller (eds), *Catalogus translationum et commentariorum*, vol. 5 (Washington (DC): Catholic University of America Press, 1984) 26f., 37–39.
141 Mooi, KDE 273.

citations, one of Origen and two of Chrysostom. Irenaeus and Basil are cited frequently, but there is no evidence for Calvin's significant knowledge of them before the 1540s. Of Gregory Nazianzen he betrays little knowledge. The large number of citations of Athanasius reflect knowledge of his life but only the most rudimentary knowledge of his theology.[142]

We have found evidence for the editions that Calvin used of pseudo-Clement, Irenaeus and Basil. Calvin's Chrysostom edition is already known. It has become abundantly clear that Calvin read the Greek fathers in Latin. This has been established for pseudo-Clement, Irenaeus, Eusebius, Basil, Chrysostom, Socrates, Sozomen and Theodoret. The only exception is the Greek quotation from Gregory Nazianzen.[143] How did Calvin the humanist justify this? Presumably he distinguished between the study of the Bible (for which the original languages were indispensable) and the study of the church fathers (for which a translation would suffice). This might be like a modern biblical scholar who would study the biblical text in the original but be happy to make use of an English translation of a German commentary. For the present study Calvin's and other sixteenth-century works have been consulted in the original, works of modern Calvin scholarship have often been consulted in translation. The need to return *ad fontes* is more compelling for the primary than the secondary sources.

142 This is, of course, only a partial examination of Calvin's use of the Greek fathers. Other fathers significant for him include Chrysostom, Cyril, Origen and the church historians.

143 Pirckheimer's Latin translation of this work had been published in 1521 (Way, 'Gregory Nazianzen', 153, 192) and Calvin's use of the Greek might indicate that he did not have access to the Latin.

4

❧❧❧

Calvin's Use of
Bernard of Clairvaux

Bernard of Clairvaux has been appreciated and appropriated by Christians of many different traditions in the centuries since his death. One of his admirers was the sixteenth-century reformer John Calvin. Calvin's works contain numerous references to four medieval writers.[1] Two of these, Lombard and Gratian, he cited because their works were standard textbooks of the time. Two others, Gregory the Great and Bernard, he cited because of his appreciation for them. Of these, it is Bernard whom Calvin most appreciates. He cites Bernard forty-one times between 1539 and 1559,[2] i.e. for most of his literary career. But Bernard does not appear in his earliest works. By 1536 Calvin had acquired a significant grasp of the fathers. He was also familiar with Lombard and Gratian and, to a lesser extent, Gregory, but had yet to cite Bernard.

I. THE 'REUTER THESIS'

What role did Bernard play in the development of Calvin's thought and its mature expression? Employing a correct method is essential if we are to answer this question accurately. Use of a faulty method can lead to misleading results, as can be seen from the works of Karl Reuter, who sees Bernard as one of the major influences upon Calvin. He reaches this conclusion by relying heavily upon historical speculation and upon a comparison of the thought of Calvin and Bernard. Very different results are reached by carefully examining Calvin's citations of Bernard.

When was Calvin's first exposure to Bernard? Hyma claimed that Calvin came to know the fathers and leading medievals during his four

---

This chapter originally appeared as 'Calvin's Use of Bernard of Clairvaux' in K. Elm (hrsg.), *Bernhard von Clairvaux: Rezeption und Wirkung im Mittelalter und in der Neuzeit* (Wolfenbütteler Mittelalter-Studien, Band 6) (Wiesbaden: Harrassowitz, 1994) 303–32. Section I has been expanded slightly and there are some revisions throughout.

---

1 Cf. chapter 2, above, section XI; Mooi, KDE 297–338.
2 Section III lists these citations. The text of the citations will be found in section IV. In the notes below they are cited according to this list – i.e. c.IXa, cc.VIII; X, etc.

years at the *Collège de Montaigu* in Paris, a claim which was repeated by Wendel in his magisterial *Calvin*.[3] Smits was the first to apply this specifically to Bernard.[4] Reuter subsequently developed the idea at length in his *Das Grundverständnis der Theologie Calvins*,[5] which appeared in 1963. Here he argued that Calvin read Bernard (at least via the *Flores*) at the *Collège de Montaigu* at Paris, where he studied in the 1520s.[6] He suggests that Bucer may also have helped Calvin to come to know Bernard.[7] He sees Bernard as a major influence upon the 1539 *Institutio*. 'In stärkster literarischer Abhängigkeit befindet sich *Calvin*, mit der zweiten Ausgabe der Institutio beginnend, von *Bernhard*.'[8] Bernard was responsible for the shift in the opening sentence of the *Institutio* from 'doctrina' (1536) to 'sapientia' (1539).[9]

These claims are part of a larger thesis concerning Calvin's time at Montaigu and the influence upon him of John Major, a Scottish theologian who taught at Montaigu from 1526 to 1531.[10] According to Reuter, he exercised a dominant influence upon Calvin's theological development, introducing him to a wide range of thinkers such as Augustine, Bernard, Lombard and Scotus.[11]

This thesis was taken up and adopted by many subsequent authors, but it also had its critics. Most noteworthy among these is Alexandre Ganoczy, in his 1966 *Le jeune Calvin*. Ganoczy points out that Calvin's studies at Montaigu did not go beyond the field of arts and that it is most unlikely that he attended theology lectures at that stage. He points out that Reuter's case is built primarily on a study of the definitive 1559 edition of the *Institutio*, whereas the alleged influence of Major and others should have appeared in the first edition.[12] Further criticism of Reuter's thesis came in 1975 from T. H. L. Parker. He repeats Ganoczy's arguments and adds a further element. He questions the traditional dating of Calvin's studies in Paris and argues that he probably overlapped with Major at Montaigu for a year only, or maybe not at all.[13]

In 1981 Reuter responded with the publication of a further book, *Vom Scholaren bis zum jungen Reformator*.[14] He accepts the point that Calvin's studies were in the arts faculty and that he did not attend Major's lectures

---

3   A. Hyma, *The Christian Renaissance* (New York and London: Century, 1925) 283f.; idem, *Renaissance to Reformation* (Grand Rapids: Eerdmans, 1951) 380; F. Wendel, *Calvin* (London: Collins and New York: Harper & Row, 1963) 19, 126f.
4   Smits, SAOJC 1:14, followed by Mooi, KDE 327. Smits subsequently, in a private conversation in 1971, revised his opinion.
5   Neukirchen-Vluyn: Neukirchener Verlag, 1963.
6   Ibid., 17, 32.
7   Ibid., 17.
8   Ibid., 12 (his emphasis).
9   Ibid., 9–18, especially 16f. W. S. Reid, 'Bernard of Clairvaux in the Thought of John Calvin', *Westminster Theological Journal* 41 (1978–79) 143f. also claims that Bernard influenced the opening words of the *Institutio*, without reference to Reuter.
10 The larger thesis is discussed more fully in chapter 2 above, section II. The present discussion concentrates on its implications for Bernard in particular.
11 Reuter, *Grundverständnis*, 20–28, 32.
12 (Wiesbaden, 1966) 39, 186, 188–90. ET: *The Young Calvin* (Philadelpia: Westminster, 1987) 61, 173f., 175f.
13 T. H. L. Parker, *John Calvin* (London, 1975) 11, 156–61.
14 (Neukirchen-Vluyn: Neukirchener Verlag, 1981).

in the theology faculty.[15] But he continues to argue for the influence upon Calvin of his time at Montaigu, where he was taught in the tradition of the *Devotio moderna* and the anti-Pelagian branch of the *Via moderna*.[16] In 1988 T. F. Torrance also argued vigorously that John Major was a formative influence upon Calvin.[17] Qualified support for the 'Reuter thesis' has come from Alister McGrath.[18] He argues for the influence upon Calvin, while at Montaigu, of the *via moderna* and the *schola Augustiniana moderna*. But he is sceptical about the claim of the influence upon Calvin of a specific individual like Major rather than of a general late medieval theological current.[19]

What of the influence upon Calvin of Bernard in particular? On this matter Reuter's claims have become stronger rather than weaker. He claims that at Montaigu in general, and through Major in particular, Calvin was exposed to the Augustinian anti-Pelagianism of the late Middle Ages and to the 'bernhardinisch-devote' tradition of piety and spiritual training. Where the latter is concerned, this is a matter of practice, of spiritual exercises and discipline, as much as of ideas.[20] He also claims that at Montaigu Calvin was exposed to the writings of Bernard.[21] He usually suggests a considerable exposure, but once qualifies this by stating that Calvin must have known at least anthologies from Bernard's writings, such as the *Flores*.[22]

Turning to the first edition of the *Institutio*, Augustine and Bernard are, according to Reuter, 'die für Calvin zunächst einmal nächstliegenden literarischen, geistlichen und theologischen Quellen'.[23] Calvin has been influenced by 'die augustinisch-bernhardinisch-devote Mystik'.[24] This is more often described as the 'bernhardinisch-devote Frömmigkeit'.[25] Reuter describes an aspect of Calvin's theology in 1536, 'die ohne die bernhardinisch-devote und augustinisch-franziskanische Frömmigkeit und auch Theologie kaum denkbar ist'.[26] As regards Calvin's exposure to this tradition, 'es konnte zu keiner anderen Zeit so sehr von Calvin Bezitz ergreifen wie zu derjenigen, als er das Gymnasium montis acuti besuchte'.[27]

---

15 Ibid., 1 *et al.* But he also points to Calvin's statement that his father made him turn from the study of philosophy to law. He suggests that this may mean that Calvin commenced at Montaigu the study of scholastic theology (ibid., 37).
16 Reuter, *Vom Scholaren*, 4–12, *et al.*
17 T. F. Torrance, *The Hermeneutics of John Calvin* (Edinburgh, 1988) 80–95.
18 A. E. McGrath, 'John Calvin and Late Mediaeval Thought. A Study in Late Mediaeval Influences upon Calvin's Theological Development', *Archiv für Reformationsgeschichte* 77 (1986) 58–78; idem, *The Intellectual Origins of the European Reformation* (Oxford: Blackwell, 1987) 94–106; idem, *A Life of John Calvin* (Oxford: Blackwell, 1990) 36–47.
19 McGrath, *Intellectual Origins*, 101–106; idem, 'John Calvin', 63–78; idem, *Life of Calvin*, 39–47.
20 Reuter, *Vom Scholaren*, 16–18, 25, 30f., 56, 62f., 122, 127, 136.
21 Ibid., 16, 18, 30, 32, 56, 114, 127.
22 Ibid., 63f., cf. 122.
23 Ibid., 20.
24 Ibid., 58.
25 Ibid., 30, 102, *et al.*
26 Ibid., 72.
27 Ibid., 203.

Reuter sees evidence in the 1536 *Institutio* for Calvin's exposure not just to a Bernardine tradition but to the writings of Bernard himself.[28] 'Schon in der Erstausgabe der Institutio fällt eine gewisse Kenntnis Bernhards auf.'[29] Reuter expounds an aspect of the young Calvin 'die ohne den Einfluß von Schriften Bernhards und der Imitatio schon im Gymnasium montis acuti nicht denkbar erscheint'.[30] To summarize, Reuter sees Bernard as a major influence upon the young Calvin. At Montaigu Calvin was exposed to the 'bernhardinisch-devote' tradition in general and to the writings of Bernard in particular. He must have read at least the *Flores*. Bernard was an important source for the first edition of the *Institutio*.

On what grounds does Reuter make these claims? His case rests upon a twofold foundation: the circumstances of Calvin's studies at Montaigu[31] and the many parallels which he discerns between the thought of Bernard and the young Calvin.[32] But how adequate is this?

First, the circumstances of Calvin's studies at Montaigu. It would be hard to dispute that Calvin was there exposed to the 'bernhardinisch-devote' tradition. But must he have read the writings of Bernard? Clearly he *may* have done so, but we cannot simply assume that he did. Again, if he did, how extensive and how significant was this? For a boy in his mid-teens to be forced to read something does not have the same significance as, say, an ardent young man of twenty-four studying in a friend's library to prepare himself for his theological career. Even if Calvin did read Bernard at Montaigu, we cannot *assume* that it made a significant impression upon him.

What about the alleged parallels between Bernard and the young Calvin? This is where Reuter places most of his emphasis and it is the weakest part of his case. Suppose there are profound parallels between the thought of Bernard and Calvin? What does this prove? Not necessarily that Calvin had even heard of Bernard, let alone that Bernard was his source. It could be that Bernard's ideas reached Calvin via an intermediary source, such as the *devotio moderna* to which Calvin *was* exposed at Montaigu and whose influence upon Calvin Reuter stresses.[33] It could be that Bernard and Calvin are similar because they are both independently following an earlier source, such as Augustine. It could be that they are similar because they both belong to a broader theological tradition, such as medieval Augustinianism. Similarities and parallels prove no more than that Bernard is *one possible* source for the theology of the young Calvin. This weakness is apparent as Reuter expounds his thesis. Some of the parallels are so general that they prove little more than the fact that Bernard and Calvin were both orthodox Christians.[34]

---

28 Ibid., 30, 61f., 63–65, 102, 114, 121, 135, 138, 143, 145, 176.
29 Ibid., 102.
30 Ibid., 114.
31 Cf. nn. 20–22, above.
32 Reuter, *Vom Scholaren*, 64f., 73, 114, 127, *et al.*
33 A clear example of an intermediary source is found in *Inst.* 2:2:5 (OS 3:247, n. 4). Calvin there cites Peter Lombard for the threefold definition of liberty which comes ultimately from Bernard. The idea may be Bernard's, but the source is Lombard.
34 Cf. Reuter, *Vom Scholaren*, 127, for some parallels which are very general.

The missing element in both of Reuter's books is a study of how Calvin *cites* Bernard. There is an extensive bibliography at the end of each book, but these contain hardly any of the many studies of Calvin's *use* of the fathers, such as the magisterial works of Mooi or Smits.[35] This lacuna points to a fundamental defect in methodology. In one place he does refer to Calvin's use of earlier writers, listing the authors cited in Calvin's Seneca commentary. But this is done in an uncritical fashion and without reference to a study which has shown how much Calvin was dependent upon other people's collections at this point.[36]

Returning to Bernard, in the first book Reuter makes passing reference to two of Calvin's citations of Bernard,[37] but otherwise ignores them. In the second book there are again passing references to five of Calvin's citations,[38] but these are so brief that they are likely to be missed by all but the most careful readers. The author places no weight upon them, wisely given the paucity of Bernardine citations in Calvin prior to 1543. Indeed, he absolves himself from any obligations in this area. He maintains Bernard's influence upon the young Calvin, 'ohne daß eine direkte literarische Abhängigkeit nachgewiesen werden kann, auch nicht nachgewiesen zu werden braucht. Die gleichlautende Verwendung der Termini und die Verwandtschaft in der Sache selbst entscheidet'.[39] Back to the alleged parallels.

Here an important methodological question needs to be faced. How significant is it that Calvin does not name a particular writer? Ganoczy criticizes Reuter's first book in part on the grounds that most of the alleged late-medieval influences upon Calvin are not named in the 1536 *Institutio*.[40] He has rightly been criticized for this. McGrath argues that for Calvin, unlike the young Luther, there was no point in naming late-medieval scholastic authors.[41] When Calvin cites earlier writers he is not declaring which writers have influenced him nor even necessarily stating his sources in the way of the modern footnote. In his citations of the fathers he is above all appealing to authorities.[42]

Where does that leave us with *Bernard*? Reuter gives a reason why Calvin might not have named Bernard. He shows how in the *fromme Traktatliteratur*, such as the *Imitatio Christi*, sources are named rarely or not at all. 'Calvin hielt es sogar auch dann mit dieser Üblichkeit, wenn er katholische Zeitgenossen, unmittelbare katholische Gewährsmänner,

---

35 Mooi, KDE; Smits, SAOJC.

36 Reuter, *Vom Scholaren*, 89f. F. L. Battles, 'The Sources of Calvin's Seneca Commentary' in G. E. Duffield (ed.), *John Calvin* (Appleford: Sutton Courtenay, 1966) 38–66.

37 Reuter, *Grundverständnis*, 191, 195. On p. 191 he inaccurately attributes c.IX to the 1559 *Institutio*.

38 Reuter, *Vom Scholaren*, 16, n. 61 is probably meant to refer to c.II; p. 156, n. 1305 appears to be a reference to c.XXXIXb, although the wrong source in Calvin is given; p. 156, n. 1312 refers to c.XI; p. 163, n. 1361 refers to cc.III and II; p. 185, n. 1517 refers to c.I.

39 Ibid., 138.

40 Ganoczy, *Le jeune Calvin*, 189; ET: 175.

41 McGrath, *Intellectual Origins*, 102–104. Cf. idem, *Life of Calvin*, 37–39; Torrance, *Hermeneutics*, 81.

42 Cf. chapter 2, above, section IV.

sowie anderes katholisches Schrifttum ungenannt sein ließ, wo immer er auch mit aus ihnen fruchtbare Förderung auf dem Weg vom Scholaren zum jungen augustinisch gesinnten Reformator empfangen hatte und weiterhin empfing'.[43] McGrath and Reuter, warn us against building too much upon silence, even though Bernard was not a late-medieval theologian and the *Institutio* does not belong to the category of *fromme Traktatliteratur*.

If the circumstances of Calvin's study at Montaigu do not demand a significant exposure to Bernard himself, if alleged parallels prove very little, if failure to name an author does not prove ignorance of him, to what can we turn? With Bernard we *do* have hard evidence, in the form of Calvin's citations. We must not fall into the trap of assuming that his references to Bernard *exhaust* his knowledge of him. But we can legitimately turn to his use of Bernard for evidence of his *attitude to* him and of the *type of* knowledge of Bernard that he has. Calvin's use of Bernard comes in four stages: 1539, the 1543 *Institutio*, 1543 to 1558 and the 1559 *Institutio*.

Bernard is not mentioned in the 1536 *Institutio*. But he appears three times in the 1539 edition, which was nearing completion in October 1538.[44] Calvin quotes Bernard's definition of *liberum arbitrium*. But there are two reasons why this is no indication of Bernardine influence. First, Calvin disapproves of Bernard's definition. Secondly, the definition appears with others from (pseudo-)Augustine and Anselm. The same three passages appear together in a number of earlier works and it can hardly be a coincidence that Calvin follows suit.[45] No evidence here either for Calvin's reading of Bernard or for Bernard's influence upon him. In his second citation Calvin accuses Bernard of semi-Pelagianism and of departing from the teaching of Augustine. This misrepresentation of Bernard could be derived from Gabriel Biel, who was also one of the possible sources for the first citation.[46] It is clear that Calvin's grasp of Bernard's theology was somewhat defective at this stage and that he was no great admirer of Bernard. After two disapproving citations Calvin concludes more positively ('neque vero inepte') with a brief summary of one aspect of Bernard's teaching in the *De gratia et libero arbitrio*.[47] There is one other Bernardine citation in the *Responsio ad Sadoletum* of 1539, a passing reference to the fact that Bernard protested against papal and clerical corruption.[48]

What can be deduced from this? One cannot argue that Calvin knows no more of a writer than he quotes. Torrance sounds an important warning here regarding Calvin's knowledge of figures such as Bernard:

> Calvin's indebtedness to their thought cannot be measured simply by the passages where they are mentioned by name, for Calvin's language is often saturated with that of others in such a way that it is

43 Reuter, *Vom Scholaren*, 178.
44 Cc.I-III. Cf. OS 3.XI.
45 Cf. chapter 5, below, at nn. 151–53.
46 Cf. chapter 5, below, at nn. 154–56.
47 C.III.
48 C.IV.

clear that they affected him deeply in his early formative years when he was acquiring his primary instruments of thought and speech.[49]

The identification of Calvin's sources by finding linguistic parallels is, if anything, even more precarious than the use of alleged parallels of thought.[50] But Torrance is certainly right to maintain that Calvin's knowledge of a writer is not to be *limited* to his use of him. It would be wrong to suggest that Calvin knew no more of Bernard in 1539 than he cites. But it is surely not wrong to turn to the citations to see *what sort of* knowledge of Bernard Calvin had in 1539.

Two of the four 1539 citations are disapproving, one of which is taken from an intermediate source and the other of which misrepresents Bernard and possibly comes from an intermediate source. The remaining two are brief and in one instance extremely general. The extent and the nature of the 1539 citations do not encourage the view that Calvin was profoundly influenced by Bernard at that stage. This does not prove that there was no such influence, but it does place a heavy burden of proof on any claim to such influence. Until the 1543 *Institutio* Calvin's citations are all vague, no references are given and none can be related with any certainty to a specific passage of Bernard, except for the definition of freewill, which appears to have an intermediary source. We do not find much evidence for the claim that 'in stärkster literarischer Abhängigkeit befindet sich *Calvin*, mit der zweiten Ausgabe der *Institutio* beginnend, von *Bernhard*'.[51]

In the next edition of the *Institutio*, published in 1543, all has changed. There are eight citations in which Calvin quotes at length from four of Bernard's sermons and from his work *De consideratione*.[52] It is clear that Calvin is by now familiar with Bernard. Bernard is cited extensively and approvingly, to support the points being argued by Calvin. There are long and appreciative quotations from Bernard's works.

What follows from this? Comparing Calvin's use of Bernard in the 1539 and 1543 editions it is hard to resist the following conclusion. In 1539 Calvin's knowledge of Bernard was slight and inaccurate. He could cite Bernard as an example both of the medieval departure from Augustinian truth and as a witness to that truth. By 1543 he had read a significant quantity of the Bernardine corpus and could quote from it at length to present Bernard as a medieval witness to the truth. It is noteworthy that four of the new quotations in 1543 are incorporated into sections consisting mainly of 1539 material.[53] This confirms the impression that Calvin's

49 Torrance, *Hermeneutics*, 81.
50 For a critique of Torrance's use of this argument, cf. chapter 2, above, at n. 52. Reuter also uses the linguistic argument (*Vom Scholaren*, 46f., 179, 261). In the last of these passages he lists the vocabulary that Calvin shares with the *Imitatio* and acquired at Montaigu. Apart from the fact that some of the terms (e.g. *crucis Christi, patientia, conversio, simplicitas, miseria*) are hardly rare, Reuter goes on to say that Erasmus, Budé, Augustine, Bonaventure and Bernard also share the same vocabulary. The most impressive linguistic parallels between two writers are no proof of dependence unless they are peculiar to those two writers. Neither Reuter nor Torrance make any attempt to demonstrate such peculiarity.
51 Reuter, *Grundverständnis*, 12 (his emphasis).
52 Cc.IX–XVI.
53 Cc.IX–XII.

knowledge of Bernard was not very great at the time of the 1539 *Institutio*. Calvin's first serious exposure to Bernard came between the writing of the second and third editions of the *Institutio*, during his time at Strassburg, from 1538 to 1541. This conclusion concerns not the nebulous influence of a 'bernhardinisch-devote' tradition, where Reuter may well be correct, but Calvin's direct literary encounter with Bernard, about which Reuter makes equally firm assertions, which are unfounded.

When did Calvin first encounter Bernard? There are four possibilities. Calvin may have read Bernard at Montaigu and this could have been the source of his 1539 citations. Certainly he was exposed to the 'bernhardinisch-devote' tradition at Montaigu and this may have included a first-hand encounter with the writings of Bernard himself. Another possibility is that Calvin read Bernard during his time at Angoulême in 1534. Here he spent some months of leisure with access to the library of his friend Louis du Tillet and with the desire to prepare himself for his work as a reformer.[54] Access, leisure and inclination all coincide. A third possibility is his time at Basel preparing the first edition of the *Institutio*. Finally, it is even possible that Calvin had read no Bernard until his stay in Strassburg. The earliest citations, in the 1539 *Institutio*, could have been inserted after his arrival at Strassburg. In favour of this possibility is the slightly confused attitude to Bernard in this edition – both hostile and favourable. This is more easily understood if Calvin had only recently begun to read Bernard. The other 1539 citation, in his reply to Sadolet, is very similar to a comment made by Bucer.[55]

There are a number of possibilities for Calvin's earliest encounter with Bernard, ranging from Montaigu to Strassburg. But if the impression left by the 1539 *Institutio* is accurate, Calvin's knowledge of Bernard at that point was so slight that it is neither possible nor important to know when and where he acquired it.

In his first book, Reuter suggests that Calvin's early acquaintance with Bernard may have been via the *Flores* and that Bucer may have helped him with his knowledge of Bernard.[56] Study of the 1539 citations shows that they betray no greater knowledge of Bernard than could easily be derived from the *Flores*.[57] It is possible that Calvin's earliest reading of Bernard was via the *Flores*, but all that has been shown is that Calvin's vague and general use of Bernard in 1539 does not *demand* greater knowledge than that available in the *Flores*, not that he actually read them. Bucer is a distinct possibility. It was at Strassburg that Calvin's serious reading of Bernard began. Bucer himself had a modest knowledge of

---

54 E. Doumergue, *Jean Calvin. Les hommes et les choses de son temps*, vol. 1 (Lausanne: Bridel, 1899) 370. Parker, *Calvin*, 31, points out that Calvin 'could hardly have spent more than four or five months there', but this is ample time to acquire a superficial knowledge of Bernard.

55 C.IV is very similar to a comment in Bucer's 1530 *Epistola Apologetica* (C. Augustijn, P. Fraenkel and M. Lienhard (eds), *Martini Buceri Opera Latina*, vol. 1 (Leiden: E. J. Brill, 1982), 101f. But anyone with a basic knowledge of Bernard could have made such a comment.

56 Reuter, *Grundverständnis*, 17, 32.

57 Cf. chapter 5, below, at nn. 110f. It has already been argued that cc.I; II come from an intermediate source.

Bernard.[58] It is possible that a couple of Calvin's Bernardine citations are derived from Bucer.[59] But Bucer's use of Bernard is slight compared with Calvin's and Bucer's role would have been no more than to point Calvin in the direction of Bernard. The influence of Gropper and the inter-confessional colloquies is also significant.[60]

Why bother to spend so much time considering Reuter's thesis? There are several reasons. First, it is being claimed, by Reuter and a number of others who have followed his thesis, that Bernard played a major role in the early development of Calvin's thought. If the evidence contradicts rather than supports this thesis, then it is important to put the historical record straight. But there is a wider issue at stake. Reuter's is not the only such thesis. The methodological issues involved have a wider relevance to other instances of alleged influence, such as that of others upon Calvin or Bernard's alleged influence upon others.

II. CALVIN'S USE OF BERNARD[61]

(a) The Citations and their Source

What image of Bernard does Calvin present in the 1543 *Institutio*? Calvin's eight citations fall into two distinct groups. First there are four substantial quotations from the sermons relating to the doctrine of justification by faith. Here Bernard warns against presuming on our own merits. In and of ourselves we are nothing. But that is only half of the story because God has set his heart upon us. Therefore, 'nos sumus: sed illius dignatione, non nostra dignitate'.[62] So our trust is to be in Christ alone. Security and rest are to be found in Christ's wounds. We are to boast in God's promises, indeed our merit is to hope in him. Our righteousness comes from Christ's righteousness and our merit is Christ's compassion and mercy.[63]

Calvin also appeals to Bernard in his attack upon the condition of the Roman Catholic church. He refers to Bernard's attacks on clerical corruption. [64] He mentions Bernard's opposition to the undermining of due church order by the centralization of power at Rome, quoting specific complaints from the *De consideratione*.[65] He also quotes at length from Bernard in his opposition to the temporal claims of the papacy.[66] Thus

---

58 The indices of Bucer's *Opera Latina* and *Deutsche Schriften* so far published (Gütersloh and Paris, 1955ff.; Leiden, 1979ff.) reveal a modest use of Bernard. Bucer's and Parker's handwritten collection of patristic passages contains ten references to Bernard, six of which are in Bucer's handwriting (P. Fraenkel (ed.), *Martini Buceri Opera Latina*, vol. 3 (Leiden, etc.: E. J. Brill, 1988), 69, 86, 158, 160, 160f., 171).

59 Cf. chapter 5, below, at nn. 158, 164, for two instances where Bucer anticipated one of Calvin's citations. In neither instance is it *necessary* to postulate dependence upon Bucer.

60 Cf. chapter 5, below, at nn. 159f., 163.

61 The themes of this section are covered more fully in my *Calvin and Bernard of Clairvaux* (Studies in Reformed Theology and History New Series no. 1) (Princeton: Princeton Theological Seminary, 1996).

62 C.IX.

63 Cc.X; XII.

64 C.XIII.

65 Cc.XIV; XV.

66 C.XVI.

there are two sides to Calvin's use of Bernard in the 1543 *Institutio*. There is the somewhat negative appeal to Bernard as a witness against Roman corruption. Apart from a brief repeat of one of these passages,[67] Calvin does not continue with this use of Bernard. On the other hand, there is the positive appeal to the spirituality of Bernard as Calvin expounds his doctrine of justification by faith. This approach to Bernard is developed further in the next significant wave of Bernardine material, in the definitive 1559 edition of the *Institutio*.

The third stage of Calvin's use of Bernard covers the period between the 1543 and 1559 editions of the *Institutio*. Bernard is cited fourteen times during this period. Four of these citations are found in Calvin's response to Pighius's *De libero arbitrio*.[68] Calvin claims that when it comes to the bondage of the will, Bernard is predominantly on his side over against Pighius. There are a further four brief citations found in other polemical works against Rome and drawn from material already used in the 1543 *Institutio*.[69] Two more are found in polemical works against the Anabaptists, from 1544 and 1545, and concern the issue of soul sleep.[70] These involve new material which Calvin does not use again.

The remaining citations from this period are found in Calvin's exegetical works. In commenting on 1 Corinthians 3:15 in 1546 Calvin numbers Bernard among those fathers who had the right foundation but mixed good with bad material in building upon it.[71] Calvin is following a Protestant exegetical tradition of referring this passage to the fathers.[72] There is a brief quotation from Bernard in Calvin's 1554 commentary on Genesis 3:6.[73] In a sermon on Deuteronomy 32, preached in 1556, Calvin accuses the papists of honouring Bernard and others as fathers, but rejecting the good parts of their teaching.[74] Finally, there is a brief quotation of a Bernardine wordplay in Calvin's 1557 commentary on Psalm 55:13–15.[75]

What do these very diverse citations tell us about Calvin's study of Bernard? They cohere well with external evidence. When Calvin returned to Geneva in 1541 he had to sell most of his books. He seems to have left behind the copy of Bernard which he had read at Strassburg, either because it was not his own or because he had sold it.[76] Calvin's citations from 1543 to 1550 support this supposition. Four of them simply reflect his reuse of material from the 1543 *Institutio*. The four in the 1543 reply to Pighius reflect a good knowledge of Bernard, but are themselves brief, unlike the great majority of patristic citations in that work. This coheres well with the theory that these citations are based on Calvin's memory of his reading

---

67　C.XXIII takes up c.XIVh.
68　Cc.V-VIII. This work *appeared* before the 1543 *Institutio*, but was written after the latter (CO 6.XXIII).
69　Cc.XVII; XXI-XXIII.
70　Cc.XVIII; XIX.
71　C.XX.
72　Cf. chapter 5, below, at nn. 131–34.
73　C.XXIV.
74　C.XXV.
75　C.XXVI.
76　Cf. chapter 5, below, at nn. 7–12.

of Bernard at Strassburg from 1538 to 1541. Textual evidence indicates that the two anti-Anabaptist quotations were not derived from an *Opera omnia*, but probably from a fifteenth-century edition of Bernard's sermons and letters.[77] The reference to Bernard in the 1 Corinthians commentary is merely a comment on him. None of the citations from 1543 to 1550 suggest that Calvin was reading the *Opera omnia* of Bernard after his return to Geneva from Strassburg in 1541.

Calvin's quotations in the 1559 *Institutio* probably come from the 1552 Basel edition of the *Opera omnia Bernardi*.[78] This is supported by the proximity of Basel to Geneva, by the fact that a copy of this edition, possibly Calvin's own, was already in the library of the Genevan *Académie* in 1572[79] and by the date at which new Bernardine material appears in Calvin's works. After a gap of seven years, Bernard reappears in Calvin's 1554 Genesis and 1557 Psalms commentaries, probably the first fruit of Calvin's renewed reading of Bernard, in the Basel edition. That reading bore fruit in the definitive 1559 edition of the *Institutio* where there are many quotations from Bernard.

The fourth stage of Calvin's use of Bernard comes with the 1559 *Institutio*. Here Bernard is cited fifteen times.[80] Although this is almost twice the number of citations in the 1543 edition, the actual bulk of citation is less as Calvin's quotations have become briefer. Most of the new historical material in the 1559 *Institutio* is taken from Calvin's polemical treatises of the 1550s, against anti-Trinitarianism and the Lutheran doctrine of the real presence in particular. The new Bernardine material does not fit into this pattern. Bernard is quoted for support in the doctrines of freewill and grace, justification by faith and predestination, continuing the interests of the 1539 *Institutio*. The new quotations are incorporated into material which is predominantly from 1539 and, to a lesser extent, from 1543.

(b) The Role of Bernard

What is the significance of these Bernardine citations? There is one place where the Bernardine addition can be said to modify the previous text. In the 1543 edition Calvin stressed the need to be severe with ourselves and to acknowledge our sins. In 1559 this receives the important pastoral qualification that our grief for sin should be neither perpetual nor excessive. This qualification concludes with a long quotation from Bernard.[81] The substance of the qualification is found in the Bernard passage and it is possible that Calvin's reading of Bernard in general and of this passage in particular moved him to add this pastoral counsel. But apart from this one instance, the Bernardine citations in 1559 add no new ideas. They testify to Calvin's deepening appreciation of Bernard, not to Bernard's significant influence upon his theology.

This raises an important question. Why did Calvin cite Bernard? What status did Bernard have for him? This can be seen clearly from the citations.

---

77 Cf. chapter 5, below, at nn. 34–37.
78 Cf. chapter 5, below, at nn. 83–86.
79 A. Ganoczy, BAC 188.
80 Cc.XXVII–XLI.
81 C.XXXIV.

A clear progression can be discerned through three different approaches to Bernard. In the first two citations Calvin is critical of Bernard. The second approach begins with the third citation in the 1539 *Institutio* which is appreciative, beginning 'neque vero inepte Bernardus'. This sets the pattern for Calvin's future use of Bernard. This use is primarily apologetic, as with Calvin's use of the fathers in general. In at least thirty of the forty-one Bernardine citations Calvin is appealing to Bernard for support against an opponent. If the measurement is by length, rather than the number of citations, more than six-sevenths of the citations fall into this category. This use of Bernard begins in 1539 and continues to the end. It comes in two forms: the appeal to Bernard as a historical witness to the state of the church in his time and (more commonly) the appeal to Bernard as a theological witness to the truth during the Dark Ages.

With Calvin's renewed reading of Bernard from the 1552 Basel edition we find a new approach to him. From 1554 we have quotations from Bernard without any discernible apologetic motive.[82] Calvin was quoting Bernard simply because he had expressed something well, in an elegant style. Calvin's humanist training had instilled in him a lifelong concern for good style, for expressing the truth clearly and persuasively. In this concern he found an ally in Bernard. While we find no citations before 1554 where this is Calvin's primary motive, a number of the earlier quotations may well have been chosen at least partly with this motive in mind. It is noteworthy that a significant number of Bernardine word plays are found in the earlier quotations.[83]

What status did Bernard have for Calvin? This also is clearly seen from his citations. The words of introduction to the quotations grow more appreciative over the years. It is also significant to see the contexts in which Bernard is quoted. Thirteen different times he appears with a total of thirteen fathers other than Augustine.[84] Augustine appears on eight of these occasions and a further nine times he appears alone with Bernard.[85] The formulae used to introduce Bernard indicate that Calvin saw him as witness to Augustinian truth during the Middle Ages. In one instance Calvin claims that his doctrine is not new but is that of Augustine which was shut up in the cloisters of monks for almost a thousand years.[86] This last point is also illustrated by considering the other medieval authors that appear with Bernard. In the first two citations, which are disapproving, he is criticized together with Anselm, Peter Lombard, Thomas Aquinas and others. Thereafter he is set *against* Lombard and scholasticism, against the *Donatio Constantini* and other later papal claims.[87]

One citation is very important for Calvin's attitude to Bernard. In keeping with his use of the fathers in general,[88] he quotes Bernard mainly

---

82 Cc.XXIV; XXVI; XXXII; XXXIV, certainly; cc.XXVII; XXXVII; XXXVIII; XL, probably.
83 Cc.III; IXc; Xa(3x), XIIc; XIVb, e(2x), f; XVIf; XXII(2x).
84 Cc.I; V; VII; XII-XV; XVII-XX; XXIII; XXV.
85 Cc.I; VII; XII; XVII-XX; XXV with others; cc.II; VI; X; XI; XXIV; XXVIII; XXIX; XXXV; XXXVII alone.
86 C.XXVIIIe.
87 Cc.XVI; XXVIII; XXXIII.
88 Cf. chapter 2, above, section IV.

for support and rarely disagrees with him. But this does not imply that there was little in Bernard with which Calvin disagreed. In his exposition of 1 Corinthians 3:15 Calvin refers the passage to Cyprian, Ambrose, Augustine 'et similes' and adds 'ex recentioribus' Gregory, Bernard 'aliosque eius notae'.[89] These saints aimed to build on Christ but often turned away from the right method of building. There are a number of points to be drawn from this passage. First, Bernard is listed with the fathers, as elsewhere he is counted among the 'anciens docteurs'.[90] Calvin would probably have concurred with Mabillon's description of him as 'ultimus inter patres, sed primis certe non impar'.[91] Secondly, Calvin's appeal to the fathers in general, and to Bernard in particular, does not indicate total agreement with them. Thirdly, this qualification applies even to Calvin's beloved Augustine, whom he cites some two thousand times and whom he several times claims as 'totus noster' on specific points.[92]

(c) Calvin's Accuracy

Calvin's use of Bernard consists primarily, though not exclusively, in an appeal to him for support in theological controversy. How valid was this appeal? How accurate is Calvin's interpretation of Bernard? There is no space to consider this fully here and it has been examined thoroughly elsewhere.[93] But a summary of the conclusions reached and some general observations are in order.

First, the question of accuracy of quotation. Calvin's quotations are rarely exact.[94] Normally there are many minor variations. These come for a variety of reasons. Calvin seems often to have quoted from memory and this leads to inaccuracy. Again, he sometimes abbreviates passages when he quotes them. He also adapts them by changing parts of speech, etc. But are there theologically motivated inaccuracies? A careful study has revealed eight instances when the textual inaccuracy is of minor theological significance. But this does not necessarily mean that they are theologically motivated. In four of the eight instances the inaccuracy can be traced to the sixteenth-century edition that Calvin was using.[95] In all of the instances the effect of the inaccuracy is no more than slightly to heighten the impact of the passage.

Two other points need to be mentioned here. First, Calvin did not claim total support from Bernard. In one citation he claims not Bernard's total support but only that were Bernard to settle the issue, he would fare considerably better than his opponent (Pighius).[96] Secondly, Calvin on

---

89 C.XX.
90 C.XVIII. He appears also in lists of 'vetusti ecclesiae scriptores' (c.XII) and 'veteres' (c.XIX), but there Bernard is added to an earlier collection of patristic quotations, so we must be cautious in claiming that Calvin saw him there as one of the fathers.
91 PL 182:26.
92 Cf. chapter 2, above, nn. 157f.
93 Cf. Lane, *Calvin and Bernard*, chapter 3.
94 Only cc.XIVd; XVIf; XXVIIIb; XXIX are exact. Cc.XVIe; XLb differ from the modern edition but follow the sixteenth-century *Opera omnia* exactly.
95 Cc.Xa; XIVf, h; XVIIIa; XIXa; XXII; XXXVIII; XL. With cc.Xa; XVIIIa; XIXa; XXII the fault lies with the sixteenth-century edition.
96 C.V.

occasions leaves in his Bernardine quotations material with which he profoundly disagrees. His quotations from *De consideratione* include the statements that the pope has *plenitudo potestatis* and has received the keys of the kingdom of heaven.[97] If Calvin had been seeking to twist Bernard in his favour he would certainly not have included these statements.

There are other ways to distort than by misquotation. It is noteworthy that Calvin never uses pseudo-Bernard, no mean feat considering the bulk of *spuria* in circulation. This does not mean that Calvin made his own critical judgments concerning authenticity. Almost all of the *Opera omnia Bernardi* of his time contained warnings about which works were and were not genuine. The diligent reader could see which works were genuine. But the fact remains that most of Calvin's contemporaries either did not notice this or did not care. Another feature that marks Calvin out from many of his contemporaries is the way in which he lets Bernard speak for himself. The majority of his quotations are simply extracts from Bernard with a minimum of interpretative comment from Calvin himself. His comments are usually a brief formula of introduction: 'Bernardus vero', or 'cum Bernardo respondeo', or 'praeclare enim Bernardus', or 'quanto rectius Bernardus', or 'cui pulchre succinit Bernardus', to give but a few.

On the whole Calvin's quotations, if loose, represent fairly what Bernard said. On the whole, Calvin's interpretation is correct in that Bernard meant more or less what Calvin claimed that he meant. But there remains one other major form of misrepresentation, namely selectivity. How representative is the Bernard that Calvin presents? This question can be answered at a variety of levels. First, Calvin quotes from a limited but not totally unrepresentative range of Bernard's works. The most significant omission is of the works on monasticism. Apart from these, the major works not mentioned are *De diligendo deo, De gradibus humilitatis et superbiae, Vita Sancti Malachiae* and the *Sermones de diversis*. Secondly, and more importantly, there is the range of topics cited. Calvin focuses on topics, such as grace and freewill and church corruption, which were of major interest to Bernard. But he also ignores areas of central importance to Bernard. Apart from one indirect reference,[98] one could read Calvin without even realizing that Bernard was a monk. He also ignores the specifically mystical teaching of Bernard, though he quotes often from the *Sermones in Cantica*. Thus Calvin draws only on those sides of Bernard which accord with his own interests. This involves a significant sector of Bernard's thought, but not the whole nor even the most central part.

Finally, this points to the most basic question. How representative of Bernard is the portrait presented by Calvin? It has to be recognized that Calvin's portrait is highly selective. He has followed the standard approach of the apologist, namely to quote what suits him and to pass over what does not. Calvin ably presents many of the more evangelical strands of Bernard's teaching. These strands are there and are substantially as Calvin portrays them. On the topics of sin, freewill, grace and predestination Bernard broadly supports Calvin's stand against contemporary semi-Pelagianism and semi-Augustinianism, which is not of course

97 Cc.XIVh; XVIc.
98 C.XXVIIIe.

to say that there are no differences between them. With the doctrines of justification and merit Calvin could justly appeal to one side of Bernard's teaching, though there is another side of his teaching on these subjects which is manifestly not in harmony with Calvin. Bernard protested against corruption in the church, as Calvin shows, but his basic view of the church and the papacy was very different from Calvin's. When we consider other sides of Bernard, such as his monasticism and his mysticism, we see how partial is Calvin's portrait of him.

If Bernard offered support to any one group in the sixteenth century it was to those Catholic humanists who sought to recover Augustinian doctrine, to embrace much of the Protestant doctrine of justification and to reform the church, but all within the framework of loyalty to the pope and the Roman Catholic church. Seripando and others at Trent appealed to Bernard in support of their view of justification, quoting some of the same passages as did Calvin.[99] It can broadly be stated that where Calvin found Bernard congenial it was usually where his own interests coincided with those of the Catholic humanists.

Calvin's portrait of Bernard was selective and apologetic. But it does not follow that he was merely a ruthless polemicist culling from Bernard the most advantageous proof texts. His use of Bernard was decidedly occasional and he did not call upon him whenever he felt the need of support, nor even whenever Bernard had support to offer. Some of the passages which he quoted could well have been used by him for additional support in other contexts. Furthermore, even Calvin's apologetic quotations are often chosen for literary as well as polemical reasons. This is even clearer in those passages which are quoted for no discernible apologetic reason but purely to illustrate a point. Calvin began to read and quote Bernard for apologetic purposes, but as time went on he grew to appreciate and use him for his own inherent value.

III. CALVIN'S BERNARDINE CITATIONS

Citation Number	Calvin Reference OS	CO^{100}	Bernard Source[101]	BO	PL	Type [102]	Topic [103]
1539 *Institutio*							
C.I	2:2:4	3:246 1:318	*Gra* 2:4	3:169	182:1004	q	a
C.IIa	2:2:6	3:248 1:319	*Gra*[104]			s	a

99 CT 5:335, 353, 374, 562, 620f.; 12:620, 703.
100 For the 1539 and 1543 *Institutio*, references are to the original edition in CO 1, not to the 1559 edition in CO 2.
101 This is given only where it can be ascertained with reasonable certainty, not where it is merely one possible source among others. OS footnotes have been used to trace sources, but they contain many minor inaccuracies and the conclusions reached here are sometimes substantially different.
102 q = quotation (accurate or loose); p = paraphrase of a longer passage; s = summary of Bernard's teaching, not of any particular passage; c = comment on Bernard; s/c, etc. = combination of more than one type.
103 a = sin and grace; b = justification; c = predestination; d = state of the departed; e = clergy and papacy; f = transubstantiation.
104 This does not refer to any one passage in *Gra, pace* OS. Cf. chapter 5, below, at nn. 154–56, for possible sources.

Citation Number	Calvin Reference	OS	CO	Bernard Source	BO	PL	Type	Topic
C.IIb	2:2:6	3:248	1:319				c	a
C.III	2:3:5	3:277	1:339	Gra[105]			s/c	a

1539: *Responsio ad Sadoletum*

C.IV		1:476	5:403	Csi[106]			s/c	e

1543: *Defensio doctrinae de servitute arbitrii*

C.V	Lib. 2		6:291				s/c	a
C.VI	Lib. 4		6:333	Gra[107]			s	a
C.VII	Lib. 4		6:334f.	Gra[108]			s	a
C.VIII	Lib. 6		6:378	Gra[109]			s	a

1543: *Institutio*

C.IXa	3:2:25	4:35f.	1:463f.	Ded 5:3f.	5:390f.	183:531	q	b
C.IXb	''	4:36	1:464	Ded 5:5	5:391	183:532	q	b
C.IXc	''	''	''	Ded 5:7f.	5:394	183:533f.	q	b
C.Xa	3:12:3	4:210	1:748	SC 61:3	2:150	183:1072	q	b
C.Xb	''	''	''	SC 61:5	2:151	183:1073	q	b
C.Xc	''	''	''	QH 15:5	4:479	183:246	q	b
C.XI	3:13:4	4:219	1:754	Ded 5:6f.	5:393	183:533	q	b
C.XIIa	3:15:2	4:241	1:770	SC 68:6	2:200	183:1111	q	b
C.XIIb	''	''	''	SC 68:6	''	''	c+q	b
C.XIIc	''	''	''	SC 68:6	''	''	c+q	b
C.XIII	4:5:12	5:84	1:590	Csi[110]			s/c	e
C.XIVa	4:7:18	5:121	1:619	Csi			s/c	e
C.XIVb	''	''	''	Csi 1:4:5	3:398	182:732	q	e
C.XIVc	''	''	''	Csi 1:10:13	3:408f.	182:740f.	p	e
C.XIVd	''	''	''	Csi 4:2:4	3:451	182:774	q	e
C.XIVe	''	''	''	Csi 4:2:5	3:452	182:775	q	e
C.XIVf	''	''	''	Csi 4:4:11	3:457	182:780	p	e
C.XIVg	''	''	''	Csi 3:2:6–12	3:435ff.	182:76lff.	s/c	e
C.XIVh	''	5:121f.	1:619f.	Csi 3:4:14	3:442	182:766	q	e
C.XIVi	''	5:122	1:620				c	e

105 This is based not on one single passage (*pace* OS) but on ideas found through much of *Gra*, especially 6:16, 18–20, 8:24–26. Similar ideas are found in Bernard's *Sent* 3:21, 60 (BO 6/2:78, 98) but Calvin would not have been thinking of this.

106 There are a number of works attacking papal and clerical corruption, two of which are cited by OS. In the light of the reference to Eugenius and Calvin's later usage it is likely that he had *Csi* in mind.

107 Calvin's point is found in *Gra* 4:9, 10:35. In the 1539 *Institutio* c.III is immediately followed and in the 1559 *Institutio* c.XXX is immediately preceded by the point here discussed, but with no reference to Bernard.

108 *SC* 81 and 82 come the closest to Calvin's point (the necessity of sin) and the former sermon is quoted in 1559 (cc.XXVIII; XXX). In *Gra* Bernard denies that humanity is under necessity (2:5, 3:7, etc.), but Calvin is probably thinking of Bernard's teaching that fallen humanity has lost freedom from sin (3:7, 4:10, etc.).

109 For the source, cf. on c.III, of which this is a repeat.

110 OS cites *Mor* as the source. But as Calvin never refers to *Mor* and quotes widely in this edition from *Csi*, which is an adequate source for this brief allusion to Bernard's criticism of the clergy, the latter is the likely source (especially 1:10:13, 3:1:5, 3:2:6–12, 3:3:13, 3:4:14, 16, 3:5:19f.; 4:2:2–5, 4:5:13, 15, 4:6:20).

Citation Number	Calvin Reference	OS	CO	Bernard Source	BO	PL	Type	Topic
C.XVa	4:7:22	5:125	1:622	Csi[111]			s/c	e
C.XVb	"	5:126	1:622f.	Csi[112]			s/c	e
C.XVIa[113]	4:11:11	5:206	1:654	Csi 2:6:10	3:418	182:748	q	e
C.XVIb	"	"	"	Csi 1:6:7	3:402	182:736	q	e
C.XVIc	"	5:206f.	"	Csi 1:6:7	"	"	q	e
C.XVId	"	5:207	"	Csi 2:6:9	3:416f.	182:747	q	e
C.XVIe	"	"	"	Csi 2:6:10f.	3:418	182:748	q	e
C.XVIf	"	"	"	Csi 2:6:11	"	"	q	e
C.XVIg	"	"	"				c	e

1544 *Articuli facultatis parisiensis cum antidoto*

C.XVII	Art. 4		7:13	SC 61:5	2:151	183:1073	q	b

1544 *Instruction contre les anabaptistes*

C.XVIIIa			7:126	OS 2:8	5:348	183:468	q	d
C.XVIIIb			"	OS 3:1	5:349	"	q	d
C.XVIIIc			"	OS 2&3			c	d

1545 *Psychopannychia*

C.XIXa			5:215	OS 2:8 & 3:1	5:348f.	183:468	p[114]	d
C.XIXb			"	OS 3:1	5:349f.	183:469	q	d
C.XIXc			"	OS 2&3			s	d
C.XIXd			"				c	d

1546 *Commentarii in priorem epistolam ad Corinthios*

C.XX	3:15		49:357				c	

1547 *Acta synodi tridentinae cum antidoto*

C.XXI	Sess. 6		7:457	Ded 5:7	5:393	183:533	q	b
C.XXII	Sess. 6		7:479	SC 61:3	2:150	183:1072	q	b
C.XXIII	Sess. 7		7:506	Csi 3:4:14	3:442	182:766	p	e

1554 *Commentarius in Genesim*

C.XXIV	3:6		23:63	Ep 1:3[115]	7:4	182:72	p	a

1556[116] *Sermons sur le Deuteronome*

C.XXV	Serm. 182		28:713				c	

111 These general references to Bernard's criticisms of the papacy are clearly based on Csi, especially on the passages quoted in cc.XIV; XVI.
112 Cf. previous footnote.
113 J. Raitt, 'Calvin's Use of Bernard of Clairvaux', *Archiv für Reformationsgeschichte* 72 (1981) 101, n. 31 accuses me of failing to note that the first part of c.XVI (i.e. c.XVIa&b) dates from 1559 and not from 1543. In fact, CO, OS, and the 1543 original (p. 226) all show that c.XVI in its entirety dates from 1543.
114 C.XIXa is a paraphrase of c.XVIIIa-b.
115 This passage comes closest to Calvin. *Gra* 8:25 and *Ann* 1:1 are also similar, but not as close.
116 Sermon 182 was preached on 3 June 1556 (CO 28:708) but not published until 1567. As it was not published until after Calvin's death and not by Calvin, it has been dated by its original delivery and not, as with all the other works, by its publication.

Citation Number	Calvin Ref.	OS	CO	Bernard Source	BO	PL	Type	Topic
1557 *Commentarius in librum Psalmorum*								
C.XXVI	55:13–15		31:540	*VI p P* 2:5[117]	5:212	183:343	q	
1559 *Institutio*								
C.XXVII	2:1:4	3:232	2:179	*SC* 28:5	1:195	183:923	p	
C.XXVIIIa	2:3:5	3:278	2:214	*SC* 81:7	2:288	183:1174	q	a
C.XXVIIIb	''	''	''	*SC* 81:7	''	''	q	a
C.XXVIIIc	''	''	''	*SC* 81:7	''	''	q	a
C.XXVIIId	''	''	''	*SC* 81:9	2:289	183:1175	q	a
C.XXVIIIe	''	''	2:214f.				c	a
C.XXIX	2:3:12	3:288	2:222	*SC* 21:9	1:127	183:876	q	a
C.XXX	2:5:1	3:298	2:230	*SC* 81:7	2:288	183:1174	p	a
C.XXXI[118]	2:5:14	3:315	2:243	*Gra*			s	a
C.XXXII	2:16:1	3:482f.	2:368	*SC* 15:6	1:86	183:846f.	p	b
C.XXXIIIa	3:2:41	4:52	2:432	*Ann* 1:1	5:13	183:383	q	b
C.XXXIIIb	''	''	''	*Ann* 1:3	5:14f.	183:383f.	p	b
C.XXXIV	3:3:15	4:72	2:446	*SC* 11:2	1:55f.	183:824f.	q	b
C.XXXVa	3:11:22	4:206	2:551	*SC* 23:15	1:149	183:892	q	b
C.XXXVb	''	''	2:551f.	*SC* 22:6 & 22:11	1:132f., 137	183:880, 884	p	b
C.XXXVIa	3:12:3	4:210	2:555	*SC* 13:4	1:71	183:836	q	b
C.XXXVIb	''	4:210f.	''	*SC* 68:6	2:200	183:1111	q	b
C.XXXVIc	''	4:211	2:555f.	*SC* 68:6	''	''	q	b
C.XXXVII	3:12:8	4:215	2:559	*SC* 13:5	1:71f.	183:836	p	b
C.XXXVIII	3:21:1	4:370	2:679f.	*SC* 78:4	2:269	183:1161	q	c
C.XXXIXa	3:22:10	4:392	2:697	*Ep* 107:4	7:270	182:244	q	c
C.XXXIXb	''	''	''	*Ep* 107:5	7:270f.	182:245	q	c
C.XXXIXc	''	''	''				c	c
C.XLa	3:24:4	4:415	2:715	*SC* 23:15	1:148f.	183:892	q	b/c
C.XLb	''	''	''	*SC* 23:16	1:149	183:893	q	b/c
C.XLI	4:17:15	5:360	2:1014				s	f

IV. TEXT OF CALVIN'S BERNARDINE CITATIONS

The source of each citation in Calvin's works and, where relevant, its Bernardine source will be found in Section III. The text of each citation has been checked against the sixteenth-century edition in which it first appeared.[119]

---

117 Mabillon and Migne number this sermon as *VI p P* 3, but their *VI p P* 2 is not found in the best MSS and is probably inauthentic (BO 5:VII).
118 This is the one instance where a passage has been allowed as a Bernardine citation although Bernard himself is not named. This is because the ascription to Augustine is incorrect and the passage is a repeat of cc.III;VIII. For its source, cf. on c.III.
119 Differences in spelling and punctuation have not been noted.

C.I

Obscurius Bernardus, dum vult argute loqui, qui ait esse consensum, ob voluntatis inamissibilem libertatem, et rationis indeclinabile iudicium.

C.II

a   sicut Bernardus bonam quidem voluntatem opus Dei[120] esse asserens, homini tamen hoc concedit, ut motu proprio bonam eiusmodi voluntatem appetat.

b   Sed istud ab Augustini mente procul abest, a quo tamen sumpsisse partitionem videri vult Lombardus [De libero arbitrio.].

C.III

Neque vero inepte Bernardus, qui velle nobis omnibus inesse docet: sed velle bonum, profectus: velle malum, defectus. Ideo simpliciter velle, hominis: male velle, corruptae naturae: bene velle, gratiae.

C.IV

Bernardus quanta vehementia in Eugenium omnesque suae aetatis episcopos fulminat? At quanto saeculi illius conditio hac praesenti tolerabilior?

C.V

Nec vero Bernardum proferre alibi dubitat: cuius arbitrio si definienda esset controversia, si non prorsus totum obtinerem, longo tamen intervallo essem superior.

C.VI

Neque id est nostrum commentum. Sic ante nos Augustinus, sic Bernardus loquuti sunt.

C.VII

Nunc vero post eius lapsum, necessitatis iugum, a quo alias soluti essemus atque immunes, nobis impositum, ipse, et Prosper, et Bernardus, uno ore tradunt.

C.VIII

Nam quantum ad praesentem quaestionem, Bernardum sequutus tria consideranda proposueram: velle per se, aut simpliciter; deinde male et bene velle.

C.IX

a   Nec aliter disserit Bernardus, quum hoc argumentum ex professo tractat, Homilia in dedicatione templi quinta. Dei (inquam) beneficio nonnunquam de anima cogitans, videor mihi in ea veluti duo quaedam contraria invenire; si ipsam, prout in se est et ex se, intueor: de ea nihil verius dicere possum, quam ad nihilum esse redactam. Quid modo necesse est singulas eius miserias numerare, quam sit onerata peccatis, offusa tenebris, irretita illecebris, pruriens concupiscentiis, obnoxia passionibus, impleta illusionibus, prona semper ad malum, in vitium omne proclivis,

---

120 'opus Dei' is the 1559 reading. OS fails to note that all earlier editions read 'Dei opus'.

postremo ignominiae et confusionis plena? Nimirum si ipsae quoque iustitiae omnes ad lumen veritatis inspectae, velut pannus menstruatae inveniuntur, iniustitiae deinceps quales reputabuntur [Iesa. 64. c. 6]? Si lumen quod in nobis est, tenebrae sunt, ipsae tenebrae quantae erunt [Matth. 6. c. 23]? Quid igitur? sine dubio vanitati similis factus est homo: in nihilum redactus est homo: nihil est homo. Quomodo tamen penitus nihil est quem magnificat Deus? Quomodo nihil, erga quem appositum est cor divinum? Respiremus fratres. Etsi nihil sumus in cordibus nostris, forte in corde Dei potest aliquid latere de nobis. O Pater misericordiarum, o Pater miserorum, quomodo apponis erga nos cor tuum? Cor enim tuum ubi est thesaurus tuus. Quomodo autem thesaurus tuus sumus, si nihil sumus? Omnes gentes quasi non sint, sic sunt ante te: in nihilum reputabuntur. Nimirum ante te: non intra te: sic in iudicio veritatis tuae, sed non sic in affectu pietatis tuae. Nimirum vocas ea quae non sunt, tanquam sint; et non sunt ergo, quia quae non sunt, vocas: et sunt, quia vocas. Licet enim non sint, quantum ad se: apud te tamen sunt, iuxta illud Pauli, Non ex operibus iustitiae, sed ex vocante [Rom. 9. c. 12].

b   Deinde mirificam esse hanc connexionem dicit utriusque considerationis. Certe quae inter se connexa sunt, se invicem non destruunt.

c   Quod etiam in conclusione apertius declarat his verbis, Iam si utraque consideratione diligenter inspexerimus nos quid sumus: imo in una quam nihil, in altera quam magnificati: puto temperata videtur gloriatio nostra: sed forsan magis aucta est solidata quidem[a], ut non in nobis sed in Domino gloriemur. Nimirum si cogitamus, si decreverit salvare nos, statim liberabimur: iam in hoc respirare licet. Sed in altiorem speculam ascendentes, quaeramus civitatem Dei, quaeramus templum, quaeramus domum, quaeramus sponsam[b]. Non oblitus sum[c]: sed cum metu et reverentia dico, Nos inquam sumus: sed in corde Dei. Nos sumus: sed illius dignatione, non nostra dignitate.

---

a) *1543–50* tamen   b) *VG 1545 sqq.* le secret du mariage qu'il a avec nous   c) Non – sum: *VG 1545 sqq.* en ce faisant nous n'oblirons point l'un pour l'autre

C.X

a   Bernardus vero, Et re vera, ubi tuta firmaque infirmis requies et securitas, nisi in vulneribus Salvatoris? tanto illic securior habito, quanto potentior est ad salvandum. Fremit mundus, premit corpus, diabolus insidiatur. Non cado, quia fundatus sum supra firmam petram. Peccavi peccatum grave. Turbatur conscientia: sed non perturbabitur, quia vulnerum Domini recordabor [Super cant. serm. 61].

b   Postea ex iis concludit, Meritum proinde meum miseratio Domini; non sum plane meriti inops, quandiu non fuerit ille inops miserationum. Quod si misericordiae Domini multae, multus ergo[d] peraeque sum in meritis. Nunquid iustitias meas cantabo? Domine meminero iustitiae tuae solius. Ipsa enim est et mea, nempe factus est mihi iustitia a Deo.

c   Item alibi, Hoc totum hominis meritum, si totam spem ponat in eum qui totum hominem salvum facit [In Psal.[e] Qui habit. ser. 15].

---

d) *1543–50* ego   e) In Ps. > *1543–54*

C.XI

Bernardus quoque, Quis poterit salvus esse? dicunt discipuli Christi. At ille, Apud homines impossibile hoc est, sed non apud Deum. Haec tota fiducia nostra, haec unica consolatio, haec tota ratio spei nostrae. Sed de possibilitate certi, de voluntate quid agimus? Quis scit an odio vel amore dignus sit [Eccles. 9. a. 1]? Quis cognovit sensum Domini, aut quis consiliarius eius fuit [1. Cor. 2. d. 16]? Hic iam plane fidem nobis subvenire necesse est: hic oportet succurrere veritatem: ut quod de nobis latet in corde Patris, per Spiritum reveletur, et Spiritus eius testificans persuadeat cordibus nostris quod filii Dei sumus. Persuadeat autem vocando et iustificando gratis per fidem: in quibus nimirum velut medius quidam transitus est ab aeterna praedestinatione ad futuram gloriam [Serm. 5. in dedicat. templi.][a]

---

a) [Serm. –]: *1553–61 supra ante* [Eccles. –] *exstat.*

C.XII

a   Citavi quidem antea ex Bernardo sententiam[a], Ut ad meritum satis est de meritis non praesumere: sic carere meritis, satis est ad iudicium [supra canti. sermo.[b] 68].

b   Sed continuo addita interpretatione, duritiem vocis satis emollit, quum dicit, Proinde merita habere cures: habita, data noveris: fructum speres Dei misericordiam: et omne periculum evasisti, paupertatis, ingratitudinis, praesumptionis. Foelix Ecclesia cui nec merita sine praesumptione, nec praesumptio sine meritis deest.

c   Et paulo ante abunde ostenderat quam pio sensu uteretur. Nam de meritis, inquit, quid sollicita sit Ecclesia, cui de proposito Dei firmior securiorque existit gloriandi ratio? non potest seipsum negare Deus: faciet quod promisit. Sic[c] non est quod quaeras, quibus meritis speremus bona? praesertim quum audias, Non propter vos, sed propter me [Ezech. 36. e. 22, f. 32]. Sufficit ad meritum, scire quod non sufficiant merita.

---

a) Cit. – sent: *1543–54* Dicit quidem alicubi Bernardus   b) cant. ser.> *1559*   c) *sic 1543–54; 1559–61 falso* Si

C.XIII

Tempore Bernardi res aliquanto magis prolapsae erant: sed videmus etiam quam acerbis obiurgationibus invehatur in totum ordinem: quem tamen credibile est fuisse tunc non paulo integriorem quam nunc sit.

C.XIV

a   Itaque videmus qualis fuerit et quam prodigiosa Romae omnium sacrorum profanatio, et totius Ecclesiastici ordinis dissipatio Bernardi aetate.

b   Conqueritur ex toto orbe Romam confluere ambitiosos, avaros, simoniacos, sacrilegos, concubinarios, incestuosos, et quaeque istiusmodi monstra, ut Apostolica authoritate vel obtinerent honores Ecclesiasticos vel retinerent [Lib. 1. De conside. ad Eugenium]:

c   fraudem, et circumventionem, et violentiam invaluisse. Eum iudicandi modum qui tunc usitatus erat, execrabilem esse dicit: nec modo Ecclesiae, sed foro indecorum. Clamat plenam esse ambitiosis Ecclesiam: nec esse qui magis exhorreat flagitia perpetrare quam latrones in spelunca quum spolia viatorum distribuunt.

d   Pauci (inquit) ad os legislatoris: ad manus omnes respiciunt. Non immerito tamen. Omne Papale negotium illae[c] agunt [Circa finem libri 4].

e   Quale est quod de spoliis ecclesiarum emuntur, qui dicunt tibi, Euge, euge? pauperum vita in plateis divitum seminatur: argentum micat in luto: accurritur undique: tollit illud non pauperior, sed fortior: aut qui forte citius praecurrit. A te tamen mos iste, vel potius mors ista, non venit; utinam in te desinat. Inter haec tu pastor procedis, multo et pretioso circumdatus ornatu. Si auderem dicere, daemonum magis quam ovium pascua haec. Scilicet sic factitabat Petrus: sic Paulus ludebat.

f   Curia tua recipere bonos magis quam facere consuevit. Mali enim illic non proficiunt, sed boni deficiunt.

g   Iam quos appellationum abusus refert, nemo pius sine magno horrore legat [Lib. 3].

h   Tandem sic de effraeni illa Romanae sedis cupiditate in iurisdictione usurpanda concludit, Murmur loquor et querimoniam communem Ecclesiarum. Truncari se clamitant ac demembrari. Vel nullae vel paucae admodum sunt quae plagam istam aut non doleant, aut non timeant. Quaeris quam? subtrahuntur Abbates Episcopis, Episcopi Archiepiscopis, etc. Mirum si excusari hoc queat. Sic factitando, probatis vos habere plenitudinem potestatis: sed iustitiae non ita. Facitis hoc quia potestis, sed utrum etiam debeatis quaestio est. Ad honorem quibusque suum gradumque conservandum positi estis, non invidendum.

i   Haec pauca ex multis referre libuit, ut partim videant lectores quam graviter tunc Ecclesia concidisset, partim etiam ut agnoscant, quanto in moerore ac gemitu pios omnes tenuerit isthaec calamitas.

---

c) *1543* illi

C.XV

a   Verum ne singula persequi et excutere cogar, iterum istos appello qui hodie Romanae sedis patroni et optimi et fidelissimi haberi volunt, ecquid pudeat ipsos praesentem statum Papatus defendere: quem constat centuplo corruptiorem esse quam Gregorii et Bernardi seculis fuerit: qui tamen tunc sanctis illis viris tantopere displicebat.

b   Bernardus vero quas fundit querimonias, quos edit gemitus dum suae aetatis vitia intuetur? Quid igitur, si hoc nostrum ferreum seculum, et siquid est ferro deterius, inspiceret[b]? Quae ista est improbitas, non modo pertinaciter tueri velut sacrosanctum ac divinum, quod uno ore sancti omnes semper improbarunt: sed eorum quoque testimonio abuti ad defensionem Papatus, quem constat fuisse illis prorsus incognitum? Quanquam de tempore Bernardi fateor tantam fuisse tunc corruptionem rerum omnium, ut non fuerit multum nostro dissimile.

---

b) Quid – insp.: *VG 1545 sqq.* Que diroit-il donc sil voyoit (*VG 1545–51* véoit) ce qui se faict de ce temps, auquel la mechanceté sest debordée du tout, comme en un deluge

C.XVI

a Primum cum Bernardo respondeo, Esto ut alia quacunque ratione hoc sibi vendicet, non tamen Apostolico iure. Neque enim Petrus quod non habuit dare potuit: sed dedit successioribus quod habebat, sollicitudinem Ecclesiarum [Lib. De consider. 2[e]].

b Quum vero dicat Dominus ac Magister, se non esse constitutum inter duos iudicem [Luc. 12. b. 14], non debet servo ac discipulo indignum videri, si non iudicet universos.

c Loquitur autem Bernardus de iudiciis civilibus: subiungit enim[f], Ergo in criminibus, non in possessionibus potestas vestra: quoniam propter illa, non propter has accepistis claves regni caelorum. Quaenam tibi videtur maior dignitas, dimittendi peccata, an praedia dividendi? nulla comparatio. Habent haec infima et terrena iudices suos, Reges et Principes terrae. Quid fines alienos invaditis? etc.

d Item, Factus es superior (Eugenium papam alloquitur) ad quid? non enim ad dominandum, opinor. Nos igitur, ut multum sentiamus de nobis, meminerimus impositum ministerium, non dominium datum. Disce sarculo tibi opus esse, non sceptro, ut opus facias Prophetae [Lib. De consider. 2][a].

e Item, Planum est, Apostolis interdicitur dominatus. I ergo tu, et tibi usurpare aude aut dominans Apostolatum, aut Apostolicus dominatum.

f Et continuo post, Forma Apostolica haec est, dominatio interdicitur: indicitur ministratio.

g Haec quum ab homine sic dicta sint ut ipsam veritatem loqui omnibus palam sit, imo quum sine ullis verbis res ipsa pateat: nihil tamen puduit Romanum Pontificem in Concilio Arelatensi decernere, supremum ius utriusque gladii sibi competere iure divino.

---

e) *sic 1543–54; 1559–61 falso* 25   f) *VG 1545 sqq.* + parlant au Pape   a) *1553–54* [Ibidem.]

C.XVII

Item cum Bernardo, [2]) meritum omne nostrum esse miserationes Domini: vel, ut clarius loquamur, concludimus, post Basilium Magnum, . . .

---

2) Bern. serm. 6. super cantica.

C.XVIII

a Sainct Bernard: La doulceur qu'ont maintenant les ames des sainctz est grande, mais elle n'est pas encore parfaicte: car elle se parfera quand ilz seront assis sur les thrones comme iuges. Quand elles sont despouillées de leur corps, elles sont incontinent introduites à repos, mais non point à la gloire du Royaume.

b Et au sermon suyvant il poursuit encor ce propos, disant qu'il y a troys estatz de l'ame. Le premier au corps, comme en un tabernacle, le second apres la mort, comme au portail du temple, le troisiesme au ciel avec son corps glorieux.

c   Qui en voudra savoir d'avantage, qu'il lise le second et le troisiesme sermon du iour de tous les sainctz.

C.XIX

a   Bernardus vero, homiliis duabus habitis in festo omnium sanctorum, ubi ex professo hanc quaestionem tractat, sanctorum animas corporibus exutas, adhuc in atriis Domini stare docet, ad requiem admissas, non autem ad gloriam.

b   In illam, inquit, beatissimam domum nec sine nobis intrabunt, nec sine corporibus suis: id est, nec sancti sine plebe, nec spiritus sine carne.

c   Et multa alia in hanc sententiam.

d   Qui autem in coelo eas collocant, modo non attribuant illis resurrectionis gloriam, nihil ab ea sententia dissident: sicut Augustinus ipse facere alicubi videtur.

C.XX

Quales etiam fuerunt multi ex sanctis, Cyprianus, Ambrosius, Augustinus, et similes: adde etiam si libet, ex recentioribus, Gregorium et Bernardum, aliosque eius notae, qui, quum haberent hoc propositum ut in Christo aedificarent, a recta tamen aedificandi ratione saepe aberrarunt. Tales dicit Paulus salvos fieri posse, sed hac lege, si Dominus eorum ignorantiam absterserit, et repurgaverit eos ab omni sorde.

C.XXI

Praeclare enim Bernardus: [2] Fidem hic nobis subvenire necesse est: hic oportet succurrere veritatem: ut quod de nobis latet in corde patris, per spiritum reveletur: et spiritus persuadeat cordibus nostris, quod filii Dei simus. Persuadeat autem, vocando et iustificando gratis per fidem.

––––––

2) Serm. 5. in dedic. templi.

C.XXII

Nam, ut praeclare Bernardus, si turbetur conscientia, non perturbabitur, vulnerum Domini memor. [1] Illic enim tuta firmaque infirmis requies, et securitas.

––––––

1) Super cantica serm. 16.

C.XXIII

Scribit Bernardus, communem suo tempore fuisse querimoniam, truncari et mutilari ecclesias, quod romanus episcopus omnium potestatem ad se trahendo ordines confunderet. [3]

––––––

3) Bernard. de consid. ad Eugen. libr. 3.

C.XXIV

Atque ut taceamus de brevitate temporis, illa Bernardi admonitio memoratu digna est: Quum tam horribile praecipitium in paradiso accidisse legamus, quid nos facturi sumus in sterquilinio?

C.XXV

Il est vray que par honneur ils diront bien sainct Augustin, sainct Ambroise, S. Bernard nos peres: mais quand on leur allegue ce qui est là trouvé de bon, ils les detestent: que s'ils les tenoyent auiourd'huy, ils seroyent aussi bien bruslez que les Martyrs lesquels nous voyons estre si cruellement traittez par les papistes.

C.XXVI

Quod genus hostium, (ut dicit Bernardus) neque fugere neque fugare datur.

C.XXVII

Itaque recte Bernardus ianuam salutis aperiri nobis docet, quum hodie Evangelium auribus recipimus: sicuti illis fenestris, dum Satanae patuerunt, mors admissa fuit[a].

----

a) ianuam – fuit: *VG 1560* que la porte de salut est en noz oreilles quand nous recevons l'Evangile, comme c'ont esté les fenestres pour recevoir la mort

C.XXVIII

a Augustino subscribens Bernardus ita scribit, Solus homo inter animalia liber: et tamen interveniente peccato, patitur quandam vim et ipse: sed a voluntate, non a natura, ut ne sic quidem ingenita libertate privetur. Quod enim voluntarium, etiam liberum.

b Et paulo post, Ita nescio quo pravo et miro modo ipsa sibi voluntas peccato quidem in deterius mutata, necessitatem facit, ut nec necessitas (quum voluntaria sit) excusare valeat voluntatem, nec voluntas (quum sit illecta) excludere necessitatem. Est enim necessitas haec quodammodo voluntaria.

c Postea dicit nos premi iugo, non alio tamen quam voluntariae cuiusdam servitutis: ideo pro servitute esse miserabiles, pro voluntate inexcusabiles: quia voluntas, quum libera esset, servam se peccati fecit.

d Tandem concludit, Ita anima miro quodam et malo modo sub hac voluntaria quadam ac male libera necessitate et ancilla tenetur et libera: ancilla, propter necessitatem: libera propter voluntatem: et, quod magis mirum magisque miserum est, ideo rea, quod libera: eoque ancilla, quo rea: ac per hoc, eo ancilla, quo libera [Serm. super Cantica 81.].

e Hinc certe agnoscunt lectores nihil me novum afferre, quod olim ex piorum omnium consensu prodidit Augustinus, et mille fere annis postea in claustris monachorum retentum fuit.

C.XXIX

Cui consentit Bernardus, Ecclesiam ita loquentem inducens, Trahe quodammodo invitam, ut facias voluntariam: trahe torpentem ut reddas currentem [Serm. 2. in Can.].

C.XXX

quod idem Bernardus quoque scite docet, nos ideo miseriores esse, quod voluntaria est necessitas: quae tamen nos sibi addictos ita constringit, ut servi simus peccati, sicuti ante retulimus [Ser. 81. in Cantica.].

C.XXXI

sed ne foveat in nobis ignaviam, sic Dei actionem cum nostra conciliat ut velle sit a natura, bene autem velle a gratia.

C.XXXII

Et memoratu digna est illa Bernardi admonitio, non modo lucem sed cibum quoque esse nomen Iesu: oleum etiam esse, sine quo aridus est omnis animae[c] cibus: salem esse, sine cuius conditura insipidum est quicquid proponitur[d]: denique esse mel in ore, in aure melos, in corde iubilum, et simil medicinam: et quicquid disputatur insulsum esse, nisi ubi sonat hoc nomen [Bern. in Cant. Serm. 15].

---

c) > *VG 1560*   d) sine – prop.: *VG 1560* pour donner goust et saveur à toute doctrine, qui autrement seroit fade

C.XXXIII

a   Quanto rectius Bernardus: Testimonium, inquit, conscientiae, quod piorum gloriam vocat Paulus [2 Cor. 1. c. 12], in tribus consistere credo. Necesse enim primo omnium est, credere quod remissionem peccatorum habere non possis nisi per indulgentiam Dei: deinde quod nihil prorsus habere queas operis boni nisi et hoc dederit ipse: postremo quod vitam aeternam nullis potes operibus promereri nisi gratis detur et illa [Sermo 1. in Annuntiatione].

b   Paulo post subiicit, haec non sufficere, sed esse quoddam fidei initium: quia credendo peccata non posse remitti nisi a Deo, simul tenere oporteat remissa nobis esse donec etiam Spiritus sancti testimonio persuasi simus salutem nobis esse repositam: quia Deus peccata condonat, merita ipse donat, et praemia idem redonat, non posse gradum in illo principio figere.

C.XXXIV

Qua de re utilis etiam est admonitio Bernardi, Necessarius dolor pro peccatis si non sit continuus. Suadeo reflectere pedem interdum a molesta et anxia recordatione viarum vestrarum, et evadere ad planitiem serenae memoriae beneficiorum Dei. Misceamus absynthio mel, ut salubris amaritudo salutem dare queat: cum immisto dulcore temperata bibetur: et si de vobis in humilitate sentitis, sentite et de Domino in bonitate [Ser. 11. in Cant.].

C.XXXV

a   Cui respondent praeclarae Bernardi sententiae, Non peccare, Dei iustitia est: hominis autem iustitia, Dei indulgentia [Serm. 23. in Cant.].

b   Ante autem asseruerat, Christum nobis esse iustitiam in absolutione, ideoque solos esse iustos, qui veniam ex misericordia consequuti sunt [Serm. 22.].

C.XXXVI

a   Similiter ubi pacem sibi retinens, gloriam relinquit Deo. Tibi, inquit, illibata maneat gloria: mecum bene agitur si pacem habuero. Abiuro gloriam prorsus: ne si usurpavero quod meum non est, perdam et oblatum [Serm. 13. in Cant.].

b   Apertius etiam alio loco, De meritis quid sollicita sit Ecclesia? cui de
     proposito Dei firmior suppetit securiorque gloriandi ratio? Sic non est
     quod quaeras, quibus meritis speremus bona: praesertim quum audias
     apud Prophetam, Non propter vos faciam, sed propter me, dicit Dominus
     [Ezech. 36. e. 22. f. 32]. Sufficit ad meritum scire quod non sufficiant merita:
     sed ut ad meritum satis est de meritis non praesumere, sic carere meritis
     satis ad iudicium est [Serm. 68][a].

c   Quod merita libere usurpat pro bonis operibus ignoscendum est
     consuetudini. In fine vero[b] consilium eius fuit terrere hypocritas, qui
     peccandi licentia contra Dei gratiam proterviunt: sicuti mox se explicat,
     Foelix Ecclesia cui nec merita sine praesumptione, nec praesumptio absque
     meritis deest. Habet unde praesumat, sed non merita. Habet merita, sed
     ad promerendum, non praesumendum. Ipsum non praesumere nonne
     promereri est? Ergo eo praesumit securius quo non praesumit, cui ampla
     materies gloriandi est, misericordiae Domini multae.

---

a) [Serm. –]: *1559–61 supra ante* [Ez. – 32] *exstat.*[121]   b) In – vero: *VG 1560* et en
condamnant ceux qui n'ont point de merites

C.XXXVII

Cui pulchre succinit Bernardus, servis infidis comparans superbos, qui meritis
suis vel minimum arrogant: quia laudem gratiae per se transeuntis improbe
retinent, perinde acsi paries radium se parturire dicat quem suscipit per
fenestram [Ser. 13. in Can.].

C.XXXVIII

Quid quod nobis inde emergit Ecclesia, quae alioqui, ut recte docet Bernardus,
non posset inveniri, nec inter creaturas agnosci? quia miro utroque modo latet
intra gremium beatae praedestinationis, et intra massam miserae damnationis
[Serm. in Can. 78].

C.XXXIX

a   Recte enim Bernardus, Amici (inquit) seorsum audiunt, quibus et loquitur,
     Nolite timere pusille grex: quia vobis datum est nosse mysterium regni
     caelorum. Qui sunt hi? Utique quos praescivit et praedestinavit conformes
     fieri imagini Filii sui; magnum secretumque innotuit consilium, Novit
     Dominus qui sui sint, sed quod notum erat Deo, manifestatum est
     hominibus: nec alios sane dignatur tanti participatione mysterii, nisi eos
     ipsos quos fore suos praescivit et praedestinavit [Ad Thomam
     praepositum Beverlae[a], epist. 107].

b   Paulo post concludit, Misericordia Dei ab aeterno usque ad aeternum
     super timentes eum: ab aeterno, ob praedestinationem: in aeternum, ob
     beatificationem: altera principium, altera finem nesciens.

---

a) *1559–61 falso:* Benerlae

---

121 Note a) does not appear to make sense. First, there are so many differences in the
     positioning of marginal references not noted by OS that there appears to be no
     reason for noting this one. Secondly, the marginal reference to Serm. 68 is in fact in
     the normal position, at the beginning of the relevant citation.

c   Sed quid Bernardum citare testem opus est, quando ex magistri ore audimus, non alios videre nisi qui sunt ex Deo [Iohan. 6. e. 46]?

C.XL

a   Qua de re apposite Bernardus; postquam enim de reprobis loquutus est, Stat (inquit) propositum Dei, stat sententia pacis super timentes eum, ipsorum et dissimulans mala, et remunerans bona: ut miro modo eis non modo bona, sed et mala cooperentur in bonum. Quis accusabit electos Dei? sufficit mihi ad omnem iustitiam, solum habere propitium cui soli peccavi. Omne quod mihi ipse non imputare decrevit, sic est quasi non fuerit.

b   Et paulo post, O verae quietis locus, et quem non immerito cubiculi appellatione censuerim, in quo Deus non quasi turbatus ira, nec velut distentus cura prospicitur, sed probatur voluntas eius in eo bona et beneplacens et perfecta. Visio ista non terret, sed mulcet: inquietam curiositatem non excitat sed sedat: nec fatigat sensus, sed tranquillat. Hic vere quiescitur. Tranquillus Deus tranquillat omnia, et quietum aspicere quiescere est.

C.XLI

Bernardi quidem aetate, etsi durior invaluerat loquendi ratio, trans-substantiatio tamen nondum agnita erat.

5

❧❧❧

Calvin's Sources of
Bernard of Clairvaux

I. INTRODUCTION

Bernard of Clairvaux (1090–1153) was one of Calvin's favourite medieval writers. From the 1539 to the 1559 editions of the *Institutio* Calvin referred to him forty-one times, quoting most of his greatest writings.[1] Initially and primarily he used him polemically, but he also grew to appreciate him for himself and later quoted him purely for illustration.

Calvin's sources of Bernard are of interest not only in themselves but also for their wider implications. While it does not necessarily follow that he knew other ancient writers by the same means there is some antecedent likelihood that he did. The conclusions of this chapter will, especially when used together with the results of other such studies,[2] contribute to a deeper

---

This chapter originally appeared as 'Calvin's Sources of St. Bernard' in *Archiv für Reformationsgeschichte* 67 (1976) 253–83. (Most of the internal cross-references were corrupted at the editorial stage.) Twenty-five years of further study in the area have led to two significant changes. A wider search has revealed considerably more partial overlaps between Calvin's citations and other works. But at the same time I am persuaded that in 1976 I gave too much weight to such alternative sources and that the evidence is stronger than I then claimed that, with minor exceptions, Calvin's source for Bernard was the *Opera omnia*.

---

1 For the range of writings cited by Calvin, see the previous chapter. For a list of the citations and for the text of the citations, see sections III and IV of that chapter. They are referred to below according to that list: c.I, c.Xb, etc.
2 There have been relatively few studies which examine the specific editions or intermediary sources used by Calvin. Apart from chapters 1, 3, 6, 8f. of the present work, the following should be noted: I. Backus, 'Calvin's Judgment of Eusebius of Caesarea: An Analysis', *Sixteenth Century Journal* 22 (1991) 419–37; idem, 'Calvin and the Greek Fathers' an as yet unpublished paper given at the Seventh International Congress on Calvin Research (Seoul, 1998); F. L. Battles, 'The Sources of Calvin's Seneca Commentary' in G. E. Duffield (ed.), *John Calvin* (Appleford, Abingdon: Sutton Courtenay, 1966), 38–66; A. Ganoczy and K. Müller, *Calvins Handschriftliche Annotationen zu Chrysostomus* (Wiesbaden: Franz Steiner, 1981); L. Smits, SAOJC 1:196–220; W. N. Todd, *The Function of the Patristic Writings in the Thought of John Calvin* (New York: Union Theological Seminary ThD thesis, 1964) 66, 76f., 107–109, 125–30; J. N. Tylenda, 'Calvin and the Avignon Sermons of John

appreciation of Calvin's scholarly methods. His seriousness as a scholar will be affected by the results. Furthermore, if his knowledge of Bernard was derived from other authors this could have implications for the sources and influence of his thought as a whole, not just of isolated quotations.

It cannot be assumed that Calvin had only one source for Bernard: he may have used different sources at different times, or for different works of Bernard. The former possibility can be checked both by the evidence of the citations themselves and by evidence of Calvin's circumstances.

There are ten passages of Bernard which appear in slightly different forms at different times in Calvin's writings. With nine of these the differences are of no significance in choosing between possible texts that Calvin might have used.[3] The tenth passage varies slightly between the 1543 *Institutio* and later editions.[4] The same variation is also found among the printed editions and among the manuscripts.[5] But this does not prove a change of source between editions. First, this variation is typical of the countless changes which arose from printers' errors and corrections.[6] Secondly, Calvin would hardly have changed a minor point like this while leaving uncorrected his many other far greater inaccuracies in quotation. Finally, the change in 1545 is quite simply the correction of a grammatical error. Neither in this variation nor in the others is there any evidence for a change in Calvin's source. When Calvin quoted a passage twice he probably took the second quotation from the first or from memory, especially when, as in most of the above examples, the first quotation came in the *Institutio* and the second elsewhere.

The external evidence is more conclusive. In 1543 Calvin excused the paucity of quotations in his 1539 *Institutio* by the plea that he had quoted from memory, having only one (borrowed) volume of Augustine at hand.[7] The 1539 *Institutio* was largely complete by October 1538[8] so Calvin was short of books that year. Apart from this evidence, the paucity of his quotations of Bernard up to this time, in contrast with those of other patristic writers, makes it unlikely that Calvin had his own copy of Bernard when he went to Strassburg. Furthermore, it is known that he was

---

XXII', *Irish Theological Quarterly* 41 (1974) 37–52; A. Zillenbiller, *Die Einheit der Katholischen Kirche: Calvins Cyprianrezeption in seinen ekklesiologischen Schriften* (Mainz: Philipp von Zabern, 1993) 68–100. Ganoczy, BAC contains much relevant material about editions that Calvin might have used. Useful information can also be derived from the introductions and notes to some editions of Calvin's writings.

3   *SC* 61:3 in cc.Xa; XXII; *SC* 61:5 in cc.Xb; XVII; *SC* 68:6 in cc.XIIa; XXXVIb; cc.XIIb; XXXVIc; cc.XIIc; XXXVIb; *Csi* 3:4:14 in cc.XIVh; XXIII; *Ded* 5:7 in cc.XI; XXI. There are small changes between editions in cc.IIa; IXc; Xb; XIIc. The first of these is not noted in OS which gives the reading of the 1559 edition. All earlier editions read 'Dei opus' for 'opus Dei'. The differences introduced by French translations are of no significance for the present question.

4   C.XIVd. The 1543 edition reads 'illi' and later editions have 'illae'.

5   Cf. n. 28, below, for the editions; BO 3:451 for the manuscripts.

6   As may be seen by a brief perusal of the textual apparatus of OS 3–5.

7   CO 6:336 (*Def. adv. calumn. Pighii*). He goes on to describe himself as 'ita libris destitutus'. On this claim, cf. J.-F. Gilmont, *Jean Calvin et le Livre Imprimé* (Geneva: Droz, 1997) 185f.

8   CRF 5:134, cited in OS 3:XI.

extremely poor at Strassburg and it is possible that he even had to sell some of his own library while there.[9] Far from having gained a copy of Bernard at Strassburg he would probably have been forced to sell his copy had he brought one with him. Even if, despite all these problems, he ended his stay at Strassburg with a copy of Bernard he could have been forced to sell it to cover the expenses of his return to Geneva. It is therefore almost certain that the copy of Bernard which Calvin used at Strassburg did not travel to Geneva with him.

This conjecture is supported by an examination of Calvin's citations. In the 1543 *Institutio* (which was mostly written at Strassburg, where Calvin probably found his Bernardine material) Bernard is cited at length, but this changes with his return to Geneva. The four citations in Calvin's 1543 *Defensio doctrinae de servitute et liberatione arbitrii* are brief and vague and suggest that Calvin was relying on memory of earlier study of Bernard and had no text at hand.[10] The only new Bernardine material in the next few years comes in two anti-Anabaptist works of 1544 and 1545 and, as we shall see, was not taken from an *Opera omnia*.[11] The next new material comes in two commentaries, from 1554 and 1557,[12] followed by a mass of new material in the 1559 *Institutio*. This suggests a renewed exposure to Bernard in the 1550s.

II. PRINTED EDITIONS

A printed edition of Bernard would have been Calvin's most obvious source. Bernard was often printed in the fifteenth and sixteenth centuries and there are many editions that Calvin could have used.[13] The first genuine work appeared between 1470 and 1475 while the *editio princeps* of the *Opera omnia* was printed in 1508 at Paris by Jean Petit.[14] From 1470 to 1508 there was a steady stream of 'partial' editions (containing some, but

---

9 E. Doumergue, *Jean Calvin. Les hommes et les choses de son temps*, vol. 2 (Lausanne: Bridel, 1902) 455–57; J. Pannier, 'Calvin à Strasbourg', *Revue d'histoire et de philosophie religieuses* 4 (1924) 509f. Cf. CRF 5:307, 6:30–32, cited by Doumergue. Doumergue argues that while Calvin certainly sold the books that he had inherited from Olivétan and also sold copies of his own works, there is no explicit reference to Calvin's selling from his *own* library while at Strassburg (2:457, n. 1). But absence of evidence is not evidence of absence and it is not unlikely that in the circumstances he was forced to sell some of his own books.
10 Cc.V-VIII. The *Def. adv. calumn. Pighii* appeared before the 1543 *Institutio*, but was not started until late 1542, by when the latter was almost complete (CRF 7.410, cited in OS 3:XIX-XX).
11 Cc.XVIII; XIX. Cf. at nn. 34f., below.
12 Cc.XXIV; XXVI.
13 These are listed in section VII, below. The items of BBJ are referred to by their numbers as J3, etc. J*510, e.g. is an edition which is similar to J510 but with substantial differences.
    The editions can be variously grouped according to their editor(s) or according to publishers, but for the purposes of this comparison such groupings have been ignored. Our interest is only in textual variations in a small number of passages, which can easily arise by accident.
14 It is uncertain which of J3, J7, J15, J20 and J30 is the earliest. J15 is *Homiliae super missus est* from '1472?' (BBJ 8). Details of the others are in section VII, below. The *editio princeps* of the *Opera omnia* is J350, the alleged edition of 1500 (J239) not existing.

not all, of the Bernardine corpus) but thereafter the great majority of editions were *Opera omnia*. The *Bibliographia Bernardina* lists thirty-five from Calvin's lifetime but not all of these existed. Throughout this period there were significantly more editions of the *Flores* and pseudo-Bernard than of the genuine Bernard.[15]

Calvin's quotations have been compared with all available editions.[16] While the aim is to detect the edition which comes closest to Calvin's, a direct comparison of the citations with his text would be a most insensitive test as he departed widely from them all in many places.[17] Instead, the editions and Calvin's text have been compared with the modern critical edition.[18] The variations of each ancient edition from it have been noted and compared with Calvin's text. The edition whose variations are most in accord with Calvin is most likely to have been the one that he used.[19] This depends, naturally, not just on the quantity of the variations but also on their significance. The omission of a whole sentence in one edition outweighs a number of minor verbal differences in others. Differences of spelling and punctuation have not been considered as they are trivial in comparison with other variations and are less likely to be followed in quotation.

In 1539 Bernard is cited three times in the *Institutio* but the one quotation is too short to contain any disputed readings.[20] Before the 1543 edition there is one more citation but this is not a quotation.[21]

The 1543 *Institutio* contains quotations which can be tested. The *Sermones in Cantica* are quoted twice.[22] Calvin was clearly not using a partial edition.[23] With one minor exception there are no differences between the *Opera omnia*.[24]

---

15 The *Flores* contain genuine Bernardine passages as well as much pseudo-Bernard but they do not give an accurate impression of his teaching. Cf. ESB 187.
16 See section VII, below for details of the editions. Many, but not all, of Calvin's quotations are long and precise enough to contain some of the textual variations of the editions.
17 Calvin quoted Bernard from memory and (by modern standards) very loosely. Thus in a quotation spanning ten lines there may be many differences between Calvin and the text of Bernard. By comparison, the differences between the various editions are minor in the extreme. But where Calvin sides with some editions against others these differences are significant.
18 J. Leclercq *et al.* (eds), *Sancti Bernardi Opera* (Rome, 1957ff.) (BO).
19 It might be thought that the results would vary if a different text were taken as normative, but this is not so. With any two editions the aim is to discover which varies less from Calvin. The method used in fact measures their deviation from Calvin relative to a norm (BO). As the norm is the same for both editions, that edition which departs less from Calvin will also depart less relative to the norm. This will be true whatever norm is taken.
20 Cc.I-III, of which the first is a quotation.
21 C.IV. On the date of cc.V-VIII, cf. n. 10, above.
22 *SC* 61 and 68 (cc.Xa-b; XII).
23 J299 does not contain either sermon; J68 and J240 number sermon 68 wrongly as 69 (Calvin has the correct number); J60, J68, J162, J207 and J240 have significant variations against both Calvin and the *Opera omnia*.
24 J422 reads 'merito' for 'meritum' in *SC* 61:5 (c.Xb), against Calvin and the other *Opera omnia*, but Calvin could easily have corrected this spelling mistake himself.

With the *De consideratione*, which is quoted twice,[25] the results are similar. The *Opera omnia* vary three times together from the critical edition in favour of Calvin's text.[26] The other editions all contain a number of significant variations from Calvin peculiar to them.[27] Two of the *Opera omnia* are slightly more likely to have been used by Calvin than the others as they vary an extra time in favour of his text.[28]

There are quotations from two of Bernard's sermons.[29] The partial editions are again excluded by their many and significant variations from Calvin and the *Opera omnia*. One variation from the critical edition is shared by all of the *Opera omnia* and most of the other editions.[30] Apart from this there are extra variations in five of the *Opera omnia*, which leaves one of them closer to Calvin than the rest.[31]

If Calvin used a printed edition for the 1543 *Institutio* it was certainly an *Opera omnia*. Some editions are more likely than others,[32] but there can be no certainty about which one he used.

Between 1543 and 1559 there are fourteen citations of Bernard in Calvin's works, but five are taken from the 1539 and 1543 *Institutio*, two are comments on Bernard and not references to his writings and five do not provide sufficient quotation to test the edition used.[33] The two remaining quotations, of two of Bernard's sermons for All Saints' Day, appear in anti-Anabaptist works of 1544 and 1545 and are the only testable quotations outside the *Institutio*.[34] The *Opera omnia* cannot be Calvin's

---

25 Cc.XIV; XVI.

26 Most significant is 'monstra' in place of 'monstruosa genera' in *Csi* 1:4:5 (c.XIVb).

27 Including J386 which appeared in 1515 after some of the *Opera omnia*. It is the type of edition that is significant, not the date.

28 J476 reads 'praecucurrit' for 'praecucurrit' in *Csi* 4:2:5 (c.XIVe). Calvin could easily have made this correction himself. J422 has 'illi' for 'illae' in *Csi* 4:2:4 (c.XIVd). But Calvin's 'illi' is probably a printer's error (see at nn. 4–6, above).

29 *QH* 15 (c.Xc); *Ded* 5 (cc.IX; XI).

30 'Impleta' for 'plena' in *Ded* 5:3 (c.IXa), against Calvin. J61, J180 and J181 have 'plena' but none of these could be Calvin's source as they all have many deviations from Calvin and the *Opera omnia*. 'Plena' is found with 'confusio' in the Vulgate of Ezek. 16:7, 22 and with 'ignominia' in Ezekiel 16:39 and 23:29. Calvin *could* have seen the allusion to Ezekiel 16 and supplied 'plena' from there but this is unlikely. Calvin's translation of these verses in his lectures on Ezekiel contains none of the three words.

31 J423 omits 'si' in *Ded* 5:4 (c.IXa) ('Et si nihil sumus'), against Calvin; J*462 and J484 read 'iustitiae' for 'iniustitiae' in *Ded* 5:3 (c.IXa), also against Calvin; J422 has 'sunt' for 'sint' in *Ded* 5:4 (c.IXa), against Calvin while J422 and J388 have 'salvaret' for 'salvare' in *Ded* 5:7 (c.IXc), against Calvin and 'cognovit' for 'novit' in *Ded* 5:7 (c.XI), with Calvin. All but the last could very easily have been corrected by Calvin as they can be seen to be mistakes. The last change could also have been made by Calvin as it is in accord with the Vulgate of both 1 Corinthians 2:16 (to which Calvin here refers) and Romans 11:34 (which Bernard was actually citing) and with the translation in his commentaries on both passages. This leaves J388 as marginally the most likely edition.

32 J423, J*462 and J484 are less likely than the rest. J388, J422 and J476 are more likely than the others, with J388 the most likely.

33 From 1539 *Institutio*: c.VIII. From 1543 *Institutio*: cc.XVII; XXI-XXIII. Comments: cc.XX; XXV. Insufficient quotation: cc.V-VII (summary); c.XXIV (paraphrase); c.XXVI (no textual variants).

34 *OS* 2 & 3 (cc.XVIII-XIX). These quotations are not themselves anti-Anabaptist. Cf. A. N. S. Lane, *Calvin and Bernard of Clairvaux* (Studies in Reformed Theology and History New Series no. 1) (Princeton: Princeton Theological Seminary, 1996) 73–76.

source because they all omit a crucial phrase, which Calvin could not have supplied independently.[35] This is striking confirmation that Calvin did not bring to Geneva the edition that he used at Strassburg. Most of the partial editions are also excluded by a number of significant variations. Of the three partial editions which do have the crucial missing phrase, one numbers the sermons wrongly.[36] This leaves just two editions, from 1495, which do differ slightly from Calvin's text, but could be his source.[37] Calvin was clearly not dependent upon an *Opera omnia* for these citations, but might have been using one of these two partial editions.

Most of the new citations in the 1559 *Institutio* come from the *Sermones in Cantica*.[38] The partial editions are again excluded by a number of significant deviations from both Calvin and the *Opera omnia*. There are more differences than hitherto between the *Opera omnia*. Two of them deviate significantly, against Calvin.[39] Six others have minor verbal differences.[40] Calvin is slightly less likely to have used one of these than one of the remaining editions.

There is not much evidence for the one sermon quoted in 1559.[41] The *Opera omnia* are all the same and the other editions differ only slightly. Two of them can be excluded as they number the sermon wrongly.[42] These are, interestingly, the same two that were a possible source for the 1544/45 quotations. The others are less likely than an *Opera omnia* to have been Calvin's source in the light of his usage elsewhere in the 1559 *Institutio* and because of slight extra variations against Calvin.

C.XVIII is in French. The work was translated into Latin (*Brevis instructio . . . adversus errores sectae Anabaptistarum* (Strassburg: W. Rihel, 1546)) but unfortunately the relevant material was omitted, so there is no Latin text of c.XVIII to check against possible sources.

35 'Tertium in corpore iam glorificato' (*OS* 3:1), translated into French in c.XVIIIb.

36 J61 numbers the sermons as 3 and 4 while Calvin has the correct numbers in c.XVIIIc.

37 J180 and J181 differ from the critical edition in the following points: (1) 'Quid tamen . . . abscondita est' is omitted from *OS* 2:8. This includes two words quoted by Calvin ('multitudo dulcedinis'), but these are also found just before the passage omitted. (2) The words 'perficietur' and 'tamquam', quoted by Calvin, are omitted from *OS* 2:8. These could have been supplied by the sense of the passage. (3) 'Primum in militia . . . beatudine consummata' is omitted from *OS* 3:1. Calvin himself omits these words. (4) The word 'suis' ('sine corporibus suis'), quoted by Calvin, is omitted from *OS* 3:1. Points 1–3 refer to c.XVIII, which is in French; point 4 refers to c.XIXb, in Latin. It is by no means impossible for Calvin to have supplied the missing words (points 1, 2 and 4) and the fact that Calvin omits a clause omitted by these editions also strengthens the argument for their use. In 'Calvin's Sources of St Bernard', 258, I wrongly ruled out these two editions.

38 There are the following quotations: cc.XXVIII; XXIX; XXXIV; XXXVa; XXXVI; XXXVIII; XL.

39 J350 and J*462 have 'facias' for 'reddas' in *SC* 21:9 (c.XXIX).

40 'Mixto' for 'immixto' in *SC* 11:2 (c.XXXIV) (J350, J*462, J484, J491 and J504); 'ablatum' for 'oblatum' in *SC* 13:4 (c.XXXVIa) (J388 & J422); 'voluntare' for 'voluntariae' in *SC* 81:7 (c.XXVIIIc) (J402); 'Det' for 'Dei' in *SC* 23:15 (c.XLa) (J491 and J504). All these are against Calvin. He could easily have corrected these mistakes himself.

41 *Ann* 1 (c.XXXIII).

42 J180 and J181 number it as sermon 2 while Calvin has the correct number.

One epistle is quoted in 1559.[43] All but three of the partial editions are excluded by numbering it incorrectly.[44] The other editions are all alike except for two of the *Opera omnia* which also have the wrong number.[45]

While Calvin might have used partial editions for the single quotations of the *Sermones* and *Epistolae* he did not do so for the *Sermones in Cantica*. If he did use a printed edition it was probably an *Opera omnia* for all of the citations. Four editions may be discounted[46] but there are only minor verbal differences between the rest.

The examination of the printed editions leaves some likelihood that Calvin used an *Opera omnia* for the 1543 and 1559 *Institutio* with uncertainty over his source for the *Sermones* in 1544 and the following year. A definitive verdict must await the examination of the alternative sources: manuscripts, anthologies and other authors.

III. MANUSCRIPTS

It is not *a priori* likely that Calvin relied on manuscripts for his text of Bernard. As there was no shortage of recently printed editions he had no need to resort to the laborious means of consulting manuscripts. Calvin did sometimes refer to manuscript readings, though the evidence that he himself *consulted* manuscripts is very sparse.[47] He refers to manuscripts only for texts on which he was commentating and there is no evidence

---

43 *Ep* 107 (c.XXXIX).

44 J3 and J170 number it as 109 and 110 respectively while Calvin has the correct number. J180 and J181 do not number it at all. The three remaining editions are J58, J146 and J147.

45 J388 and J422 number it as 108. J504 has it in the correct position (between 106 and 108) but by a printer's error numbers it CXII. J388 also has 'manifestum' for 'manifestatum', against Calvin, in *Ep* 107:4 (c.XXXIXa). Two Vulgate passages are relevant. Romans 1:19 contains very similar language to Bernard, with 'manifestum', but is different in meaning. Colossians 1:26 is similar in meaning but different in language, though with 'manifestatum'. These texts were probably in Bernard's mind but are not likely to have caused Calvin to correct J388. The translation in his commentaries has 'manifestum' in Romans 1:19 but does not use either word in Colossians 1:26.

46 J350, J388, J422 and J*462. Note that J388 and J422 were the most likely editions for 1543. This supports the conclusion that Calvin changed his source (cf. at nn. 7–12, above).

47 *Comm.* Romans 2:17, 12:11; *Comm.* 1 Corinthians 7:29, cited by T. H. L. Parker, *Calvin's New Testament Commentaries* (Edinburgh: T&T Clark, 1993 – 2nd edition) 147–53. *Comm.* Philippians 3:15f., cited by A. M. Hunter, 'The Erudition of John Calvin', *Evangelical Quarterly* 18 (1946) 204. Of these, *Comm.* 1 Corinthians 7:29 is the only passage which might state that Calvin had himself consulted manuscripts. Parker (pp. 152f.) argues that it does have that implication. The nineteenth-century Calvin Translation Society translation is accurate here, but the more recent Oliver & Boyd translation is unreliable, adding to Calvin's text two sentences (in brackets) and the crucial words 'I consulted'. Parker also claims (p. 147, n. 44) that Calvin used manuscripts for his commentary on *De clementia*, citing as an example 1:3. F. L. Battles and A. M. Hugo, *Calvin's Commentary on Seneca's De Clementia* (Leiden: E. J. Brill, 1969) deny that Calvin used manuscripts (pp. 68*f.) and translate 'exemplaribus' in the cited passage as 'editions' (p. 93). Parker himself warns that *codex* and *exemplar* can at that time mean either manuscript or printed edition (p. 148, n. 45).

that he had a wider interest in them.[48] The imprecision with which he quotes Bernard makes it quite clear that he was not particularly concerned to recover the precise text. The presumption that he did not use manuscripts can be tested. The text of the *Opera omnia* does not belong to any one manuscript tradition and at times differs from all the manuscripts.[49] Thus the manuscript traditions and the editions can be checked against Calvin's text to see which comes the closest. This test will also show which tradition or traditions of Bernard's writings Calvin knew.

There is no shortage of manuscripts of Bernard.[50] Dom. Jean Leclercq, in producing his critical edition had by 1972 examined about 1,460 manuscripts, of which exactly 610 are from the twelfth century.[51] For each work they fall into distinct traditions which often correspond to different redactions. The *Recensio Morimundensis*, found in the manuscripts from the Bavarian and Austrian monasteries of the Morimond filiation, is usually the earliest redaction and forms a relatively homogeneous collection.[52] The *Recensio Claraevallensis* is the official Clairvaux text but is not as valuable as might be supposed.[53] It is the definitive version based on the final redaction of Bernard himself and shows which works are genuine. But it is not the most primitive text and has in many places been 'corrected' after Bernard's death, especially with a view to his canonization. It provides the definitive version but not the definitive text.

For each quotation the different manuscript traditions have been compared with the best printed edition[54] to see which comes closest to Calvin's text. This will reveal which tradition(s) Calvin knew and whether he is more likely to have used manuscripts than printed editions.

There are three recensions of the *Sermones in Cantica*.[55] The first was the *Recensio Morimundensis* which is an early and uncorrected text of sermons 1 to 83 only. The *Recensio Anglica* is Bernard's final revision of the sermons, containing all eighty-six in a corrected form. As the name suggests, this recension is found especially in England, which was distant and independent enough to avoid contamination by the *Recensio Claraevallensis*. This last recension arose from corrections made to the *Recensio Anglica* at Clairvaux after Bernard's death. It is rare in its pure state but has contaminated most of the other manuscripts, except those with the Morimond text. Between the Morimond and English texts there is a *Textus Medius* which arose from copies made from Bernard's original at different stages of its development and from later corrections to such texts. It is found especially in incomplete manuscripts.

48 In *Inst.* 4:7:17 Calvin refers to the archives of the 'Curia Parisiensis' but that does not prove that he had consulted them for himself (cf. OS 5:120, n. 4) and is not an example of him citing manuscripts for a work which was in print.

49 Relative to the manuscript traditions the *Opera omnia* can be considered to form one textual tradition. Cf. RESB 1:272.

50 This paragraph is based on ESB 11–40 and RESB 1–3.

51 These figures come from a private letter of 30 July 1972. In ESB 12 (1953) the figures 1444 and 608 are given.

52 For the Morimond text cf. RESB 2:19–33.

53 For the Clairvaux text cf. RESB 1:245–271, 2:35–40, 233–238, 3:310–315.

54 I.e. the edition closest to Calvin's text, as found in the previous section. All details of the text of each MS tradition will be found at the appropriate passage in BO.

55 This paragraph is based on RESB 1:213–270; BO 1:IX–XII, XV–LXVII.

For the 1543 *Institutio* the *Opera omnia* come closer to Calvin's text than the manuscripts.[56] The *Recensio Anglica* and the *Textus Medius* come the closest to Calvin's text of the manuscript traditions. In 1559 the Clairvaux text and some of the English manuscripts come as close to Calvin's text as the closest editions.[57]

There was only one recension of the *De gratia et libero arbitrio*, the text of which is relatively homogeneous.[58] Calvin's nine words of quotation in 1539 do not include any disputed readings.[59]

The recensions of the *De consideratione* are similar to those of the *Sermones in Cantica*.[60] The text of the first, the *Recensio Morimundensis*, is very homogeneous. The second, the *Recensio Secunda* is Bernard's own final revision. Those manuscripts which combine the readings of these two form a *Textus Medius*. Finally, the *Recensio Claraevallensis* is the text corrected and revised at Clairvaux after Bernard's death. There is no trace of an Italian or Roman text arising from the original copy sent to Pope Eugenius. The best editions[61] come closer to Calvin's text than do any of the manuscripts. Of the latter, some of those of the *Recensio Secunda* come the closest to Calvin.[62]

The surviving sermons of Bernard fall into two groups.[63] Some are careful literary productions, drafted in their final form by Bernard or his disciples and in some cases never preached. Others are in the form of notes, by Bernard or his hearers, of his actual preaching. The *Sermones in Cantica* and the liturgical sermons, together with the sermon *De conversione*, fall into the former group while the latter contains the *Sermones de diversis* and various *sententiae* and *parabolae*. Calvin cited only the literary sermons. These are found in five successive editions, *Brevis, Media, Longior, Perfecta* and *Claraevallensis*.[64] Not all of the sermons are to be found in each edition, the difference between the editions lying as much in the selection of sermons included as in their text. The editions *Brevis, Longior* and *Perfecta* can be dated as after 1138, 1148 and 1150, respectively. The last two dates show that Bernard revised his sermons carefully in his last years.

Calvin quoted six of Bernard's sermons. The quotations of two of these contain no disputed readings but it should be noted that these sermons appear only in the *Perfecta* and *Claraevallensis* manuscripts.[65] The *Sermo 5 in dedicatione ecclesiae*, quoted in 1543, appears in the *Longior, Perfecta* and *Claraevallensis* manuscripts. Of these some of the *Perfecta*

---

56 In SC 61:3, e.g. the MSS have 'requies' only while Calvin and the *Opera omnia* add 'securitas' (c.Xa).
57 For the closest editions see at nn. 24, 39f., above. The English MSS are those following the text of Pembroke College, Cambridge MS 9, formerly at Bury St Edmund's Abbey.
58 BO 3:XI, XVII-XXXII, 157-64.
59 *Gra* 2:4 in c.I.
60 This paragraph is based on RESB 2:129f.; BO 3:XII-XIII, XVII-XXXII, 381-92.
61 J422 and J476 (n. 28, above).
62 Those MSS which follow the text of Douai 372.
63 This paragraph is based on ESB 45-80; RESB 2:3-18, 203-260; BO 4:VIII-IX, 119-60.
64 The *Perfecta* MSS fall into three groups: those with the whole series of sermons, those with the first half only and those with the second half only.
65 *QH* 15 in c.Xc; *VI p P* 2 in c.XXVI. Both are very short. The latter is also found in the *Media* MS Tours 344 (RESB 2:215). RESB 2:209 lists the sermons found in each edition.

manuscripts come the closest to Calvin's text but the best *Opera omnia* is significantly closer.[66]

In 1544 and 1545 Calvin quoted from the second and third sermons for All Saints' Day which are found in the *Perfecta* and *Claraevallensis* and some *Media* manuscripts.[67] He was not using an *Opera omnia* but might have been using a partial edition.[68] The Clairvaux text and some of the *Perfecta* manuscripts have a serious omission.[69] Others of the *Perfecta* manuscripts differ significantly from Calvin's text, as does part of the *Media* tradition.[70] The remaining manuscripts of these two traditions come the closest to Calvin, being considerably closer than the printed editions.[71]

In 1559 Calvin quoted from the first sermon on the Annunciation which is found in all but the *Longior* manuscripts.[72] The Clairvaux text and most of the *Perfecta* manuscripts[73] come the closest to Calvin's text. The *Opera omnia* differ once from these manuscripts in word order, against Calvin.[74] It is therefore possible that Calvin used one or more of these manuscripts but the slight difference in word order is too small to demand, or even to imply, such a conclusion.

There are three early collections of the letters of Bernard: *Brevis*, which is the Morimond text, *Longior* and *Perfecta*.[75] The Clairvaux text is a later corruption. In 1559 Calvin quoted *Epistola* 107, which is in all of the collections. The manuscripts of the *Longior* and *Perfecta* traditions come slightly closer to Calvin's text than the best editions.[76] Against this must be set the fact that Calvin knew the number of *Epistola* 107, which he is unlikely to have known from a manuscript.[77] Given this, the evidence strongly favours the use of a printed edition.

For the 1543 *Institutio* Calvin is clearly more likely to have used an *Opera omnia* than manuscripts. His source for the *Sermones* in 1544 and 1545 might be a partial edition with manuscripts of the *Perfecta* tradition being more likely. The situation is more complex with the 1559 *Institutio*. For the *Sermones in Cantica* the evidence is evenly balanced while for the *Sermones*

---

66 The best MSS are those following the MSS Vercelli 184 and Tarragone 137. The best edition is J388 (n. 31, above).

67 RESB 2:209. Of the *Media* MSS, *OS* 2 appears in all listed except Leipzig 381 while *OS* 3 appears only in Tours 344 and Vienna 1074 (RESB 2:215).

68 Cf. at nn. 34–37, above.

69 The Clairvaux MSS and *Perfecta* MS Cambrai 557 omit 'Est ergo multitudo dulcedinis' in *OS* 2:8 (c.XVIIIa).

70 The *Perfecta* MSS Vercelli 184 and Troyes 832 read 'cum' for 'nec sine' and the *Media* MS Tours 344 reads 'idem' for 'id est', both in *OS* 3:1 (c.XIXb).

71 *Media* MS Vienna 1074 and *Perfecta* MSS Tarragone 137 and Gethsemani 2 (USA).

72 RESB 2:209.

73 The *Perfecta* MSS Vercelli 184 and Gethsemani 2 (USA) are less close as they add 'tibi' after 'gratis' in *Ann* 1:1 (c.XXXIIIa), against Calvin.

74 The *Opera omnia* do not vary for this quotation. They all read 'quod aeternam vitam' for 'quod vitam aeternam' in *Ann* 1:1 (c.XXXIIIa).

75 For this paragraph cf. ESB 87–93; RESB 3:307–22, 4:125–225.

76 Except for J388 and J422 the *Opera omnia* do not vary for this quotation (n. 45, above). They read 'filii Dei' in *Ep* 107:4 for the 'filii sui' of the best manuscripts and Calvin (c.XXXIXa). But Calvin could easily have corrected 'Dei' to the 'sui' of Romans 8:29.

77 There is no consistent numeration of the *Epistolae* in the MSS, according to Dom. J. Leclercq (in a private letter of 19 August 1972).

it very slightly favours the manuscripts. The evidence for the *Epistolae* would favours the manuscripts, were it not for the decisive factor of numeration. The textual evidence for 1559 is not conclusive and a final judgment must await the evidence of availability.

Three possible objections must first be met. Calvin could have used a manuscript not of the ancient traditions. It is clearly not possible to examine every existing manuscript of Bernard, to say nothing of those which have perished since Calvin's time. But as any manuscript which Calvin might have used would consist mainly of readings from the different traditions,[78] the evidence for the 1543 *Institutio* against all the traditions is significant. Secondly, it is possible that Calvin did his own textual criticism of the manuscripts and produced a text different from any individual manuscript. But it would have been ridiculous for him to have done this and then to have quoted Bernard as imprecisely as he did. Finally, this test does not take into account the possibility of Calvin using manuscripts as a secondary source, being primarily dependent upon printed editions. This cannot be checked, but nor is it important as it is his main source that is of primary interest. Whether he ever glanced at a manuscript of Bernard is of minor importance.

The textual evidence indicates that Calvin did not use manuscripts for the 1543 *Institutio*, that he could have used either a partial edition or (more likely) manuscripts in 1544 and 1545 and that he is more likely to have used an *Opera omnia* in 1559. The availability of manuscripts points in a different direction. There were many manuscripts at Strassburg and these included not a few of Bernard.[79] At Geneva there was probably little if any opportunity to consult manuscripts of Bernard.[80] This evidence does not alter the conclusion for the 1543 *Institutio* as there was no shortage of printed editions at Strassburg. But it does affect the balance of probability for 1559 where the textual evidence is inconclusive. It is possible that Calvin had copied or memorized portions of Bernard read in manuscripts at Strassburg or elsewhere on his journeys. It is also possible that he actually possessed some manuscripts of his own. Nonetheless, the evidence of availability, together with what is known of Calvin's methods, makes it fairly certain that he used an *Opera omnia* in 1559 rather than manuscripts.

Evidence of availability can also indicate *which* printed editions Calvin might have used. Until 1549 the *Opera omnia* of Bernard were printed only at Paris and Lyons and any of these editions could easily have been

---

78 Only rarely do MSS contain readings not in the ancient traditions. Such readings would be glosses or 'corrections' to make the text easier or to conform it to later Latin according to J. Leclercq (in a private letter of 30 July 1972). Cf. RESB 4:180–83.

79 C. Schmidt, *Zur Geschichte der ältesten Bibliotheken und der ersten Buchdrucker zu Strassburg* (Strassburg: C. F. Schmidt, 1882) 52–55 lists MSS of Bernard in the library of the Carthusian monastery.

80 J. Leclercq found no MSS of Bernard at Geneva (from a private letter of 30 July 1972). There are few Bernard MSS in Switzerland except in Engelberg and Fribourg. Zurich has none of the works which Calvin cited. Bern has a MS of the *Epistolae* (MS 44) but this came to Bern at a late date from France. By 1539 almost the entire contents of the pre-Reformation libraries at Geneva had gone and a library had to be begun from scratch (A. Ganoczy, BAC 2f.).

available at Strassburg.[81] For the 1543 *Institutio* the textual evidence is the most important.[82] For the 1559 *Institutio* there is more important evidence. An edition of Bernard's *Opera omnia* was published at Basel in 1552.[83] There are a number of reasons for supposing that Calvin used this particular edition. First, its date of publication fits the timing of Calvin's citations. Secondly, the links between Geneva and Basel would favour the use of this edition. Thirdly, there is a copy of this edition in the *Bibliothèque publique et universitaire* at Geneva. This volume is already to be found in the 1572 catalogue of the library of the Genevan Academy, some of whose books came from Calvin's personal library.[84] There is a distinct possibility, therefore, that this may have been Calvin's own copy. There are marks in this copy and some handwriting[85] but nothing that can be identified as Calvin's. That does not mean that it was not his copy as he did not normally mark his books.[86] This must be the most likely source for the 1559 *Institutio* though a final verdict on this or the other years must await the examination of the other possible sources.

IV. ANTHOLOGIES

It is highly unlikely that the majority of Calvin's citations of Bernard were derived from anthologies. The length and variety of his quotations confirm for Bernard the following comment on his citations in general: 'man sieht, daß sie [die Citate] der Verfasser nicht blos da und dort aufgelesen, sondern einem reichen Material, das ihm frei zu Gebot stand, entnommen hat'.[87] For Calvin to have derived his knowledge of Bernard merely from others' selections would also have been inconsistent with his humanist

---

81 Three *Opera omnia*, two from Paris and one from Lyons, have been traced with some certainty to Calvin's Strassburg. The *Bibliothèque nationale* in Paris has a catalogue from 1804 to 1806 of the material acquired by the Strasbourg *Bibliothèque de la Ville* through the Revolution (J. Rott, 'L'ancienne Bibliothèque de Strasbourg, détruite en 1870, les catalogues qui en subsistent' in *Refugium Animae Bibliotheca. Festschrift für Albert Kolb* (Wiesbaden: Guido Pressler, 1969) 433). This includes J350, J423 and J476 (MSS Fr. Nouv. Adq. 6433, fol. 394 and Fr. Nouv. Adq. 6435, fol. 102. I am indebted to Xavier Barral I Altet for this information). The first two were in the library of the house of the order of St John of Jerusalem before the Revolution (J. N. Weislinger, *Catalogus librorum impressorum in Bibliotheca Eminentissimi Ordinis Sancti Johannis Hierosolymitani asservatorum Argentorati* (Strasbourg: Simon Kürsner, 1749) 32f. lists J423 and an *Opera omnia* of Jean Petit at Paris. As these books were transferred to the *Bibliothèque de la Ville* the latter is presumably the J350 found there). The J476 probably came from one of the other religious houses at the time of the Revolution, but it could have come from the Jesuit seminary (Rott, 'L'ancienne Bibliothèque', 427; J. Gass, *Die Bibliothek des Priesterseminars in Strassburg* (Strassburg: F. X. Le Roux, 1902) 11). I am indebted to Jean Rott for guidance in the work leading to this note.
82 For the conclusions on the basis of the textual evidence cf. n. 32, above.
83 J532.
84 Ganoczy, BAC 17–19, 188. It is item 86 in the catalogue.
85 Marks on sigs. b6b, h5b-6a, xlb, Vu5a-Xx4b. Handwriting on sigs. xlb and Vu6a.
86 Ganoczy, BAC 19. Cf. pp. 51f. where he expresses the opinion that this might have been Calvin's copy.
87 J. Köstlin: 'Calvin's Institutio nach Form und Inhalt in ihrer geschichtlichen Entwicklung', *Theologische Studien und Kritiken* 41 (1868) 35.

principle of *ad fontes*.[88] It would not, however, have been inconsistent or impossible for him to have made a minor use of such sources, in addition to or before his study of the *Opera omnia*. Citations for which anthologies are feasible as his primary source are the early citations, before the 1543 *Institutio*, and the two quotations from 1544 and 1545 which may not come from a printed edition.[89] Apart from two brief citations in the commentaries,[90] the remaining citations are either in the 1543 or 1559 *Institutio* or were derived from the former. The quantity and length of the quotations in these two editions make anthologies most unlikely as a source. But *a priori* likelihood is not proof. Calvin's quotations have been checked against all available anthologies to test the relation between them. There are two groups of anthologies to be considered: collections of purely Bernardine literature and general patristic anthologies.

(a) Bernardine Anthologies

This group contains five items.[91] The *Summa de vitiis* was compiled from various works of Bernard.[92] Calvin is unlikely to have seen it as it was never printed. The *Brevis commentatio in Cantici Canticorum priora duo capita* is a work of Bernard's youth, before his more famous *Sermones in Cantica*.[93] There is some overlap between the two works, but the former is not, as used to be thought, a résumé of the latter. The mature work develops some, but not all, of the themes of the earlier work. There is no overlap with any of Calvin's citations from the sermons. The *Declamationes de colloquio Simonis cum Iesu* is also sometimes called *Sententiae exceptae ex opusculis venerabilis abbatis Claraevallis*.[94] This is a work in sixty chapters of Geoffrey of Auxerre, Bernard's secretary and biographer, who claimed that it was drawn 'e multis sermonibus sancti Patris nostri'.[95] It contains nothing that Calvin quoted. One section is relevant to two of Calvin's quotations but there is no verbal overlap. The *Flores seu sententiae ex S. Bernardi operibus depromptae* include a number of collections, three of which

---

88 Cf. Todd, *Function*, 134–37.
89 Cc.I-IV; XVIII; XIX. The brevity of the first four citations favours this. Battles shows that Calvin was heavily dependent upon anthologies for his commentary on *De clementia*. His patristic citations came mostly from the *Decretum Gratiani* ('Sources', 56). A similar use of anthologies for the 1539 *Institutio* is certainly possible. The four citations in *Def. adv. calumn. Pighii* (cc.V-VIII), after the 1543 *Institutio* was *written* (n. 10, above), are vague enough to have come from anthologies but are more likely to reflect Calvin's memory of his Strassburg reading.
90 C.XXIV (a paraphrase); c.XXVI (a quotation).
91 These are listed by F. Cavallera, 'Bernard (Apocryphes attribués à saint)', *Dictionnaire de Spiritualité*, vol. 1 (Paris: G. Beauchesne, 1937) cols 1499f. In this article the apocryphal works listed in BBJ IV-XIV are divided into four groups, including 'Extraits ou remaniements des oeuvres authentiques'.
92 BBJ IX; Cavallera, 'Apocryphes', col. 1500.
93 Cf. on this ESB 116–24, where Mabillon's later theory that it is a résumé of *SC* 1–51 is rejected. On this theory cf. Cavallera, 'Apocryphes', col. 1499. The text is in PL 184:407–36. For a more recent study, cf. T. X. Davis, 'A Further Study of the *Brevis Commentatio*' in J. R. Sommerfeldt (ed.), *Bernardus Magister* (Kalamazoo: Cistercian Publications, 1992) 187–202.
94 BBJ V; Cavallera, 'Apocryphes', col. 1499. The text is in PL 184:435–76.
95 PL 184:437.

are found in Mabillon's edition.[96] These in fact are only part of a much larger group of *sententiae* which, together with the *parabolae* and the *Sermones de diversis*, are the record in non-literary form of much of Bernard's preaching.[97] Some sermons appear both in a literary form and in a much shorter non-literary form. The latter is not a résumé or corruption of the former but rather an earlier stage of its development, or possibly a handling of the same theme on a different occasion. The *sententiae* are not among Calvin's sources of Bernard.[98]

The remaining item is the *Flores* (or *Florilegium* or *Bernardinum* or *Liber florum*) which was compiled in the thirteenth century by William, a monk of St Martin de Tournai.[99] This is not to be confused with the *Floretus sancti Bernardi* which is among the *poemata S. Bernardo adscripta*.[100] Much of the text of the *Flores* is genuine Bernard but it is systematized in a manner that is foreign to Bernard. It is not to be found in Mabillon's edition (reprinted in Migne) nor in the earlier *Opera omnia* but it was often printed in Calvin's lifetime.[101]

The *Flores* are in ten books, divided into chapters, each of which contains a few passages from Bernard. The entire work has been carefully checked as a possible source for Calvin.[102] Twenty-three of Calvin's forty-one references to Bernard are paralleled in the *Flores*[103] but this total appears more impressive than the reality. There are thousands of extracts from Bernard in the *Flores* and it would be strange for none of them to overlap with Calvin's citations. *How* they overlap is more important. In many

96 Cavallera, 'Apocryphes', col. 1500 lists PL 183:747–52, 751–58, 1197–1204. The last group contains two short extracts from Calvin's quotations (col. 1201 and c.XXXVII; col. 1202 and c.XIVe). This group is unlike the other *sententiae* in being a collection of quotations with references given. J. Leclercq comments that it 'may be a *florilegium* (XIII-XIV or XV century). But the references as they are given are surely modern, i.e. post XVII century. . . . The collection sounds rather modern' (in a private letter of 19 August 1972).

97 Cf. on these writings ESB 45–49, 73–78 and RESB 2:203f. A fuller discussion, with some unpublished texts, is in H. M. Rochais: 'Enquête sur les sermons divers et les sentences de saint Bernard', *Analecta Sacri Ordinis Cisterciensis* 18:3–4 (1962).

98 A wide selection of them has been examined and, apart from the atypical collection mentioned at two notes above, no parallels with Calvin's citations were noted. Assuming that Calvin did not scour the libraries of Europe for rare manuscripts of *parabolae* and *sententiae*, these would have been available to him only in the *Opera omnia*.

99 On the *Flores* cf. Cavallera, 'Apocryphes', col. 1499f.; ESB 187; M. Bernards, 'Zur Verbreitung der Bernhardflorilegien', *Studien und Mitteilungen zur Geschichte des Benediktiner-Ordens* 64 (1952) 234–41; idem, 'Flores Sancti Bernardi', in J. Lortz (hrsg.), *Bernhard von Clairvaux, Mönch und Mystiker* (Wiesbaden: Franz Steiner, 1955) 192–201; idem, 'Zur Überlieferung der Bernhardschriften', *Cîteaux in de Nederlanden* 5 (1954) 153–72.

100 BBJ XIII. This has been examined in J298 (Cologne: H. Quentel, 1501) and bears no relation to Calvin's use of Bernard. There are many more editions of this work listed in BBJ than there are of the *Flores*.

101 J14, J65, J221, J314, J315, J411, J457, J502, J544, J568, J569.

102 J600 (Lyons: G. Rouillius, 1570) was used, though Calvin could not have used that edition. Where the contents were important they were checked with J221 (Paris: P. Pigouchet, 1499). The only significant differences were in the marginal references which often vary between editions.

103 A further seven references are comments about Bernard or summaries of his teaching too general to be tested (cc.IV; V; XIII; XV; XX; XXV; XLI). Thus, effectively twenty-three out of thirty-four possible references are paralleled in the *Flores*.

places, part but not all of Calvin's quotation is found in the *Flores* which are not, therefore, his source.[104] Elsewhere they contain the whole passage that Calvin quoted but the text is too deviant for him to have been reliant upon it.[105] Some sections found in the *Flores* text are preceded or followed in Calvin by another quotation from the same portion of Bernard which is not also found there.[106] This is a clear indication that Calvin was not quoting from the *Flores*, with one possible exception.[107] The twelve possibly dependent citations which remain can be further reduced. Four are taken from earlier citations, not from the *Flores*.[108] Two more are citations of the *Sermones in Cantica* in 1559[109] and as the *Flores* were clearly not the source of all the citations from this work in that edition it is uneconomical to suppose that they were the source for these two.

Only six citations remain[110] but these are not unimportant. They include the first three citations, the fourth being general enough to have been based upon reading of the *Flores*, which means that Calvin need not have had any other source for Bernard before his work on the 1543 *Institutio*.[111] A brief quotation in the 1543 *Institutio* is found in the *Flores*, but this is not significant as Calvin was clearly using an *Opera omnia* at that stage.[112] Of the four citations in the 1543 *Defensio doctrinae de servitute et liberatione arbitrii*, one is taken from the 1539 *Institutio* and two could have been based on the *Flores* (one of these being a general summary) but the fourth is not found there.[113] Calvin is more likely to have been citing from memory based on his reading at Strassburg.[114] Finally, the citation from the Psalms commentary could have been drawn from the *Flores*.[115]

104 *Flores* 2:10, 5:3, 9, 20, 22, 38, 39, 6:8, 7:21, 53, 8:15, 78, 87.
105 *Flores* 2:9f., 5:22, 8:87.
106 *Flores* 2:10, 4:23f., 5:22, 38, 7:48, 8:86f.
107 *Flores* 8:86 contains the phrase which eliminated the *Opera omnia* editions as the source for c.XVIII (cf. n. 35, above). Much, but not all, of the material for this citation is found in 8:86f. It is possible (but unlikely) that Calvin retained the crucial phrase from an earlier reading of the *Flores*.
108 Cc.VIII; XXXI are drawn from c.III which could be dependent upon *Flores* 7:67 and 8:18–20. C.XVII is taken from c.Xb rather than *Flores* 5:22. C.XXX is a summary of c.XXVIIIb-c rather than dependent upon *Flores* 2:9f.
109 *SC* 15:6 (c.XXXII) in *Flores* 8:5; *SC* 23:15 (c.XXXVa) in *Flores* 5:3. The latter sermon, but not the same passage, is found in c.XL (also 1559).
110 Cc.I-III; VII; Xc; XXVI.
111 Cc.I-III could be drawn from *Flores* 10:8, 8:22–24 and 7:67 and 8:18–20, respectively. *Flores* 10:8 adds an extra phrase to the portion of *Gra* 2:4 quoted in c.I but Calvin could easily have omitted it as he anyway omits part of the passage.
112 C.Xc could be drawn from *Flores* 5:22. The *Flores*, like Calvin, omit 'suam' ('spem suam ponat'), but given the looseness of Calvin's quotations the omission of a word is not of great significance. *Flores* 5:22 also contain parts of *SC* 61:5 (quoted in cc.Xb; XVII) and *SC* 68:6 (quoted in cc.XIIa-c; XXXVIb-c), but do not contain the entire text of any one part of a citation (e.g. c.XIIa), except for c.XVII, which is taken from c.Xb. In 'Calvin's Sources of St Bernard', 269, I paid too much attention to this juxtaposition. Other anthologies also juxtapose citations similarly to Calvin and this is a very slender basis for postulating influence. Calvin was reading the *Opera omnia* for himself and was capable of making his own judgments.
113 C.VIII is a repeat of c.III; c.VII could be drawn from *Flores* 2:9f.; c.V is general enough to have been based upon reading of the *Flores*.
114 Cf. at n. 7, above, for Calvin's quoting from memory.
115 C.XXVI could be drawn from *Flores* 10:10. In 'Calvin's Sources of St. Bernard', 269 I also stated that c.XXIV could be drawn from *Flores* 2:3, which is taken from *SC*

What conclusions can be drawn from this? Clearly the *Flores* were not Calvin's primary source for Bernard, although it is possible that they were the source for his earliest citations, prior to the 1543 *Institutio*. But that this is possible is due in part to the wide scope of the extracts in the *Flores* and the brevity and imprecision of Calvin's earliest citations. For the citations in the 1543 and 1559 *Institutio* appeal to the *Flores* becomes superfluous as we know that Calvin was reading the *Opera omnia*. For the 1543 *Defensio* memory of reading Bernard at Strassburg is the more likely explanation. The *Flores* could conceivably have influenced the text of the 1544 quotation which may not be based on a printed edition.[116] They are not likely to be the source for the Psalms commentary since (as we shall see) the earlier Genesis commentary requires the use of an *Opera omnia*.

Calvin may have used the *Flores*, especially in 1539, but it must be admitted that there is no certain proof that he had even seen a copy of them. If he had at some stage read them it is possible that they may have pointed him to certain later Bernardine passages, though his quotations require more knowledge of these passages than could be obtained from the *Flores* alone. In addition, there are other possible sources for these citations, to be considered below.

(b) Patristic and Medieval Anthologies

Most of the anthologies of Calvin's time, unlike the Flores, did not confine themselves to one writer. There are many collections of patristic and medieval literature on which Calvin could have drawn. For the original version of this chapter I examined twenty-five such works. This led on to an ongoing wider study of early printed patristic anthologies and the discovery of many more such works.[117] Now a total of fifty-eight potential sources have been examined. Some of these consist of a number of entire works (or sermons) of ancient authors. None of those examined contained any Bernard.[118]

---

35. But Calvin's likely source in Bernard has since been identified more accurately. (See chapter 4, above, at n. 115.) If c.XXIV requires Calvin's use of an *Opera omnia* it then becomes redundant to postulate an alternative source for c.XXVI.

116 I.e. c.XVIII. Cf. n. 107, above.

117 So far published are 'Early Printed Patristic Anthologies to 1566: A Progress Report' in E. A. Livingstone (ed.), *Studia Patristica* 18:4 (1990) 365–70, which is now very out of date, and 'Justification in Sixteenth-Century Patristic Anthologies' in L. Grane, A. Schindler, M. Wriedt (eds), *Auctoritas Patrum. Contributions on the Reception of the Church Fathers in the 15th and 16th Century* (Mainz: Philipp von Zabern, 1993) 69–95. Most of the anthologies cited in nn. 118–27, below, went through more than one edition, but only one is mentioned, except where there are significant differences between editions. Anthologies relating to biblical books are discussed in section V.a, below.

118 The following such works were examined: Jodocus Badius, *Enchiridion pietatis amatorum* (Paris, 1521), which contains some pseudo-Bernard. Franciscus Blosius, *Margaritum spirituale* (Louvain, 1550). Johannes Cochlaeus *Speculum antiquae devotionis circa missam, et omnem alium cultum dei* (Mainz, 1549). Johannes Costerius, *De veritate corporis et sanguinis domini nostri Iesu Christi in eucharistiae sacramento* (Louvain, 1551). *Florilegium ex diversis opusculis atque tractatibus* (Mainz, 1520). Conrad Gesner, *Theologorum aliquot Graecorum veterum orthodoxorum libri* (Zurich, 1559–60). John Herold, *Orthodoxographa theologiae doctores* (Basel, 1555). idem, *Haereseologia* (Basel, 1556). *Homilie hoc est conciones populares* (Basel, 1516): Bernard

More important are the collections of *passages* from ancient writers. Some of these contain no Bernard,[119] the most noteworthy of which is the *Corpus iuris canonici*. The *Decretum Gratiani* in particular was a source for Calvin both at the beginning of and throughout his literary career.[120] Others have extracts from Bernard's writings none of which overlaps with Calvin's citations.[121] It is significant that these include Bucer's *Commonplace Book*, which suggests that his influence upon Calvin's study of Bernard at Strassburg was not great.[122] A number of other works have extracts from Bernard which overlap with one or more of Calvin's citations, but without containing the whole citation or without stating the correct source where Calvin knows that.[123]

---

is never *named* as an author, which is all that matters for our present purpose. *Homilie diversorum doctorum in evangeliaque cantantur dominicis diebus iuxta consuetudine romane ecclesie* (1526). *Illustrium virorum opuscula* (Paris, 1550). *Mikropresbutikon* (Basel, 1550). Wolfgang Musculus, *Ecclesiasticae historiae autores* (Basel, 1549). *Orationes quaedam devotissime Basilii Magni & Chrysostomi de communione Eucharistiae* (Krakov, 1555). *Piae aliquot homiliae sanctorum quorundam patrum* (Paris, c.1535). John Sichard, *Antidotum contra diversas haereses* (Basel, 1528). John Surgant, *Homeliarius doctorum* (Basel, 1493).

119 Antonius Melissa, *Sententiae sive loci communes* (Antwerp, 1555). Franciscus Blosius, *Psychagogia* (Louvain, 1549). Adriano Castellesi, *De vera philosophia* (Cologne, 1540). *Centum et xiiii sententiae patrum* (Cologne, 1531). Antonius Corvinus, *Augustini et Chrysostomi theologia* (Halle, 1539). A. Friedberg (ed.), *Corpus Iuris Canonici* (Leipzig: B. Tauchnitz, 1879 and 1881). Johann Hofmeister, *Canones sive claves aliquot* (Mainz, 1545). Philipp Melanchthon, *Sentenciae veterum aliquot scriptorum de Coena Domini* (1530) (CR 23:733–52). *Quaedam auctoritates ad misericordiam inducentes* (Mantua, 1485). *Testimonia de disciplina ecclesiae* (s.l., s.d.). Georg Witzel, *In quaestionem de igne purgatorio* (Cologne, 1545).

120 For the beginning cf. n. 89, above; for later cf. Smits, SAOJC 1:206–11.

121 Alardus Aemstelredamus, *Parasceve ad sacrosanctam synaxin* (Cologne, 1532); idem, *Selectae aliquot similitudines sive collationes* (Cologne, 1539); idem, *Paraenesis de eleemosyna* (Cologne, 1545); Bartholomaeus Amantius, *Flores celebriorum sententiarum . . .* (Dillingen, 1556); *Autoritates notabiles de castitate et moribus* (Cologne, 1505?); Jodocus Badius, *Allegoriarum moraliumque sententiarum . . . concinnata miscellanea* (Paris, 1520); Martin Bucer, *Liber locorum communium*, which was examined in Corpus Christi College, Cambridge MS 418, but has subsequently been edited by P. Fraenkel, *Martini Buceri Opera Latina*, vol. 3 (Leiden, etc.: E. J. Brill, 1988); Jacobus Magdalius, *Passio magistralis* (Cologne, 1505); Andreas Musculus, *Precandi formulae ex veterum doctorum scriptis. . . . Adiecta est instructio orandi* (Frankfurt, 1553); idem, *Precationes ex veteribus doctoribus* (Frankfurt, 1559) (very similar to the preceding); *Probatissimorum ecclesiae doctorum sententiae* (Basel, 1520); Erasmus Sarcerius, *De consensu verae ecclesiae et patrum* (Frankfurt, 1540); idem, *Locorum communium ex consensu scripturae et patrum* (Basel, 1546) (a later edition of the preceding item but very different to his *Loci aliquot communes* of 1538); Godfried Tilmann, *Allegoriae simul et tropologiae* (Paris, 1551); Timannus Borckens, *Enchiridion precationum illustrium virorum* (Wessel, 1551); Benedict Vernier, *Magnum & universale concilium* (Paris, 1554); Georg Witzel, *Sylvula dictorum ecclesiasticorum* (Mainz, 1544).

122 But cf. at nn. 134, 158, 164, below, for some evidence of possible influence.

123 Listed chronologically: (1) *Pharetra auctoritates et dicta doctorum, philosophorum et poetarum continens* (two editions have been examined: items 12907f. in L. Hain, *Repertorium Bibliographicum* (Stuttgart and Tübingen: J. G. Cotta and Paris: J. Renouard, 1826–1838) [i.e. H 12907f.]) overlaps cc.Xa; XXXIIIa; XXXIXb in sections *de Christi passione*, *de fide* and *de amore dei ad homines*, respectively. (2) Thomas Hibernicus, *Manipulus florum* (Piacenza: J. de Tyela, 1483) sig. n3b (s.v. *meritum*) has c.Xc (with a key word missing) followed by the final sentence of c.XIIc, with the source given as 'Serm 53'. (3) Dominicus Nanus Mirabellus, *Polyanthea* (Saone: Bernardinus, 1503) f. 218a (s.v. *meritum*) has the

This leaves just three anthologies. The *Unio dissidentium* of Hermann Bodius was printed at least twenty-two times between 1527 and 1566[124] and it is quite possible that Calvin handled it. There are two partial overlaps with Calvin[125] and one that covers a citation completely. Bodius is not, however, Calvin's source as the latter had quoted from the same work shortly before.[126] Finally, two anthologies (Robert Barnes's *Sentenciae ex doctoribus collectae* and Bartholomew Westheimer's *Conciliationem Sacr. Scripturae, & Patrum*) are possible as a source for a passage in the 1543 *Defensio*, as well as overlapping another citation partially.[127]

---

same quotation as the previous item (4) Johann Hofmeister, *Loci communes rerum theologicarum* (Ingolstadt: A. Weissenhorn, 1547) f. 42b, overlaps c.XXXIIIa and f. 51a covers c.XXXIXb, but not c.XXXIXa. (5) *Catholicus Consensus . . . de sola fide in Christum iustificante* (Leipzig, 1551) sig. A8b, overlaps c.XXXIIIa. (6) Bartholomew Westheimer, *Conciliationem ac consensum sacrosanctae scripturae et patrum* (Zurich: A. Gesner and R. Weissenbach, 1552) is a radical revision of the 1536 edition and on pp. 135f. overlaps c.XXVIII. (7) Andreas Musculus, *Enchiridion Sententiarum* (Frankfurt: J. Eichorn, 1552) 384, 430, overlap c.XXXIIIa; 429f. overlaps c.XXXIIIb; 388f. covers Cc.XLa; XXXVa but not c.XLb from the same sermon; 427 overlaps c.XXXVb; 428 overlaps c.XXXVIb, material which is already found in c.XIIc, a. All but the first of these pages are numbered incorrectly in the original. (8) Johann Freyesleben, *Sylva quaedam testimoniorum* in Thomas Venatorius, *De sola fide iustificante nos in oculis dei* (Nuremberg: G. Hayn, 1556) sigs. I2b, I4b-5a, repeat the extracts on pp. 384, 388f. of the previous item. (9) Andreas Musculus, *Catechesis Sanctorum Patrum ac Doctorum* (Frankfurt: J. Eichorn, 1556) 70f., 146, 145f., 72f., 120, respectively, repeat all but the last of the overlaps in his *Enchiridion*. The final passage from the latter (p. 428) is not repeated, but p.185 overlaps c.XXXVIc, from the same sermon. (10) Rodrigues Andreas, *Sententiae & exempla*, vol. 1 (Lyons: T. Pagan, 1557) 383, 418, 445, 447, overlaps cc.XXVII; XIIc and Xc; XXXII; XXXVb, respectively. With each of the two Musculus works it was, unfortunately, possible to check only the two chapters on justification and works for Calvin's citations. Given the subject matter of the citations in the 1559 *Institutio*, these chapters are the most likely source for any overlaps.

124 On his identity cf. R. Peters: 'Who Compiled the Sixteenth-Century Patristic Handbook "Unio Dissidentium"?' in G. J. Cuming (ed.), *Studies in Church History*, vol. 2 (London *et al.*: Nelson, 1965) 237–50. As the citations vary from edition to edition (idem, 'The Use of the Fathers in the Reformation Handbook "Unio Dissidentium"', *Studia Patristica* 9 (1966) 570; Lane, 'Justification in Sixteenth-Century Patristic Anthologies', 71) four editions were checked (Cologne: J. Gymnicus, 1531; Basel: B. Westheimer, 1541; Basel: N. Bryling, 1551; Constance: N. Kalt, 1601). The only difference noted was that one citation fell out in 1601. References are to the 1531 edition. It is not in the 1572 Genevan catalogue (Ganoczy, BAC) but this catalogue lacks even some books printed in Geneva (e.g. the *Bibliotheca studii theologici* printed in 1565 by John Crespin).

125 C.IXa in ch. 2 (pp. 18f.); c.XXXIII in ch. 8 (pp. 147f.). It is interesting that twelve of Bodius's twenty Bernardine extracts overlap with the *Flores* but nine of these are only partly covered by the *Flores* while there are differences in the text of the other three. This is a further warning that mere overlapping proves nothing.

126 C.XI could be dependent upon ch. 9 (pp. 202f.) for *Ded* 5:6f. but the other quotations from that sermon in c.IX (also 1543) could not have been taken from the *Unio dissidentium*. In 'Calvin's Sources of St. Bernard', 272, I suggested that Bodius might also be the source for c.VI, but Bodius does not have the specific point cited by Calvin, the comparison with God and Satan.

127 Barnes, *Sentenciae*, sig. Cviia-b could be the source for c.VI, the one citation in *Def. adv. calumn. Pighii* not covered by the *Flores* (cf. at n. 113, above). C.XXVIIIa-c, but not c.XXVIIId is covered on sigs. Cviib-viiib. References are to the Wittenberg: J. Clug, 1530 edition, which appeared under the pseudonym of Antonius Anglus. The same two passages are also found in Westheimer, *Conciliationem Sacr.*

This examination of the patristic and medieval anthologies has produced only one passage in Calvin where it is even *possible* for him to have been dependent upon an anthology.[128] This meagre result is not very impressive in that the only citation that could be derived solely from an anthology is a very brief reference in a work (the 1543 *Defensio*) containing other citations on the same theme which are not covered in any patristic and medieval anthology (although they are covered by the *Flores*). There is a much simpler explanation of all of the citations in this work – Calvin's memory of his reading of Bernard at Strassburg.

V. OTHER AUTHORS

One final potential source remains. It is possible that some of Calvin's Bernardine citations were mediated via other authors. There are three main ways in which this could have happened: through commentaries, through correspondence and through general reading.

(a) Commentaries

Bernard appears three times in Calvin's commentaries. It is possible that these citations were derived from earlier commentaries. As many as possible of the relevant commentaries between Bernard and Calvin, available in print to Calvin, have been examined. For convenience, possible parallels to these three citations in other works will also be considered at this stage.

The first such citation[129] appeared in 1546 when Calvin, commenting on 1 Corinthians 3:15, mentions Bernard as (together with Cyprian, Ambrose, Augustine and Gregory) one of those *sancti* who rightly sought to build on Christ but often turned away from the right way of building.[130] There is no question here of a source in Bernard's works, but was this interpretation of Bernard original to Calvin? Johann Bugenhagen also applied this

---

Scripturae, & Patrum (Basel: B. Westheimer, 1536) 370f., 378–80, where there is also an overlap with c.XXXIII on p. 408.

128 Of course there are probably other anthologies that I have not yet discovered and it is also not unlikely that in the many thousands of pages that I have examined I may have missed a few overlaps. But the result that has emerged from reading which includes all the major anthologies makes it extremely unlikely that there is any undiscovered passage which could be a significant source for Calvin.

129 C.XX.

130 Space permits a listing of no more than the authors of the commentaries consulted and the dates of the particular editions, except where more information is appropriate. For all three citations the following three works have been examined: *Textus biblie cum Glossa ordinaria, Nicolai de Lyra postilla, Moralitatibus eiusdem, Pauli Burgensis additionibus, Matthie Thoring Replicis* (1506–08); Hugh of St Cher, *Postilla* (1498–1502); Robertus Stephanus (1545 *Biblia*). For 1 Corinthians: Johann Bugenhagen (1530); Heinrich Bullinger (1558 – there was a 1537 edition); Cardinal Cajetan (1531); Dionysius Carthusianus (1538); Desiderius Erasmus (1535 *Annotationes*); Jacobus Faber (1531); John Gagneius (1538); Nicolaus de Gorran (1502); Claude Guilliaudus (1544); Johann Hofmeister (1545); Philipp Melanchthon (1524 and 1551); Conrad Pellican (1539); Peter Lombard (PL 191); Erasmus Sarcerius (1544); Thomas Aquinas (1541); Francis Titelmann (1540); Lorenzo Valla (1505); Ulrich Zwingli (1528).

passage to the fathers, of whom he named Cyprian, Augustine, Ambrose, Irenaeus, Tertullian and Gregory, but not Bernard.[131] As the two lists of names are similar Calvin could have drawn on Bugenhagen, himself adding Bernard to the list. This particular commentary of Bugenhagen was not in the Genevan library of 1572, but others were.[132] Melanchthon also applied this passage to Bernard and Bonaventure but his commentary appeared after Calvin's.[133] Bucer and Luther also applied this passage to the fathers (not in commentaries), actually naming Bernard.[134] This was clearly a commonplace of Protestant exegesis.

The first new Bernardine material for almost ten years comes in Calvin's 1554 commentary on Genesis.[135] In 1976 it was suggested that Calvin might have derived this brief citation from Aloisius Lippoman's *Catena in Genesim ex authoribus ecclesiasticis*, which contains a collection of patristic passages for each portion of Genesis.[136] Calvin's likely source in Bernard has since been identified more accurately and none of the possible passages is found in Lippoman. A subsequent more rigorous examination has established that there is no evidence for Calvin's use of this anthology.[137]

So what was his source? The simple answer is Calvin's reading of the 1552 *Opera omnia*. But is this feasible? Calvin lectured on Genesis from 1550 to 1551/2 and began work on his commentary in 1550. Progress on the commentary was slow, but it is likely that the beginning of chapter three (where Bernard appears) was composed before the 1552 *Opera omnia* came Calvin's way. Either way, however, the commentary was not published until 1554 and Calvin would have read through the whole work before sending it to the printer.[138] This presumably happened in 1553 or

131 *Commentarius in quatuor capita prioris epistolae ad Corinthios* (Wittenberg: J. Lufft, 1530) sigs. T8b-X4a.
132 Items 103 II and 113 I (Ganoczy, BAC, 194, 198) are other commentaries of Bugenhagen.
133 *Commentarius in epistolas Pauli ad Corinthios* (1551) (CR 15:1068). The 1524 commentary on Corinthians does not contain this comment.
134 Bucer, in his 1524 *Handel mit Cunrat Treger* (*Martini Buceri Opera Omnia: Deutsche Schriften*, vol. 2 (Gütersloh: G. Mohn and Paris: Presses Universitaires de France, 1962) 106) mentions Bernard, Gregory 'und andern lieben heyligen vaettern' under 'Yrrthumb der vaetter'. While Calvin could not have read this, Bucer could have expressed this view to him at Strassburg. Luther, in his 1533 *Von der Winkelmesse und Pfaffenweihe* (WA 38:222) states that Bernard, Gregory and Bonaventure were saved through fire. Calvin could not have read the German, but there was a Latin edition the following year.
135 C.XXIV. The following have been examined: Petrus Artopoeus (1546); Cardinal Cajetan (1539); Ambrosius Catharinus (= Lancelot Politi) (1552); Dionysius Carthusianus (1896 edition); Aloisius Lippoman (1546); Martin Luther (1544); Philipp Melanchthon (1523); Wolfgang Musculus (1554); Johannes Oecolampadius (1536); Conrad Pellican (1536); William Pepin (1528); Augustinus Eugubinus Steuchus (1529 and 1535); Thomas Aquinas (1563 edition); Franciscus Zephyrus (1572 edition); Jacob Ziegler (1548); Ulrich Zwingli (1527).
136 Lane, 'Calvin's Sources of St. Bernard', 273: 'the possibility of Calvin having used the *Catena* can by no means be discounted'.
137 See chapter 8, below, where n. 63 explains why Lippoman is not the source of the Bernard citation in particular.
138 N. Colladon, *Vie de Calvin* (CO 21:72, 75). R. Peter and J.-F. Gilmont, *Bibliotheca Calviniana*, vol. 1 (Geneva: Droz, 1991) 519–23. It should be noted, however, that Calvin delivered his Psalms commentary to the printer in batches (T. H. L. Parker, *Calvin's Old Testament Commentaries* (Edinburgh: T&T Clark, 1986) 31, n. 56).

1554, at a time when Calvin was probably reading his newly-acquired Bernard volume. The insertion of an apt quotation would not be unnatural.

In 1557 Calvin quoted from Bernard in his commentary on Psalm 55, with a play on the words *fugere* and *fugare*.[139] There are some apparent parallels.[140] The *Postilla* of Cardinal Hugh of St Cher on the biblical text quotes at this point in the Psalms a similar Bernardine wordplay, as does Petrus de Herentals in the following century. But the overlap is limited and Hugh and Peter are not actually quoting the same Bernardine source as Calvin.[141] A similar quotation also appears several times in Bucer's *Consilium theologicum privatim conscriptum*.[142] Here the text is slightly closer to Calvin's, but with no connection to the Psalms, and the passage quoted is again not the same as Calvin's. Also, Bucer's work existed only in manuscript form and the only way that Calvin could have derived the quotation from this work would have been during his time at Strassburg, more than ten years previously. The quotation appears again in Bucer's works, in his 1550 *De regno Christi*, but this time the similarity in wording reduces to no more than the play between *fugare* and *fugere*.[143] The *Flores* does have the correct passage,[144] but by far the most likely hypothesis is

139 C.XXVI. Calvin lectured on the Psalms from 1552 to 1555/6. It was also discussed in the *Congrégations* from 1555 to 1559. The commentary was written from about 1553 to 1557 (Parker, *Calvin's Old Testament Commentaries*, 30f.). Parker has suggested, verbally, that the *Congrégations* might have served as a resource for Calvin's commentaries, with many of the talented exiles supplying material for him to use. If this is so, it could account for some of Calvin's understanding of the exegetical tradition, but is unlikely to account for a rhetorical embellishment like c.XXVI.

140 The following have been examined: Gabriel Brebia (1477); Johann Brenz (1552); Martin Bucer (1554); Johann Bugenhagen (1524); Cardinal Cajetan (1530); Dionysius Carthusianus (1553); Brother Felix (1522); Mantonius Flaminius (1547); John Folengius (1549); Franciscus de Puteo (1520); Ludolphus Carthusianus (1521); Philipp Melanchthon (1553–55); Wolfgang Musculus (1551); Brother Pelbartus (1504); Conrad Pellican (1532); Jacob Perez (1506); Petrus de Herentals (1488); Peter Lombard (PL 191); Richard of Le Mans (1541, via PL 191); Reignier Snoy (1536); Francis Titelmann (1531); Johannes de Turrecremata (c.1513); Jacobus de Valencia (1506); Jerome Varlenius (1557); François Vatable (1556); Ulrich Zwingli (1532). Luther's 1513–16 *Dictata* were not printed until later but they have been examined.

141 Bernard wrote 'hostem ... nec fugere possumus ... nec fugare' (*VI p P* 2:5, BO 5:212); Calvin quoted 'genus hostium ... neque fugere neque fugare datur'; the *Postilla* reads 'amarissima ... non fugare non fugere eos potest' (vol. 2, sig. v.8a) (Basel: J. Amerbach, 1498–1502 edition); Peter has almost the same as Hugh. Peter and Hugh are quoting *SC* 33:16 (BO 1:244). Note the difference in order of *fugare* and *fugere*. Calvin's use of the word *hostis* confirms that *VI p P* 2:5 is his source. The same quotation is also found in Thomas Hibernicus, *Manipulus florum* (Piacenza: J. de Tyela, 1483) sig. c8a (s.v. *clericus*).

142 P. Fraenkel (ed.), *Martini Buceri Opera Latina*, vol. 4 (Leiden, etc.: E. J. Brill, 1988) 8, 11, 32, 176. (On the probable date of this work (1540–41), cf. pp. XIV–XXII.) The first of these quotations is 'non fugare nec fugere eos potest' (p. 8) but the rest are 'nec fugere nec fugare', with two other words in the middle in the second passage (p. 11). Bernard is not mentioned in the third passage (p. 32). The only indication of source is in the first passage (p. 8) where *SC* 77 is cited, an error for *SC* 33:16. The word *hostis*, which links Calvin's quotation with *VI p P* 2:5, does not appear.

143 *De regno Christi* 1:4 (F. Wendel (ed.), *Martini Buceri Opera Latina*, vol. 15 (Gütersloh: G. Mohn and Paris: Presses Universitaires de France, 1955) 39): 'Non fugare, non fugere eos potest', in the context of a long quotation from *SC* 33:15f.

144 Cf. n. 115, above.

Calvin is simply quoting a pleasing word play, remembered from his recent reading of the 1552 *Opera omnia*.

(b) Correspondence

Calvin's correspondence is another possible source of patristic citations. His original draft of the *Vivere apud Christum non dormire animis sanctis* (later called *Psychopannychia*) was based on notes supplied by a friend describing the Anabaptist position.[145] There was some correspondence with Neuchâtel before the writing of the 1544 *Brieve instruction contre Anabaptistes*.[146] It is possible that some of the patristic citations in these or others works were derived from letters. All the surviving letters that Calvin received, up to the date of his last citation of Bernard in the 1559 *Institutio*, have been examined.[147] There are a number of citations of the fathers together with some quotation and even the giving of references.[148] But no mention of Bernard has been found. This does not prove that Calvin did not receive useful Bernardine quotations from friends, by letter or in person, but such a supposition must remain pure conjecture.

(c) General Reading

Biblical commentaries and personal correspondence are two ways in which Calvin could have derived some of his Bernardine citations from other authors. This could also have happened through his general reading. An examination has been made of a number of works that Calvin is either certain or likely to have read and a modest number of parallels have been found. None has been found in Peter Lombard's *Libri quatuor sententiarum* which were a source for some of Calvin's other citations[149] but contain no reference to Bernard, the two being contemporaries. The editors of the critical edition of Lombard have recorded four allusions but these bear no relation to Calvin's use of Bernard.[150] Calvin's citations will be reviewed in chronological order, considering possible sources and, for convenience, reviewing parallels already found in patristic anthologies.

Calvin's first citation of Bernard is a quotation of his definition of *liberum arbitrium*. The text of the quotation is too short to decide between the different printed editions and the manuscripts. But it looks as if the source is none of these. Bernard comes in a series of definitions of the term: Origen, (pseudo-)Augustine, Bernard, Anselm, Peter Lombard and Thomas Aquinas. The Augustine, Bernard and Anselm definitions are found

145 Cf. the 1534 preface (CO 5:169f.).
146 Cf. *Epist*. 534, 538, 540 (CO 11:681f., 689, 692), written between Farel and Calvin in February to April of that year. Cf. also the dedicatory epistle at the beginning of the *Brieve instruction* (CO 7:49).
147 These are found in CO 10b-17.
148 Quotations are found in *Epist*. 590 (CO 11:781–802) and references are given in *Epist*. 1950 (CO 15:131f.). Many letters addressed to Calvin contain citations of the fathers, especially Augustine.
149 Smits, SAOJC 1:206–11. It was less often a source after 1539 (ibid., 211).
150 *Libri IV Sententiarum* (Quaracchi: Collegium S. Bonaventurae, 1916 – 2nd edition) at Lib. 3, dist. 25, c. 3; Lib. 4, dist. 3, c. 4; Lib. 4, dist. 4, c. 4; Lib. 4, dist. 6, c. 3 (pp. 668, 757, 765, 780).

together in Gabriel Biel's commentary on Peter Lombard's *Sentences*,[151] and were found by Biel in Alexander of Hales,[152] whom he cites. These definitions are also found in Johann Altenstaig's *Vocabularius theologie*, which drew heavily upon Biel's work.[153] The juxtaposition of the three definitions would indicate that Calvin acquired them either from one of these works or from some other work which mediated the same tradition. The second citation strengthens the likelihood that the source is Biel or someone in his tradition. Calvin accuses Bernard of a semi-Pelagianism of which he is not guilty.[154] Biel, unlike Alexander, expounded Bernard in a semi-Pelagian fashion,[155] so Biel or another author in his tradition is a plausible source for the second citation.[156] It is likely, therefore, that the first two citations reflect Bernard mediated via Biel or someone similar, rather than Calvin's first-hand reading of Bernard.[157] The third citation may also come via an undiscovered intermediate source or may indicate that Calvin was also reading Bernard for himself.

The one other citation from 1539 refers to Bernard's protest against clerical corruption. Bucer had made a similar comment in 1530.[158] Since this work was written at Strassburg and since that year Calvin cited Bernard for the first time, it is quite possible that Bucer pointed Calvin to this aspect of Bernard's teaching. That would then have led Calvin to read Bernard for himself and thus to the lengthy citations of the 1543 *Institutio*.

The volume of the quotations in the 1543 *Institutio* shows that Calvin had been studying Bernard's works for himself. But there are a number of

---

151 G. Biel, *Collectorium circa quattuor libros Sententiarum. Liber secundus* (Tübingen: J. C. B. Mohr (Paul Siebeck), 1984) 483, 485 (Lib. 2, dist. 25, q. unica, art. 1).

152 Alexander of Hales, *Summa theologica* Pars Ia, Lib. 2, Inq. 4, tract. 1, sect. 2, quaest. 3, tit. 3, memb. 2, cap. 2 ((Quaracchi: Collegium S. Bonaventurae, 1928) 471). Alexander's *Glossa in Quatuor Libros Sententiarum*, Lib. 2, dist. 24:5, also has the three quotations together, but the 'Augustine' quotation is incomplete ((Quaracchi: Collegium S. Bonaventurae, 1952) 209). The same is true of Bonaventure's commentary on the Sentences (Lib. 2, dist. 25, pars 1, dub. 2) (Venice, 1477 edition, sig. s6a, col. 1). The full text of the 'Augustine' quotation is found in Lombard, *Sententiae* Lib. 2, dist. 24, c. 5 (PL 192:702). While Calvin *could* have pieced his definitions together from Alexander's or Bonaventure's Sentence commentary with the help of a different passage of Lombard, sources such as Biel, Alexander of Hales or Altenstaig which have all three definitions together are more plausible.

153 J. Altenstaig, *Vocabularius theologie* (Hagenau: H. Gran, 1517) f. 134b, s.v. 'liberum arbitrium'.

154 Cf. Lane, *Calvin and Bernard*, 36–47.

155 Cf. H. J. McSorley, *Luther: Right or Wrong?* (New York *et al.*: Newman and Minneapolis: Augsburg, 1969) 210f.; L. Grane, *Contra Gabrielem* (Copenhagen: Gyldendal, 1962) 118–36.

156 Altenstaig's entry under 'voluntas' (*Vocabularius theologie*, f. 273b) is relevant to c.II, but is less complete. It is also possible that c.II could have been inspired by a misinterpretation of the quotation from Gra. 11:36 in Biel, *Collectorium* Lib. II, dist. 25, q. unica, art. 3, dub. 1 (p. 490).

157 Pighius, *De libero hominis arbitrio et divina gratia* (Cologne: M. Novesian, 1542) has two of Calvin's quotations of Bernard, but only because Pighius is seeking to refute Calvin's use of them in the 1539 *Institutio*. C.II is attacked (f. XIa) and the words of c.III are used without mention of Bernard's name (f. XIIb).

158 C.IV is parallelled in Bucer, *Epistola Apologetica* in C. Augustijn, P. Fraenkel and M. Lienhard (eds), *Martini Buceri Opera Latina*, vol. 1 (Leiden: E. J. Brill, 1982) 101f.

partial overlaps between his quotations and those of others. Parts of his quotations from Bernard's fifth sermon on the dedication of the church are found in Gabriel Biel's *Canonis misse expositio* and in Johann Gropper's *Enchiridion christianae institutionis.*[159] Again, parts of his quotation from Bernard's 61st sermon on the Song of Solomon are also found (without indication of source) in Gropper's *Enchiridion.*[160] Calvin also quotes at length from Bernard's *De consideratione*. John Wyclif cited the same work in his *Tractatus de potestate pape*, including parts of Calvin's quotations, as did Gabriel Biel in his *Canonis misse expositio.*[161] Bullinger's *Ad Ioannis Cochlei ... libellum ... orthodoxa responsio* contains part of one of Calvin's citations, but could not have influenced him as it did not appear until 1544.[162]

What does this prove about Calvin's use of Bernard in the 1543 *Institutio*? Probably not very much. It shows that Calvin was not the first to use these works, but that was obvious anyway. Apart from a very brief quotation that was covered by the *Flores*, none of these quotations could have been acquired other than by reading the works of Bernard himself. This is clearly how Calvin acquired them. But what led Calvin to turn to Bernard in the first place? Did specific people stimulate him to study Bernard and point his attention to certain passages of Bernard? There are two prime candidates. Bucer influenced Calvin at this time, but the lack of overlap with his *Commonplace Book* cautions against too readily assuming that he also influenced Calvin's use of Bernard. Bucer may have been the one to point Calvin to the *De consideratione*, which accounts for half of the citations in the 1543 *Institutio*. The other half are on the theme of justification and here the likely influence is the Hagenau–Worms–Regensburg series of colloquies in general[163] and the contact with Gropper in particular. There are two overlaps with Gropper's citations. The experience of the colloquies and the debates that took place must surely have influenced Calvin and the evangelical use of Bernard by a Roman Catholic theologian may well have stimulated and directed his interest.

There was just one citation in Calvin's 1543 reply to Pighius that was not adequately covered by the *Flores*, the content of which is found in

---

159 C.IXa is partly covered in H. A. Oberman and W. J. Courtenay, with D. E. Zerfoss (eds), *Gabrielis Biel canonis misse expositio* (Wiesbaden: F. Steiner, 1963–67) 4:54f. (lect. 82). C.XI is partly covered by *Enchiridion*, in *Canones Concilii Provincialis Coloniensis* (Cologne: P. Quentel, 1538) f. 169b. Cc.IXa; XI were also covered in Bodius, *Unio dissidentium*, the former only partially (nn. 125f., above).

160 C.Xb is partly covered in *Enchiridion*, f. 169a. C.Xa was partly covered in the *Pharetra* (n. 123, above). Cc.Xc; XIIc were partly covered by Thomas Hibernicus, *Manipulus florum* and Dominicus Nanus Mirabellus, *Polyanthea* (n. 123, above).

161 J. Wyclif, *Tractatus de potestate pape* (London, 1907), where c.XIVe is partly covered in ch. 5 (p. 86) and c.XVIa, e-f is covered in chs 7f. (pp. 136f., 170f.) (London: Wyclif Society, 1907). C.XIVe is partly covered in Oberman, etc. (eds), *Expositio*, 1:217 (lect. 23).

162 Chapter 28 contains part of c.XIV, with a significant difference in the text, which suggests that Bullinger was not following Calvin (Zurich: Froschouer, 1544) sig. qq 2b.

163 Smits, SAOJC 1:58, maintains that the Regensburg *Acta* influenced the 1543 *Institutio*.

Bucer's 1531 *Apologie der Confessio Tetrapolitana*.[164] While Calvin could not have read this German work, Bucer could have pointed him to the Bernard material during their time together in Strassburg. But Calvin did not receive Pighius's work until he had returned to Geneva. It must also be remembered that the reply to Pighius was written after the 1543 *Institutio* and therefore after Calvin's reading of the *Opera omnia*. It is true that Calvin does not here quote Bernard at length, as in the 1543 and 1559 *Institutio*. Superficially, his use of Bernard here resembles that in the 1539 *Institutio*: brief citations on the subject of grace and freewill with no references being given. But in fact there are important differences. Whereas in 1539 Calvin is mainly critical of Bernard, here he confidently claims him as predominantly on his side. This is supported by specific appeals to his teaching. The impression is given, and is confirmed by the 1543 *Institutio*, that Calvin's knowledge extends not just to a few passages (as in the 1539 *Institutio*) but to a broad knowledge of Bernard's teaching. The brevity of the citations is most likely due to the fact that Calvin was working from his memory of reading Bernard at Strassburg. The most likely source, therefore, is Calvin's reading of the *Opera omnia*, with possible (but not very likely) influence from Bucer or from another source.

The quotations of 1544 and 1545 are strong candidates, because of their problematic nature, for being derived from Calvin's general reading. The *Opera omnia* are excluded by the omission of a phrase which Calvin quotes, but two of the partial editions are close enough to be possible as Calvin's source.[165] On the other hand, some manuscripts in the *Perfecta* and *Media* traditions come considerably closer to Calvin's text.[166] A section in the *Flores* contains the missing phrase, but does not cover the whole of Calvin's quotations.[167] Where then did Calvin find this material? The *Flores* would not suffice on its own but a partial edition is possible. A manuscript is also possible, but unlikely given Calvin's method elsewhere. It is possible that he might have put together his quotations from memory of having previously read two different versions, but this is unlikely.

What then is Calvin's source? How could he draw on the manuscript tradition without using manuscripts? One answer would be for him to derive the quotations from a printed edition of a medieval writer who had himself read Bernard in manuscript form. One possible source springs to mind. In the preface to his *Vivere apud Christum non dormire animis sanctis* (which is dated 1534 but was first published in 1542) and in the 1543 *Institutio* Calvin refers to the error of pope John XXII on the matter of the faithful departed and cites Jean Gerson as his source.[168] Since the Bernard

---

164 C.VI is covered by M. Bucer, *Opera Omnia: Deutsche Schriften*, vol. 3 (Gütersloh: G. Mohn and Paris: Presses Universitaires de France, 1969) 241f. It was also covered by Barnes, *Sententiae* and Westheimer, *Conciliationem* (see n. 127, above).
165 See at nn. 34–37, above.
166 See at nn. 67–71, above.
167 See n. 107, above.
168 CO 5:171f.; OS 5:130 (4:7:28). For more details on the Gerson source, cf. Tylenda, 'Calvin and Avignon Sermons', 48f. The material surrounding the John XXII debate would be a likely source were it not that Calvin clearly misunderstood John's position (Lane, *Calvin and Bernard*, 74f.). For that debate, cf. G. Hoffmann, *Der Streit über die selige Schau Gottes (1331–38)* (Leipzig: Hinrichs'sche Buchhandlung,

quotations under consideration appear shortly after, in 1544 and 1545, and since Gerson drew heavily on Bernard, he would appear to be a prime suspect. Examination of his works has not, however, proved fruitful.[169] This is perhaps not surprising since if Gerson had been Calvin's source one would have expected the Bernard quotations to appear in the 1542 edition. There were a number of writings on the issue of soul sleep in the years prior to Calvin's work and it is possible that one of these might have provided the quotations, but a search through these writings has been fruitless.[170] Outside of these works, part of one of the quotations has been found in Gabriel Biel.[171]

There is another factor that suggests that the quotations are derived from Calvin's own reading of Bernard. The Bernard quotation in 1544 is added to a series of patristic quotations taken from the 1542 *Vivere apud Christum non dormire animis sanctis.*[172] Calvin in 1544 merely adds a Bernard citation to an existing dossier. This is precisely what he did with the justification citations in the 1543 *Institutio* (based on his Strassburg reading) and in the 1559 *Institutio* (following his renewed reading of Bernard from 1552).[173] Adding an extra illustrative quotation from Bernard, which makes no new point, is just what Calvin tends to do after reading Bernard for himself. The provisional verdict must be that Calvin used a partial edition, but further research may yet uncover an intermediary medieval source, such as Occam or Biel.

Some of the citations from the 1559 *Institutio* are partially paralleled in anthologies.[174] But no parallels have been found in other authors, with one major exception. Calvin quotes relatively briefly (for him) from Bernard's

---

1917), which mentions Calvin on pp. 74, 177f. For documents from the time H. Denifle, *Chartularium Universitatis Parisiensis*, vol. 2:I (Paris: Delalain, 1891) 426–41, has been examined but yielded nothing.

169 These have been checked in two ways. Likely items in his *Opera* (Basel, 1518) have been examined and all of the Bernard references in J. Gerson, *Oeuvres Complètes*, 10 vols (Paris, etc.: Desclée, 1960–73) have been checked via the index of names. It is clear that Gerson was not the source for these or any other of Calvin's Bernard citations.

170 For accounts of the literature cf. J.-U. Hwang, *Der junge Calvin und seine Psychopannychia* (Frankfurt, etc.: Peter Lang, 1991) 118–27, 161–78; T. George, 'Calvin's *Psychopannychia*: Another Look' in E. J. Furcha (ed.), *In Honor of John Calvin, 1509–64* (Montreal: Faculty of Religious Studies, McGill University, 1987) 305–12; H. A. Oberman, '*Initia Calvini*: The Matrix of Calvin's Reformation' in W. H. Neuser (ed.), *Calvinus Sacrae Scripturae Professor. Calvin as Confessor of Holy Scripture* (Grand Rapids: Eerdmans, 1994) 140–45.

171 The second half of c.XVIIIa has been found in Oberman, etc. (eds), *Expositio*, 3:106 (lect. 67). Lecture 67 is on the relevant topic and includes discussion of Bernard's teaching and reference to *OS* 2 and 3 (3:114–16).
    Some of the works of Occam in opposition to Pope John XXII have been examined, without success: *Compendium errorum Johannis XXII*; *Defensorium contra errores Johannis Papae XXII*.

172 The quotations of CO 7:125f. are taken entirely from CO 5:214f.

173 Lane, *Calvin and Bernard*, 15f., 19f.

174 Cc.XXVII; XXXII; XXXV by Andreas, *Sententiae*; c.XXVIII by Barnes, *Sententiae* and Westheimer, *Conciliationem*; cc.XXXV; XXXVI; XL by Musculus, *Enchiridion* and *Catechesis*; cc.XXXV; XL by Freyesleben, *Sylva*; c.XXXIXb by *Pharetra* and Hofmeister, *Loci communes* (see nn. 127, 123, above).

first sermon on the Annunciation[175] and here there are a remarkable number of parallels. This must be one of the most quoted Bernardine passages in the sixteenth century, if not the most. The following examples are doubtless far from complete. In each case the quotation partly overlaps with Calvin, unless otherwise indicated. Prior to the Reformation it appears in the *Pharetra*, which was first printed in about 1475, and was quoted by Gabriel Biel.[176] Luther cited it five times.[177] It appears twice in his 1515–16 lectures on Romans, which were not published at the time.[178] It comes again in his 1517 lectures on Hebrews.[179] Luther also quotes it in a written response submitted to Cardinal Cajetan at their meeting in Augsburg in October 1518.[180] Finally, Luther refers to the sermon, without quoting it, in his 1527 lecture on 1 John 4:10.[181]

That same year the first edition of Bodius, *Unio Dissidentium* was published, containing a passage from the sermon.[182] This anthology had a significant influence upon the subsequent development of the genre in the sixteenth century.[183] Following Bodius's lead, a further nine anthologies prior to 1559 include the sermon.[184]

In 1531 Melanchthon twice quotes it in his *Apologia Confessionis Augustanae*.[185] The following year it appears in the introduction to his commentary on Romans.[186] A few years later it appears in the fourth of the Wittenberg Articles.[187] After a long history of Protestant usage it was taken up by the eirenic Catholic theologian Johann Gropper and appears in his *Enchiridion* (1538).[188] It also appears in the Regensburg Book of 1541, the

175 C.XXXIII.
176 *Pharetra*, section *de fide*. Biel loosely quotes part of the material covered in c.XXXIIIa in his 1484–88 *Canonis misse expositio* (Oberman, etc. (eds), *Expositio*, 2:442).
177 F. Posset, '*Bernardus Redivivus*: The *Wirkungsgeschichte* of a Medieval Sermon in the Reformation of the Sixteenth Century', *Cistercian Studies* 22 (1987) 239–49, discusses Luther's use of the sermon. Cf. also P. Manns, 'Zum Gespräch zwischen M. Luther und der katholischen Theologie' in T. Mannermaa, A. Ghiselli and S. Peura (hrsg.), *Thesaurus Lutheri* (Helsinki, 1987) 135–37, 143–47. T. Bell, 'Testimonium Spiritus Sancti – An Example of Bernard-Reception in Luther's Theology', *Bijdragen, Tijdschrift voor Filosofie en Theologie* 53 (1992) 62–72; idem, *Divus Bernhardus. Bernhard von Clairvaux in Martin Luthers Schriften* (Mainz: Philipp von Zabern, 1993) 31–38, 66f., 91–106, 133–37.
178 On 8.16 (WA 56:79, 369f., cf. 57/I:189f.).
179 On 5.1 (WA 57/III:169).
180 WA 2:15f.
181 WA 20:746.
182 Ch. 8 (pp. 147f.). See n. 124, above, for the edition used.
183 Cf. Lane, 'Justification in Sixteenth-Century Patristic Anthologies', 77–85.
184 For six of these, cf. nn. 123, 127, above. In addition to the passages noted there: Westheimer, *Conciliationem* (Basel, 1536) 444 (not overlapping Calvin); Hofmeister, *Loci communes* (Ingolstadt, 1547) f. 178a-b (not overlapping Calvin); B. Westheimer, *Conciliatio Patrum et Conciliorum* (Zurich: J. Gesner, 1563) 172f., 184; Guy de Brès, *Le baston de la foy chrestienne* (Lyons, 1555) ff. 37b-38a, 60a-62a; A. Musculus, *Catechismus* (Frankfurt: J. Eichorn, 1555) f. 30a-b; idem, *Catechesis* (Frankfurt, 1556) 122, 162f., 173f. (not overlapping Calvin).
185 Articles 12, 27 (CR 27:549, 633).
186 CR 15:520.
187 G. Mentz (hrsg.), *Die Wittenberger Artikel von 1536* (Leipzig: A. Deichert, 1905) 30f.
188 *Enchiridion*, ff. 169a,170b. The marginal reference in 170b is to 'Ann serm 2' but the citation is from *Ann* 1:1 and overlaps c.XXXIIIa.

chief author of which was Gropper.[189] A further occurrence which can be traced to Gropper is in Benedetto of Mantua's *Beneficio di Cristo* (1543).[190] According to Tommaso Bozza, this quotation, together with others, is taken from Gropper's *Enchiridion*.[191] In the same year the sermon is quoted in the new edition of Melanchthon's *Loci Communes*.[192] Melanchthon also quotes from it (but without overlapping Calvin's quotation) in his preface to the second volume of Luther's *Opera omnia* (Wittenberg, 1546), stating that it influenced the young Luther.[193] That same year, the sermon was quoted by no less than five different participants at the Council of Trent, during the debates on the doctrine of justification, twice overlapping with Calvin.[194]

What does this prove? Calvin's use of the sermon comes after a long tradition of quoting it. Calvin quotes from the same parts of the sermon as others, but his quotation is not fully covered by anyone else's. Clearly his discovery of the passage was not independent of the use of it by others. But caution must be exercised here. Calvin would certainly have encountered it in 1541 at the Regensburg Colloquy, via the Regensburg Book. But he does not himself make use of it in his next edition of the *Institutio*, the 1543 edition which contained much new Bernardine material. He waits eighteen years before incorporating it into the 1559 edition. This shows that while Calvin's use of Bernard may have been influenced by others, in the last resort (at least from the time of the 1543 *Institutio*) it was his own personal interpretation and not a copy of other people's Bernard dossier.

Doubtless a further examination of sixteenth-century literature would reveal other parallels to Calvin's citations, almost all incomplete. But the not inconsiderable range of literature so far surveyed has yielded no clear evidence of influence except for the first citation of 1539. The quotations of 1544/45 were probably taken from a partial edition, but may be derived from an as yet undiscovered late medieval author who read Bernard in manuscripts. This evidence greatly reinforces the conviction that, from

189 G. Pfeilschifter (hrsg.), *Acta Reformationis Catholicae Ecclesiam Germaniae Concernentia Seculi XVI*, vol. 6 (Regensburg: F. Pustet, 1974) 30–54 has the three surviving drafts of the article on justification. *Ann* 1 appears in the first of these only (37f.). For Gropper's authorship, cf. H. Eells, 'The Origin of the Regensburg Book', *Princeton Theological Review* 26 (1928) 358–64. R. Stupperich, 'Der Ursprung des Regensburger Buches von 1541 und seine Rechtfertigungslehre', *Archiv für Reformationsgeschichte* 36 (1939) 88–116, shows how the fifth article on justification (where the Bernard quotations are found) is drawn from Gropper's *Enchiridion*.
190 Benedetto da Mantova, *Il Beneficio di Cristo*, Corpus Reformatorum Italicorum (Florence: G. C. Sansoni and Chicago: Newberry Library, 1972) 80f.
191 T. Bozza, *Nuovi Studi sulla Riforma in Italia. I. Il Beneficio di Cristo* (Rome: Storia e Letteratura, 1976) 370–73.
192 CR 21:748.
193 CR 6:159. Bell, 'Testimonium Spiritus Sancti', assesses the accuracy of this claim and decides in Melanchthon's favour, apart from the question of dating.
194 By Cardinal Seripando (CT 5:374, 12:634), Aloisius Lippoman (CT 5:460), Franciscus Visdomini (CT 5:533f.), Richard of Le Mans (CT 5:539), Diego Laynez (CT 5:620), *De certitudine gratiae* (CT 12:702). Cf. Lane, *Calvin and Bernard*, 70. C.XXXIIIa is overlapped by Laynez and c.XXXIIIb is slightly overlapped by Lippoman. Johannes Consilii also responds to the quotation of Richard of Le Mans (CT 5:546).

the time of the 1543 *Institutio,* apart from the 1544/45 quotations, the one significant source for Calvin is his own reading of the *Opera omnia* of Bernard. He was not unaware of other people's use of Bernard and doubt-less not uninfluenced by this, but it is clear that the lengthy quotations in the 1543 and 1559 editions of the *Institutio* are the fruit of his own extensive reading of Bernard.

VI. CONCLUSION

What then were Calvin's sources for his citations of Bernard? A fairly clear picture has emerged. His first quotation, in the 1539 *Institutio,* was drawn from Altenstaig or Biel or from some other work in the same tradition. The three remaining citations from that year do not reveal much knowledge of Bernard. They could have been derived from a wide range of printed editions or from the *Flores* or from a second-hand knowledge of Bernard derived from a number of possible sources. It is neither possible nor very important to know where this minimal understanding of Bernard originated.

The 1543 *Institutio,* by contrast, shows that Calvin had studied the *Opera omnia* of Bernard for himself. This edition was nearing completion in January 1542 and it is likely that the Bernardine material was written at Strassburg. It is not certain which edition Calvin used but he almost certainly left it behind when he returned to Geneva. The choice of *some* of the passages quoted *may* have been influenced by others, especially by the debates at the colloquies and Gropper in particular.

The quotations in the 1543 *Defensio* are probably drawn from memory of reading at Strassburg. The only other fresh material before 1554 comes in the enigmatic quotations of 1544 and 1545. He probably used a 'partial' edition, but might have read them in a late-medieval author. The other citations in this period were all taken from the 1543 *Institutio* except for Calvin's comment in the 1546 1 Corinthians commentary, which was a commonplace of the Protestant exegetical tradition.

The first sign of new material comes in the 1554 Genesis and 1557 Psalms commentaries. No alternative sources have been found and these appear to be the first-fruits of a renewed reading of the *Opera omnia.* Their dates support the theory that Calvin acquired the 1552 Basel edition of the *Opera omnia* still in the Genevan library and with it resumed his study of Bernard. An *Opera omnia,* probably this copy, was also the source for the 1559 *Institutio.* The new citations in this edition are not related to Calvin's particular interests at this time[195] which would suggest that the reason for adding them was a renewed reading of Bernard.

This study has shown beyond any reasonable doubt that Calvin's main use of Bernard, in the 1543 and 1559 *Institutio,* is drawn from his own reading of the *Opera omnia.* It has also shown with a high degree of likelihood that Calvin drew at least one quotation from the Biel-Altenstaig tradition. It is possible that the quotations in the 1544 and 1545 anti-Anabaptist works may have been drawn from an as yet undiscovered intermediary source. Some of the other citations, notably those before 1543

195 Cf. Mooi, KDE 191.

and those outside the *Institutio, may* be derived from other sources. But the possibility of this may be due entirely to their brevity, which also makes it impossible to be sure one way or the other. There is a possibility that the *selection* of a number of Calvin's citations is derived from others' works even if the *text* of the quotation is not. Either way, we see that Calvin's prime source of Bernard was the *Opera omnia* and that there are probably a number of other intermediary influences rather than sources. Thus Calvin read Bernard especially during his time at Strassburg and during the final decade or so of his life at Geneva, each time in an *Opera omnia*.

VII. BIBLIOGRAPHY OF EDITIONS OF BERNARD UP TO 1559[196]

The only editions listed are those in Latin up to 1559 (the date of Calvin's last citation) that contain works cited by Calvin. For the meaning of J3, etc. see n. 13, above. There are many minor verbal errors in BBJ but space does not permit an account of these. Places and dates which are deduced rather than explicitly stated in the edition are put in brackets. Under 'Publisher' are also listed those whose device appears on the title-page and those who bore the cost of an edition. It should be noted that sometimes at Paris or Lyons the same edition was published simultaneous by a number of printers in joint editions varying only in the title-pages and/or colophons. See, for example J379/ J*379, J462 / J*462 / J**462, J526 / J527 / J*527 and probably J484/ J*484 and J508/J*508/J*510.

Under 'Source(s)' are listed the libraries whose copies have been examined. Where more than is listed, the comparison with Calvin's text has usually been made from one only, the other volumes being consulted in order to check whether they were the same edition.[197] The following abbreviations are used:

a   Bornem-aan-de-Schelde (Belgium): Abdij Sinte Bernaerdts
b   Cambridge: Caius College
c   Cambridge: Christ's College
d   Cambridge: Clare College
e   Cambridge: Corpus Christi College
f   Cambridge: Pembroke College
g   Cambridge: St John's College
h   Cambridge: Sidney Sussex College
i   Cambridge: Trinity Hall

196   The following abbreviations are used: H = Hain, *Repertorium Bibliographicum*; C = W. A. Copinger, *Supplement to Hain's Repertorium Bibliographicum* (London: Henry Sotheran, 1895–1902); R = D. Reichling, *Appendices ad Hainii-Copingeri Repertorium Bibliographicum* (Munich: J. Rosenthal, 1905–11); GW = *Gesamtkatalog der Wiegendrucke* (Leipzig: K. W. Hiersemann, 1925–40); IA = *Index Aureliensis* (Baden-Baden: Valentin Koerner *et al.*, 1965ff.). H n = item n in Hain, etc. H-C n means an edition that appears in both Hain and Copinger.
197   In the first years of this study, in the early 1970s, I did not make such full bibliographical notes on each edition as in later years. It is possible, therefore, that in my early searches I may, for example, have missed instances where more than one publisher produced editions in the same place and the same year. Since these are likely to be joint editions any such omission is probably not serious.

j   Cambridge: University Library
k   Geneva: Bibliothèque publique et universitaire
l   London: British Library
m   Munich: Staatsbibliothek
n   Oxford: Bodleian Library
o   Oxford: Corpus Christi College
p   Oxford: Jesus College
q   Oxford: Merton College
r   Oxford: New College
s   Oxford: Queen's College
t   Oxford: St Edmund Hall
u   Oxford: St John's College
v   Paris: Bibliothèque nationale
w   Poitiers: Bibliothèque municipale
x   Strasbourg: Bibliothèque nationale et universitaire
y   Tübingen: Universitätsbibliothek
z   Vienna: Nationalbibliothek

BBJ no.	GW/IA[198]	Contents	Place: Publisher, Date	Source(s)
J3	GW 3923	Epistolae et tractatus	[Strassburg: H. Eggestein, c.1470–80]	l, n
J7	GW 3905	Opuscula	[Cologne, c.1470–80]	j, l
J20	GW 3913	De consideratione	[Utrecht: N. Ketelaer and G. de Leempt, c.1473–74]	j, l, n, v
J30	GW 3940	Sermones	Mainz: P. Schöffer, 1475	j, l, n, y
J37	GW 3914	De consideratione	Augsburg: A. Sorg, 1477	j, l, n, s, y
J56[199]	H-C 2888	De consideratione	Zwolle, 1481	–
J58	GW 3924	Epistolae	Brussels: [Fratres Vitae Communis], 1481	j, l, n
J60	GW 3934	Sermones in Cantica	Rostock: Fratres Communis Vitae, 1481	l
J61	GW 3941	Sermones	Brussels: [Fratres Vitae Communis], 1481	j, l, n
J62	GW 3942	Sermones	Speier: P. Drach, 1481–82	l, n, v, w, y
J64[200]	H 2842	Sermones	[Speier: P. Drach, post-1481]	–
J68	GW 3935	Sermones in Cantica	Pavia: N. Girardengus, 1482	l, n, v
J76[201]		Sermones	Speier: P. Drach, 1484	–
J78	GW 3916	De consideratione	[Zwolle: P. van Os, c.1484–95]	j, v
J88	GW 3915	De consideratione	Zwolle: P. van Os, 1486	j, l
J146	GW 3926	Epistolae	Basel: [N. Kessler], 1494	l, n
J147	GW 3925	Epistolae	Paris: [P. Levet], 1494	j, l, n, r, v

198 Where the edition is listed in GW or IA the item number is here given (without the IA prefix 117.). Where it appears in neither but is in Hain, that number is given instead.
199 'Édition fort douteuse' (BBJ 18). 'Wohl irrtümlich für Nr 3915' (= J88) (GW 3:668).
200 This is actually H-C 2846 (= J62), according to GW 3:684. (GW mistakenly states that H 2842 rather H 2846 is in Copinger as well as Hain.) BBJ refers to a copy in 'Dresdo-Neostad'.
201 This is the same as J62 and J64 according to BBJ 25.

BBJ no.	GW/IA	Contents	Place: Publisher, Date	Source(s)
J149[202]	H-C 2874	Epistolae et sermones	Paris, 1494	–
J162	GW 3936	Sermones in Cantica	Paris: [P. Levet], 1494	r, v
J163[203]		Sermones in Cantica	Venice, 1494	–
J168	GW 3943	Sermones	[Paris: P. Levet, c.1494–95]	l, v
J170[204]	GW 3927	Epistolae et tractatus	Milan: L. Pachel, 1495	j, l, m
J172	GW 3907	Opuscula	Brescia: A. and J. Britannico, 1495	l
J173	GW 3908	Opuscula	Venice: S. Brevilaqua, 1495	l
J174[205]		Opuscula	Paris, 1495	–
J177[206]	H 2858a	Sermones in Cantica	Strassburg, 1495	–
J178[207]	H 2847	Sermones	1495	–
J179	GW 3944	Sermones	Basel: N. Kessler, 1495	l, m, n, y
J180	GW 3946	Sermones et epistolae	Milan: L. Pachel, 1495	l
J181	GW 3945	Sermones et epistolae	Venice: J. Emerich, 1495	l, o
[208]	GW 3918	De consideratione	Rouen: [M. Morin, c.1495–98]	l, v
J192[209]	H 2923	Opuscula	Paris: J. Bouyer and G. Boucher, 1496	–
J195[210]		Sermones in Cantica	Strassburg: M. Flach, 1496	–
J207	GW 3937	Sermones in Cantica	Strassburg: M. Flach, 1497	l, y
J208[211]	H 2851	Sermones	Strassburg: M. Flach, 1497	–
J239[212]		Opera omnia	Lyons, 1500	–
J240	GW 3938	Sermones in Cantica	Brescia: A. Britannico, 1500	l, n, y
J242[213]		De consideratione	[Paris]: J. Petit, [c.1500]	–
J243[214]		De consideratione	[Paris?: J. Petit, c.1500]	–
J253[215]	GW 3917	De consideratione	[Paris: P. Levet, c.1495–96]	–

202 'Hanc editionem re vera exstitisse dubitamus; composita enim esse videtur ex . . . [J 147] atque ex . . . [J 286]'. (BBJ 42). GW 3925 (J147) claims to be H-C 2874. The details in Copinger (*Supplement*, 1:84) clearly describe J147 = GW 3925.

203 'Sub hac editione – ni fallimur – latet . . . [J162]' (BBJ 45).

204 The limited details given by BBJ, which are taken from H 2873, contain an abbreviated colophon and translate the date into Roman numerals. GW 3927, which describes the three copies that I have seen, identifies itself as H 2873, and therefore J170.

205 BBJ mentions one source but 'hujus editionis aliud vestigium nullibi reperitur' (p. 50). H, C, R and GW are silent.

206 This is probably H-C 2859 (= J207), according to GW 3:681.

207 This is H-C 2848 (= J179), according to GW 3:685.

208 This is not in BBJ (but cf. n. 217, below).

209 GW 3:665 refers to this edition (with Poitiers wrongly substituted for Paris) citing Hain and Panzer and adding 'Fälschung'.

210 'Haec editio prorsus concordat cum Flachiana. Vid. N. 207' (i.e. J207) (BBJ 55).

211 'Wahrscheinlich irrtümliche Vermengung des Anfangs von Nr 3944 [J179] mit der Schlusschrift von Nr 3937 [J207]' (GW 3:687).

212 'Sic Olearius I.129 – reliqui tacent idque merito!' (BBJ 65).

213 This might be a faulty entry for J254. GW 3919 is clearly J254 – both refer to the same copy in the Staatsbibliothek at Munich. Yet GW also refers to 'Pellechet 2134' which is J242. BBJ mentions a copy in 'biblioth. monast. Eremi B. M. V'.

214 H, C, R and GW do not mention it. If it did exist (which is unlikely) it would probably have been similar to the other partial editions, which Calvin clearly did not use.

215 The text of this edition is probably similar to that of J254 which Calvin did not use (cf. following note). BBJ refers to a copy at Lyons; GW refers to copies at Lyons and in four other places.

BBJ no.	GW/IA	Contents	Place: Publisher, Date	Source(s)
J254[216]	GW 3919	De consideratione	Paris: F. Baligault / J. Petit, c.1498–1500	m
J255[217]		De consideratione et alia	Rouen, [c.1475]	–
J285[218]		De nomine Iesu	[fifteenth century?]	v
J286[219]	H 2855	Sermones in Cantica	fifteenth century	–
[220]	C 959	Sermones, sermones in Cantica et epistolae	Paris: J. Petit, 1500	–
J299	IA 441	Opuscula	Speier: P. Drach, 1501	j, l
J310	GW 3920	De consideratione	[Paris: J. Poitevin / D. Roce, c.1500–02]	l
J317	IA 450	Opuscula	Venice: L. de Giunta, 1503	l
J330[221]		De consideratione	[Paris]: D. Roce, [c.1505]	–
J348[222]		Epistolae	Hagenau, 1508	–
J350	IA 471–73[223]	Opera omnia	Paris: J. Petit, 1508	c, t
J379	IA 485	Opera omnia	Paris: B. Rembolt / J. Petit, 1513	b, l
J*379[224]		Opera omnia	Paris: B. Rembolt / J. Petit, 1513	j
J383[225]		Opera omnia	Lyons: J. Clein, 1514	–

216 'Ist seitengetreuer Nachdruck von Nr 3917' (= J253) (GW 3:670).
217 BBJ gives various sources but 'recentiores autem prorsus negant' (p. 69). This may be a garbled description of GW 3918, at n. 208, above.
218 This item contains extracts from *SC* 15, part of which Calvin cited in 1559 (c.XXXII). Details in BBJ are very abbreviated. Calvin quoted often from *SC* in 1559 and this reference probably came from the same source as the others.
219 'Aus den widerspruchsvollen Angaben bei Weislinger scheint hervorzugehen, dass es sich um Nr 3937 [J207] handelt' (GW 3:678).
220 'Wohl eine der Pariser Ausgaben für Jean Petit aus dem Anfang des 16. Jh'. (e.g. J350?) (GW 3:687).
221 'Brit. Mus. Catal. "Berg" 176' (BBJ 85). This refers to the old British Museum catalogue where the relevant item is J310.
222 BBJ's only source is Weislinger, *Catalogus librorum impressorum*, 23, where no more details are given than here. There is no mention of this edition in IA. Even if it existed other evidence indicates that Calvin used an *Opera omnia* rather than partial editions in 1559.
223 IA 117.472 and 473 give different parts of the same titlepage and give the printer's name in its French and Latin forms. IA 117.471 is 'Seraphica scripta', 'Parisiis 1508: Andreas Bocardus'. J350 is called the seraphic edition (BBJ 92) because the words 'seraphica scripta' appear in the colophon, which also mentions the labours of Andreas Bocardus.
224 This is the same as J379 except that the device on the title page is of B. Rembolt instead of J. Petit, with a further difference in the text beneath the devices. The colophons are identical and mention both names. There is no difference in the text of the passages quoted by Calvin. IA makes no mention of this variation of J379.
225 This edition 'nunquam exstitit' and is probably an error for J388 (BBJ 99). IA makes no mention of it. It is not mentioned in J. Baudrier, *Bibliographie Lyonnaise*, 12 vols (Lyons: Brun and Paris: Picard, 1895–1921) or S. von Gültlingen, *Bibliographie des Livres Imprimés à Lyon au seizième siècle*, 4 vols (Baden-Baden and Bouxwiller: Valentin Koerner, 1992–96). In J388 the date is found in the colophon only and it is possible that J383 represents an earlier batch of the same printing, but as the date is *April* 1515 this is not very likely. If it did exist its readings are probably similar to those of J388.

BBJ no.	GW/IA	Contents	Place: Publisher, Date	Source(s)
J386	IA 490	De consideratione	Paris: venundatur a R. Chaudiere, 1515	l
J388	IA 489	Opera omnia	Lyons: J. Clein, 1515	l, m
J389[226]		Opera omnia	Venice, 1515	–
J402	IA 497	Opera omnia	Paris: J. Petit, 1517	l, n, p, u, y
J422	IA 505	Opera omnia	Lyons: J. Clein, 1520	k, l
J423[227]	IA 507	Opera omnia	Lyons: J. Mareschal/ O. Martin, 1520	b, k
J436[228]		Opera omnia	Paris: B. Rembolt, 1521	–
J444[229]		Opera omnia	Lyons: J. Clein, 1524	–
J452	IA 519	Opera omnia	Paris: C. Chevallon/ B. Rembolt, 1527	n
J*462[230]	IA 525	Opera omnia	Lyons: J. Mareschal, 1530	j
J**462[231]	IA 525	Opera omnia	Lyons: J. Mareschal/ Vincent de Portonariis, 1530	i
J462[232]		Opera omnia	Lyons: [J. Mareschal]/ J. de Giunta, 1530	–
J463[233]		Opera omnia	Venice: J. de Giunta, 1530	–
J472	IA 532	De gratia et libero arbitrio	Paris: A. Augereau, 1534	z
J473[234]		Opera omnia	Lyons: J. Clein, 1534	
J476	IA 536	Opera omnia	Paris: C. Chevallon, 1536	y
J484	IA 540	Opera omnia	Lyons: N. Petit, 1538	a
J*484[235]		Opera omnia	Lyons: J. Giunta, 1538	–

226 'Scriptum esse videtur "Venetiis" pro "Lugduni"' (= J388) (BBJ 102). IA makes no mention of it.
227 The two copies examined differed considerably in the layout, but not the content, of the colophon. There was no difference in the text of the passages quoted by Calvin.
228 'Fortasse errore typi pro anno 1527' (= J452) (BBJ 115). IA makes no mention of it.
229 This is probably an error for J422 (BBJ 117). IA makes no mention of it. It is mentioned neither in Baudrier, Bibliographie nor in von Gültlingen, Bibliographie.
230 The title page is as J462, except that BBJ 121 adds: 'Lugduni apud Jacobum de giuncti'. IA identifies it as 'Janauschek 462 (?)'.
231 This appears to be identical to the previous item, except that on the title page the printer's device (of Vincent de Portonariis) is different and the line identifying place and printer is missing. The colophon is identical in both editions, with details of place and printer. This can be taken to be a joint edition with J*462.
232 Cf. the note before last. Janauschek had not himself seen a copy. It is mentioned neither in Baudrier, Bibliographie nor in von Gültlingen, Bibliographie. If it existed it was presumably a joint edition with J*462. On the assumption that it most probably had the same colophon as J*462 and J**462 I have included J. Mareschal among the printers.
      According to BBJ 'Est editio Lamberti Campestris et Laurentii Dantisceni ... Vid. N. 422' (p. 121). But for the passages tested the text of J*462 agrees with J350 rather than J422. The editions fall into different groupings according to editor, format, place of origin, etc. These are significant for the layout and contents of the edition but not always for individual readings.
233 'Nobis autem persuasum est, latere sub illa Lugdunensem ejusdem anni. Cfr. N. 462' (BBJ 121). IA makes no mention of it.
234 BBJ doubts its existence (p. 123). IA does not mention it. It is mentioned neither in Baudrier, Bibliographie nor in von Gültlingen, Bibliographie.
235 There is copy in the Biblioteca Nacional at Madrid (Catálogo Colectivo de Obras Impresas en los Siglos XVI al XVIII existentes en las Bibliotecas españolas. Sección I: Siglo XVI (Madrid, 1972: Edición Provisional). It is probably a joint edition with J484.

BBJ no.	GW/IA	Contents	Place: Publisher, Date	Source(s)
J486[236]	IA 543	Opera omnia	Paris: C. Chevallon, 1540	v
J491	IA 547	Opera omnia	Lyons: J. Giunta, 1544	a
J492[237]		Opera omnia	Paris, 1544	–
J495[238]		Opera omnia	Paris, 1545	–
J504	IA 549	Opera omnia	Lyons: J. Giunta, 1546	m
J508[239]		Opera omnia	Paris: J. Roigny, 1547	g, q
J*508[240]		Opera omnia	Paris: Hugues and heirs of Aimon de La Port, 1547	–
J*510[241]	IA 551	Opera omnia	Paris: C. Guillard and G. des Boys, 1547	f
J510	IA 552	Opera omnia	Paris: C. Guillard and G. des Boys, 1548	m
J515	IA 553	Opera omnia	Venice: ad signum spei, 1549	m, o
J518[242]		Opera omnia	Lyons, 1550	–
J519[243]		Opera	Venice, 1550	–
J526[244]	IA 557	Opera omnia	Paris: A. Petit, 1551	–
J527[245]		Opera omnia	Paris: C. Guillard and G. des Boys, 1551	p, x, y
J*527[246]		Opera omnia	Lyons: Hugues de La Port, 1551	–
J532	IA 559	Opera omnia	Basel: J. Hervagius, 1552	c, d, e, h, k, l, y

236 'Même édition que le no *117.536 [J476] avec un nouveau titre' (IA 4.63). In the passages quoted by Calvin the texts are the same.
237 BBJ mentions one source but 'reliqui fontes altum tacent!' (p. 128). IA does not mention it.
238 'Hanc editionem unquam exstitisse ... vehementer dubitamus' (BBJ 128). IA does not mention it.
239 IA 117.551 is described as 'Janauschek 508 (diff.)', but the details given fit J*510.
240 *Catálogo Colectivo* lists this edition with copies at Soria and Toledo. It is probably a joint edition with J508 and/or J*510.
241 This is the same as J510 but is dated a year earlier. There is no difference in the text of the passages quoted by Calvin. It is mentioned under J508 in n. 1. On IA, cf. the note before last.
242 'Sic Olearius I.129, praeter quem nemo' (BBJ 133) IA does not mention it. It is mentioned neither in Baudrier, *Bibliographie* nor in von Gültlingen, *Bibliographie*.
243 BBJ sees this as an error for J520, an edition of *Opuscula* (p. 133) IA does not mention it.
244 This appears to be a joint edition with J527 (cf. next note), which means that its readings would be the same. Failure to see this edition is not too important as it is not the textual evidence that is decisive between the *Opera omnia* in 1559. IA mentions copies at Berlin, Salzburg and Utrecht and *Catálogo Colectivo* mentions a copy in Madrid.
245 'Eadem editio cum praecedenti apud Audoënum Parvum vendita' (BBJ 135). IA does not mention it.
246 R. Cataldi, *Melliflui Doctoris Opera. Le edizioni delle opere di san Bernardo di Clairvaux dei sec. XV-XVIII della Biblioteca Statale del Monumento Nazionale di Casamari e di altre Biblioteche cistercensi* (Casamari: Biblioteca Statale del Monumento Nazionale di Casamari, 1992) 36–39, contains details including a reproduction of the title-page, an illustration and an initial capital. These are completely identical to J527 (including damaged and misaligned type) except for the bottom half of the title page, which includes printer's device and details. This is presumably, therefore, a joint edition with J526 and J527 and may be assumed to have the same readings. This edition is also listed in *Catálogo Colectivo*, with copies in Madrid and Valencia.

BBJ no.	GW/IA	Contents	Place: Publisher, Date	Source(s)
J533[247]		Opera omnia	Colognen, 1552	–
J534[248]		Opera omnia	Paris, 1552	–
J553[249]		Opera omnia	Lyons, 1558	–
J554[250]		Opera omnia	Venice, 1558	–

247 BBJ mentions one source but 'plura prorsus latent' (p. 136). IA does not mention it.
248 BBJ mentions one source but 'alia desiderantur' (p. 136). IA does not mention it.
249 'Sic Caveus – ceteri silent!' (BBJ 140). IA does not mention it. It is mentioned neither
     in Baudrier, *Bibliographie* nor in von Gültlingen, *Bibliographie*.
250 'Est editio Basileensis Hervagii a. 1552 impressa' (=J532) (BBJ 140). IA does not
     mention it.

6

❧❧❧

Calvin and the Fathers in his
Bondage and Liberation of the Will

I. INTRODUCTION

How did Calvin use the fathers in his *Bondage and Liberation of the Will*?[1] How did he work at his desk? How did he handle the fathers? In the first part of the chapter we will seek to ascertain which works of the fathers Calvin actually used in composing his *Bondage and Liberation of the Will*. In the second, shorter, part we will examine his hermeneutical principles. But why the church fathers in this rather than in some other work of Calvin's? Not only does it contain more patristic citations than any other of Calvin's works apart from the *Institutio*, but it actually contains more than any three such works.[2] This is not surprising since a major thrust of

---

This chapter originally appeared as 'Calvin and the Fathers in *Bondage and Liberation of the Will*' in W. H. Neuser and B. G. Armstrong (eds), *Calvinus Sincerioris Religionis Vindex. Calvin as Protector of the Purer Religion* (Kirksville (MO): Sixteenth Century Journal Publishers, 1997) 67–96. Editorial errors in the original have here been corrected and significant new material has been added.

---

1 This title will be used for his *Defensio sanae et orthodoxae doctrinae de servitute et liberatione humani arbitrii adversus calumnias Alberti Pighii Campensis*. It is the title of the English translation, edited by me and translated by G. I. Davies (Grand Rapids: Baker and Carlisle: Paternoster, 1996). I am also editing this work for the new *Opera recognita* series, published by Droz.
   For details of the controversy, cf. P. Pidoux, *Albert Pighius de Kampen, Adversaire de Calvin, 1490–1542* (Lausanne: Lausanne University BTh thesis, 1932); L. F. Schulze, *Calvin's Reply to Pighius* (Potchefstroom: Pro Rege, 1971); G. Melles, *Albertus Pighius en zijn Strijd met Calvijn over het Liberum Arbitrium* (Kampen: Kok, 1973). Neither Calvin nor Pighius mentions the exchange between Luther and Erasmus on this issue and there is no internal evidence to suggest that either of them had the earlier debate in mind. Pighius attacks Luther's *Assertio omnium articulorum* but does not mention his *De servo arbitrio*.
2 For these figures, cf. the tables in R. J. Mooi, KDE 365–97. While his figures may not be not 100 per cent accurate, they suffice for comparative purposes like this. Following Mooi's figures, the 1559 *Institutio* has 866 citations; the *Bondage and Liberation of the Will*, 310; *Def. c. err. Serveti*, 108; the three replies to Westphal, 194; *Diluc. explic. Heshusii*, 99; *Comm. I & II Corinthians*, 98; *De praed.*, 98; *Art. fac. Par.*, 81. For a different comparison, the 1539 *Institutio* has 301, the 1543 edition has 418 *new* citations.

Calvin's controversy with Pighius was the dispute about the teaching of the fathers, especially Augustine. It is not just the number of citations that reflects this emphasis, but the quantity of material as well. In the third book, for example, about a third of the text is composed of patristic quotation.

How did this work come to be written? In his 1539 *Institutio* Calvin twice claimed that apart from Augustine, the early fathers are so confused, vacillating and contradictory on the subject of free choice that almost nothing can be determined with certainty from their writings.[3] This claim so incensed the Dutch Roman Catholic theologian Albert Pighius that he devoted much of the first six books of his *De libero arbitrio* to refuting it.[4] Calvin made haste to reply. Pighius's work was published in August 1542. Calvin was concerned that his reply be ready in time for the 1543 Frankfurt Book Fair (1 to 20 March), which meant that he had, according to his own testimony, barely two months in which to write it.[5] The work was published by February;[6] so which two months did Calvin have in mind? Since he was already engaged in the work on 15 December,[7] it could not have been the two months immediately prior to the Book Fair. He was more likely to be thinking of December and January, the two months in which it would need to be written in order to be ready for Frankfurt. If we allow for an element of rhetorical exaggeration in the two-month claim, we can safely conclude that the work was written during November, December and January.

It is possible that during some of this time Calvin was released from preaching, except for one Sunday sermon. Such a dispensation was granted to Calvin by the City Council on 11 September 1542.[8] This was not because his normal load was too heavy[9] but in order to free him (together with Claude Roset) for the task of recodifying the Genevan laws and constitution.[10] However, it seems that the draft that Calvin and Roset had been asked to prepare was completed by 2 October, so Calvin presumably

---

3 OS 3:245, 251 (*Inst.* 2:2:4, 9).
4 *De libero hominis arbitrio et divina gratia* (Cologne: M. Novesian, 1542). Pighius returns to Calvin's claim on ff. 10b, 28a, 32b, 35b, 36b and in many other places.
5 Calvin stated early in the work that he had to be brief because of the pressure of time, with barely two months before the Book Fair (CO 6:236). A. L. Herminjard, CRF 8:341, n. 1, gives the dates of the Fair. In a letter to Farel of 15 December 1542 Calvin states that he is replying to Pighius and wishes the work to appear at the next Book Fair (CRF 8:221; CO 11:474).
6 On 31 January Simon Sulzer wrote from Bern thanking Calvin for what is generally understood to be a copy of the work, perhaps unbound (CRF 8:256, n. 1; CO 11:501, n. 1). On 16 February Calvin wrote to Melanchthon announcing its recent publication (CRF 8:286f.; CO 11:515).
7 Cf. n. 5, above.
8 *Annales* for 11 September 1542, taken from the *Registres du Conseil* (CO 21:302). I am grateful to William Naphy for drawing my attention to the fact that Calvin had a 'sabbatical' around this time.
9 *Contra* T. H. L. Parker, *Calvin's Preaching* (Edinburgh: T&T Clark, 1992) 60.
10 W. Walker, *John Calvin* (New York: Schocken, 1969 – revised edition) 275f. On the constitution, cf. R. M. Kingdon, 'Calvin et la Constitution Genevoise' in *Actualité de la Réforme* 12 (Geneva: Labor et Fides, 1987) 209–19; idem, 'Calvinus Legislator: The 1543 "Constitution" of the City-State of Geneva' in W. H. Neuser (hrsg.), *Calvinus Servus Christi* (Budapest: Ráday-Kollegium, 1988) 225–32.

resumed weekday preaching from that date.[11] It is unlikely, therefore, that Calvin worked on his reply to Pighius during the period that his preaching load was lightened. It does seem, however, that he probably had no other writing commitments while responding to Pighius.[12]

II. WORKS USED BY CALVIN

Which patristic works does Calvin use? He names or cites twenty-five of Augustine's works, three of pseudo-Augustine and thirty-three from nineteen other authors[13] – quite an impressive array of patristic learning, one might think. But we must not jump to hasty conclusions. It would be rash to assume that Calvin *at that stage* handled all or even most of these works. First, the response to Pighius was written in a couple of months. Indeed Calvin complains not only about the brevity of the time available, but also about the weight of other responsibilities with which he continued to be burdened, in contrast to the leisure available to his Roman Catholic antagonists like Pighius,[14] so we can expect to find evidence of haste and must expect our author to take short cuts. Secondly, Calvin was short of cash and books during his stay at Strassburg.[15] It is likely that he built up his library during his time at Geneva, but by the time he began to answer Pighius he had been back in Geneva for little over a year. It is unlikely, therefore, that he had a large library at his disposal.

11 R. M. Kingdon, 'Calvin and the Government of Geneva' in W. H. Neuser (hrsg.), *Calvinus Ecclesiae Genevensis Custos* (Frankfurt, etc.: Peter Lang, 1984) 60, gives 2 October as the terminus for Calvin's release from preaching. I am grateful for help in this matter from Robert Kingdon who, in a private letter of 12 September 1995, explains that the latter date is based upon the submission of the draft by Calvin and Roset, as recorded by A. Roget, *Histoire du Peuple de Genève depuis la Réforme jusqu'à l'Escalade* (Geneva: Jullien, 1870–83) 2:63, presumably drawing upon the *Registres du Conseil*. Kingdon also states that the Consistory registers show that Calvin attended all of the meetings of the Consistory for this period (7, 14 and 21 September). This suggests that Calvin was released only from weekday preaching and not from other duties. He was certainly not released from other duties while responding to Pighius, as can be seen from the complaints noted at n. 14, below. On 17 November 1542 the City Council granted Calvin 'ung bossot de vin vieulx de celluy de lhospital' in recognition of the pains that he was taking on behalf of the city (CO 10a:125, drawing on the *Registres du Conseil*). This reinforces the conclusion that Calvin's labours over the constitution were completed before he embarked upon his reply to Pighius in November.
12 An examination of Calvin's other works from around this time (R. Peter and J.-F. Gilmont, *Bibliotheca Calviniana*, vol. 1 (Geneva: Droz, 1991) 104–43) suggests that those works published in 1542 would all have been completed, that the 1543 *Institutio* was probably already with the printer and that he was unlikely to have begun any of the other works published in 1543.
13 See the table of works in section VI, below. Note there the different categories of works included. Works which are possible or even likely, but not certain, sources (such as Bernard's *Sermones in Cantica* in CO 6:334f.) have not been included. To include such works could extend the list indefinitely and make it highly subjective and unreliable.
14 CO 6:229–32, 236. For the competing claims on Calvin's time, cf. J.-F. Gilmont, *Jean Calvin et le livre imprimé* (Geneva: Droz, 1997) 353.
15 Cf. at nn. 51f., below. For precise details of Pighius's extensive library, cf. M. E. Kronenberg, 'Albertus Pighius, Proost van S. Jan te Utrecht, zijn Geschriften en zijn Bibliotheek', *Het Boek* 28 (1944–46) 125–58. Pighius also had money problems (ibid. 119–21).

In examining Calvin's citations we will adopt a hermeneutic of suspicion, assuming that he did not have a particular work to hand unless
there is clear evidence to the contrary. We will consider alternative sources
available to Calvin. First, some of the passages that he cites are simply
taken from Pighius. If, in responding to a quotation in Pighius, Calvin
gives no indication of knowing more of the work than is found in Pighius,
we may safely assume either that he did not have the original to hand or
that he did not bother to turn to it. Secondly, some passages are simply
drawn from the 1539 *Institutio*, which Pighius was attacking. If Calvin
betrays no more knowledge of the work than is already found in the 1539
Institutio, we may again safely assume either that he did not have the
original to hand or that he did not bother to turn to it. Thirdly, some works
are cited in a very imprecise manner. One is left with the impression that
Calvin has in the past read the work, but does not at present have it open
before him – either because he does not have it or because of haste. Finally,
and much harder to assess, is the possibility that some of the quotations
may be derived from an intermediary source, such as an anthology. In
order to establish this, one needs more substantial evidence than just the
fact that Calvin's quotation is also found in another work.[16]

(a) Augustine

Applying this hermeneutic of suspicion, how wide a selection of works
does Calvin have to hand? He cites twenty-five Augustinian works.[17]
Twelve of these he quotes at such length that one must conclude that he
had them before him. Ten of these, it will come as no surprise, are anti-
Pelagian works. The others are the *Retractationes* and the *Epistolae*, to four
of which (all anti-Pelagian) he must have turned.[18] But how did he use
these works? Did he constantly turn to them for quotations? Detailed study
of the quotations yields the following conclusions. Occasionally he clearly
had the volume open before him. This can be seen where there is a sus-
tained volume of quotation from one work,[19] or where he refers to the
position of the text in the volume.[20] On other occasions the quotations

---

16 F. L. Battles, 'The Sources of Calvin's Seneca Commentary' in G. E. Duffield (ed.),
    John Calvin (Appleford, Abingdon: Sutton Courtenay, 1966) 38–66, shows the use of
    intermediary sources by Calvin at that stage. L. Smits, SAOJC 1:206–11, notes
    Calvin's use of Lombard and Gratian in his early years, but detects none in the
    Bondage and Liberation of the Will. A. Zillenbiller, *Die Einheit der Katholischen Kirche:
    Calvins Cyprianrezeption in seinen ekklesiologischen Schriften* (Mainz: von Zabern, 1993)
    75–81 gives evidence for Calvin's use of Gratian as a source in the *Prefatory Address*
    to the *Institutio*, which is later recycled in the *De scandalis*. Chapter 5, above, section
    IV, shows that there is little evidence for Calvin's use of anthologies in his Bernard
    citations. My own examination of Lombard and Gratian has yielded no evidence
    that Calvin was dependent upon either of them in this work.
17 See the table of works in section VI, below. For the Augustinian and pseudo-
    Augustinian material I am immensely indebted to the work of Smits, SAOJC, vol. 2,
    in tracing sources. My own study, concentrating on one work only of Calvin's, has
    been more thorough and my conclusions differ from his in many points of detail
    and a number of substantial points. Some of the claims made below will, therefore,
    contradict the claims made in his tables. The basis for my claims will be found in
    the translation and critical edition cited in n. 1, above.
18 *Epistolae* 46f., 105, 107 in his edition, numbered 194, 214f., 217 today.
19 E.g. from *De praedestinatione sanctorum* in CO 6:320–23.
20 Cf. at nn. 71, 74, below.

are briefer and looser. Here it is likely that Calvin read Augustine for material in response to a particular point and then quoted from memory as he wrote.

With six of the works, there is no evidence that Calvin used them. With two of these, Calvin discusses Pighius's quotations without any indication that he has gone back to the original. With an additional three works Calvin discusses Pighius's quotations, drawing on material from the *Retractationes*, but giving no indication that he has gone back to the original. Why should he have neglected to go to the originals? One explanation would be that he did not have them to hand. This is possible with two of the works, but the other three are found in the same volume of the Erasmian editions as the *Retractationes*.[21] There is a simpler explanation. These are works of the early Augustine and Calvin's concern in discussing them is simply damage limitation. His aim is no more than to cast doubt on Pighius's appeal to them, his own attack coming from the later writings of the mature Augustine. He, therefore, has neither the need nor the time to study these early writings. To unravel the complexities of Augustine's *De libero arbitrio* would have taken even Calvin more time than he could then afford. Finally from the sixth work, the *Confessiones*, Calvin once quotes Augustine's famous prayer:[22] 'Give what you command....' He need not have turned to the *Confessiones* for this since it had already been quoted in the 1539 *Institutio*[23] and was also available via Augustine's anti-Pelagian works.[24]

That leaves seven other works which Calvin might have used. These will be discussed in alphabetical order. From the *De civitate dei* there is a brief and rather loose quotation.[25] This is probably taken from memory and almost certainly from earlier reading.[26] Calvin would not have scoured such a long work merely in order to give a single inaccurate three-line quotation.[27] The *Enarrationes in Psalmos* is four times named,[28] but always with less than four lines of quotation and generally not very accurately. This also looks like quotation from memory of earlier reading. Another possibility for these brief quotations is that Calvin kept a book of quotations, as did some other reformers.[29] Annette Zillenbiller argues that he must have done so because he is dependent upon Bucer's *florilegium*,

---

21 *De libero arbitrio*, *De quantitate animae* and *De vera religione* are in the first volume, together with the *Retractationes*. The other two, *De duabus animabus* and *De actis cum Felice Manichaeo*, are in volume six, together with *De haeresibus*, a work which we will shortly maintain that Calvin used. The assumption that Calvin used an Erasmian edition is justified below.

22 Quoted in CO 6:348.

23 OS 3:305 (*Inst.* 2:5:7).

24 *De dono perseverantiae* 20:53.

25 In CO 6:304.

26 For Calvin's earlier use of this work, cf. Smits, SAOJC 2:159–63.

27 Here and throughout, the number of lines is counted in the original 1543 edition, where lines are slightly longer than those in CO.

28 In CO 6:337, 342, 353, 386.

29 Bucer's handwritten collection is in the library of Corpus Christi College, Cambridge and has been edited by P. Fraenkel, *Martini Buceri Opera Latina*, vol. 3 (Leiden: E. J. Brill, 1988). Comparison of this with Calvin's works does not encourage the idea that Calvin was influenced by it and it was not, of course, available to him when he wrote his *Bondage and Liberation of the Will*.

which was *handwritten*, in his 1543 *Institutio*.[30] But the latter work was largely completed by January 1542,[31] and the most likely explanation, *if* Calvin is dependent upon Bucer's *florilegium*, is that he made use of it while he was still at Strassburg. So the verdict to date must be that there is no evidence that Calvin compiled his own book of quotations. But absence of evidence is not evidence of absence and Zillenbiller has reminded us that this is a question which must continue to be posed and investigated.

From the *Enchiridion* Calvin thrice cites a passage earlier quoted in the 1539 *Institutio*.[32] He also adds a new, lengthy and accurate quotation from another passage, which he quotes a second time, more briefly.[33] This seems to be clear evidence that he turned to the work. The passage concerns the interpretation of Romans 9:16, which was in dispute, and Calvin may have been drawn to it from memory or via the Scripture index of the Augustine *Opera*, where it is found.

Augustine's *In evangelium Johannis tractatus* is named five times by Calvin. Three times Calvin is simply repeating a quotation from the 1539 *Institutio* and a fourth time he does so and adds extra material quoted by Pighius.[34] The fifth time the work is simply named as one of the sources for Augustine's statement that God crowns his gifts in us.[35] We can assume that Calvin knew this from his earlier reading of the sermons or via an intermediate source[36] – it is unlikely that he searched through them there and then to check whether this quotation might appear.[37]

One double citation of the *Contra Faustum Manichaeum* is simply drawn from Pighius.[38] But there is also a brief quotation, which appears nowhere else in Calvin's writings.[39] Since Calvin first began to quote this work in his 1543 *Institutio*,[40] which was largely completed by the time he took up his pen in response to Pighius, this two-line quotation is probably drawn from the memory of earlier reading.

Calvin repeatedly cites Augustine's *De haeresibus* as a source of knowledge about early heresies.[41] The only reason that one might question whether Calvin has the volume in front of him is the fact that he makes mistakes, attributing to the Montanists and Priscillianists ideas of which other heretics are accused. This clearly suggests that Calvin is working from memory. But since this book is not directly cited prior to

30 Zillenbiller, *Einheit der Katholischen Kirche*, 82–100.
31 OS 3:XIX-XX.
32 In CO 6:293, 295, 336, cf. OS 3:250 (*Inst.* 2:2:8).
33 In CO 6:343f., 392.
34 In CO 6:265, 314f., 315, 380. Cf. OS 3:249f., 254, 305 (*Inst.* 2:2:8, 11, 2:5:7).
35 In CO 6:337.
36 It is cited in Peter Lombard, *Sententiae* Lib. 2, dist. 27, c. 6 (PL 192:718f.). Calvin also cited Augustine's work repeatedly in the 1539 and 1543 *Institutio* (Smits, SAOJC 2:189–97), so probably knew of the passage from that reading.
37 The index volumes to the Erasmian editions list other sources for the saying, but none from the sermons on John.
38 In CO 6:300.
39 In CO 6:358. Cf. Smits, SAOJC 2:197.
40 Cf. Smits, SAOJC 2:197–99.
41 In CO 6:260, 262–64.

our present work[42] it is likely that the memory is of reading done specifically to answer Pighius. Thus the inaccuracies would reflect the pressure of time rather than the inaccessibility of the original.

Finally, Calvin twice briefly cites the *Contra Julianum*, expanding even briefer references from the 1539 *Institutio*.[43] It is hard to be sure whether he has returned to the work or whether he is relying upon the memory of his earlier reading.

Where does this leave us? It appears that Calvin turned to the works of Augustine for fourteen or fifteen works, making use of at least five of the ten volumes of the Erasmus edition. Despite this, his reading was confined to the anti-Pelagian writings and the *Retractationes*, apart from brief forays into the *De haeresibus*, necessitated by Pighius's attack on that front, and the *Enchiridion*. Given the subject-matter and the time constraint, it is hardly surprising that Calvin did not read more widely.

What of pseudo-Augustine? Calvin cites only three works, each in response to Pighius's use of them. Two of them that he quotes at length he clearly had before him. These are found in those volumes of the Erasmian edition that he used for genuine works. The third he knew only through Pighius.[44]

(b) Augustine Edition Used

Which edition of Augustine did Calvin use? This question has been addressed by Luchesius Smits.[45] He notes that the choice is between the edition of Johann Amerbach at the beginning of the century and that of Erasmus, first published in 1528/29 and subsequently revised.[46] Before considering the evidence he notes three *a priori* reasons why Calvin should have used one of the Erasmian editions. His early humanist education, his humanist commentary on Seneca's *De clementia* and his ongoing humanist inclinations would all have disposed him towards them. Secondly, his other writings contain evidence of his acquaintance with the latest works of humanist scholarship. Finally, Calvin's links with Basel would have predisposed him to the Erasmus edition, first published there. This last argument is perhaps less persuasive, not just because Amerbach's edition had also been published at Basel but also because factors like quality and, even more important, availability would presumably be much more important than place of publication.

Smits then proceeds to the evidence for the Erasmian editions. First, in discussing works of dubious authenticity Calvin showed independence

---

42 Cf. Smits, SAOJC 2:206f. Smits sees some parallels with the 1539 *Institutio*, but this work is not named and no knowledge of it is there *required*. Calvin mentions the work in the 1534 preface to his *Psychopannychia* (CO 5:170f.), but gives the *Decretum Gratiani* as an intermediate source. Gratian is not the source for Calvin's extensive citations here.

43 In CO 6:294, 354. Cf. OS 3:249, 275 (*Inst.* 2:2:8, 2:3:4).

44 Cf. at n. 65f., below.

45 Smits, SAOJC 1:196–205.

46 On these editions, cf. J. de Ghellinck, *Patristique et Moyen Age*, vol. 3 (Gembloux: J. Duculot, Brussels: Édition Universelle and Paris: Desclée de Brouwer, 1948) 371–92; Smits, SAOJC 1.197–201. In this chapter the 1528/29 edition, is called 'the Erasmus edition'; it and its subsequent revisions are called 'Erasmian edition(s)'.

of judgment, but in fact always reached the same conclusion as Erasmus, for ill as well as for good.[47] Secondly, Calvin uses for Augustine's sermons on the Psalms the title coined by Erasmus: *Enarrationes*. Again, where there are textual variants, Calvin always follows Erasmus's reading against that of Amerbach.

These arguments may be accepted as sound, though with qualifications. The *a priori* arguments show why Calvin might have preferred to use an Erasmian edition; they do not prove that he was actually able to do so. There is often a gulf between the editions that we would like to use and those that are actually available to us. The appeal to variant readings is legitimate, but must be used with caution. Those who have examined Calvin's quotations in detail will be aware that he often quotes very loosely, so we must be cautious about using differences in wording as evidence. Smits claims that Calvin always follows Erasmus over against Amerbach and then proceeds to give four examples. He says that he could continue the list, but gives no indication of how many such examples he has found,[48] which makes it hard to assess the strength of his argument.

There is another, more fundamental, weakness in Smits' case. Implicit is the assumption that Calvin used the same edition of Augustine throughout his literary career. But this assumption is a presumption. We might reasonably suppose that while in one place Calvin used just the one edition, though if that edition was not his own personal copy there is no guarantee that he might always have had access to the same one. But until such time as Calvin possessed his own copy of Augustine's works, we must suppose that he used a different set in each place. Even when he did come to possess his own copy, he might subsequently have been forced to part with it, especially at the time of his various moves to and from Geneva.

There is solid evidence to support these reservations. Calvin almost certainly used different editions of the works of Bernard during his time at Strassburg and during his later time at Geneva.[49] This shows the danger of assuming that Calvin used the same edition throughout. Where Augustine is concerned, Calvin himself is explicit. He had to respond to Pighius's charge that in the 1539 *Institutio* he failed to name all of the fathers who oppose him on a particular point.[50] Calvin justifies himself in part on the grounds that he had no books to hand at that time, 'except one volume of Augustine which had been given to me on loan'. He proceeds to state that he had then been destitute of books.[51] While it suited Calvin's purpose to exaggerate his destitution, his claim broadly fits what is known of his poverty at Strassburg.[52] It is quite possible, therefore, that by the end of his stay at Strassburg[53] Calvin was using a copy of Augustine different both from the one(s) he had used before his stay in the city and from the

47 For the details, cf. Smits SAOJC 1:183–96.
48 Ibid., 1:204f.
49 Cf. chapter 5, above, at nn. 7–12.
50 *De libero arbitrio* f. 63a w.r.t. the 1539 *Institutio*, OS 3:299:1–8 (*Inst.* 2:5:2).
51 CO 6:336. On this claim, cf. Gilmont, *Jean Calvin et le livre imprimé*, 185f.
52 Cf. chapter 5, above, at n. 9.
53 This leaves open the possibility that he may have brought a copy of Augustine to Strassburg and have been forced to sell it there. Cf. the previous note.

one(s) that he used on his return to Geneva. Our goal here is not to discover one edition which Calvin used always, but simply to establish which edition of Augustine Calvin used for one particular work: his *Bondage and Liberation of the Will.*[54]

Smits seeks not just to show that Calvin used an Erasmian edition but also to establish *which* of these editions he used. By the time that Calvin came to respond to Pighius there were four available.[55] The first edition was begun by Johann Froben at Basel and, after his death, completed by his sons in 1528 and 1529.[56] Three years later, in 1531 and 1532, Claude Chevallon at Paris printed a further edition with some corrections by Jacobus Haemer, together with some newly discovered sermons.[57] In 1541, also at Paris, Yolande Bonhomme and Charlotte Guillard printed another edition.[58] Finally, Hieronymus Froben and Nikolaus Episcopius produced another edition at Basel, with corrections by Martin Lipsius, between 1541 and 1543.[59]

How might one discover which of the Erasmian editions Calvin used? Smits relies entirely upon one passage, which conveniently for us occurs in the work that we are considering. We will explore a number of possible indicators, also seeking positive proof that Calvin was not using the Amerbach edition. We will examine first the inconclusive evidence, then the evidence which excludes the Amerbach edition and finally the evidence that might indicate *which* Erasmian edition Calvin used.[60]

First, Calvin quotes (loosely) a number of passages from the *De haeresibus.* Two of these are not found in the earliest manuscripts,[61] but were found in both the Amerbach and Erasmian editions. Secondly, there is a small but vital textual variant in a quotation from the *De correptione et gratia.* Calvin has 'inseparabiliter' where there is an alternative reading 'insuperabiliter'.[62] Since Calvin's reading weakens the desired force of the quotation, it is unlikely that he would have introduced the variant himself. Unfortunately though, his reading is found in both the Amerbach and Erasmian editions. Thirdly, Calvin queries the authorship of *Sermon* 236, denying that the style is Augustine's and conceding no more than the

---

54 One might have hoped that Calvin's copy of Augustine would have ended up in the Genevan library, as probably did his copy of Bernard (chapter 5, above, at nn. 83–86), but the library contains Peter Martyr's copy (A. Ganoczy, BAC 183). In 1569 the library sold some of the books that had belonged to Calvin and Peter Martyr (ibid., 18f.). It may well have sold Calvin's copy either because it was older (a conclusion reached below for the edition used in this work) or because it was not a complete set (a possibility that is also considered below).
55 Cf. n. 46, above.
56 IA 110.175.
57 IA 110.201.
58 IA 110.258.
59 IA 110.256.
60 For the Amerbach, 1528/29 and 1541 editions, the copies in the Cambridge University Library have been examined; for the 1541/43 edition, the copy in the British Library; for the 1531/32 edition, the copies in both libraries.
61 CO 6:260, 262, quoting from *De haeresibus* 1 and 11 (PL 42:26, n. 1 and 42:28, n. 3). In the former passage, Calvin reads 'Selene' where Augustine read 'Helen' (PL 42:25, n. 1). The Amerbach and Erasmus editions read 'Selene'. Intriguingly, the French translation of Calvin reads 'Heléné'.
62 CO 6:324, citing *De correptione et gratia* 12:38 (PL 44:940, n. 1).

possibility that this might be an early work of Augustine.[63] His doubts were well founded since this is in fact Pelagius's *Confession of Faith to Pope Innocent!*[64] The Erasmian editions do not indicate that this particular sermon is spurious, but there are general health warnings both at the beginning of the *Sermons* volume and at the beginning of the *Sermones de Tempore*, which indicate that not all of the sermons are genuine. But none of this helps us to discover which edition Calvin was using. The work is quoted by Pighius who, unusually, gives no indication of his source.[65] Calvin is totally dependent upon Pighius's quotation and clearly has no idea about the identity of this work, other than that it is alleged to be by Augustine.[66]

One instance marginally favours the Erasmian editions. Calvin denies the authenticity of the *Hypognosticon*, citing 'the established opinion of the learned'.[67] The Amerbach edition states that the work is not found in the *Retractationes*, but adds that it is still useful. The Erasmian editions clearly state that it is not by Augustine and give reasons why.

Two other instances strongly favour the Erasmian editions. First, Calvin discusses the pseudo-Augustinian *De dogmatibus ecclesiasticis* and gives reasons why it is not authentic. The Erasmian editions, unlike Amerbach, make clear its inauthenticity, but, as Smits notes,[68] Calvin's reasons are independent of Erasmus's and more developed. Furthermore, Calvin notes that the author refers to pope Innocent as 'magister' and speaks of the African synods of Milevis and Carthage, but the document itself refers to the author not as Innocent but as 'magister in epistola ad Milevitanum concilium'.[69] How did Calvin know that the *magister* was Innocent? Erasmus's *censura*, found in all of the Erasmian editions, states that chapter 25 is pope Innocent's letter to the council. Here, then, is further evidence that Calvin was working with an Erasmian edition. Finally, there is in another work a textual variant between the Amerbach and Erasmian editions where Calvin follows the latter.[70]

Most significantly, there are two passages that might indicate *which* Erasmian edition Calvin used. The first is used by Smits as the sole item of evidence to settle the issue. Calvin cites a passage from *De correptione et gratia* and then introduces another extract with the words 'five lines earlier he had said'.[71] As Smits notes, in all the Erasmian editions save the first the text is divided into two columns and so it is in the latter only that one needs to return only five lines to reach the second extract.

63 CO 6:319.
64 PL 39:2181, n. b.
65 Perhaps he did not know it. Peter Lombard, *Sententiae* Lib. 2, dist. 28, c. 8 has a very similar quotation, missing the last line, attributed to Jerome 'in Explanatione fidei Catholicae ad Damasum' (PL 192:718f.). Pighius may have derived it from some such source.
66 CO 6:319, following Pighius, *De libero arbitrio* f. 58a. ('ex quadam ad populum concione, quae Augustino adscribitur').
67 CO 6:306.
68 Smits, SAOJC 1:187f.
69 CO 6:318, citing *De dogmatibus ecclesiasticis* 25 (PL 58:986).
70 Amerbach has 'quicquid', Erasmus and Calvin have 'quisquis' in *De correptione et gratia* 7:12, quoted in CO 6:342. Cf. PL 44:923, n. 3. This is one of Smits' textual variants (SAOJC 1:205).
71 CO 6:293f., citing *De correptione et gratia* 13:42. Cf. Smits, SAOJC 1:204.

This simple test appears to settle the case. But the simplicity is only apparent. How does one arrive at the total of five lines? Does one measure from the beginning or the end of the first passage and does one measure back to the beginning or the end of the second passage? It is yet more complicated. The first passage is a loose quotation in which only two words are adjacent in both quotation and original. The second passage is a paraphrase in which only two words come from the original. So from where to where does one count the gap? According to where the measurements are taken, the 1528/29 Erasmus edition yields results of four or five lines, the later editions yield results varying between six and ten lines (at least seven lines for the 1541 edition). If this were the only piece of evidence, it would favour the first edition – but only marginally.

Apart from the question of what to measure, one must ask whether 'five lines earlier' is intended as a precise mathematical measure or just another way of saying 'a few lines above'. On two other occasions Calvin makes similar statements where we know precisely which volume he had before him: Pighius's *De libero arbitrio*. Once he claims that Pighius contradicts himself ten lines later.[72] He then, after a brief summary of what follows, paraphrases a short passage which begins exactly ten lines after the end of the first. Another time Calvin claims that Pighius contradicts what he had said twenty lines previously.[73] Having summarized a passage of nine lines long, he proceeds to summarize an earlier passage which is eight lines long. The gap between the two is twenty lines. So to move from the beginning of the passage first summarized to the end of the second requires a move of twenty-one lines, while to move from the end of the passage first summarized to the beginning of the second requires a move of thirty-six lines.

There are two ways of interpreting this evidence. If we think that Calvin was seeking to give precise measurements, this would mean that when measuring distances *backwards* he did so by measuring the *gap* between the two passages. If the Augustine passage is measured this way, the 1528/29 Erasmus edition has a gap of just three lines, the 1531/32 and 1541/43 editions have gaps of exactly five lines, while the 1541 edition has a gap of six lines. By this way of measuring, the first Erasmus edition turns out to be the least likely. Alternatively, it may be that Calvin was not concerned to measure distances precisely. The fact that he speaks in terms of five, ten and twenty lines would support this contention, though the evidence allows all three measurements to be taken literally. If he was being precise throughout, the evidence *excludes* the 1528/29 edition; if not, the evidence from the Augustine passage does not significantly favour the 1528/29 edition over the other editions, in which case we must look elsewhere.

There is a second passage, not noted by Smits. Calvin is arguing with Pighius about the interpretation of Augustine's *De libero arbitrio*. He responds to a quotation made by Pighius by inviting him to 'turn the page'

72 CO 6:301, w.r.t. Pighius, *De libero arbitrio* f. 47b.
73 CO 6:367f., w.r.t. Pighius, *De libero arbitrio* f. 80a-b.

to another passage, which he proceeds to quote.[74] As these two passages are twenty-two columns apart in Migne, this would seem to indicate that Calvin was using not the Erasmus edition but a microfiche version. But in fact Calvin has inadvertently alerted us to the fact that he was using not the *De libero arbitrio* itself, but the extracts from it found in the *Retractationes*. What happens when we turn from one passage to the other in the Erasmian editions? In the 1541/43 Basel edition the two passages are found on the same page. In the 1528/29 Erasmus edition they are found on facing pages. In the other two editions they are on opposite sides of the same leaf, so that one literally has to turn the page over to move from the one to the other. This strongly favours these two editions.

Where does this leave us? The 1541/43 edition seems to be excluded. This also follows from its date. Some of the volumes were not published until 1543, which is too late since Calvin appears to have completed his work by February of that year. What of the 1528/29 Erasmus edition? One might argue that 'turn the page' is as likely to be metaphorical as 'five lines earlier'. But there is a difference. In the one case the issue is *how many* lines one has to move up the page; in the other case the issue is *whether* or not one needs to turn the page. The evidence again clearly excludes the 1528/29 edition.

My judgment is that Calvin used not the 1528/29 Erasmus edition but one of the two Paris editions. If Calvin (as he says) did not have a copy while at Strassburg and if he bought one in Geneva (rather than borrowing one), the 1541 edition appeared at just the right time. On the other hand, if we take the 'five lines earlier' as a precise measurement of the gap between the two passages, the 1531/32 edition is indicated.[75]

(c) Other Fathers

What of the thirty-three works by other authors?[76] Here would appear to be evidence of a wide range of patristic learning. But those who read the treatise will be struck by the paucity of reference to other fathers compared to the wealth of material on Augustine. This paucity cannot be explained solely by the fact that the others do not support Calvin to the same extent as does Augustine.

Nineteen of the thirty-three works are easily eliminated. With five Calvin is simply discussing his citation in the 1539 *Institutio*, providing no

---

74 CO 6:296 with quotations from Augustine, *De libero arbitrio* 3:3:7 and 3:18:51. It might be argued that 'turn the page' means 'turn a handful of pages' from one passage to the other in the *De libero arbitrio*, but since the whole point is the closeness of the two passages, this is very unlikely. It is also excluded by the fact that Calvin's next words are 'Then he adds', followed by a quotation not from *De libero arbitrio* but from the *Retractationes*.

75 Another possibility, which should not be discounted, is that Calvin possessed the first volume of one edition (with the *Retractationes*) and the seventh volume of another edition (with *De correptione et gratia*). We cannot simply assume that Calvin had a complete set of the *Opera omnia*. He claims that while preparing the 1539 *Institutio* he had only one volume of Augustine to hand (CO 6:336). But if one edition (like the 1531/32 or 1541 editions) fits all of the evidence it is most likely that he did have a complete set, or at least that all of the volumes that he used were from the same edition.

76 See the table of works in section VI, below.

evidence of any further knowledge of the work. With a further eight Calvin contents himself simply with discussing the quotation given by Pighius, providing no evidence of any further knowledge of the work. Another four are drawn from Augustine's works.[77] One is taken from both the 1539 *Institutio* and Pighius and another one from Augustine as well as these two.

This leaves fourteen works, some of which can also be eliminated. Calvin refers to Eusebius's references to the correspondence of Clement of Rome, which was not itself available in the west at that time.[78] He appeals to Bernard without mentioning any source.[79] His citations are based upon the *De gratia et libero arbitrio*, which Calvin cited in the 1539 *Institutio*. Here he appears to be drawing upon memory of earlier reading.[80] There is a brief and loose quotation from Theodoret's *Historia ecclesiastica*.[81] Both the text of the quotation and Calvin's general usage indicate that he was reliant upon Cassiodore's *Historia tripartita*. He had made good use of this work prior to 1543[82] and the present brief reference was probably drawn from memory of that study.

Three other works can be considered together. Calvin shows some knowledge of the contents of the pseudo-Clementine *Recognitiones*.[83] Since he had never before referred to this work it appears that he now turned to it in order to combat Pighius's claims. We shall shortly return to the question of which edition he might have used. In opposition to Clementine authorship he cites both Eusebius's *Historia ecclesiastica* and Rufinus's *De adulteratione librorum Origenis*, found as the epilogue to his Latin translation of Pamphilus's *Apologia pro Origene*.[84] There was nothing new in opposing the authenticity of the *Recognitiones*. This had been done by Johannes Trithemius, drawing on a comment made by Gratian.[85] But where did Calvin find the two witnesses for the opposition? They are found together in *later* compilations of evidence,[86] but a search of literature available to Calvin has failed to find them. There is no good reason to question that Calvin read them for himself. By this time he was certainly familiar with Eusebius and may here have been quoting him from

---

77 The entire discussion of Cyprian (CO 6:282f.) and most of the discussion of Ambrose (CO 6:287) is based upon Augustine's quotation of and interpretation of these authors.

78 In CO 6:262.

79 In CO 6:291, 333, 334f., 378.

80 This is also confirmed by the evidence that Calvin did not bring to Geneva the edition of Bernard that he used at Strassburg and did not acquire another copy until the 1550s (chapter 5, above). It is possible that the citation in CO 6:334f. is based upon the *Sermones in Cantica*, which Calvin quoted extensively in the 1543 *Institutio*, largely completed by this time.

81 In CO 6:276.

82 Cf. Mooi, KDE 292–96. Theodoret and Cassiodore have been counted as two separate works.

83 In CO 6:261.

84 In CO 6:261f.

85 J. Trithemius, *Catalogus Scriptorum Ecclesiasticorum* (Cologne: P. Quentel, 1531) f. 2a, citing *Decretum Gratiani* Pars 1, dist. 15, c. 3, §. 29 (PL 187:76). It is also declared to be apocryphal by J. Driedo, *De ecclesiasticis scripturis et dogmatibus* Book 4, ch. 5, pt. 5 (Louvain: R. Rescius, 1533) 602.

86 E.g. PG 1:1159–1162, taken from a work of A. Gallandi of the 1760s.

memory.[87] The reference to an obscure work of Rufinus is more suspicious, but there is a simple explanation: it is found in at least some of the contemporary editions of Origen's works.[88] Calvin's use of Origen prior to 1543 was not excessive, but wide enough to suggest that Calvin had read his works.[89] It is not unlikely that he may at the same time have read Rufinus's *De adulteratione librorum Origenis*. Since there was no particular reason why someone interested in pseudo-Clement should think to look at Rufinus, the chances are that the brief reference here is from memory of that earlier reading.

This leaves seven works. How many of these did Calvin consult while preparing his response to Pighius? Calvin undoubtedly used Basil. Pighius quoted from two works by Basil.[90] Calvin responds to Pighius's quotations, adds some more material from one of the works and quotes from two more works.[91] We can be more precise about what happened because there were different translations of Basil. Pighius was using the Latin translation by Raphael Maffei Volaterranus, which appeared in five editions of Basil's *Opera* between 1515 and 1531.[92] Calvin, by contrast, in the passages that he cites, uses the translation by Janus Cornarius in the edition of the *Opera omnia* published in 1540 by Froben at Basel.[93] This fits the hypothesis propounded above. Calvin built up his patristic library on his return to Geneva. How better to start than by purchasing the fresh translation of Basil recently published by Froben at Basel?

There are four remaining works which Calvin might have used. Pighius quotes from Ambrose's *De Jacob et vita beata*.[94] Calvin discusses Pighius's quotations and then adds two short (three-line) quotations of his own. As he had twice cited this general passage in the 1539 *Institutio*,[95] it is clear that he was already familiar with it. Whether he was now quoting from memory or turned again to the text is not clear, though there is a clue that implies that he did have the work at hand. He notes that he is quoting 'ex

---

87 Cf. Mooi, KDE 289–92; I. Backus, 'Calvin's Judgment of Eusebius of Caesarea: An Analysis', *Sixteenth Century Journal* 22 (1991) 419–37. The Greek text of Eusebius was not published until 1544, so Calvin was dependent upon the Latin translation by Rufinus, printed in 1473 and many times thereafter (*Die Griechischen Christlichen Schriftsteller der ersten drei Jahrhunderte*, vol. 9/3 (Leipzig: Hinrichs'sche Buchhandlung, 1903) XLIII, CCLVI).

88 It is found, together with Pamphilus's *Apologia pro Origene* in the *Opera omnia* of Origen published at Paris in 1522 by Parvus, Badius and Resch. Pighius quotes Origen via Pamphilus's *Apologia* (*De libero arbitrio* ff. 22a-24a).

89 Cf. Mooi, KDE 209–12.

90 Pighius, *De libero arbitrio* f. 33a-b.

91 In CO 6:284–86.

92 IA 114.428, 440, 448f., 486. Cf. I. Backus, *Lectures humanistes de Basile de Césarée* (Paris: Institut d'Études Augustiniennes, 1990) 15–27.

93 *Omnia D. Basilii Magni ... Opera* (Basel: H. Froben and N. Episcopius, 1540) (IA 114:485). On this edition, cf. Backus, *Lectures humanistes*, 43–48, 232–38. Knowledge of which editions were used is quite important because they vary considerably (ibid., 9, 27, 48). The 1572 catalogue of the Genevan library contains Peter Martyr's copies of the 1532 Greek and the 1552 Latin editions of Basil (Ganoczy, BAC 168, 181).

94 Pighius, *De libero arbitrio* ff. 34b-35a.

95 OS 3:333, 506 (*Inst.* 2:7:7, 2:16:18).

eadem pagina, ex qua sumpsit Pighius quod adducit'.[96] If this statement is accurate, it would suggest that he had the volume open before him; if it is inaccurate, it would suggest that he was relying on memory. There were six editions of Ambrose between 1506 and 1539 and in two and only two of these, both published by the Chevallons in Paris, Pighius's and Calvin's quotations are found on the opposite sides of the same leaf.[97] Calvin's claim would thus be literally true if we allow 'pagina' here to mean leaf rather than side. That this translation is possible is shown by the contemporary French translation of the earlier passage where Augustine is cited, which renders 'cur non vertit paginam?' as 'Que ne tourne-il le fueillet . . .?'.[98]

Calvin cites Jerome repeatedly.[99] But all save one of these citations are drawn from the 1539 *Institutio*, Pighius or Augustine. The one exception is a brief statement about Jerome's *Epistola* 133.[100] Calvin already knew this letter since he had cited it in the 1539 *Institutio*,[101] so was probably here referring to it from memory. That he did not have Jerome to hand is confirmed by the way that he handles Pighius's material. He parries it without saying much at all about Jerome, which suggests either that he had no access to Jerome or that he had no time to turn to him.[102]

Tertullian's *De praescriptione haereticorum* is also cited. Calvin displays a definite knowledge of this work, but never quotes more than a single sentence[103] and makes mistakes.[104] This suggests that he was citing from memory without consulting the text.[105]

Finally, Calvin repeatedly cites Irenaeus.[106] Mostly he makes general statements about the *Adversus haereses*, but he also twice quotes from the work.[107] The first quotation is loose enough for Mooi to suggest that Calvin

---

96 CO 6:287. The 1572 catalogue of the Genevan library contains Peter Martyr's copy of the 1555 edition of Ambrose (Ganoczy, BAC 182).
97 The editions are IA 104.633, 644, 648, 651, 662, 663. IA alleges another edition in 1526 (104.647), citing the Nuremberg Stadtbibliothek as its only source. There are a number of suspicious features about this entry and a letter from the Stadtbibliothek has confirmed that the copy referred to (Theol. 172.2° and 173.2°) is not a 1526 Basel edition but is in fact the 1516 Basel edition (IA 104.644). In both the 1529 Claude Chevallon and the 1539 Gervase Chevallon Paris editions (nos. 651 and 663) the quotations are found on f. 289a&b.
98 CO 6:296. Cf. at n. 74, above. The French is found on p. 325 of the *Recueil des opuscules* (Geneva: B. Pinereul, 1566).
99 In CO 6:267, 286, 291, 299, 336.
100 In CO 6:267.
101 OS 3:299 (*Inst.* 2:5:2).
102 In CO 6:286. In his later works of 1543–44 (excluding the 1543 *Institutio*) Calvin shows more knowledge of Jerome (cf. CO 6:446, 516; 7:18, 22, 28, 38, 104; 9:827), which might suggest that the problem here is lack of time rather than lack of access. The 1572 catalogue of the Genevan library contains Peter Martyr's copy of the 1553 edition of Jerome (Ganoczy, BAC 179).
103 Which he twice does in CO 6:275.
104 He gives a faulty chapter reference (CO 6:260); he incorrectly claims that Tertullian lists all of the bishops of Rome to his time (CO 6:261) and that he commented on the small number of bishops in succession to the apostles up to his time (CO 6:278).
105 The 1572 catalogue of the Genevan library contains Peter Martyr's copy of the 1550 edition of Tertullian (Ganoczy, BAC 177).
106 In CO 6:260f., 274f., 278, 281f., 288, 290, 339.
107 In CO 6:275, 282.

quoted from memory having shortly before read the text,[108] but the second is longer (eleven lines) and more accurate. It appears, therefore, that Calvin had the text of Irenaeus to hand and this likelihood is reinforced by an examination of Calvin's other citations.[109]

It may be possible to identify the editions of pseudo-Clement and Irenaeus used by Calvin, if not the actual copy. In the debates with Servetus, recorded in the 1554 *Defensio orthodoxae fidei de sacra Trinitate*, Calvin and Servetus refer repeatedly to both writers, giving page and even line numbers. Servetus five times cites from the *Recognitiones* and Calvin four times cites alleged early papal letters, which were found in the editions of Clement. There are four potential editions prior to 1553, of which only the 1526 edition fits the page numbers.[110] With Irenaeus there are even more citations by Servetus and Calvin with page numbers and even, twice, line numbers. The five potential editions prior to 1553 have been examined and the page and line numbers in the Servetus debate fit both the 1528 and the 1534 Froben editions.[111] Can we decide which of these two editions Calvin used? The list of volumes that were sent to the Swiss churches together with the documents of the Servetus trial includes 'ung aultre livre intitule Opus D. Irenaei episcopi Lugdunensis, imprime a Basle par Froben lan 1528'.[112] Also, the 1528 edition is found in the 1572 Genevan Library catalogue, bound together with the 1526 edition of pseudo-Clement that Calvin used.[113] It is unlikely that there were many copies of pseudo-Clement in Geneva, which increases the likelihood that the library copy was Calvin's, which in turn increases the likelihood that the Irenaeus edition was also his. It is possible, to put it no stronger, that

---

108   Mooi, KDE 196, n. 3.
109   Cf. chapter 3, above, section III.b.
110   CO 8:514 (Servetus); 8:534 (Calvin). The potential editions are Basel: J. Bebel, 1526 (IA 140.921); Basel: [J. Bebel], 1536 (IA 140.923); Lyons: Hugues and heirs of Aimon de La Port, 1544 (IA 140.924); Paris: J. Roigny, 1544 (IA 140.925). I have checked all of these except IA 140.924, but it is clear from the pagination of that edition that it could not be the source. There is one place where Calvin gives the wrong page number, 76 instead of 56. This is clearly a typographical error as the next reference, to page 60, comes 'paulo post'.
111   CO 8:510–14, 530, 532, 542 (Servetus); 8:530, 533 (Calvin). The potential editions are Basel: J. Froben, 1526 and 1528; Basel: H. Froben and N. Episcopius, 1534 and 1548; Paris: V. Gaultherot, 1545 and three other 1545 Paris editions (Petit, Regnault and Dupuys). (Cf. O. Reimherr with F. E. Cranz, 'Irenaeus Lugdunensis' in V. Brown with P. O. Kristeller and F. E. Cranz (eds), *Catalogus Translationum et Commentariorum*, vol. 7 (Washington (DC): Catholic University of America Press, 1992) 31.) I have checked all of these except the last three Paris editions which, according to ibid., 37, form 'four issues' together with the other 1545 edition and which, according to the catalogue of the Bibliothèque Nationale in Paris, have the same number of pages as it. The 1526, 1545 and 1548 editions do not fit the page numbers. The 1528 and 1534 editions both fit exactly except for one place (CO 8:513) where p. 20 should read pp. 19f. (a slip that Servetus could easily have made).
112   CO 8:804. I am grateful to David Wright for drawing my attention to this passage.
113   Ganoczy, BAC 168. The Genevan library also had Peter Martyr's copy of the 1548 edition of Irenaeus (BAC 180). Were the passages cited by Servetus and Calvin marked in the volume? Irena Backus has kindly checked the Irenaeus/pseudo-Clement volume at Geneva and reports that while she saw no underlinings in pseudo-Clement there were some (very few) in Irenaeus. There were, apparently, no marginal notes.

he used the copies of Irenaeus and pseudo-Clement that found their way into the Genevan Library.

What works of non-Augustinian fathers did Calvin consult in preparing his response to Pighius? The evidence indicates that he used the 1540 Froben edition of Basil's works, editions of Irenaeus and pseudo-Clement (perhaps the copies currently bound together in the Genevan library) and that he turned briefly to Ambrose. Otherwise there is no indication that Calvin consulted any other patristic writings outside Augustine.

Finally, Calvin quotes from a number of councils: those of Carthage, Milevis and Orange. The number and length of the quotations leave no doubt that he has the source before him. The Council of Orange, which he cites extensively, is found not in the editions of Jacobus Merlin but first in Peter Crabbe's two-volume *Concilia omnia*.[114] All of the present citations from the councils can be found in the first volume of that work. Smits noted that almost all of Calvin's citations of the canons of Orange and the African councils appear in works published in 1543. Apart from repetitions of these citations, there are only three exceptions, from 1541, 1544 and 1547.[115] This would indicate that Calvin studied them soon after his return to Geneva, which reinforces the conclusion that he had a copy of Crabbe to hand, rather than relying on earlier reading, from Strassburg say.

(d) Conclusion

What conclusion have we reached? Here is Calvin's second most important work as regards his use of the fathers. He cites twenty-eight works of Augustine or pseudo-Augustine, thirty-three from nineteen other authors and three councils – a grand total of sixty-four works. How many books did he have to hand for this task? The evidence indicates that he had ten volumes at hand: five of Augustine's (1531/32 or 1541) *Opera omnia*, editions of Irenaeus and of pesudo-Clement (probably the 1526 and 1528 editions), the 1540 Basel edition of Basil, a (1529 or 1539) Chevallon edition of the works of Ambrose and the first volume of Crabbe's 1538 *Concilia*. Otherwise there is no firm evidence for the use of any other patristic sources. Thus this work may have been written with the help of as few as ten patristic volumes. But it is important to be clear about what is and is not being claimed. There is no firm evidence that Calvin used more than ten patristic volumes. In other words, there is no need to postulate the use of more than ten volumes to account for the evidence that we have. But this is not to be confused with the statement that Calvin definitely used only ten volumes. Absence of evidence is not evidence of absence and it . may be that Calvin consulted a further twenty volumes. But if he did consult further volumes, they had no discernible effect upon the final outcome.

114 Smits, SAOJC 1:232. This work was published by Peter Quentel at Cologne in 1538. Cf. also OS 5:113, n. 1. The medievals relied on compilations for their knowledge of the councils and these, including the most influential, the ninth-century pseudo-Isidorian *Decretals*, did not include Orange. Thus the canons of this council were unknown and unquoted from the tenth century to the publication of Crabbe (H. Bouillard, *Conversion et grace chez S. Thomas d'Aquin* (Paris: Aubier, 1944) 98–102, 114–21).
115 Smits, SAOJC 1:229f.

Why is this? Two reasons were noted at the beginning. First is lack of availability. At some stages in his career Calvin may have had access to a wide range of books, as during his stay with Louis du Tillet or his time at Basel. At other times this would not have been true and the early years at Geneva must have been among the most barren. Second is lack of time. *The Bondage and Liberation of the Will* was written in haste and Calvin did not have time to check all of his references or to follow up all of the issues that interested him. There is also a third reason. On this topic Calvin turns to Augustine for support. Where the writings of the other fathers or the young Augustine are concerned, his main aim is to parry Pighius's attack. There was little to be gained by discussing them at length.

Confirmation of this is found with Chrysostom. Calvin contributes nothing beyond what was said in the 1539 *Institutio* with the exception of one reference to a passage quoted by Pighius. Yet it is likely that Calvin had a copy of Chrysostom to hand, even if he did not use it. His copy of the 1536 edition of Chrysostom's works, complete with his own under-linings and marginal notes, is at present in the Genevan library.[116] The passages marked by Calvin appear especially in the 1543 *Institutio*,[117] which would suggest that Calvin had been reading Chrysostom not long before the time that he wrote his response to Pighius. But if he already possessed the volumes by this stage, why did he not use them? Probably because there was no point, because no amount of interpretation would bring Chrysostom into line with Calvin on this issue. Already, in the 1539 *Institutio* he had criticized Chrysostom's views, so there was no need to delay further with him.

III. CALVIN'S READING

Having sought to ascertain which works Calvin consulted in writing his *Bondage and Liberation of the Will*, we can now ask a different question. Which works was Calvin reading anyway around this time? There is a simple method to test this. From the works used we can eliminate all of those which Pighius introduced into the debate and all of those derived from an intermediary source.[118] What remains is a list of twelve works that Calvin introduced into the debate. The fact of his doing so might indicate that he was then reading these works or had recently done so.

Five of the works are by Augustine. Two of these are anti-Pelagian works which Calvin had already used for the 1539 *Institutio*.[119] He is likely to have turned to these in his intense use of the anti-Pelagian works while responding to Pighius. Another is the *De haeresibus*, which Calvin here cites directly for the first time.[120] Calvin's use of it probably reflects not prior reading but the need to challenge Pighius's equating of his views

---

116 Cf. Ganoczy, BAC 182; A. Ganoczy and K. Müller, *Calvins handschriftliche Annotationen zu Chrysostomus* (Wiesbaden: Franz Steiner, 1981).

117 Ganoczy and Müller, *Calvins handschriftliche Annotationen*, 24–27, 162.

118 Some citations are drawn from the 1539 *Institutio*; some are taken from Augustine; some come from another source, such as Eusebius or Cassiodore. For details, see the table of works in section VI, below.

119 *De dono perseverantiae* and *De perfectione iustitiae hominis*.

120 Cf. n. 42, above.

with those of the early heretics. The other two Augustinian works are the *De civitate dei* and the *Enarrationes in Psalmos*. From the former there is only one brief sentence of quotation, too little to suggest recent reading, but the three brief quotations from the latter, probably drawn from memory, could well indicate that Calvin had recently been reading it.[121]

Of the non-Augustinian works, four do not necessarily indicate Calvin's *current* reading. Calvin's citations of Eusebius and Rufinus over the question of the Clementine *Recognitiones* probably come from memory of earlier reading of Eusebius and Origen.[122] The citation of Theodoret via Cassiodore probably reflects memory of earlier reading of the latter.[123] Calvin also cites Tertullian's *De praescriptione haereticorum*, the only time before 1550 that he does so. This might suggest that he might have been reading it at around this time, but there are indications to the contrary. The brevity of his quotations and the mistakes that he makes[124] suggest that his encounter with the work was less recent. It may well be that the book was brought into the debates at the colloquies of 1539 to 1541 at which Pighius, who had recently been quoting from it,[125] was present. Calvin's knowledge of this work may derive from that time.

In 1545 François Baudouin wrote to Calvin announcing that he had tried unsuccessfully to send him a copy of Tertullian's *Opera*, presumably the 1545 Paris edition.[126] It might appear, therefore, that Calvin did not have a copy prior to that time (hence the nature of his use of Tertullian in 1543) and that his serious reading of Tertullian began after Baudouin eventually sent the 1545 edition, but the other evidence does not fit this theory. First, between 1545 and 1553 Calvin cites Tertullian a mere seven times, compared to ten times prior to the *Bondage and Liberation of the Will*, eleven times in that work and a further three times in 1543 and 1544.[127] Also, Tertullian is cited repeatedly in the 1554 *Defensio orthodoxae fidei de sacra Trinitate*, by and against Servetus. Page and line numbers are given and these show that it is the 1528 Basel, not the 1545 Paris, edition that Calvin is using.[128] This result is confirmed by the list of volumes that were

---

121 It is suggested, above, that Calvin may have relied on memory for citations from *In evangelium Johannis tractatus*, *Contra Faustum Manichaeum* and *Contra Julianum*. The brevity of Calvin's citations of these works does not encourage the idea that he had recently been reading them.

122 Cf. nn. 83–89, above.

123 Cf. nn. 81f., above.

124 Cf. nn. 103f., above.

125 Pighius does not cite this work in his *De libero arbitrio*, but he did cite it on the present topic in his 1538 *Hierarchiae ecclesiasticae assertio* (P. Polman, *L'Élément historique dans la controverse religieuse du XVIe siècle* (Gembloux: J. Duculot, 1932) 288; P. Fraenkel, *Testimonia Patrum* (Geneva: E. Droz, 1961) 279).

126 CO 12:231. Cf. Chapter 1, n. 62, above.

127 Following Mooi's figures (KDE 365–81), but excluding the Genesis commentary which he wrongly dates as 1550. In fact Mooi's figures underestimate the number before 1543 and exaggerate the number from 1545 to 1553.

128 I have examined the six relevant editions known to me: Basel: J. Froben, 1521; Basel; H. Froben and N. Episcopius, 1528; Basel: H. Froben and N. Episcopius, 1539; Paris: C. Guillard, 1545; Paris: J. Roigny/C. Guillard, 1545; Basel; H. Froben and N. Episcopius, 1550. Page numbers are given in Servetus's references (CO 8:507–11, 514f., 522, 525f., 528–30, 542f.) and Calvin's (CO 8:527–29). Line numbers are given in CO 8:510, 525, 528f., 543.

sent to the Swiss churches together with the documents of the Servetus trial, which includes 'Opera Tertuliani, imprimees a Basle Ian 1528, mense martio'.[129] Calvin cites Tertullian continuously and modestly until he is forced to engage more fully with him by Pighius and (especially) Servetus.[130]

Three works remain. As mentioned, Calvin's appeals to the African councils almost all appear in 1543. This would indicate that he was probably studying Crabbe's 1538 edition at around this time, maybe having only recently acquired a copy.[131] Finally, Calvin quotes from two works of Basil which had not previously entered the debate. These are drawn from the recently published Cornarius translation.[132] Why did he quote these two works? The choice of one is not surprising since it was entitled *De libero arbitrio*. A perfunctory glance at the Basil volume could have led Calvin to this work. But the other work is less obvious. Calvin quotes from Basil's *Homiliae in Psalmos*. Why this work? The quotation is not especially relevant and contributes little to the argument. The natural interpretation is that Calvin was at this time reading Basil and so introduced a quotation from a passage that he remembered.[133] This conclusion is strengthened by the fact that prior to his response to Pighius and including the 1543 *Institutio* (which was almost finished by this time) Calvin's citations of Basil are rare and extremely brief.[134] It is likely that Calvin was at around this time beginning his first serious reading of Basil.

What conclusion have we reached? There is clear evidence that Calvin at this time was studying two books: the Crabbe edition of the councils and the Cornarius translation of Basil. He makes good use of these in his response to Pighius, introducing works which had not previously been used either in his 1539 *Institutio* or in Pighius's attack on it. Apart from these two books, there is little evidence of Calvin's reading, other than the study of Augustine's anti-Pelagian works and his *De haeresibus* needed to answer Pighius. There is evidence of earlier reading of the *Enarrationes in Psalmos*, but no clear indication that this reading was recent. The same applies to Tertullian's *De praescriptione haereticorum*, the use of which does not indicate recent reading.

IV. CALVIN'S USE OF THE FATHERS

In the final part of the chapter we will consider the manner in which Calvin uses the fathers in his *Bondage and Liberation of the Will*. Calvin and Pighius differed fundamentally concerning the relation between Scripture and tradition. Calvin maintained that he was defending God's truth against

---

129 CO 8:804. I am grateful to David Wright for drawing my attention to this passage.
130 For more on Calvin's use of Tertullian, cf. my forthcoming 'Tertullianus totus noster? Calvin's Use of Tertullian'.
131 Cf. at nn. 114f., above.
132 Cf. at nn. 91, 93, above.
133 This is paralleled by the way in which Calvin acquired the 1552 Basel edition of Bernard's works and two years later began to introduce new Bernardine material (chapter 4, above, at nn. 78f.).
134 In CO 1:442, 508, 646, 891; 5:181, 394; 9:834. Cf. chapter 3, above, section III.d.

Pighius's attacks.[135] But where is this truth to be found? For Calvin, God's truth is the 'sure truth of Scripture', the light of truth shining in the word of God.[136] The rule of faith is to be sought in the Word of God, in Scripture, in the oracles of God, not in tradition.[137] The teaching of the fathers has value, but is always open to correction in the light of Scripture.[138] Pighius, however, regarded the consensus of the tradition of the Catholic Church as normative. Scripture without the definitions of the church is obscure and is a nose of wax which can be turned this way and that by heretics. A norm for correct belief is required and is found in the tradition of the church, which is the pillar and bulwark of the truth. Indeed, he goes so far as to say that any scripture that goes against tradition is to be disregarded.[139] There is a certain irony in this. Pighius maintains that Scripture is obscure, but that the fathers nonetheless managed to interpret it correctly. Calvin, on the other hand, maintained that Scripture is clear, but that most of the fathers had nonetheless failed to grasp its meaning, at least on this issue.[140]

Calvin responds to Pighius's charges by accusing him of exalting human tradition above God's Word. His approach involves twisting Scripture to make it conform with human decisions, and thus subordinating it to them. It is true that heretics distort Scripture, as did Satan when tempting Christ. But the latter in his response relied on Scripture alone. Calvin also defended his stance from other passages of Scripture.[141] The underlying issue is the nature of the true church. For Pighius this is the institutional Catholic Church, which cannot err and whose teaching is the true Christian faith. For Calvin the true church is that which adheres to the Word of God.[142] Here is the fundamental divide of the Reformation.

(a) Other Fathers

This issue of the relation between Scripture and tradition was also fought out in the arena of the early fathers. Pighius claimed their support for his approach.[143] Calvin denies this. Irenaeus, he claims, regarded Scripture as normative.[144] Tertullian's own practice does not match what he says in his

---

135 CO 6:235–37. For this paragraph especially, a computer word search has been used to examine Calvin's use of *consensus, definitio, evangelium, oraculum, scriptura, verbum* and *veritas*.
136 CO 6:271, 273f., 277, 327f., 347f., 391.
137 CO 6:267–71.
138 CO 6:276–78. Cf. chapter 2, above, section VI.a.
139 Pighius, *De libero arbitrio* ff. 18b-19a, 20a-21b, 58b, 84a-b. Pighius repeatedly referred to the Bible as a nose of wax (Polman, *L'Élément historique*, 286f.).
140 I am grateful to Graham Davies for this observation.
141 CO 6:267–74, 277, 288, 326, 373f. Calvin uses the phrase *sola scriptura* with approval (6:268) and chides Pighius for rejecting the principle of *nuda scriptura* (6:269). But of course neither of these was yet a slogan in the way that *sola scriptura* was to become. Cf. A. N. S. Lane, 'Sola Scriptura? Making Sense of a Post-Reformation Slogan' in P. E. Satterthwaite and D. F. Wright (eds), *A Pathway into the Holy Scripture* (Grand Rapids: Eerdmans, 1994) esp. 298.
142 Pighius, *De libero arbitrio* f. 58b; CO 6:326f.
143 Pighius, *De libero arbitrio* ff. 21b-22a.
144 CO 6:274f.

De praescriptione and, furthermore, he himself falls into error.[145] Origen's essentials of the faith include opinions now regarded as heretical.[146] Calvin also goes onto the attack by citing Constantine's words to the council of Nicea and by appealing to Augustine.[147] He does, however, concede that there is value in the agreement of the churches concerning matters of faith, as long as Scripture remains the norm. Where the agreement of the churches is added, it is an exceptional witness to seal the certainty of our faith.[148] Thus, just as the Spirit bears witness to Scripture, yet the church and rational proofs are secondary helps, so also the agreement of the churches can be a secondary confirmation of Christian doctrine.[149]

The dispute over the fathers falls into two distinct halves: Augustine and the other fathers. This distinction had already been made by Calvin in the 1539 *Institutio*, where he twice claimed that apart from Augustine, the early fathers are so confused, vacillating and contradictory on the subject of free choice that almost nothing can with certainty be ascertained from their writings.[150] Pighius devoted much of his second book to refuting this claim. In return, he claimed the clear and universal consent of the orthodox fathers for his own belief in free choice.[151] Calvin responded in a variety of ways.

First, he clarified what it was that he had claimed. He had been completely frank in the 1539 *Institutio* about the fact that the fathers exalted human powers excessively, through the pressure of Greek philosophy and for fear of encouraging laziness. He also stood by his claim that their teachings were obscure and inconsistent, in particular about the limits of human power.[152] But by this he had meant that they differed from one another, not that they were internally inconsistent, though he also maintained that these fathers were confused inasmuch as they failed to take fully into account the effects of the Fall.[153]

Secondly, he engages in a protracted discussion of the teaching of the fathers: Origen, pseudo-Clement, Tertullian, Irenaeus, Cyprian, Hilary, Basil, Jerome, Ambrose and Chrysostom.[154] There is a standard reply that he uses. Where Pighius cites a passage which suggests that free choice is unimpaired, Calvin presents him with a dilemma. Either the father was referring to *unfallen* human nature (in opposition to Gnosticism, say), in which case the passage is irrelevant, or he had failed to distinguish between human nature as created and fallen, in which case he was heretical by the standards of later Catholic orthodoxy.[155]

Calvin concludes his discussion of these fathers with a number of observations. First, in opposition to Pighius's claim, he maintains that the

---

145 CO 6:275f., 277f.
146 CO 6:277f., 291.
147 CO 6:276.
148 CO 6:276f. Cf. CO 6:288.
149 For further reasons why Calvin needed to dispute the teaching of the fathers rather than appeal to Scripture alone, cf. chapter 2, above, section V.
150 Cf. n. 3, above.
151 Pighius, *De libero arbitrio* ff. 21a-b., 58b.
152 CO 6:284, w.r.t. OS 3:244 (*Inst.* 2:2:4).
153 CO 6:291f.
154 CO 6:280–91. Bernard is mentioned in the conclusion (291), but not previously.
155 CO 6:280–85, 290, w.r.t. Origen, Tertullian, Irenaeus, Hilary and Basil.

only consensus of the church is that which is in accord with the Word of God.[156] Such a dogmatic dismissal of the historical evidence would, of course, render superfluous all the preceding discussion of the fathers, so Calvin does not stop there. He proceeds to question what is meant by the consensus of the church. Merely to produce badly selected quotations here and there from six or eight patristic writings does not suffice. The common agreement of the church is not found in the private opinions of a few writers.[157]

These vague statements are made more specific in one particular instance. Calvin juxtaposes a series of statements from Hilary, quoted by Pighius, and canons from the council of Orange that condemn those views. He then challenges Pighius's claim that Hilary represents the official tradition of the church.[158] The council of Orange so effectively undermined Pighius's claim that Calvin twice returns to it.[159] It also encouraged him to claim against Pighius that there is no such thing as a lasting consensus of teaching in the church on this matter.[160] Finally, Calvin quotes Augustine's observation that those who wrote before the rise of the Pelagian controversy are not the best guides because they were not forced to address the points at issue.[161]

Calvin concludes his second book by briefly surveying the disputed fathers.[162] The Clementine *Recognitiones* are counterfeit. Irenaeus and Tertullian wrote about human nature as originally created. Ambrose and Basil, he claims, offer little support to Pighius. Origen is an unreliable witness.[163] This leaves Pighius with Hilary (who is refuted by the council of Orange), Jerome (who was more careful after the rise of Pelagius) and Chrysostom (whom Calvin would not defend). Finally, Calvin claims that Bernard, mentioned elsewhere by Pighius, is predominantly on his side.

In addition to appealing to the consent of the fathers, Pighius seeks to identify the Reformers' teaching with that of the early heretics.[164] Calvin denies the charge, contrasting his own teaching with that of the heretics as set out by Augustine.[165] He also regularly accuses Pighius of Pelagianism,[166] as well as once calling him a Manichee.[167]

---

156 CO 6:288.
157 CO 6:277, 288.
158 CO 6:288f.
159 CO 6:305, 363f.
160 CO 6:289f.
161 CO 6:290.
162 CO 6:290f.
163 Calvin accuses Origen of heresy, drawing on the judgment of Jerome (CO 6:291), but was unaware that Origen had been condemned by an ecumenical council, an argument that he could not have failed to use had he been aware of it. He also refers to 'those crazy ideas of Tertullian and Origen which we all equally reject' (CO 6:278), but shows no awareness that Tertullian's status as a Catholic church father might be questioned.
164 Pighius, *De libero arbitrio* ff. 16b-17b, 19a, 72b-73a.
165 CO 6:260–64, 308f., 350f.
166 CO 6:304, 336, 338f., 360, 363–65, 372, 384, 397.
167 CO 6:361. On the justice of this charge, cf. A. N. S. Lane, 'Bondage and Liberation in Calvin's Treatise against Pighius', in J. H. Leith and R. A. Johnson (eds), *Calvin Studies IX* (Davidson (NC): Davidson College and Davidson College Presbyterian Church, 1998) 35.

(b) Augustine

Calvin, in the 1539 *Institutio*, claimed the support of Augustine, a claim which Pighius denies. He accuses Calvin of quoting Augustine out of context and without understanding him, of quoting mutilated passages contrary to Augustine's meaning.[168] Calvin was stung by this charge and took care that his third book would not face such an accusation.[169] He quotes lengthy passages with reference to their context. He concludes the book with extended quotations from some of Augustine's last works and ends by stressing that these are not mutilated, maimed statements.[170] Calvin also responds by accusing Pighius of twisting Augustine and, in one place, of inserting his own phrase into a quotation.[171]

But the dispute over Augustine hung on more than accusations of dishonest exegesis. Both men recognized the importance of discerning the changes in Augustine's position. Pighius divided his writings into three groups: those before the Pelagian controversy, those written during the heat of the controversy and those written on the subject without polemical heat.[172] Calvin was happy to accept this division, though with one qualification.[173] Pighius tried to minimize the effect of the anti-Pelagian works by suggesting that Augustine's teaching there was sometimes excessively one-sided because of his polemic. He wanted, therefore, to place more reliance upon the works from the third stage. This was an unwise move in that Augustine's last writings are more consistently 'Augustinian' than some of the earlier anti-Pelagian writings. It is interesting that neither writer acknowledges the fact, noted by Augustine himself, that the fundamental shift in his thought took place not with the beginning of the Pelagian controversy but nearly twenty years earlier, in the mid-390s.[174]

Pighius quotes at length from Augustine's anti-Manichean works.[175] Calvin responds, mainly by interpreting these in the light of Augustine's *Retractationes*.[176] The author of the *Retractationes* and Calvin both had the same aim: to bring these writings as far as possible into harmony with Augustine's mature views. For each of them, this is essentially an exercise in damage limitation. Many statements about freewill are referred to human nature as originally created, on the grounds that this was the issue against the Manichees. Augustine himself excused the paucity of reference to original sin and the corruption of fallen human nature on the grounds that he was then debating the Manichees, who did not accept the Old Testament.[177] As a last resort, Calvin concedes that the young, anti-

---

168 Pighius, *De libero arbitrio* ff. 37a-b, 64a.
169 He responds to these charges in CO 6:292–94, 337 w.r.t. the specific passages mentioned by Pighius.
170 CO 6:320–26.
171 CO 6:299, 307, 314f.
172 Pighius, *De libero arbitrio* ff. 37b-38a. This distinction is different from that reported in J. van Oort, 'John Calvin and the Church Fathers' in I. Backus (ed.), *The Reception of the Church Fathers in the West*, vol. 2 (Leiden, etc.: E. J. Brill, 1997) 678f.
173 CO 6:294, 297.
174 *De praedestinatione sanctorum* 4:8. Cf. E. TeSelle, *Augustine the Theologian* (London: Burns & Oates, 1970) 156–65, 176–82.
175 Pighius, *De libero arbitrio* ff. 38b-47a.
176 CO 6:294–301.
177 CO 6:297.

Manichean Augustine still had much to learn about grace, a deficiency that the Pelagian controversy would help to resolve.[178]

Pighius then moves to the anti-Pelagian works.[179] Calvin is very happy to fight on this ground, though he rejected Pighius's attempt to weaken the force of these writings.[180] Here it is Pighius who is on the defensive, accusing Augustine of a sophistry unworthy of him.[181] Calvin responds with a thorough examination of the works cited by Pighius, as well as others of Augustine. He argues that where Augustine speaks of fallen humanity as free, he means by this not that good and evil are equally in our power, but rather that our choices are voluntary. This is true despite our being subject to a necessity to sin. Finally, Pighius turns to the third group of writings. Calvin finds much material for his cause here and suggests that the whole controversy should be settled on the basis of Augustine's last works.[182]

Much of the battle revolved around language. Augustine, when his views changed, continued to affirm both free will and free choice, but redefined them. This enabled him to claim considerable continuity both with earlier writers and with his own early writings, as in the *Retractationes*. Calvin, like Luther, adopted a different strategy. Already in the 1539 *Institutio* he affirmed that he believed in the freedom of the will as it was understood by Augustine, but did not wish to retain the term.[183] Calvin repeats this in his response to Pighius, defining precisely the senses in which the will is and is not free.[184] But Pighius treats passages where Augustine affirms free choice as refutations of Calvin and the latter has to devote much energy to refuting this. There might have been less heat and more light had Calvin been willing to follow Augustine's approach and to affirm free choice, while defining it carefully.

V. CONCLUSION

What conclusions can we draw? Here is Calvin's second most important work as regards his use of the fathers. He makes use of at least seven, probably nearer ten, patristic volumes. He also draws on his extensive earlier reading of the fathers and at least some current reading. Drawing on these resources, and making the most of the material presented by his opponent, he puts together an impressive case – the more impressive when one remembers the shortness of time at his disposal. He displays a thorough mastery of the anti-Pelagian Augustine. With the other fathers he shows himself a skilled debater who could argue a good case with minimal resources at his disposal.

---

178 CO 6:297, 301.
179 Pighius, *De libero arbitrio* ff. 47a–53a.
180 CO 6:301–12.
181 Pighius, *De libero arbitrio* f. 47b; CO 6:301f.
182 CO 6:312–26.
183 OS 3:249–51 (*Inst.* 2:2:7f.).
184 CO 6:279f., 292f., 311–13. Cf. A. N. S. Lane, 'Did Calvin Believe in Freewill?' *Vox Evangelica* 12 (1981) 72–90; Lane, 'Bondage and Liberation in Calvin's Treatise against Pighius', 16–45.

VI. WORKS USED IN CALVIN'S
BONDAGE AND LIBERATION OF THE WILL

This is a list not of suspected patristic allusions but of (1) works *named* by Calvin (not marked); (2) works not named but clearly cited by Calvin (marked with a *); (3) works named by Pighius and referred to by Calvin (marked with a #); (4) works clearly quoted by Pighius, without naming them, and referred to by Calvin (marked with a §); (5) works named by Calvin in the 1539 *Institutio* and here referred to by him (marked with a ¶); (6) unnamed but clear intermediate source of Calvin's quotation (marked with a ◊)

Author	*Work*	*Used?*	*Source*[185]
Augustine	**Confessiones*	No	*Inst.*
	Contra duas epistolas Pelagianorum	Yes	Erasmus vol. 7
	Contra Faustum Manichaeum	Probably not	Pighius + Memory
	Contra Julianum	Cannot say	Erasmus vol. 7 or Memory
	De actis cum Felice Manichaeo	No	Pighius
	De civitate dei	Probably not	Memory
	De correptione et gratia	Yes	Erasmus vol. 7
	De dono perseverantiae	Yes	Erasmus vol. 7
	De duabus animabus	No	Pighius; *Retr.*
	De gratia Christi et de peccato originali	Yes	Erasmus vol. 7
	De gratia et libero arbitrio	Yes	Erasmus vol. 7
	De haeresibus	Yes	Erasmus vol. 6
	De libero arbitrio	No	Pighius; *Retr.*
	De natura et gratia	Yes	Erasmus vol. 7
	De peccatorum meritis et remissione	Yes	Erasmus vol. 7
	De perfectione iustitiae hominis	Yes	Erasmus vol. 7
	De praedestinatione sanctorum	Yes	Erasmus vol. 7
	De quantitate animae	No	Pighius
	De spiritu et littera	Yes	Erasmus vol. 3
	De vera religione	No	Pighius; *Retr.*
	Enarrationes in Psalmos	Probably not	Memory
	Enchiridion	Yes	Erasmus vol. 3
	Epistolae	Yes	Erasmus vol. 2
	Retractationes	Yes	Erasmus vol. 1
	Tractatus in evangelium Johannis	Probably not	*Inst.*; Pighius; Memory
Pseudo-Augustine	*De dogmatibus ecclesiasticis*	Yes	Erasmus vol. 3
	Hypognosticon	Yes	Erasmus vol. 7
	§Sermo 236	No	Pighius

---

185 The sources identified are: (1) memory of earlier reading (= Memory); (2) 1539 *Institutio* (= *Inst.*); (3) volume x of Erasmian edition of Augustine (= Erasmus vol. x); (4) Pighius, *De libero arbitrio* (= Pighius); (5) Augustine, *Retractationes* (= *Retr.*); (6) Augustine (for other authors) (= Augustine); (7) Specific editions (named) for other authors; (8) P. Crabbe, *Concilia omnia* (= Crabbe).

Author	Work	Used?	Source
Ambrose	*De fuga saeculi*	No	Augustine
	*/#De Jacob et vita beata	Yes	Chevallon edition
	Expositio evangelii secundum Lucam	No	Augustine
Basil	*#Constitutiones asceticae*	No	Pighius
	*/#Homiliae	Yes	Froben edition
	*Homiliae in Psalmos	Yes	Froben edition
Pseudo-Basil	**De libero arbitrio*	Yes	Froben edition
Bernard	**De gratia et libero arbitrio*	No	*Inst.* + Memory
Cassiodore	*◊Historia tripartita*	Probably not	Memory
Chrysostom	**Homilia de ferendis reprehensionibus*	No	*Inst.*
	#Homiliae in Genesim	No	*Inst.*; Pighius
	*Homiliae in Matthaeum	No	*Inst.*
Pseudo-Chrysostom	*¶Homilia in dominica I adventus domini*	No	*Inst.*
Clement	*Epistolae*	No	Eusebius, *Historia ecclesiastica*
Pseudo-Clement	*Recognitiones*	Yes	Bebel edition
Cyprian	**De dominica oratione*	No	Augustine
	*Testimonia	No	Augustine
Cyril	*§Commentarius in Johannis evangelium*	No	Pighius
Eusebius	*Historia ecclesiastica*	Probably not	Memory
Hilary	*#Tractatus super Psalmos*	No	Pighius
Irenaeus	**Adversus haereses*	Yes	Froben edition
Jerome	*§Adversus Jovinianum*	No	Augustine; *Inst.*; Pighius
	¶Dialogi contra Pelagianos	No	*Inst.*
	Epistolae	No	*Inst.*; Pighius + Memory
	#Hebraicae quaestiones in Genesim	No	Pighius
Origen	*#De principiis*	No	Pighius
Pamphilus	*#Apologia pro Origene*	No	Pighius
Peter Lombard	*¶Sententiae*	No	*Inst.*
Prosper	*#De vocatione omnium gentium*	No	Pighius
Rufinus	*De adulteratione librorum Origenis*	Probably not	Memory

Author	Work	Used?	Source
Tertullian	*Adversus Marcionem*	No	Pighius
	De praescriptione haereticorum	Probably not	Memory
Theodoret	**Historia ecclesiastica*	No	Edition of Cassiodore
Council of Carthage (416)		Yes	Crabbe
Council of Milevis (416)		Yes	Crabbe
Council of Carthage (418)		Yes	Crabbe
	Concilium Africanum	Yes	Crabbe
Council of Orange (529)		Yes	Crabbe

7

❦

The Influence upon Calvin
of his Debate with Pighius

I. INTRODUCTION

In the winter of 1542 to 1543 Calvin was engaged in controversy with the Dutch Roman Catholic theologian Albert Pighius (or Pigge). Calvin's *Defensio sanae et orthodoxae doctrinae de servitute et liberatione humani arbitrii adversus calumnias Alberti Pighii Campensis*, which will hereafter simply be referred to as *The Bondage and Liberation of the Will*, has received relatively little attention, but is an important work.[1] This chapter will examine the extent to which Calvin might have been influenced by his debate with Pighius, especially by his use of the fathers and of Aristotle.[2]

First, a word about the controversy. The second edition of Calvin's *Institutio*, which appeared in 1539 had seventeen chapters. Two of these concern us here: chapter two on *the knowledge of humanity and free choice* and chapter eight on *the predestination and providence of God*. When this edition appeared, Bernardus Cincius, the Roman Catholic bishop of Aquila, showed it to cardinal Marcello Cervini. They agreed that this work was more dangerous than the other 'Lutheran' writings and showed it to Pighius.[3] He wrote a response to these two chapters, which was published

This chapter originally appeared as 'The Influence upon Calvin of his Debate with Pighius' in L. Grane, A. Schindler, M. Wriedt (eds), *Auctoritas Patrum II. New Contributions on the Reception of the Church Fathers in the 15th and 16th Centuries* (Mainz: Philipp von Zabern, 1998) 125–39.

---

1 The Latin text is found in CO 6:229–404. Quotations below are taken from the English translation: John Calvin, *The Bondage and Liberation of the Will* (Grand Rapids: Baker & Carlisle: Paternoster, 1996), edited by A. N. S. Lane, translated by G. I. Davies. I am also editing this work for the new *Opera recognita* series, published by Droz. All references to the work below will be by CO column numbers, which are given in both of these editions.

2 The first edition of this chapter contained 'a brief summary of Calvin's use of the fathers in this work' (127f.) which is redundant here in the light of chapter 6, above.

3 C. Schultingius, *Bibliothecae catholicae et orthodoxae, contra summam totius theologiae calvinianae in Institutionibus Ioannis Calvini, et Locis Communibus Petri Martyris* (Cologne, 1602) 1:39f.; H. Jedin, *Studien über die Schriftstellertätigkeit Albert Pigges* (Münster: Aschendorff, 1931) 163 (Pighius's own account of this).

179

in August 1542, his *De libero hominis arbitrio et divina gratia, Libri decem*.[4] Of the ten books, the first six respond to Calvin's second chapter, the remaining four to chapter eight.

Calvin, when he saw Pighius's work, felt a pressing need to respond, lest the evangelical cause be lost by default. He wanted his reply to be ready in time for the 1543 Frankfurt Book Fair, which meant that he had time to answer only Pighius's first six books, on free choice.[5] Some time in February 1543 he published his *Bondage and Liberation of the Will*. It was Calvin's intention to write an answer to the remaining four books, on providence and predestination, in time for the 1544 Book Fair.[6] But in the meantime Pighius had died, so Calvin decided to drop the project, so as 'not to insult a dead dog'.[7] But the controversy over predestination did not cease and in 1551 it burst into life at Geneva itself, as Calvin's doctrine was attacked by Jerome Bolsec.[8] Calvin responded to Bolsec, while also settling the old score with Pighius, in his *De aeterna praedestinatione dei*, which appeared in 1552.[9]

Why consider Calvin's use of the fathers in this particular work? This work contains more patristic citations than any other of Calvin's works apart from the *Institutio* and indeed contains more citations than any three such works.[10] This is not surprising as a major thrust of his controversy with Pighius was the dispute about the teaching of the fathers, especially Augustine. It is not just the *number* of citations that reflects this emphasis. In Book 3, for example, about a third of the text is composed of patristic quotation. Calvin is concerned throughout, so far as possible, to claim the support of the fathers:

> I declare that I am not at war with the ancient fathers – only with Pighius and those like him, whether dogs or pigs, who some of the time befoul the sacred saving truth of God with their vile, filthy snouts, and at other times trample it underfoot or tear it with poisonous teeth or pursue it with their barking.[11]

What of the influence of this debate upon Calvin's thought and writings? Calvin is fully aware of progress at least in the outward expression of his teaching. When Pighius notes the differences between Luther and

---

4 Cologne: M. Novesian, 1542.
5 CO 6:229f., 233f., 236f.
6 CO 6:404.
7 *Concerning the Eternal Predestination of God* (tr. J. K. S. Reid) (London: James Clarke, 1961) 54.
8 For a full account of the Bolsec controversy, cf. P. Holtrop, *The Bolsec Controversy on Predestination from 1551 to 1555* (Lewiston (NY), Queenston (Ontario) and Lampeter: Edwin Mellen, 1993).
9 Geneva: J. Crespin, 1552. Cf. n. 7, above.
10 For these figures, cf. the tables in R. J. Mooi, KDE 365–97. While his figures may not be 100 per cent accurate, they suffice for comparative purposes like this. On Mooi's figures, the 1559 *Institutio* has 866 citations; *The Bondage and Liberation of the Will*, 310; *Def. c. err. Serveti*, 108; the three replies to Westphal, 194; *Diluc. explic. Heshusii*, 99; *Comm.* 1 and 2 Corinthians, 98; *De praed.*, 98; *Art. fac. Par.*, 81. For a slightly different comparison, the 1539 *Institutio* has 301, the 1543 edition has 418 *new* citations.
11 CO 6:331.

Melanchthon over the question of the absolute necessity of all events Calvin explains (away) the difference as follows:

> Concerning ourselves we gladly admit what tradition says that Solon used to boast about himself: that we learn every day as we grow old, or at any rate hasten towards old age. But why does Pighius demand of us that we declare that we have taught error, when even now we persevere steadily in our adherence to that totality of doctrine which we have always avowed? It is indeed possible that we use different ways of speaking, that almost every one of us has his own manner of speaking which is different from that of others. But why could we not be allowed something that has been the common practice of everyone in every generation? This too I recognize without reluctance, that when our works are reprinted we improve what was rather coarse, we soften what was too harshly expressed, we clarify obscure points, we explain more fully and at greater length what was too compressed, we also strengthen our argument with new reasons, and finally, where we fear the danger of causing offence, we also tone down and soften our language. For what would be the point of living if neither age nor practice nor constant exercise nor reading nor meditation were of any benefit to us? And what would be the point of making progress if it did not result in some profit reaching others also? On the contrary, if Pighius does not know it, I should like it to be absolutely clear to him that we strive night and day to shape our faithfully transmitted teachings into a form which we also judge will be the best.[12]

How could one discern such influence? There are three procedures that will be used. First, Calvin makes claims in his *Bondage and Liberation of the Will* about his earlier teaching. But a knowledge of historical theology teaches us that claims like 'the church has always taught' need to be assessed critically. This will be done with Calvin's claims. Secondly, the teaching of *The Bondage and Liberation of the Will* will be examined carefully for evidence of new developments. Finally, almost all of the material from chapter two of the 1539 *Institutio* is incorporated into the later editions. In these editions new material is also added, which will be examined carefully.[13] The aim will be to trace the influence upon Calvin of this debate in general and of his interaction with the fathers and with classical philosophy in particular.

II. CLAIMS ABOUT EARLIER TEACHING

Calvin repeatedly rebuts Pighius's accusations with claims about his previous teaching. The task of editing an English translation of this

---

12 CO 6:250.
13 The OS edition has hundreds of textual footnotes relating to the material from chapter two of the 1539 edition, mostly concerning minor verbal alterations. These changes have been examined for evidence of theological revision and, in particular, for evidence of any influence from the debate with Pighius. This examination has revealed nothing of interest.

work[14] has involved tracing all of Calvin's sources, both for his citations of others and for his references to his own earlier teaching. Every claim regarding his earlier teaching has been tested and precise references given. There emerges just one point where Calvin's claim is seriously open to question. In response to Pighius's appeal to the early fathers he states: 'We do not deny that man was created with free choice, endowed as he was with sound intelligence of mind and uprightness of will.'[15] In the context of Pighius's appeal to Augustine Calvin makes a more explicit claim regarding his earlier teaching: 'Pighius lays down that man was made with free choice. We accept this, and did not wait for him to demand this of us; we have always owned this belief.'[16] The acknowledgement that Adam was created with free choice is explicit in the 1559 *Institutio*.[17] But in the 1539 edition the nearest that Calvin comes is the acceptance of Augustine's teaching that Adam's original freedom was 'posse non peccare'.[18] Where Calvin explains why he prefers not to follow Augustine in affirming *liberum arbitrium* he does so on the grounds that fallen humanity is in bondage to sin.[19] Since this objection would not apply to Adam before the Fall Calvin is justified in his claim that he never *denies* 'that man was created with free choice'. But it is not until the 1559 edition that he positively affirms what he earlier did not deny.

III. NEW DEVELOPMENTS IN
THE BONDAGE AND LIBERATION OF THE WILL

The Bondage and Liberation of the Will is the fullest discussion that Calvin ever devotes to the issue of the bondage of the will. It is not surprising, therefore, that it contains new developments. Some of these will be considered here, especially those relating to Augustine and Aristotle.

Luther, in the early years of the Reformation, was unremittingly hostile towards the use of Aristotle in theology. Compared with the medieval scholastics, Calvin made little use of Aristotle but he was not unwilling to invoke Aristotelian distinctions when these suited his purpose, as with his discussion, in 1539, of the four causes of salvation.[20] His *Bondage and Liberation of the Will* is of interest because he there makes a larger than usual use of Aristotle, though as always his use remains occasional rather than systematic.[21]

14 Cf. n. 1, above.
15 CO 6:263.
16 CO 6:296.
17 *Inst*. 1:15:8.
18 *Inst*. 2:3:13.
19 *Inst*. 2:2:8 (1539).
20 *Inst*. 3:14:17.
21 For Calvin's use of Aristotle, cf. I. Backus, '"Aristotelianism" in some of Calvin's and Beza's Expository and Exegetical Writings on the Doctrine of the Trinity, with particular reference to the terms οὐσία and ὑπόστασις' in O. Fatio and P. Fraenkel (eds), *Histoire de l'exégèse au XVIe siècle* (Geneva: Droz, 1978) 351–60; J. C. McLelland, 'Calvin and Philosophy', *Canadian Journal of Theology* 11 (1965) 42–53, esp. 46–48; V. L. Nuovo, *Calvin's Theology: A Study of its Sources in Classical Antiquity* (New York: Columbia University PhD dissertation, 1964); C. Partee, *Calvin and Classical Philosophy* (Leiden: E. J. Brill, 1977) via index.

In one place Calvin introduces a extended discussion of Aristotle. First, he makes a statement about Aristotle's understanding of 'necessity'.[22] Then, shortly after, he quotes Aristotle's discussion, in his *Nicomachean Ethics*, of circumstances in which the will becomes impotent.[23] Here Calvin takes the battle onto the enemies' ground, showing that even the philosopher beloved of the medieval scholastics offers support for his doctrine of the bondage of the will. This is doubly significant in that it is contrary to the approach of the *Institutio*. There, Aristotle is mentioned as the patron of an argument used *against* Calvin's position but is never cited for support on this topic.[24]

This use of Aristotle could be described as opportunistic, in that it provides further ammunition for Calvin but does not actually affect the case that he is arguing. But elsewhere Calvin makes use of Aristotelian distinctions as a vital part of his argument. Pighius seeks to identify the Protestant doctrine of the bondage of the will with the teaching of the Manichees and other early heretics that evil is a part of human nature as initially constituted.[25] Calvin responds to this charge with two distinctions. First, he differentiates between human nature as created by God in the beginning, which is good, and human nature as it has become through Adam's Fall, which is evil.[26] Secondly, in order to make this clearer, Calvin repeatedly invokes the Aristotelian distinction between substance and accidents.[27] The Manichees taught that evil is part of the substance of human nature, is inherent to it through its origin. The Reformers teach that human nature was created good and that while it has become evil, this evil is 'accidental'. This use of the Aristotelian distinction is fundamental to Calvin's argument. It is, one might say, not merely accidental to it but part of its substance. 'Without this distinction it is not surprising if [Pighius] gets everything confused.'[28]

This distinction is more explicit in *The Bondage and Liberation of the Will* but is not absent from the *Institutio*. In 1539 Calvin denied that the corruption of humanity flowed from nature. 'We deny that it has flowed from nature in order to indicate that it is an adventitious (*adventitiam*) quality which comes upon (*acciderit*) man rather than a substantial (*substantialem*) property which has been implanted from the beginning.' The Manichees are repudiated for imagining 'substantialem in homine malitiam'.[29] The Aristotelian distinction is less explicit than in *The Bondage and Liberation of the Will*, but is clearly implicit. In one of the rare 1550 additions to this material Calvin notes that 'the contagion does not take its

---

22 CO 6:335.
23 CO 6:335f.
24 *Inst.* 2:5:2 (1539).
25 CO 6:262f.
26 CO 6:259, 263f.
27 CO 6:263, 264, 284, 290, 331, 361, 381. In CO 6:351, 361 Calvin repudiates those who teach that evil is part of the 'essentia' of human nature.
28 CO 6:361. The distinction referred to is that between human nature as created whole and its *accidental* corruption, thus combining the two distinctions mentioned in this paragraph.
29 *Inst.* 2:1:11 (OS 3:240; LCC 20:254).

origin from the substance of the flesh or soul'.[30] It is possible that this qualification was added because the dispute with Pighius was still in Calvin's mind and he wanted to remove any possibility of misunderstanding.

Calvin also develops other similar and related contrasts. Pighius accused Calvin, because of his use of Ezekiel 36:26, of teaching that conversion involves the destruction of the faculty of the will and its replacement by another. He cites, against Calvin, Ambrose's statement that the substance of the heart is not removed. Calvin mocks this, insisting that he had never taught the destruction or removal of the substance of the heart or will. What is changed in conversion is not the faculty or substance of willing, nor is it merely the actions of the will. It is rather something in-between, the quality or 'habit' (*habitus*) of the will.[31] These contrasts are related to the distinction between substance and accidents, as is shown when Calvin shortly after refers to the '*accidental* qualities' of the soul.[32]

Calvin's use of the word 'habit' is significant. This was a scholastic technical term that was used to describe 'a kind of predicamental quality in that it is a modification of the substance not easily changed'.[33] Calvin repeatedly contrasts it with substance.[34] Elsewhere he uses it in a less technical way, as we talk of having good or bad habits.[35] Interestingly, although Calvin maintains that the distinction between substance and habit was the plain teaching of his 1539 *Institutio*, he fails to introduce it into any edition of that work.[36] But while the term does not appear in the *Institutio* the point that it makes, that the faculty of the will is not destroyed, is taken up in the 1559 edition, as we shall see later.

Finally, Calvin also uses the Aristotelian distinction between form and matter. The human will is described as the matter, which receives its form – a bad form from the corruption of original sin, a good form from the operation of grace.[37] The explicit distinction occurs just twice, but should not be forgotten on the numerous occasions where Calvin talks of the will being 'formed' by grace.[38] In the 1539 *Institutio* Calvin uses the word to describe the views of the philosophers[39] and also uses it of the work of grace.[40] In particular, Calvin claims that God by his grace bends, forms and directs the human heart and will to righteousness, claiming Augustine's support. Pighius objected strongly to this and Calvin defends

30 *Inst.* 2:1:7 (LCC 20:250).
31 CO 6:377–79, 392.
32 CO 6:381. Emphasis not in the original.
33 R. J. Deferrari, *A Latin-English Dictionary of St Thomas Aquinas* (Boston: St Paul, 1960) 453–56. While Calvin does use the term habit, unlike the medieval scholastics he never refers to grace as a habit.
34 CO 6:378f. Cf. CO 6:336.
35 CO 6:304f., 380.
36 The Latin word *habitus* occurs once (from 1543), in *Institutio* 4:4:9, where it probably simply means habit in today's colloquial sense and is translated 'exemplary life' (LCC 21:1077).
37 CO 6:312, 391f.
38 CO 6:314, 316, 329, 342f., 345, 353, 374f., 380, 389.
39 *Inst.* 2:2:2.
40 *Inst.* 2:3:6, 13, 2:5:5, 14.

himself, claiming that he 'could easily cite over two hundred passages from Augustine where he uses those words'.[41]

There is an interesting place where Calvin and Pighius dispute the interpretation of Augustine. Augustine, in his *De correptione et gratia*, contrasts the gift to Adam of *posse non peccare* with the gift to redeemed humanity of *non posse peccare*. But *when* is the latter given? In the 1539 *Institutio* Calvin claimed that it is given here and now and that Augustine is not 'speaking of a perfection to come after immortality'.[42] His aim was not, of course, to defend any form of perfectionism but rather to defend his belief that grace is efficacious, that it so works that the sinner is not able to decline. Pighius protests vehemently, arguing that this latter grace (*non posse peccare*) is to be given after the final resurrection. Calvin spends longer on this passage than on any other patristic passage in *The Bondage and Liberation of the Will* and gives ground on the issue. He concedes that the *fullness* of what Augustine describes is reserved for the resurrection, but maintains that it also applies to the present situation. He argues at length, from the wider context in Augustine, that the latter clearly intended the passage to refer to 'the present situation of the saints'.[43]

Calvin's concession is not reflected in the *Institutio*. In 1539 Calvin had rejected the idea that Augustine was thinking of the future. He had also made a significant change in his Augustinian quotation. Augustine contrasted the first freedom given to Adam (*posse non peccare*) with the *last* (*novissima*) freedom (*non posse peccare*).[44] Calvin changed this to a contrast between the first freedom and *our* freedom, implying that it refers to our freedom in this life.[45] In the 1541 French translation he had gone further and called the interpretation of it as referring to the future a mockery of the Sorbonists. In *The Bondage and Liberation of the Will*, by contrast, he claims that he does not deny 'that the *fulness* of that perfection which [Augustine] there describes does not yet exist, nor is to be hoped for before the resurrection'.[46] But this qualification is not reflected in the later editions of the *Institutio*, where the only modification in the text strengthens rather than qualifies the rejection of the future interpretation. This is now called Peter Lombard's false interpretation.[47]

IV. NEW MATERIAL ADDED TO LATER EDITIONS OF THE *INSTITUTIO*

As well as revising the material from 1539, Calvin also added new material in later editions, especially in 1559. The 1543 edition was probably complete by the time that Calvin responded to Pighius, although it did

---

41 CO 6:374. A computer check of Augustine's use of these words confirms that he does indeed frequently use them as Calvin states.
42 *Inst*. 2:3:13.
43 CO 6:401–404. For a brief discussion of whose interpretation of Augustine is correct, cf. A. N. S. Lane, 'Bondage and Liberation in Calvin's Treatise against Pighius' in J. H. Leith and R. A. Johnson (eds), *Calvin Studies IX* (Davidson (NC): Davidson College and Davidson College Presbyterian Church, 1998) 43–45.
44 *De correptione et gratia* 12:33 (PL 44:936).
45 *Inst*. 2:3:13 (OS 3:289).
46 CO 6:401. Emphasis not in the original.
47 *Inst*. 2:3:13.

not appear until after the latter work.[48] Peter Fraenkel has argued that 'Calvin ait incorporé dans l'*Institution* de 1543 surtout des matières réunies en 1539–41'.[49] There is unlikely, therefore, to be any significant influence of the debate with Pighius on the 1543 edition, though the possibility of a few last-minute revisions cannot be excluded. In fact relatively little new material is added to chapter 2 of the 1539 edition in the following, 1543, edition and even less in the 1550 edition. The substantial revision of the material comes in the definitive, 1559, edition and it is in that edition that we are most likely to find evidence of debate with Pighius from a decade and a half earlier. The significance of the new material will be examined, edition by edition.

Of the new material in the 1543 edition, some is also found in Calvin's *Bondage and Liberation of the Will*. This common material consists entirely of citations from Augustine. Four quotations in the *Institutio* are also found in *The Bondage and Liberation of the Will*.[50] A further quotation is summarized (but not quoted) on three occasions in *The Bondage and Liberation of the Will*.[51] Two other quotations overlap in the two works, both having material not found in the other work.[52] In the *Institutio* Calvin mentions Augustine's *De natura et gratia* and the passage, which is correctly identified in the *Opera selecta* footnotes, is quoted in *The Bondage and Liberation of the Will*.[53] Finally, a passage is quoted in the *Institutio* to which indirect reference is made in *The Bondage and Liberation of the Will*.[54]

What conclusions can be drawn from this? First, the common material consists simply of illustrative citations from Augustine. These do not introduce new ideas not found already in the 1539 *Institutio*. Secondly, is the influence from the 1543 *Institutio* to *The Bondage and Liberation of the Will* or vice versa? The 1543 *Institutio* was nearing completion when Calvin returned to Geneva in 1541, before Pighius's work had even appeared, but it was not published until March 1543, in Strassburg. Certainly the new material in the 1543 *Institutio* could be a source for *The Bondage and Liberation of the Will*. The reverse is also possible in that Calvin while responding to Pighius at the end of 1542 might have decided to add some last-minute Augustinian material into the new edition of his *Institutio*.

Is there any other way of determining the direction of the influence? There is one valuable clue. Two of the common quotations merely overlap, which means that each contains material not found in the other. This means that there is no question of either simply being copied from the other. The only point of uncertainty, therefore, concerns whether Calvin's attention was drawn to the quotation by his work on the *Institutio* or by his work on *The Bondage and Liberation of the Will*. There is no way to be sure whether Calvin added new patristic material to the 1543 *Institutio* while preparing

---

48 OS 3:XIX-XX.
49 P. Fraenkel, 'Trois passages de l'Institution de 1543 et leurs rapports avec les colloques interconfessionels de 1540–1541' in W. H. Neuser (hrsg.), *Calvinus Ecclesiae Genevensis Custos* (Frankfurt, etc.: Peter Lang, 1984) 153.
50 *Inst.* 2:2:8, 2:3:7. CO 6:293, 303f., 311, 313, 358.
51 *Inst.* 2:2:8. CO 6:303, 307, 338.
52 *Inst.* 2:3:7, 12. CO 6:310, 344.
53 *Inst.* 2:3:5. CO 6:300.
54 *Inst.* 2:5:2. CO 6:337.

The Bondage and Liberation of the Will or whether he drew upon his reading for the former while preparing the latter. In addition to the nine patristic citations that overlap *The Bondage and Liberation of the Will* there are a further nine in the relevant portion of the 1543 *Institutio* which have no overlap. The fact that the new citations are divided equally between those overlapping and those not overlapping could perhaps be taken as an indication that the evidence is equally divided and that a verdict is impossible.

There is little new material added in 1550 to the section that concerns us. Two Augustinian quotations, found in *The Bondage and Liberation of the Will*, are added.[55] The anti-Manichean addition, denying the substantial evil of the soul, has already been noted.

The most significant additions come in the definitive, 1559 edition and concern the issue of the destruction of the will. If conversion is a new creation, does it involve the destruction of the will? In the 1539 *Institutio* Calvin at times appears to teach this. God destroys (*aboleat*) our depraved will and substitutes a good will from himself. It is wrong to suggest that the will obeys grace as a voluntary handmaid.[56] The heart of stone is replaced by a heart of flesh so that 'whatever is of our own will is effaced. What takes its place is wholly from God'.[57] God does not merely assist the weak will but he makes (*efficere*) the will.[58] Chrysostom's statement that 'whom he draws he draws willingly' is to be rejected.[59] In short, the beginning of regeneration is 'to wipe out what is ours'.[60] If Calvin was understood to teach that grace destroys the will he must himself bear at least part of the blame. But in fact he qualified this teaching. After the last-quoted passage he adds that Augustine rightly taught that grace does not destroy the will but rather repairs it. This will is said to be made new (*nova creari*) inasmuch as its corrupt nature is entirely changed.

Despite these qualifications, Calvin was accused by Pighius of teaching that grace destroys the will.[61] Calvin retorted by accusing Pighius of wilfully misunderstanding him, but his explanation of his teaching is so much fuller and clearer than the 1539 *Institutio* that Calvin must bear at least part of the blame for Pighius's misunderstanding. Calvin reaffirms that in conversion 'whatever belongs to our will is abolished and what takes its place is entirely from God' and that 'conversion is the work of God alone'.[62] Pighius had interpreted this to mean that God destroys the substance or faculty of the will itself.[63]

Calvin was angered by this interpretation and clarified his meaning at length. As has already been seen, he invokes the idea of the habit of the

---

55 *Inst.* 2:5:17. CO 6:343f., 354.
56 *Inst.* 2:3:7.
57 *Inst.* 2:3:6.
58 *Inst.* 2:3:9.
59 *Inst.* 2:3:10 (LCC 20:303).
60 *Inst.* 2:5:15 (LCC 20:335).
61 Pighius did not allow sufficiently for the element of humanist exaggeration in Calvin's rhetoric. Cf. R. W. Richgels, 'Scholasticism Meets Humanism in the Counter-Reformation. The Clash of Cultures in Robert Bellarmine's Use of Calvin in the *Controversies*', *Sixteenth Century Journal* 6:1 (1975) 61–66.
62 CO 6:375f.
63 Pighius, *De libero arbitrio* f. 89a-b.

will, which lies between the substance or faculty of will and its individual acts. For support in this distinction he turns to a passage of Bernard which he had quoted in 1539, which distinguishes between the will itself, an evil will and a good will. The first of these signifies the faculty or substance of the will. The other two signify qualities or habits of the will. The faculty of will is permanent in humanity, but the evil will comes from the Fall and the good will from regeneration. The will remains as created, the change taking place in its habit, not its substance.[64] It is true that 'everything which is ours should be obliterated' but this means 'what we have in ourselves apart from God's creation' – i.e. 'the corruption which abides not in some part of us but throughout our nature'. Sin has affected the whole of human nature so that fallen humanity cannot think, choose, will, attempt or do anything but evil. It is in this sense that all that is ours is destroyed and renovated.[65]

Calvin also qualified his earlier rejection of Chrysostom's saying that God draws us willingly. He accepted the statement of Ambrose that those who serve Christ or Satan do so voluntarily, while quickly adding that those whom Christ wishes to will the good he causes to do such by his Spirit. Christ does not draw us violently or unwillingly, says Augustine, and we therefore follow him of our own accord (*sponte*) but of a will which he has made. Chrysostom's mistake was not to teach that we follow voluntarily but to suppose that we follow in a movement that is all our own.[66] Finally, in conversion 'it is certain that it is we who will when we will, but it is he who causes us to will the good. It is certain that it is we who act when we act, but it is he who, by giving the will fully effective powers, causes us to act'.[67] 'It is not that we ourselves do nothing or that we without any movement of our will are driven to act by pressure from him, but that we act while being acted upon by him.'[68]

The fuller teaching of Calvin's *Bondage and Liberation of the Will* leaves its mark on the 1559 *Institutio*. The statement about that 'whatever is of our own will is effaced' is qualified:

> I say that the will is effaced; not in so far as it is will, for in man's conversion what belongs to his primal nature remains entire. I also say that it is created anew; not meaning that the will now begins to exist, but that it is changed from an evil to a good will.[69]

Augustine is quoted with approval to the effect that when God acts upon us we also act. 'He indicates that man's action is not taken away by the movement of the Holy Spirit, because the will, which is directed to aspire the good, is of nature.'[70] The qualification to the destruction of the will that is found in 1539 is further reinforced:

64 CO 6:377f., 381, 392.
65 CO 6:380f.
66 CO 6:395f.
67 CO 6:330, quoting Augustine.
68 CO 6:337.
69 *Inst.* 2:3:6 (LCC 20:297).
70 *Inst.* 2:5:14 (LCC 20:334).

But even if there is something good in the will, it comes from the pure prompting of the Spirit. Yet because we are by nature endowed with will, we are with good reason said to do those things the praise for which God rightly claims for himself.[71]

In the 1539 *Institutio* Calvin came dangerously close to teaching the destruction of the will. Pighius's challenge on this point, so vehemently rejected by Calvin, did cause him to qualify his teaching, first in his *Bondage and Liberation of the Will* and later in the 1559 *Institutio*. The reason why he allows himself to be moved in this direction is that the debate concerned the teaching of Augustine, for whom he had such a high regard.

V. CONCLUSION

Pidoux points out that Calvin in responding to Pighius claims to do no more than 'reprendre à nouveau ce qu'il avait déjà une fois exprimé dans l'Institution'. He agrees with Calvin that the content of the two works is substantially the same. Calvin's aim was to dispel Pighius's misinterpretations of the *Institutio*, although Pidoux concedes that new elements are not entirely absent and that the exposition is developed at certain points.[72] The present study has confirmed Pidoux's statement. There is substantial continuity between the 1539 *Institutio* and the 1543 treatise, while at the same time that which was implicit (free choice before the Fall) is made explicit, Aristotelian terminology (substance, accidents, habit, form) is employed to clarify Calvin's teaching, a passage of Augustine is expounded more carefully and the teaching of Ambrose and Augustine is affirmed in opposition to the idea that the human will is destroyed in conversion. Calvin's engagement with Aristotle and the fathers in opposition to Pighius enabled him to express the same teaching as before, but with greater clarity and subtlety.

---

71 *Inst.* 2:5:15 (LCC 20:335).
72 Pidoux, *Albert Pighius*, 119f.

8

❦

Did Calvin Use Lippoman's
Catena in Genesim?

I. INTRODUCTION

Twenty years ago I wrote an article about the sources of Calvin's knowledge of Bernard of Clairvaux.[1] One of the possible sources examined was the *Catena in Genesim ex authoribus ecclesiasticis* published in 1546 by bishop Aloisius Lippoman.[2] There were two possible sources for Calvin's solitary Bernard citation in his Genesis commentary.[3] As a test, all other non-Augustinian patristic citations in the Genesis commentary were checked. Nine of these were not found in the *Catena*, twelve were. There were also pairings of quotations found in both Calvin and Lippoman. The tentative conclusion that was reached was that 'the possibility of Calvin having used the *Catena* can by no means be discounted'.[4]

More recently Richard Gamble, in examining the sources of Calvin's Genesis commentary, has pursued the matter further. Gamble used Calvin's exposition of Genesis 6:14 as a test case and concluded that although 'the significance of these materials may not be overdrawn ... [they] do suggest that Calvin quite heavily worked with Lippoman's *Catena*'. It is, according to Gamble, 'a possible source'.[5]

This chapter originally appeared as 'Did Calvin Use Lippoman's *Catena in Genesim?*' in *Calvin Theological Journal* 31 (1996) 404–19. The following chapter examines a wider base of citations and gives a more accurate indication of Calvin's likely sources. Where this qualifies statements made in the present chapter that has been noted. Some other minor inaccuracies have also been corrected.

---

1 A. N. S. Lane, 'Calvin's Sources of St. Bernard', *Archiv für Reformationsgeschichte*, 67 (1976) 253–83.
2 Paris, Charlotte Guillard. In the notes this will simply be called *Catena* and references will be by folio number. Lippoman (d. 1559) was a papal diplomat and theologian, who was bishop of various sees. For details of his life, cf. A.-P. Frutaz, 'Lipomano', in M. Viller (ed.), *Dictionnaire de Spiritualité*, vol. 9 (Paris: Beauchesne, 1976) 858–60. For details of his polemical works, cf. F. Lauchert, *Die italienischen literarischen Gegner Luthers* (Freiburg, etc.: Herder, 1912) 569–84.
3 On 3:6 (CO 23:63). But on this see further n. 63, below.
4 Lane, 'Calvin's Sources of St. Bernard', 273.
5 R. C. Gamble, 'The Sources of Calvin's Genesis Commentary: A Preliminary Report', *Archiv für Reformationsgeschichte* 84 (1993) 211, n. 23, where the passages mentioned in Lane, 'Calvin's Sources of St. Bernard', 273, n. 140, are further explored.

II. METHODOLOGY

The time has come for a more critical approach to this topic. How can we test whether or not Calvin actually used Lippoman? Mere parallels will not suffice. There might be endless parallels without any dependence. If Lippoman draws extensively from Augustine's works on Genesis (as he does) and if Calvin was familiar with them (as he was) and had them at hand as he prepared his exposition of Genesis (which is most likely), then it would be remarkable indeed if no parallels were to be found. Again, any patristic citation which is firmly linked to the passage being expounded could be derived from any previous commentator who had mentioned it. In other words, if Calvin and Lippoman both mention Jerome's comment on Genesis 23:16, this might reflect Calvin's own knowledge of Jerome or his dependence upon another earlier commentator who had cited Jerome. Since there is nothing remarkable about mentioning Jerome's comment on Genesis 23:16 when expounding Genesis 23:16, the fact that two separate commentators do so falls far short of demonstrating dependence.

There are two types of parallel that may be more significant. The first is a common patristic citation which is not specifically related to the passage being expounded. Here we have the coincidence that two different commentators have chosen to insert this particular citation at the same point. Such parallels are worthy of greater attention. But if the citation is one with which Calvin was already familiar, we must be cautious before declaring dependence. Also, the use of the citation at that particular point may turn out to be a commonplace of the exegetical tradition. Another type of parallel that may be significant is where both commentaries juxtapose the same sets of quotations. This might indicate dependence, though one first needs to ask whether other more likely sources have already juxtaposed these quotations or whether the juxtaposition was so obvious that anyone with the different authors in front of him would be likely to think of juxtaposing them.

For the present study all of Calvin's references to Josephus and to the fathers have been sought in Lippoman. These are *explicit* citations, where the father is named. This is the only objective way to conduct the study. To include suspected allusions would be to bias the study in the direction of the allusions that one happens to suspect. Also, if Calvin and Augustine, say, are both commenting on Genesis, the number of potential allusions will be endless. Restricting the study to explicit citations is not to deny that Calvin is elsewhere influenced by patristic exegesis; it is simply to state that we cannot be sufficiently certain about such influence for it to provide a safe basis to test whether or not Calvin used Lippoman. One group of explicit citations has, however, been excluded: those references to Jerome which are in fact to the Vulgate.[6]

---

6 This is true of some of the Jerome citations listed by Mooi, KDE 381. Mooi states that Calvin never names Jerome in connection with the Vulgate translation (p. 136), which is not true inasmuch as references to Jerome in Calvin's Old Testament commentaries sometimes refer to the Vulgate.

In addition, all of Calvin's classical references have been sought in Lippoman. So also have other vaguer references, such as to 'the papists', 'the Jews' or 'the fathers'. Again, where Calvin refers to a group like the Pelagians or the Manichees, Lippoman has been checked.[7] These different types of references will together be referred to as 'miscellaneous references', to distinguish them from the explicit citations of a named father. A few of these references have yielded positive results and these will be considered first.

No attempt has been made, however, to compare the exegetical views contained in Lippoman with those of Calvin. The magnitude of the task would be immense, unless it were limited to an arbitrarily selected sample.[8] Also, the value would be slight. By definition, Lippoman is conveying not new exegetical insights but those of the tradition. To demonstrate that Calvin derived any particular interpretation from Lippoman one would need to show that he did not find it elsewhere, a nearly impossible task. It is where Calvin names a source that one is on the safest ground. Where the name is specific, the test is the most valuable; where it is vague ('the Jews', 'the papists') it is less significant, but worth checking.

Tracing parallels between Calvin and Lippoman does not of itself prove dependence. Are there other, more likely sources of Calvin's knowledge? There are five more definite sources. First, Calvin repeatedly cites Luther[9] who is one contemporary commentator that we can say with absolute certainty was used by Calvin. But we cannot assume that Calvin had access to *all* of Luther's lectures on Genesis. These were published in four volumes, from 1544 to 1554.[10] The first volume predates Calvin's exegesis of Genesis; the last volume clearly appeared too late to be used. What of the other two? Of Calvin's four references to Luther, three appear in the first volume, the fourth in the second volume. This suggests that Calvin had at least the first two volumes before him and therefore had access to Luther's exposition of Genesis 1:1–25:10. As it happens, all of the instances where Luther might be the source of a citation fall within these chapters, which reinforces the view that Calvin had access to these two volumes only.[11]

Secondly, Calvin five times refers to Augustine's *Quaestiones in Heptateuchum*. This includes two passages not covered by Lippoman or

---

7 There are fewer Augustine citations than listed by Smits, SAOJC 2:131f. This is because he includes suspected allusions. All of these are actually considered under the references to the Manichees, the papists, etc.

8 For an example of such a comparison, between Luther, Calvin and Dionysius the Carthusian on Genesis 32:24–32, cf. D. C. Steinmetz, 'Calvin as an Interpreter of Genesis' in W. H. Neuser and B. G. Armstrong (eds), *Calvinus Sincerioris Religionis Vindex* (Kirksville (MO): Sixteenth Century Journal Publishers, 1997) 53–66.

9 CO 23:113 (twice), 169, 170, 193 on 6:3, 11:10–26, 27, 13:14f., respectively.

10 The volumes are: *In Primum Librum Mose Enarrationes* (Wittenberg, 1544) [chs 1–11:26]; *In Genesin Enarrationum ... Tomus Secundus* (Nuremberg, 1550) [chs 11:27–25:10]; *In Genesin Enarrationum ... Tomus Tertius* (Nuremberg, 1552) [chs 25:11–36:43]; *In Genesin Enarrationum ... Tomus Quartus* (Nuremberg, 1554) [chs 37–50]. All are found in WA 42–44.

11 Calvin's Luther citations have also been checked to confirm that he is not referring to Luther's *In Genesin, Mosi Librum Sanctissimum ... Declamationes* (Hagenau: Ioan. Secerius, 1527) which is found in WA 24.

Luther.[12] Given that it was Calvin's regular practice, in his exegetical works, to make use of Augustine[13] and the extent of his use of Augustine in general, it is a safe assumption that he had this work in front of him.[14]

Thirdly, Calvin also cited Jerome's *Hebraicae quaestiones in Genesim* and his *Liber de situ et nominibus locorum hebraicorum*. These citations are all covered by Lippoman but, given Calvin's regular use of Jerome in his exegesis,[15] it is likely that Calvin had these works before him.[16] But if on other grounds it is decided that he used Lippoman, the latter might then reasonably be seen as the source of this Jerome material.

Fourthly, there are Chrysostom's homilies on Genesis. These are cited only once, but Chrysostom is, together with Augustine and Jerome, one of three fathers that Calvin most often cites in his exegesis.[17] Also, Calvin possessed a copy of Chrysostom's works, which survives with his markings.[18] It would be unwise therefore to argue Calvin's dependence upon Lippoman on the basis of a citation from a work which we know Calvin to have possessed and to have read.

Finally, some of the citations in the Genesis commentary are already found in earlier works of Calvin himself. These may justly be treated as definite sources in that any such earlier citation removes the need to postulate Lippoman as the source of Calvin's knowledge.

It will be assumed, therefore, that Calvin had these works of Luther, Augustine, Jerome and Chrysostom before him and they will be regarded as definite sources. They, together with Calvin's own earlier works, will be examined as possible sources for the material in common between Calvin and Lippoman. If this material is found in these works of Luther, Augustine, Jerome or Chrysostom, which Calvin almost certainly used, or in Calvin's earlier writings there is no need to postulate the influence of Lippoman's work, for Calvin's use of which there is no evidence at all apart from the parallels. Having eliminated those parallels which are also found in Luther, Augustine, Jerome, Chrysostom or Calvin's earlier writings, we will examine those which remain.

---

12 CO 23:123, 470. Regarding the latter, Smits (SAOJC 2:132) suggests an alternative source (*Serm. Verb. Dom.* 122:4:4, PL 38:683:4–5) but this passage, unlike that in the *Quaestiones in Heptateuchum*, does not contain all that is needed for Calvin's citation.

13 Mooi, KDE 371, 377, 380f., 393–95.

14 There are four other works of Augustine on Genesis to be considered. *De Genesi contra Manichaeos* and *De Genesi ad litteram* are each cited once (CO 23:9f., 38) The other two works, *Locutiones in Heptateuchum* and *De Genesi ad litteram imperfectus liber*, have been checked for the passages which might indicate Lippoman's influence, without result.

15 Mooi, KDE 371, 377, 380f., 393–95.

16 (In fact the following chapter shows that Calvin need not have used Jerome's *Liber de situ et nominibus locorum hebraicorum*.) Jerome's *Liber interpretationis hebraicorum nominum* is not cited. It has been checked for the passages which might indicate Lippoman's influence, without result.

17 Mooi, KDE 371, 377, 380f., 393–95, but Chrysostom is cited almost entirely for New Testament exegesis.

18 A. Ganoczy and K. Müller, *Calvins Handschriftliche Annotationen zu Chrysostomus* (Wiesbaden: Franz Steiner, 1981). There are considerable markings on the Genesis homilies, including a number on Homilies 8–10, the source of Calvin's citation (ibid., 58–66). None of the markings is actually on a passage which makes the point cited by Calvin, but some are very close (ibid., 58f., 61, 65).

Before considering the specific parallels, it is worth noting the bulk of Lippoman's work. There are just over 433 large folios and the total number of extracts is somewhere between 6,000 and 10,000.[19] Given such a large number, a few parallels with Calvin may not be so remarkable. In Calvin's Genesis commentary there are twenty-two references to Augustine and twenty-four references to other fathers and Josephus. This is a tiny number compared with the mass of material in Lippoman. But the more significant statistic is the proportion of those forty-six references also found in Lippoman (nearly a half). Whether or not this overlap is purely a coincidence is the topic of this chapter.

Finally, a word about the origin of the commentary. Calvin lectured on Genesis from 1550 to 1552.[20] In the summer of 1550 he started work on his commentary, but as he was delayed by the pressure of other work it did not finally appear until 1554.[21] Does the extended time that Calvin spent on Genesis mean that for citations at the beginning of the volume a source not later than 1550 must be sought? Not necessarily. Calvin includes on 3:6 a citation of Bernard which is probably derived from his reading of the 1552 Basel edition of Bernard's works.[22] This shows that even at the beginning of the commentary citations can be drawn from books published after 1550.

III. MISCELLANEOUS CITATIONS

(a) 'The Jews'

Calvin's Genesis commentary contains a good number of references to the views of 'the Jews'. A few of these are to be found in Lippoman. On 1:26 Calvin opposes the Jewish interpretation that when God says 'Let us' he was talking to the earth or to angels. Lippoman quotes Basil's and Chrysostom's references to the Jewish interpretation, which mention the angels, but not the earth.[23] On 3:1 Calvin criticizes David Kimchi's interpretation of a Hebrew phrase. The view concerned is found in Lippoman, but without mention of Kimchi.[24] In both of these instances there is a parallel, but Calvin knows more than is to be found in Lippoman. On 4:23 Calvin relates a Jewish legend, which is also related by Lippoman.[25] Finally, on 9:5 Calvin mentions that the Jews distinguish four different kinds of homicide, *three* of which are set out in Lippoman.[26]

---

19 Not all of these are patristic, though most are. More recent expositors, like Cajetan, are included.

20 T. H. L. Parker, *Calvin's Old Testament Commentaries* (Edinburgh: T&T Clark, 1986) 29; CO 21:72, 75.

21 In the 1996 version of this chapter I referred incorrectly to the role of des Gallars in the writing of the commentary. For more on this cf. the following chapter, n. 5.

22 For evidence that Calvin did not draw this citation from Lippoman, cf. n. 63, below. For evidence that he was using the 1552 edition of Bernard, cf. chapter 5, above.

23 #2 (where #n means citation n, as listed in section VI, below). In *Catena*, 39a-b Chrysostom and Basil reject the Jewish view that 'we' means God and the angels. Luther (WA 42:42f.) gives the same information and mentions the earth as well.

24 #7. In *Catena*, 79a, the *Auctor Catenae* (i.e. Lippoman himself) mentions the Jewish view, without naming Kimchi.

25 #8. In *Catena*, 116a Rabanus Maurus recounts the same story.

26 #15. Luther mentions all four, drawing on Nicholas of Lyra (WA 42:358f.).

These four parallels are not significant. Three of them are insufficient to account for Calvin's knowledge and the fourth is found in Luther.[27] There is no reason to postulate Lippoman as a source for these citations, especially since Calvin mentions the views of the Jews on many other occasions,[28] for which there must be some source other than Lippoman.

(b) The Classics

Calvin did not cite only the Jews. His Genesis commentary is even richer in material from the classics.[29] None of the citations noted has been found in Lippoman.

(c) The Papists

Calvin repeatedly in his Genesis commentary opposes views which he attributes to 'the papists' or 'the papacy' or brands as 'papal'.[30] The majority of these simply refer to Roman Catholic beliefs and practices, but a minority refer to Catholic interpretation of specific passages of Genesis.[31] Some of these might go back to the fathers and indeed Smits attributes one to Augustine.[32] Lippoman, as a 'papist' author was a potential source of such views. In fact there are two just places where there are loose parallels, but these are not close enough for Lippoman to be Calvin's source.[33]

(d) Heresies

Calvin refers to the Manichees and the Pelagians in the course of his Genesis commentary and Smits gives references to Augustine for each of these citations.[34] There is also a reference to the Anthropomorphites[35] and to Novatus and the Novatians.[36] Lippoman does not mention these heresies (at the appropriate point), whether via Augustine or via any other source.

In his commentary on Genesis 1:1 Calvin mentions the Arians and Sabellianism. This is not in fact a direct reference to these heresies but a

---

27 #8; WA 42:235.
28 CO 23:34, 86, 88, 96f., 105, 113, 141, 163, 170, 177f., 230f., 267, 298f., 318, 321, 511. (See the following chapter for further Jewish citations.)
29 CO 23:23, 40–43, 46, 89f., 102, 116, 123, 159, 163–65, 172, 189, 196f., 201, 219, 277f., 325, 345, 461.
30 CO 23:120, 134, 152, 203, 255, 290, 318, 319, 394, 396, 404, 585, 594. (See the following chapter for further such citations.)
31 CO 23:152, 203, 290, 318, 319, 394, 396, 585, 594 on 9:23, 14:18, 20:7, 22:15f., 28:17, 28:20, 48:16, 49:5f.
32 CO 23:120; Smits, SAOJC 2:131.
33 (1) #16. Calvin criticizes those papists who seek to cover the deformity of their idol, the filth of the whole impure clergy with the cloak of Shem and Japeth; Lippoman contains material which compares the garment to the sacraments, which is not really the same point. (2) #30. Calvin states that the papists justify the invocation of the dead; Lippoman cites Augustine (*Locutiones in Heptateuchum* 1:204 (CCSL 33:401f.)) to the effect that not just God but human beings are to be invoked. In fact the source is probably the 1548 *Interim*, which makes the point mentioned here and is rejected by Calvin (CO 7:583, 653). Calvin had already countered this 'papist' argument in the 1539 *Institutio* 3:20:25 (OS 4:330).
34 CO 23:55, 61, 62, 113. Smits, SAOJC 2:131.
35 CO 23:26.
36 CO 23:474.

theological critique of a particular viewpoint – that because the Hebrew for God, *Elohim*, is plural there is a reference in this verse to the Trinity. This view is found in Lippoman.[37]

(e) Vague References

Finally, there are some vaguer references which may or may not be to the fathers. On 1:26 Calvin says that *nonnulli Patrum* were deceived in thinking that they could combat Arianism by stating that Christ alone is God's image. Lippoman quotes a passage of Ambrose which has some relevance.[38] On 3:6 Calvin refers to the traducian view of the origin of the soul as an ancient fiction of certain authors. Smits sees a reference to Augustine.[39] Lippoman makes no mention of this doctrine. On 14:18 Calvin criticizes the ancient writers of the church for locating the parallel between Christ and Melchizedek in the fact that the latter offered bread and wine. The views of Jerome, Chrysostom, Eucherius and Ambrose, as set out by Lippoman, are relevant.[40] But Calvin had already made exactly the same charge in his response to the 1548 *Interim*, so was aware of it before starting work on Genesis.[41] On 23:7 Calvin criticizes those who excuse their idolatry by making a distinction between *dulia* and *latria*. Lippoman cites a passage from Augustine where he asks how Abraham could have 'adored' the people of the land (Latin *adoravit* in Genesis 23:7) given that we should worship God alone. In his answer he uses the word λατρεύσεις.[42] But Calvin did not need to refer to Augustine or to Lippoman for the distinction between *dulia* and *latria*, which he had already incorporated into his *Institutio*.[43] Shortly after, Calvin accuses the canonists of rashly adopting an opinion of Jerome. Lippoman cites Jerome, but makes no reference to the canonists.[44]

Thus far, just four parallels have been found where Lippoman gives sufficient information to account for Calvin's citation. Two of these were known to Calvin already or are found in Luther.[45] This leaves just two parallels that might point to Calvin's dependence upon Lippoman. The first is his reference to the theory that Genesis 1:1 points to the doctrine of the Trinity.[46] It is possible to identify the source of this reference with some degree of certainty. Shortly before, Calvin criticizes Augustinus Eugubinus Steuchus for maintaining the error that unformed matter has existed from eternity. To what is Calvin referring here? Steuchus did indeed teach, in his *Cosmopoeia*, that there are three heavens and that the most transcendent of these, the *coelum empyrium* is eternal.[47] But it is unlikely that Calvin

---

37 #1.
38 #4.
39 CO 23:62. Smits, SAOJC 2:131.
40 #19. The reference to *veterum commentum* later in col. 202 is to the same point.
41 Calvin in his response to the 1548 *Interim* accuses his opponents of boasting that Athanasius, Ambrose, Augustine and Arnobius thus interpreted Genesis 14 (CO 7:579f., 644). Also, Luther had made the same point (WA 42:536–38).
42 #25.
43 *Inst.* 1:12:2, from 1550 (OS 3:106f.).
44 CO 23:326, on 23:16–20; *Catena*, 260a.
45 #8, #19.
46 #1.
47 In his 1535 *Cosmopoeia*. Cf. T. Freudenberger, *Augustinus Steuchus aus Gubbio* (Münster i. W.: Aschendorff, 1935) 219–30.

could have so misunderstood this as to accuse Steuchus of teaching the eternity of unformed matter.[48] In fact Calvin is referring to another work of Steuchus, his *Recognitio Veteris Testamenti ad Hebraicam Veritatem.*[49] In commenting on Genesis 1:1 (*creavit*) Steuchus does not exactly teach the eternity of unformed matter, but he does allow that the Hebrew word *bârâ* need not imply creation *ex nihilo.*[50] Calvin's opposition to the idea of eternal unformed matter immediately follows his own claim that *bârâ* must mean creation out of nothing.[51] Thus it seems likely that Calvin is thinking of Steuchus's *Recognitio* at this point. Calvin's critique of those who see a reference to the Trinity in Genesis 1:1 follows a few sentences after his critique of Steuchus. The point criticized is found in Steuchus immediately after the discussion of *creavit.*[52] Thus it is almost certainly Steuchus again who is being criticized here so there is no reason to suppose any influence of Lippoman's *Catena*.

Secondly there is Calvin's criticism of those fathers who thought to combat Arianism by stating that Christ alone is God's image.[53] All that Lippoman offers in support of this is a passage from Ambrose's *Hexaemeron* which refers to Christ as *solus* the image of God, but makes no mention of Arianism.[54] There is little evidence here to support Calvin's use of Lippoman. First, this passage is not *sufficient* to prompt Calvin's statement because Ambrose is only one father and does not mention Arianiasm. Secondly, even if Calvin did have Ambrose in mind (which is unlikely), he would not have needed to turn to Lippoman for this passage. In the 1543 *Institutio* he referred to Ambrose's *Hexaemeron* in a manner that implies familiarity with its contents.[55] Calvin could easily have remembered or turned again to this passage when expounding Genesis 1 in 1550.

The miscellaneous citations have produced no passage where there is any reason for postulating dependence upon Lippoman.

IV. EXPLICIT PATRISTIC CITATIONS

(a) Augustine

There are twenty-two explicit citations of Augustine. Just seven of these are also found in Lippoman. Three of these are found in Augustine's

---

48 R. Stauffer, 'L'exégèse de Genèse 1,1–3 chez Luther et Calvin', in *In Principio: interpretations des premiers versets de la Genèse* (Paris: Études Augustiniennes, 1973) 256–58, maintains that Calvin is referring to this teaching of Steuchus, while acknowledging that it is difficult to see why his attack was so imprecise.

49 Venice: Aldus and A. Socerus, 1529. There was a 1531 edition published by Sebastian Gryphius at Lyon, a copy of which was found in the library of the Genevan Academy in 1572 (A. Ganoczy, BAC 231).

50 *Recognitio*, 6b-7a (1529 edition).

51 CO 23:14f.

52 *Recognitio*, 7b (1529 edition).

53 #4.

54 *Hexaemeron* 6:7:41–43 (PL 14:257f.) in *Catena*, 40a-b. In the 1996 version of this chapter I referred also to a passage from Origen, but this has so little relevance to Calvin's point that it should not have been mentioned.

55 *Inst.* 1:14:20 (OS 3:170).

Quaestiones in Heptateuchum.[56] Calvin cites two more passages from this work which are not found in Lippoman,[57] which is therefore unlikely to be his source. A further three citations are from Augustine's *De civitate dei*, a work with which Calvin was already familiar. This work also Calvin cites twice more where Lippoman does not.[58] Furthermore, one of the passages from *De civitate dei* found in Lippoman is also found in Calvin's commentary on Acts 7:14, which appeared in 1552, two years before the Genesis commentary.[59] The seventh common Augustine passage is from the *De Genesi ad litteram.*[60] This also is found earlier. In the 1539 *Institutio* Calvin cites Eucherius's comment on the tree of life. In the 1550 edition he adds Augustine's name.[61] Thus the juxtaposition of the two, which is found in Lippoman, is already found in the 1550 *Institutio*.

Both the Acts commentary and the 1550 *Institutio* appear after the publication of Lippoman's *Catena* and it is not impossible that Calvin was already reading the latter in preparation for his exposition of Genesis. But the 1550 *Institutio* was nearly complete in February 1550 and in April Beza was writing to Calvin conveying Melchior Wolmar's thanks for his copy.[62] Thus it is unlikely that the Augustine citation was added to the *Institutio* as a result of Calvin's preparation of his Genesis exegesis. Also, given that Calvin cites the *De civitate dei* a further two times independently of Lippoman, it is likely that he is drawing upon his own knowledge of the work rather than relying upon Lippoman. All three citations from this work common to Calvin and Lippoman clearly relate to the passage being expounded, so there is no further need to account for the fact that they both cite the *De civitate dei* at the same point. There is, therefore, no need to postulate use of Lippoman in order to account for Calvin's Augustine citations.

(b) Other Fathers

Apart from Augustine, there are twenty-four explicit patristic citations, including two from Josephus. Fifteen of these are also found in Lippoman,[63]

---

56 One of the three (#20) is given by Lippoman under the heading 'Augustinus & Ambrosius', so Calvin could not have been sure from Lippoman alone what was to be attributed to Augustine. But for that citation Calvin could have been dependent upon Luther (WA 43:145). In another of the three (#28) Calvin's citation overlaps with one from his 1540 Romans commentary (CO 49:82, on 4:19).

57 #10b and CO 23:470.

58 CO 23:9f., 25.

59 #29, cf. CO 48:137.

60 #6a.

61 *Inst.* 2:2:9 (OS 3:251f.).

62 R. Peter and J.-F. Gilmont, *Bibliotheca Calviniana*, vol. 1 (Geneva: Droz, 1991) 373.

63 In Lane, 'Calvin's Sources of St. Bernard', 273, I proposed *Catena*, 88b, 97b as the source for the Bernard citation in CO 23:63, on 3:6. There are two reasons for questioning this. First, the Lippoman passages are under 3:8–13 and 3:17–19, rather than 3:6. This study involves looking for sources at the same position in Lippoman as in Calvin, which is where we would expect them if Calvin was using Lippoman. Secondly, it was there stated that 'Calvin was paraphrasing rather than quoting and these two passages are as likely to have been his source as anything else in Bernard's writings'. Further research has shown that the most likely sources are Bernard's *Ep* 1:3, *Gra* 8:25 and *Ann* 1:1 (BO 7:4, 3:184, 5:14). These are significantly closer than the nearest passage in Lippoman, *Div* 28:7 (BO 6/1:209) (*Catena*, 88b).

for eleven of which there is no reason to suspect that Calvin used Lippoman. Four are from Jerome's *Hebraicae quaestiones in Genesim*, which Calvin was most likely using.[64] A Josephus citation is found both in Luther and in Jerome's *Liber de situ et nominibus locorum hebraicorum*. As Calvin immediately proceeds to cite the latter, this is the probable source for Josephus as well.[65] Another citation is of Chrysostom,[66] whose works Calvin possessed and presumably consulted for this commentary. A reference to Eucherius is already found in the 1539 *Institutio*.[67] Augustine is explicitly named as the source for one reference to Origen[68] and another is found already in Calvin's commentary on Galatians 4:22f., which appeared in 1548.[69] Finally, an Ambrose citation refers to the death of Sarah and comes at the appropriate point in Ambrose's *De Abraham*.[70] Apart from the fact that Calvin would be likely to read this work of Ambrose when expounding this portion of Genesis, the identical passage is cited in the 1536 dedicatory epistle to Francis I[71] with the chapter number being added in the 1539 edition.[72] Clearly Calvin was familiar with this passage long before Lippoman's *Catena* was published.

This leaves four citations, two each from Origen and Jerome. One of the Origen citations is found in Luther.[73] The remaining three citations are not to be found in Calvin's definite sources. How significant are these? The one remaining Origen citation is simply to the effect that (with reference to the Ark) he boldly sports with allegories.[74] Such a brief comment could easily reflect indirect knowledge or memory of reading from years previously. In his 1548 Galatians commentary Calvin demonstrated some knowledge of the contents of Origen's homilies on Genesis. This knowledge could easily extend to the fact that Origen allegorized the Ark. None of the Origen citations require Calvin to have renewed access to Origen, either by reading the Genesis homilies or via Lippoman. He may have done one or the other, but there is no firm evidence to show that he did.

The two Jerome citations both refer to his letter to 'Evagrius' [= Evangelus] concerning Melchizedek.[75] This was an important letter and the index to the editions of Jerome gives easy access to it via the name Melchizedek. There is nothing surprising about Calvin citing it at this point.

---

64 One of these four (#22) might be a reference either to the *Hebraicae quaestiones in Genesim* or to the Vulgate. If it is the latter, the case for dependence upon Lippoman disappears. This citation is also found in Luther (WA 43:205f.).

65 #13 is found in Jerome immediately after #14 and in WA 42:338f. (The following chapter shows that both are found in Steuchus's *Recognitio*.)

66 #3. (The following chapter argues that Calvin did not actually use Chrysostom's homilies *when preparing* this commentary.)

67 #6b and *Inst.* 2:2:9 (OS 3:251f.).

68 #9 and #10a, b.

69 #21; CO 50:236.

70 #24.

71 OS 1:28.

72 OS 3:19.

73 #5; WA 42:67–69.

74 #18.

75 #17 and #18.

There remains one last piece of evidence to be considered. As stated earlier, the juxtaposition of citations may be significant. Calvin seven times juxtaposes patristic citations.[76] Two of these juxtapositions are also found in Lippoman. But the first is already found in the 1550 *Institutio*[77] and in the second one of the passages is found immediately after the other.[78] Two other juxtapositions, each of one Origen and two Augustine citations, are found in Lippoman without the second Augustine citation.[79] But in the first of these instances Calvin explicitly states that Origen's position is to be found in the Augustine passages. In the other instance we find the one Origen passage in Lippoman for which we have not yet located an alternative source. This is the only juxtaposition that might point towards Calvin's reliance upon Lippoman. But it has already been noted that this citation affirms no more than that Origen boldly allegorized the Ark and that we do not need to postulate reading of Lippoman to account for such meagre knowledge.

V. CONCLUSION

Thirty-two possible parallels[80] between Calvin's citations and Lippoman's *Catena* have been examined. Closer examination has led to the conclusion, for each of these parallels, either that Lippoman could not have been Calvin's source or that there is another more likely source. Since the original suggestion that Calvin used Lippoman was based entirely on such parallels, there no longer remains any reason for postulating Calvin's dependence upon Lippoman.

The evidence does not, therefore, encourage the hypothesis that Calvin used Lippoman's *Catena*. There is, of course, no evidence that he did not, just a lack of any convincing evidence that he did. To put it differently, there is no evidence that Calvin knew anything that he might have learnt from Lippoman and that is not already accounted for by the sources that we know him to have used. In establishing this it has not even been necessary to speculate about possible alternative sources, such as Nicholas of Lyra's *Postilla*.

What follows from this? Three things. First, the rumour that the present author started over twenty years ago[81] has been laid to rest. Secondly, some positive discoveries have been made about what sources Calvin *did* use. Some of these appear in this chapter; more will be found in the following chapter. Finally, the lesson has been demonstrated that one should be very cautious before inferring dependence on the basis of mere parallels, however impressive these may at first sight appear to be.

---

76 CO 23:9f., 25f., 38, 63, 123 (twice), 136f.
77 #6a-b.
78 #13 is found in Jerome immediately after #14. (The following chapter shows that both are found in Steuchus's *Recognitio*.)
79 #9 and #10a; #11a and #12.
80 I.e. those listed in section VI, below, counting #6a&b, as separate parallels. #10b and #11b are not actually parallels.
81 Cf. n. 4, above.

VI. POSSIBLE PARALLELS

This list contains all of the passages mentioned in the text where Calvin might be dependent upon Lippoman. As CO is not fully reliable for Calvin's references these have all been checked in the 1554 original.

Where more than one work is cited in the same portion of text these have been reckoned as the same citation (e.g. 6a, b). For the purpose of tracing the sources, each separate reference must of course be counted separately.

Where the information in Lippoman is insufficient for Calvin's citation the reference is put in brackets.

	CO 23	Genesis	Source: Calvin's text + [actual]	Lippoman	Possible source[82]
1	15:21–33	1:1	colligere solent	5b	Steuchus
2	25:28–36	1:26	Iudaei	(39a-b)	WA 42:42f.
3	26:35–38	1:26	Chrysostomus [*Homiliae in Genesim* 8:3f. 9:2–4, 10:3f.]	41a-b	Chrysostom
4	27:20–23	1:26	nonnulli Patrum	(40a-b)	
5	37:9–13	2:8	Origenes	58b	WA 42:67–69
6a	38:51–54	2:9	Augustinus [*De Gen. ad Lit.* 8:4:8]	62a	1550 *Inst.* (OS 3:251f.)
6b	38:51–54	2:9	Eucherius	61a, 62a	1539 *Inst.* (OS 3:251f.)
7	57:12–23	3:1	David Kimhi	(79a)	
8	100:49–55	4:23	Iudaei	116a	WA 42:235
9	123:8–10	6:14–17	Origenes [*In Genesim Homiliae* 2:2]	130b	Augustine (#10a&b)
10a	123:10–12	6:14–17	Augustinus lib. *de Civitate Dei* 15 [15:27:3]	130b	Augustine
10b	123:10–12		et lib. 1 *Quaestionum in Genesin* [QH 1:4]	–	Augustine
11a	123:44–48	6:14–17	Augustinus, lib. 15 *de Civitate Dei* [15:26]	132a	Augustine
11b	123:44–48		[lib.] 12 *adversus Faustum* [12:14]	–	WA 42:310:3–7
12	123:48f.	6:14–17	Origenes [*In Genesim Homiliae* 2:3–6]	132b-133a	
13	136:55–137:1	8:3–5	Josephus	142a	Jerome (PL 23.860f.)
14	137:1–2	8:3–5	Hieronymus [*Loc. hebr.* (PL 23.859)]	142a	Jerome
15	146:22–23	9:5	Iudaei	(150b)	WA 42:358f.
16	152:18–20	9:23	papistae	(157a)	
17	201:20–22	14:18	Hieronymus *ad Evagrium* [= *Ep.* 73:2–10]	188b-189a	Jerome
18	201:26–29	14:18	Hieronymus [= *Ep.* 73:7]	189a	Jerome
19	202:29–41	14:18	vetustis ecclesiae scriptoribus	189a-190b	*Interim*; WA 42:536–38
20	299:42–45	21:8	Augustinus [*Quaest. Hept.* 1:50]	(243b)	WA 43:145

82　See the following chapter for a more reliable guide to sources.

	CO 23	Genesis	Source: Calvin's text + [actual]	Lippoman	Possible source
21	302:25–29	21:10–13	Origenes [*In Genesim Homiliae* 7:2–6]	246a-b	*Comm.* Gal. 4:22f.
22	315:11–12	22:2	Hieronymus [*Hebr. quaest. in Gen.* 22:2]	251a	Vg.; Jerome; WA 43:206
23	317:41–42	22:12	Augustinus [*Quaest. Hept.* 1:58]	254b	Augustine
24	322:46–49	23:2	Ambrosius [*De Abraham* 1:9:80]	258b	1536 *Inst.* (OS 3:19)
25	325:6–9	23:7	pueriliter nugantur	(259a-b)	
26	326:10–15	23:16–20	Hieronymus [*Hebr. quaest. in Gen.* 23:16]	260a	Jerome
27	326:26–29	23:16–20	Hieronymus [*Hebr. quaest. in Gen.* 23:16]	ibid.	Jerome
28	343:35–38	25:1–5	Augustinus [*Quaest. Hept.* 1:35, 70]	272a	*Comm.* Rom. 4:19
29	561:47–49	46:8–27	Augustinus [*de Civitate Dei* 16:40]	403b	cf. *Comm.* Acts 7:14
30	585:31–34	48:16	papistarum inscitia	(413a)	*Interim* (CO 7:583, 653)
31	588:32–34	48:22	Hieronymus [*Hebr. quaest. in Gen.* 48:22]	414b	Jerome

9

⁓⁂⁓

The Sources of the Citations in Calvin's Genesis Commentary

I. INTRODUCTION

This chapter builds on two earlier studies. In a paper delivered at the International Congress on Calvin Research in 1994 I examined the sources of Calvin's 1543 *Bondage and Liberation of the Will*.[1] That study showed how a wide range of patristic citations can be accounted for by the use of fewer than ten volumes. The present study will seek to do the same for the Genesis commentary. It also arises out of an article questioning whether Calvin used Lippoman's *Catena in Genesim*.[2]

A word about the origin of the commentary.[3] Calvin lectured on Genesis from 1550 to 1552.[4] In the summer of 1550 he started work on his commentary, but it was delayed by the pressure of other work, appearing

---

This chapter originally appeared as 'The Sources of Calvin's Citations in his Genesis Commentary' in A. N. S. Lane (ed.), *Interpreting the Bible. Historical and Theological Studies in Honour of David F. Wright* (Leicester: Apollos, 1997) 47–97. Subsequent research has served to strengthen the conclusions of the first edition. A number of further potential sources have been examined, none of which Calvin is likely to have used. I am grateful to David Steinmetz and David Wright for helpful comments on the first edition. I am also most grateful to Graham Davies who examined a number of Hebrew sources for me. Max Engammare has kindly let me see the page proofs of his introduction to M. Engammare (ed.), *Jean Calvin, Sermons sur la Genèse (1–20)* Supplementa Calviniana vol. XI/1–2 (Neukirchen-Vluyn: Neukirchener Verlag, 1999). I have also been helped by discussing these issues with him at length, face to face and by E-mail.

---

1 Chapter 6, above.
2 Chapter 8, above. The results of the present chapter strengthen the conclusion that Calvin did not use Lippoman, but some of the detailed conclusions of the earlier chapter have been revised.
3 Cf. R. Peter and J.-F. Gilmont, *Bibliotheca Calviniana. Les œuvres de Jean Calvin publiées au XVIe siècle*, 2 vols (Geneva: Droz, 1991 and 1994) 1:519–23. Calvin also preached on Genesis, starting in 1559, but as these sermons come after the commentary they are of no interest for our present purposes.
4 T. H. L. Parker, *Calvin's Old Testament Commentaries* (Edinburgh: T&T Clark, 1986) 29; CO 21:72, 75.

finally in 1554.[5] It should be noted how little time Calvin had for this work. During these years he published an average of over twelve volumes a year.[6] Assuming that the lectures on Genesis lasted approximately two years, Calvin had two weeks for each chapter – on top of all of his preaching, correspondence, pastoral and administrative work, in addition to all of his other publications. The indications are that he had an hour or less to prepare each lecture.[7] The revision of the lectures for publication would have been equally rushed. Whatever his natural inclinations might have been, Calvin did not have the leisure to study a wide range of authors. It should not surprise us to find that a good number of his apparently wide-ranging citations can be traced to a small number of sources.

Does the extended time that Calvin spent on Genesis mean that for citations at the beginning of the volume a source prior to 1550 must be sought? Not necessarily. Calvin includes on 3:6 a citation of Bernard which is probably derived from his reading of the 1552 Basel edition of Bernard's works.[8] This shows that, even at the beginning of the commentary, citations can be drawn from books published after 1550.

The Genesis commentary was reprinted as part of Calvin's 1563 Pentateuch commentary.[9] It is important to be clear what Calvin already knew in 1554 so, while the *Calvini Opera* editions has been used, all citations have been checked against the first edition itself, to the extent of verifying their presence there without necessarily checking for every textual variation. This has shown that the *Calvini Opera* edition must be used with caution.[10]

---

5 Parker, *Calvin's Old Testament Commentaries*, 25f. There Parker states, on the basis of the title page of the 1572 French edition, that this commentary was completed in collaboration with Nicholas des Gallars. He has subsequently (in personal conversation) revised this judgment, accepting the advice of Jean-François Gilmont that the later title page is unreliable. The Isaiah commentary certainly was produced by such collaboration (Peter and Gilmont, *Bibliotheca Calviniana*, 1:404f.). It would not seriously affect our present inquiry if this should also have happened with the Genesis commentary as des Gallars' role was essentially scribal and Calvin checked the finished product. While the style might be des Gallars' and while he *may* have inadvertently misrepresented Calvin's view on occasions, he is unlikely to have taken it upon himself to add in his own citations.

6 Peter and Gilmont, *Bibliotheca Calviniana*, 1:332–543.

7 Jean Budé notes in his preface to Calvin's lectures on the Minor Prophets that he with difficulty found half an hour to prepare a lecture (cited by M. Engammare, 'Calvin connaissait-il la Bible?', *Bulletin de la Société de l'Histoire du Protestantisme Français* 141 (1995) 165, n. 8); Colladon, in his *Vie de Calvin*, notes that Calvin usually had less than an hour to prepare his lectures (CO 21:109, cited by Parker, *Calvin's Old Testament Commentaries*, 21); Calvin, writing to Farel in 1554, comments that the hour for the lecture was approaching and that he had not yet been able to prepare (CO 15:148, cited by Engammare, ibid.).

   J.-F. Gilmont, *Jean Calvin et le livre imprimé* (Geneva: Droz, 1997) 353, lists some of the distractions that Calvin faced while he tried to write.

8 For evidence that Calvin was using the 1552 edition of Bernard, cf. chapter 5, above.

9 Peter and Gilmont, *Bibliotheca Calviniana*, 2:1013–16.

10 CO 23 contains the occasional textual note drawing attention to differences between the editions (e.g. CO 23:13f.). This could easily lead the unwary reader into assuming that the 1554 edition conforms to CO except where indicated, which is far from true. This study has revealed a number of unnoted textual differences, most strikingly between CO 23:618:22–32 and p. 332 of the 1554 edition.

It is important to be clear about the question being tackled. The ultimate aim is to determine which sources Calvin used when preparing his Genesis commentary.[11] But how should one discover that? The obvious method, to compare Calvin's comments with those of his predecessors, is fraught with difficulties. First, to do this properly it is necessary to make the comparison for a substantial portion of the commentary, not just for isolated passages. Secondly, unless one does this for *all* of the commentaries available to Calvin one can easily be led astray. For obvious reasons, many commentators say similar things about the same passage. If one compares Calvin with just one or two of his predecessors one may be impressed with what at first sight appear to be impressive parallels, but, in fact, are mere commonplaces of the exegetical tradition. The time needed to make a suitably comprehensive study along these lines is very considerable, which is presumably why it has not so far been attempted.

The approach of the present study is more modest. The aim is to determine, so far as is possible, the sources of Calvin's *citations*. We will be investigating his sources not by examining alleged parallels with other commentaries but by examining texts where Calvin openly *refers* to the views of others, whether by name (e.g. Augustine) or more vaguely (e.g. the Jews). When looking at Calvin's own views one can never be sure to what extent they are derived from others or original to him; when looking at his citations of others one knows by definition that there is a source to be found. If one can identify those sources one then knows at least some of the works that Calvin used while preparing his commentary. The present study will yield some very specific conclusions, which will provide a firm basis for the ongoing task of determining the sources of Calvin's exegetical views.

We will not, of course, presume that because Calvin *names* a particular source he has actually read or even set eyes upon the source himself. The study of his response to Pighius revealed that Calvin named and even exegeted texts that he did not actually have before him.[12] Calvin was hardly less busy by the time he came to prepare his Genesis commentary.[13] We must expect, therefore, that he will take short cuts in preparing his commentary. He did not have the leisure of the professional scholar to sit down for hours consulting every available source. Also, we must be realistic about the range of books available to Calvin at Geneva, which in intellectual terms was very different from Paris, Basel or Strassburg. Calvin's use of resources would have been curtailed by limitations of

11   For an attempt at answering this question, cf. R. C. Gamble, 'The Sources of Calvin's Genesis Commentary: A Preliminary Report', *Archiv für Reformationsgeschichte* 84 (1993) 206–21. Gamble has been working on a fuller study of this question, nearing completion. We have been working independently, without collaboration, on this issue.

12   Cf. chapter 6, above, section II.a, c.

13   Gilmont has estimated the number of words written by Calvin himself each year and published in his lifetime, excluding sermons, lectures and correspondence (*Jean Calvin et le Livre Imprimé*, 371–73). The total for 1542 and 1543, the relevant years for the response to Pighius, is 180,700; for the years 1550–54, the relevant years for the Genesis commentary, the total is 945,000. This gives averages of 90,350 and 189,000 words per year, respectively.

opportunity as well as by limitations of time. In this study, therefore, we will apply a hermeneutic of suspicion. For example, if Calvin once cites from a more obscure writer and the same citation is found in Luther's commentary which Calvin definitely used, the citation of the obscure writer is in itself no evidence that Calvin had read him. The aim will be to account for Calvin's citations by postulating the smallest necessary number of sources. This is not to deny that Calvin's reading *prior to* the preparation of the commentary was wide, but it is to question how many sources he had time and opportunity to use *whilst actually preparing* the commentary. Where, for example, Calvin cites a passage of Augustine which has no particular link to Genesis and for which no intermediate source has been found, the most natural explanation is that this is drawn from his memory of earlier reading of Augustine.[14]

We should not assume that Calvin's sources remain constant throughout the commentary. There are various reasons for doubting this. Some of Calvin's sources did not cover the whole of Genesis. A brief glance at the appendixes will show that Calvin's citations are not spread evenly throughout the commentary. When looking at sources that Calvin definitely did use we will also need to ask whether he used them for all of the commentary or for part only.

As wide as possible a range of commentaries available to Calvin[15] have been examined in the preparation of this article and these are listed at the end. The reader will be disappointed, but hardly surprised, to hear that I have not read every one of these commentaries from cover to cover. The method adopted has been to examine them as potential sources for Calvin's citations. In some instances it becomes quickly apparent that the commentary does not supply the right sort of material and a thorough reading has been unnecessary. Other sources, of which Calvin clearly made considerable use, have been examined thoroughly. But in no case is it claimed that a commentary has been examined absolutely exhaustively and that every last instance where it might be a source for Calvin's citations has been traced. While with Calvin's major sources the aim has been to find as many parallels as possible, the greater priority has been to find at least some plausible source for every citation. Obviously there will be other potential sources that I have not examined, whether because of ignorance, lack of access or the shortness of life. This should not be considered to invalidate the conclusions of the present chapter until such time as another source is found which actually contains Calvin's citations, especially those not yet accounted for.

---

14 For Calvin's ability to make later use of remembered earlier reading, cf. N. Colladon, *Vie de Calvin* (CO 21:109).

15 Making use of the bibliography in A. Williams, *The Common Expositor. An Account of the Commentaries on Genesis 1527–1633* (Chapel Hill: University of North Carolina Press, 1948) 269–77. The colophon of Wolfgang Musculus's Genesis commentary (Basel: Hervagius, 1554) is dated September (sig. Eee4a); the colophon of Calvin's commentary is dated July. We can assume, therefore, that Calvin did not use Musculus, a disappointing conclusion as Musculus could account for some of Calvin's more elusive citations. It is also assumed that Calvin used neither the German commentaries of Corvinus (1541) or Linck (1543), nor the Italian commentary of Brucioli (1540 and 1546).

One factor has been borne in mind when considering sources. The 1572 catalogue of the library of the Genevan Academy survives.[16] Some of Calvin's books ended up in this library. If a work is found there it might be Calvin's copy or it might explain why the library did not take Calvin's copy, having one already. If, on the contrary, a work is not found there one must ask why the library chose not to take Calvin's copy. This is not an infallible guide, but it does affect the balance of probability that Calvin used a particular source. To avoid introducing an unwarranted bias, I have ignored this evidence until the very end. In other words, it has been used to confirm conclusions already reached but not to dictate conclusions in advance.

A variety of types of citations will be considered, in the following order. First to be considered will be the small number of Calvin's named references to contemporary authors. Second will be his references to different translations of Genesis. This will point to some sources which are important for other types of citation. Next will come named references to patristic authors, which for the purposes of this study will include Josephus. Related to the patristic citations are the few references to ancient heresies, such as Arianism. The commentary is rich in Jewish citations and also contains a number of references to the pope or 'papists'. Finally there are two types of looser references. First there are unnamed references to a specific group such as the fathers or the Anabaptists. Secondly there are numerous vague references to the views of others, described in loose terms simply as 'nonnulli' or 'alii'. This group is by far the largest and in order to contain the scope of the study such citations have been examined for the first eleven chapters only. All of Calvin's likely sources have been checked against these citations and where a source accounts for many of them this is a strong confirmation that Calvin was using it. While these citations have been used as confirmatory evidence it is not the goal of this chapter to trace the source of every such vague reference. For each of these eight types of citation, details of each citation are listed in the appendixes at the end of the chapter, with an indication of their probable source.

Apart from the last category of vague references the aim has been to consider every single citation fitting into each category, but it would be rash to claim that no citations have been overlooked.[17] The occasional minor lapse need not, however, be serious. The aim is to find clues which point to Calvin's sources and it is possible for the detective to catch the criminal without necessarily making use of every single clue.

Two other types of citation should also be mentioned. Calvin's Genesis commentary is rich in material from the classics, including proverbial sayings. These were sought in the potential sources that have been examined but no significant intermediate sources were found, other than Erasmus's *Adages*. Including these citations would significantly lengthen the chapter without making any contribution towards tracing Calvin's

---

16 A. Ganoczy, BAC.
17 I am grateful to John Dawson, one of my students, for reading through Genesis 1–11 checking for citations that I might have missed. Use of a CD ROM with the English text of Calvin's commentary has confirmed my fallibility. Some extra citations have been added at the proof stage.

exegetical sources. Secondly, there are many discussions of the meanings of Hebrew words. When examining potential sources these, like the classical citations, have been considered but there has been no systematic attempt to trace their source.[18]

It also needs to be stated that we must not assume that Calvin used only those writings which he cited. Calvin, unlike modern commentators, was under no obligation to document all of his sources. Where he does refer to the interpretation of others it is more often than not in vague terms such as 'some say'. Nor does he feel obliged to refer to all that he has read, as he himself indicates:

> It is not my intention to relate the ravings or the dreams of every writer, nor would I have the reader to expect this from me; here and there I allude to them, though sparingly, especially if there be any colour of deception; that readers, being often admonished, may learn to take heed unto themselves. Therefore, with respect to this passage, which has been variously tortured, I will not record what one or another may have delivered, but will content myself with a true exposition of it.[19]

This quotation also reminds us that Calvin, *in his commentaries*, more often cites others in order to disagree with them. While in the *Institutes* and the polemical treatises Calvin is citing authorities as witnesses in his favour, in the commentaries he is dialoguing with his fellow expositors.

So how should one select which potential sources to check? Clearly all works cited by Calvin must be checked as well as works by authors that he names, such as Steuchus. Again, all of the significant patristic commentaries and sixteenth-century commentaries prior to 1554 have been checked, as have important medieval predecessors such as the *Glossa ordinaria*, Nicolaus of Lyra, Bede, Rabanus Maurus, Hugh of St Cher and Dionysius the Carthusian. Almost every medieval Latin commentary on Genesis to be found in Migne has been looked at, at least briefly. Annotated Bibles such as Münster's are obvious potential sources. Finally, Augustinus Marlorat in 1562 published at Geneva *Genesis cum catholica expositione ecclesiastica ... sive, Bibliotheca expositionum Genesews*, a compilation of extracts from the works of eleven authors.[20] This obviously post-dates Calvin's commentary, but it does reveal which authors on Genesis a French

---

18 In the first edition of this chapter I announced my intention, in collaboration with Graham Davies, to seek to determine which Hebrew Bible(s), lexicon(s) and grammar(s) Calvin used, as well as the sources of his Jewish citations, for all of his Old Testament commentaries, not just Genesis. In the light of the recent studies by Engammare and Phillips (cf. n. 51, below) the future of this project is less certain.

19 J. Calvin, *Commentaries on the First Book of Moses called Genesis*, 2 vols (Grand Rapids: Eerdmans, 1948 reprint) 1.221f. Apart from quotations, this translation has often informed the English paraphrases of Calvin's text found in this chapter.

20 (Geneva: H. Stephanus, 1562). Cf. P. Chaix, A. Dufour and G. Moeckli, *Les livres imprimés a Genève de 1550 a 1600* (Geneva: Droz, 1966 – revised edition) 54. Stephanus provides a key indicating which *authors* are being used but, unfortunately, not which of their *works*. That is usually, but not always, obvious. Also, the indications in the text as to which author is being quoted are often unreliable. Some Calvin quotations are attributed to others. The authors are: Vatable, Luther, Musculus, Calvin, Fagius, Oecolampadius, Artopoeus, Pagninus, Münster, Steuchus and Marlorat.

Reformed pastor considered most useful and which Calvin was also not unlikely to have used.

II. NAMED CONTEMPORARY CITATIONS[21]

A good place to start is with Calvin's own contemporaries, for the obvious reason that he had little or no opportunity to be acquainted with their writing through intermediary sources. A citation from Ambrose has had over a thousand years to be used by others; a citation from Luther's commentary is hot off the press.

Before considering those contemporaries explicitly cited, there is one contemporary author who is not named but may safely be considered a potential source for other, explicit, citations. That is John Calvin. If the Genesis commentary contains a citation which has earlier appeared in another work of Calvin's we need look no further for the source. The purpose of this study is to identify the sources used by Calvin *while preparing* his Genesis commentary, not the sources of his earlier works.

Calvin names four contemporary authors, three of them only once. Most significant is Luther, who is named no less than five times.[22] It is reasonably safe to assume that this is evidence for Calvin's use of Luther's commentary, something that would have been not unlikely even if there were no citations. This assumption is greatly strengthened by two facts. First, as we shall see, many of Calvin's other citations can be traced to the Luther commentary. Secondly, Calvin himself confirms this when he states, with reference to this commentary, that out of respect for Luther he had abstained more than a hundred times from naming him.[23] Calvin's first-hand knowledge of Luther is therefore certain.

This does not mean, however, that Calvin had access to *all* of Luther's lectures on Genesis. These were published in four volumes, from 1544 to 1554.[24] The first predates Calvin's exegesis of Genesis; the last volume clearly appeared too late to be used. What of the other two? First, of Calvin's four references to Luther, three appear in the first volume, the fourth in the second volume, which ends at 25:10. Secondly, all of Calvin's citations after 25:10 have been sought in Luther. This search has yielded all but nothing,[25] which suggests that Calvin had just the first two volumes before him and therefore had access to Luther's exposition of chapters 1–25:10.[26]

Secondly, commenting on the first verse of Genesis, Calvin chides Steuchus for maintaining the error that unformed matter has existed from

---

21 Named contemporary citations are listed in Appendix 1. #n = citation n in that list.
22 ##3–7.
23 CO 9:54 (*Def. sec. c. Westph.*).
24 See details in section XI, below.
25 Jews #62, 63, 65; Translations #113; Papists #27.
26 Calvin's Luther citations have also been checked to confirm that he is not refer-ring to Luther's *In Genesin, Mosi Librum Sanctissimum . . . Declamationes* (Hagenau: J. Secerius, 1527) which is found in WA 24.

eternity.[27] Augustinus Eugubinus Steuchus or Agostino Steuco was a humanist Old Testament scholar who in 1538 was appointed both absentee bishop of Chisamo in Crete and papal librarian.[28] To which of his works is Calvin referring here? Steuchus taught, in his *Cosmopoeia*, that there are three heavens and that the most transcendent of these, the *coelum empyrium* is eternal.[29] But it is unlikely that Calvin could have so misunderstood this as to accuse him of teaching the eternity of unformed matter.[30] In fact Calvin is referring to another work of Steuchus, his *Recognitio Veteris Testamenti ad Hebraicam Veritatem*.[31] In commenting on Genesis 1:1 ('creavit'), Steuchus does not exactly teach the eternity of unformed matter, but he does allow that the Hebrew word 'bârâ' need not imply creation *ex nihilo*.[32] Calvin's opposition to the idea of eternal unformed matter immediately follows his own claim that 'bârâ' must mean creation out of nothing.[33] Thus it seems likely that Calvin is thinking of Steuchus's *Recognitio* at this point. Shortly afterwards there is further confirmation that this is correct. A few sentences after the critique of Steuchus Calvin criticizes those who see a reference to the Trinity in Genesis 1:1. The point criticized is found in Steuchus immediately after the discussion of 'creavit'.[34] Thus it is almost certainly Steuchus again who is being criticized. The claim that Calvin used the *Recognitio* is based not just upon these two citations but, as will be seen, on a total of seventy-one citations where it is a possible source, in eight of which no other possible source has been found. About a quarter of the Steuchus references are also found in Münster (who used the *Recognitio*) – but the other three-quarters are not.

Thirdly, a few lines later, Calvin refers to Servetus, criticizing him for the view that the first beginning of the Word was when God commanded that there should be light.[35] Calvin was already aware that Servetus held such views, having attacked them (though without naming him) in the 1539 edition of the *Institutio*.[36] But why mention them again in the Genesis

27 #1.
28 For Steuchus, cf. F. Lauchert, *Die italienischen literarischen Gegner Luthers* (Freiburg, etc.: Herder, 1912) 315–28; T. Freudenberger, *Augustinus Steuchus aus Gubbio* (Münster i. W.: Aschendorff, 1935).
29 In his 1535 *Cosmopoeia*. Cf. Freudenberger, *Augustinus Steuchus*, 219–30.
30 R. Stauffer, 'L'exégèse de Genèse 1,1–3 chez Luther et Calvin' in his *In Principio: interpretations des premiers versets de la Genèse* (Paris: Études Augustiniennes, 1973), 256–58, maintains that Calvin is referring to this teaching of Steuchus, while acknowledging that it is difficult to see why his attack was so imprecise. Stauffer points out that earlier M. Réveillaud had, incorrectly, given Steuchus's *De perenni philosophia* as the source.
31 Venice: Aldus and A. Socerus, 1529. There was a 1531 edition published by Sebastian Gryphius at Lyon (*Augustini Steuchi Eugubini Veteris Testamenti ad veritatem Hebraicam Recognitio*) a copy of which was found in the library of the Genevan Academy in 1572 (Ganoczy, BAC 231). Both editions have been consulted but references will be to the 1531 edition, since the copy in the Genevan Academy library might be the one which Calvin used.
32 *Recognitio*, 25–28.
33 CO 23:14f.
34 *Recognitio*, 28–32.
35 #2.
36 *Inst.* 1:13:8. OS 3:118, n. 1 identifies two passages from Servetus. Cf. also Stauffer, *In Principio*, 264. The source appears to be Servetus, *De Trinitatis Erroribus Libri Septem* (s.l., 1531) f. 47a; E.T.: E. M. Wilbur (transl.), *The Two Treatises of Servetus on the*

commentary? This same issue was raised by the trial of Servetus where reference was made to Servetus's 1553 *Christianismi Restitutio*.[37] The Servetus citation, therefore, should be seen both as a recollection of earlier reading and as a byproduct of the trial.

Finally, Budé is cited for the statement that 1600 Attic drachmas are worth about 250 pounds of French money.[38] This seems to be based upon Budé's *De asse*.[39]

III. CITATIONS OF TRANSLATIONS[40]

Citations of translations are the next to be traced. By examining these we will be able to ascertain some works which Calvin clearly had before him while expounding Genesis. These will be potential sources for other types of citation.

When is a translation not a translation? In English there are two words which are clearly distinct: 'translate' and 'interpret'. Latin is less straightforward and Calvin can use many different words to mean 'translate': *vertere, legere, transferre, facere, reddere, habere, exponere, exprimere, interpretari* and others.[41] Unfortunately all of these words (even 'vertit') can be used in a looser sense than 'translate'. The situation is also complicated by the fact that Calvin is not always concerned to quote translations exactly.[42] For example, he states that Jerome's rendering of 2:18 is 'Quod sit illi simile' where the Vulgate reads 'similem sui' or 'similem sibi'. The key word is 'similem' and for the rest the sense suffices. Again, he cites the Vulgate translation of 3:1 as 'Cur dixit Deus?' when in fact it is 'Cur praecepit Deus'. It is the first word that Calvin is discussing and for the others the sense suffices. This means that in seeking the translation that Calvin is citing one has to realize that he may not be quoting it with total accuracy. Where there are significant differences between Calvin's quotation and his alleged source, that is indicated in Appendix 2, below, in a note. Readers are therefore in a position to judge for themselves whether sources are being alleged on adequate grounds.

Two criteria have been used to determine what are citations of translations. First, the context in Calvin. The aim has been to consider only

---

Trinity (Harvard Theological Studies 16) (Cambridge (MA): Harvard University Press, and London: Humphrey Milford: 1932) 75.

37 CO 8:572f. (*Def. c. err. Serveti*); M. Servetus, *Christianismi Restitutio* (Frankfurt: Minerva, 1966) 704. Cf. also CO 8:505 (proposition XXV) which refers to *Christianismi Restitutio*, 208. A quick reading of the *Restitutio* has yielded little evidence that it is the source for further citations; a more thorough search *might* reveal more.

38 #8.

39 G. Budaeus, *De asse & partibus eius* (Paris: M. Vascosan with R. Stephanus and J. Roigny, 1541) f. 44b appears to value 1600 drachmas at just 25 pounds. Maybe Calvin made a mistake in haste. I am grateful to David Wright for further help with disentangling Budé's Latin.

40 Citations of translations are listed in Appendix 2. #n = citation n in that list.

41 See Appendix 2. Listed in order of first occurrence.

42 For the (considerably worse) looseness of Calvin's biblical citations in his sermons on Genesis, cf. Engammare, 'Calvin connaissait-il la Bible?', 163–84.

those passages which are citing *someone else's* translation of the text, not
those which are simply discussing Calvin's translation, nor those which
concern the interpretation of the text rather than strictly its translation,
nor those which discuss the meaning of a Hebrew word in general rather
than its translation in this particular place.[43] Secondly, where it is not
sufficiently clear from the context in Calvin whether or not it is a
translation that is being cited, the evidence of the actual translations
available to Calvin has been allowed to influence the decision. Clearly this
could have the effect of biasing the final list in favour of the translations
examined, but this second criterion has only rarely been invoked and does
not affect the overall picture.

Finally, two types of translation have been excluded from this section:
citations of the 'Chaldaeus paraphrastes' and citations of the translations
of Jewish interpreters. These will be considered below under Jewish
citations.

The citations of translations will be considered in three parts: the
Septuagint, Jerome and the Vulgate and the remainder.

(a) Septuagint

Calvin twelve times refers to the way in which 'Graeci' or 'Graeci interpretes' translate the text,[44] all of these refering to the Septuagint. This
would appear to be a clear indication that Calvin consulted the Septuagint
while expounding Genesis. It may be that he did, but the evidence is
unclear. All twelve citations are also found in Steuchus's *Recognitio*,[45]
where we find not just the text of the Septuagint but also Calvin's comment about it, such as the statement that they have missed Moses' sense,[46]
or that they read the text incorrectly.[47] Thus while Calvin *may* have looked
at the Septuagint, if he did so it did not lead him to refer to any passage
nor to express any opinion which was not already to be found in the
Recognitio, which he was constantly using. Calvin betrays no knowledge
of or judgment about the Septuagint which he would not have found in
Steuchus.

---

43 For an alternative approach, cf. H. F. van Rooy, 'Calvin's Genesis Commentary –
Which Bible Text did he Use?' in B. J. van der Walt (pref.), *Our Reformational
Tradition. A Rich Heritage and Lasting Vocation* (Potchefstroom: Potchefstroom
University for Christian Higher Education, 1984) 203–16, where Calvin's translation
(of the first three chapters only) is compared with the Vulgate, Pagninus and
Münster translations. The advantage of this method is that there is plenty of material
to consider. The drawback is that while Calvin's translation might be very similar
to Pagninus's, for example, that does not prove that Calvin was actually dependent
upon Pagninus. If, on the other hand, Calvin states that some have translated a
passage in a certain way, he is explicitly declaring that he has seen such a translation.
It is also perhaps suspicious that only three translations are considered and that the
verdict is that Calvin was dependent upon these same three. In the final paragraph
of the article the author acknowledges the need to look at more than just three
chapters and to consider a wider range of potential sources than those available to
him (in South Africa).
44 ##1, 11, 15, 21, 33, 36, 39, 67, 88, 98, 106, 108.
45 Full details will be found in Appendix 2.
46 #33.
47 #36.

(b) Jerome and the Vulgate

Calvin refers to the Vulgate in a variety of ways: 'vetus interpres', 'Hieronymus', 'vulgaris translatio' and 'Hieronymi versio'.[48] The picture is further complicated by the fact that Jerome also discusses the text of Genesis in his *Hebraicae quaestiones in Genesim*, a work which Calvin cites explicitly. Every reference to Jerome's translation has been checked in this work as well as in the Vulgate. There are four references to Jerome discussed in this section where it could be the *Hebraicae quaestiones* that Calvin has in mind, though in every instance the Vulgate is also a possible source.[49]

Clearly other commentators also discuss the Vulgate and it is theoretically possible that Calvin could have derived his knowledge of it indirectly. But this is *a priori* unlikely and also examination of the other citations of translations will point towards a particular edition that Calvin probably used.

(c) The Remainder

A wide variety of contemporary translations have been examined as potential sources for Calvin's citations.[50] The great majority of his citations are accounted for by three volumes. A number are found in Steuchus's *Recognitio*. Many are found in the Zurich translation of 1543. Others are found in the notes of François Vatable. These notes are found, together with the Vulgate and Zurich translations, in Robert Stephanus's 1545 edition of the Latin Bible and were not otherwise printed before Calvin's Genesis commentary.[51] Finally, Calvin on occasions seems to be using

48 See Appendix 2. Listed in order of first occurrence. R. J. Mooi, KDE 136, states that Calvin never names Jerome in connection with ('in verband met') the Vulgate translation. This is not true inasmuch as references to Jerome sometimes refer to the Vulgate.

49 ##7, 37, 69, 86.

50 These are listed in section XI, below. A number of French translations have also been examined in case Calvin might have been referring to one of these and changes between editions of the Olivétan Bible have been noted. Nothing indicates that Calvin referred to French translations but it is interesting that the Olivétan Bible in 1540/46 introduces the translation 'sera armé'/'s'armera' in 41:40, a rendering rejected by Calvin (#91).

51 Cf. D. Barthélemy, 'Origine et rayonnement de la "Bible de Vatable"' in I. Backus and F. Higman (eds), *Théorie et pratique de l'exégèse* (Geneva: Droz, 1990) 385–401. In the first edition of this chapter I was unaware that this material did not appear elsewhere before 1554. It has been repeatedly claimed, since A. J. Baumgartner (*Calvin Hébraïsant et Interprète de l'Ancien Testament* (Paris: Fischbacher, 1889) 15f.) that Calvin learned Hebrew from Vatable, a claim which is rightly questioned by Max Engammare ('*Johannes Calvinus trium linguarum peritus*? La Question de l'Hébreu', *Bibliothèque d'Humanisme et Renaissance* 58 (1996) 37–39). The only times that Vatable is named in CO is in two letters *to* Calvin (11:517f., 20:582).

François Baudouin in a letter from Paris at the end of 1545, announces that he is sending (*mittimus*) Calvin 'reliquas chartas bibliorum Stephani' (CO 12:231. Cf. chapter 1, n. 62, above). Given the date and the internal evidence this quite likely refers to the 1545 Stephanus Bible (which appeared in five fascicules/volumes), though cf. CO 12:231, n. 15 for other possibilities. Darryl Phillips concludes that Calvin used the 1545 Stephanus Bible for his lectures on Lamentations (*An Inquiry into the Extent of the Abilities of John Calvin as a Hebraist* (Oxford: Oxford University DPhil thesis, 1998) 226f., 261f.).

either the Latin translation or the notes of Sebastian Münster's Latin Bible. These three volumes are sufficient to account for all but six of Calvin's citations of translations, including those of the Septuagint and Jerome.

What of the remaining six? These will be considered individually. One is a reference to Luther, whom we know Calvin to be using.[52] Another is found in Fagius's *Exegesis*, a work which is a likely source of some of Calvin's other (especially Jewish) citations.[53] Another claims that 'communiter vertunt interpretes' where the translations give the same sense in different words. One translation does, however, come close to Calvin's wording, Fagius's *Thargum*, a work which is a likely source of some of Calvin's Jewish citations.[54] One has been found only in Pagninus's translation and dictionary.[55] Another has been found in one place only: as a variant reading in Servetus's revision of the Pagninus translation.[56]

This points to the distinct, and intriguing, possibility that Calvin used the Servetus edition, a suggestion that elicited surprise or disbelief in some readers of the first edition of this chapter. What is the evidence apart from the fact that the Servetus edition alone matches Calvin's citation this one time? There are three other places where Servetus's variant readings are a possible source, the alternatives being Münster's or Vatable's notes.[57] But since we can be certain that Calvin used Münster and Vatable this evidence counts for very little.

The internal evidence is significant but not overwhelming. The external evidence, by contrast, is more compelling. In the records of Servetus's trial mention is made of the Spaniard's notes on Isaiah chapters 7, 8 and 53 in this edition, both in the thirteenth interrogation (17 August 1553) and in Calvin's refutation of Servetus published the following February. Calvin refers not just to these three chapters but to the marginal notes in general.[58] There are not many marginal notes in the volume and it is likely that Calvin read most if not all of them in search for evidence. It is unlikely that he

---

52 #32.
53 #28.
54 #87. Calvin's text is 'non sic fieri decet'; Fagius's is 'sic enim non decebat fieri'.
55 #55. The notes in the 1557 Stephanus Bible have a similar reading (*Biblia Utriusque Testamenti* (Geneva: R. Stephanus, 1557) f. 14a) but this is not found in the 1545 Stephanus Bible.
56 #111. *Recognitio* 361 comes the nearest of other potential sources. Where Calvin and Servetus have 'principium *seminis*', it refers to the LXX reading of 'principium filiorum meorum'.
57 ##54, 68, 70.
58 For the three chapters, cf. CO 8:745f. (trial), 497f. (*Refutatio*). Max Engammare has drawn my attention to the fact that in the French edition of the *Refutatio* Calvin introduces this issue with an impersonal 'On luy mit aussi en avant un autre item' (CO 8:497, n. 3, 8:745, n. 3). He suggests that Nicolas Colladon may have been charged to study and respond to the Servetus edition. If this is true it would not prove that Calvin did not also himself read the notes at some stage, but it does show that one cannot be absolutely certain that he read them. In the *Refutatio* Calvin also states of this edition *in general* that Servetus 'margines multis perniciosis commentis inquinavit' (CO 8:552f.). The potential source of #111 is in the marginal notes.

neglected to check Genesis, the first book of the Bible and the one on which he was commenting at the time.

There are eighteen times when the Pagninus translation is one of a number of possible sources, the others being more definite, but just one where it is the only source that has been traced. The comment there is on a Hebrew word and the source might be Pagninus's dictionary rather than his translation.[59] Thus the evidence for the use of the Pagninus translation is actually weaker than that for the use of Servetus's marginal notes. Given the external evidence the most likely explanation is that Calvin read the marginal notes during the Servetus trial and that he may also have read some or all of the translation at the same time.

This leaves just one citation which has not to date been traced, though it is just possible, but not likely, that Calvin's comment may have been inspired by Pagninus's dictionary.[60] A later author, however, attributes this translation to Vatable.[61] It is not found in his notes as they appear in the 1545 Stephanus Bible, the only form in which they were then available to Calvin. It first appears in the Vatable notes of the 1557 Stephanus Bible – for the simple reason that Stephanus added to these notes extensive material from Calvin's commentary![62]

The study of the citations of translations has yielded the following conclusions. Calvin definitely used the *Recognitio*, Münster's Latin Bible[63] and the 1545 Stephanus Bible. There is evidence, soon to be confirmed, that he used the two works of Fagius. For the Servetus trial he probably read at least the marginal notes of his revision of the Pagninus translation and these seem to have left some mark on the commentary.

---

59 #55. S. Pagninus, *Thesaurus Linguae Sanctae* ([Paris]: R. Stephanus, 1548) 888 suggests the meaning 'poena & punitio' for this word, citing Genesis 15:16. See Appendix 2 for details of the other eighteen.

60 #79. Pagninus, *Thesaurus Linguae Sanctae*, 1065f.

61 M. Poole, *Synopsis Criticorum aliorumque S. Scripturae Interpretum*, vol. 1 (London: J. Flesher and T. Roycroft, 1669) 79.

62 *Biblia*, f. 28b. I am grateful to John L. Thompson for showing me his forthcoming 'Calvin's Exegetical Legacy' which draws attention to the insertion of Calvin's material into the Vatable notes.

63 Which edition of Münster did Calvin use? For the present study all three have been examined. The 1546 is longer than the 1534–35 edition, but does not thereby provide a source for any further citations. The 1551 edition is abridged and omits material which accounts for seven citations: Jews ##4, 5, 30, 31, 57, 58; Vague #77. If Calvin studied Hebrew at Basel with Münster in 1535–36 it is highly likely that he would then have bought the newly published Münster Bible. As the extra material in the 1546 edition covers no new citations it is most likely that Calvin owned and used the 1534–35 edition. It is found in the Genevan library (Ganoczy, BAC 160), but for such a standard work there is no great likelihood that this is Calvin's copy.
   Max Engammare, in a seminar given at the Seventh International Congress on Calvin Research (Seoul, 1998) presented evidence from Calvin's Genesis sermons that also indicated that he then used the 1534 edition (also in Engammare (ed.), *Jean Calvin, Sermons sur la Genèse*, in his introduction (from XLIV in the page proofs)). At Genesis 4:8 Calvin comments that the Jews 'mettent icy comme un espace en blanc'. The first, but not the second, Münster edition has a blank space of a quarter of a line in length at this point (f. a4a). This strengthens the likelihood that Calvin used the first Münster edition throughout his career.

IV. NAMED PATRISTIC CITATIONS[64]

(a) Augustine

Augustine is cited twenty-two times in Calvin's Genesis commentary. Five of these citations are of his *Quaestiones in Heptateuchum*.[65] Given Calvin's regular use of Augustine, it is safe to assume that he was working with the original, unless the same citations are found in another work which Calvin was likely to have used. In fact one of the citations is also found in Luther[66] and another had already appeared in Calvin's Romans commentary.[67] These parallels are not, however, sufficient to revise the judgment that Calvin was using Augustine for himself. Calvin does not cite the Genesis part of this work outside of this commentary, except for the one citation in the Romans commentary,[68] which would suggest that Calvin read it for the specific task of expounding Genesis.

Two other Augustinian expositions are also cited. In the Argument Calvin gives the *De Genesi contra Manichaeos* as one of two marginal references for Augustine's comment on the Manichees.[69] The same passage was cited, more briefly, both in the 1539 *Institutio*[70] and in the 1552 *De aeterna dei praedestinatione*.[71] The citation in the Genesis commentary is fuller, which suggests that Calvin possibly turned to the work again while preparing either the Genesis commentary or the *De aeterna dei praedestinatione*, having remembered the passage from the 1539 *Institutio*. Either way the citation is no evidence that Calvin made more general use of this work of Augustine's while preparing the commentary. This verdict is supported by the fact that there is no other citation of this work until later in the 1550s.[72]

Calvin also cites an opinion of Augustine and Eucherius on the tree of life, the former coming from the *De Genesi ad litteram*.[73] The Eucherius citation was already found in the 1539 *Institutio* and the reference to Augustine was added in 1550.[74] The *De Genesi ad litteram* is also cited explicitly three times in the 1539 *Institutio* and twice in the 1552 *De aeterna dei praedestinatione*.[75] Calvin is unlikely here to be depending upon his reading for the 1539 *Institutio* as he there mentioned Eucherius without

---

64 Named patristic citations are listed in Appendix 3. #n = citation n in that list. The reference to 'Iustinus' at 10:8 (CO 23:159) is to the classical author, not to Justin Martyr (*pace* Gamble, 'Sources of Calvin's Genesis Commentary', 219).
65 ##21, 34, 36, 41, 43.
66 #34.
67 #41.
68 L. Smits, SAOJC 2:237.
69 #2.
70 *Inst.* 3:23:2.
71 CO 8:312f.
72 Smits, SAOJC 2:202. Some of the 'citations' mentioned by Smits are where this work is just one of a number of possible sources for a general comment of Calvin's. In one place (CO 5:202 – *Psychop.*) Calvin refers to the relevant entry in Augustine's *Retractationes*, which is of course no evidence for Calvin's direct knowledge of this work.
73 #10.
74 *Inst.* 2:2:9. Smits, SAOJC 2:201 wrongly dates this citation as 1539.
75 Smits, SAOJC 2:201f.

Augustine. The new citations after 1550 probably reflect new reading. The 1550 *Institutio* was nearly complete in February 1550 and in April Beza was writing to Calvin conveying Melchior Wolmar's thanks for his copy.[76] It is probable that Calvin turned to this work with an eye to his imminent exposition of Genesis and that his reading also yielded citations for his revision of the *Institutio* and for his treatise on predestination. There are other passages where this work is a possible source.[77]

There are two other expositions of Genesis by Augustine: *De Genesi ad litteram imperfectus liber* and *Locutiones in Heptateuchum*. Calvin appears never to have cited these works[78] and no evidence of their use has been found from comparing them with the citations in his Genesis commentary. The last three books of the *Confessiones* are also an exposition of the first chapter of Genesis and there are some parallels with Calvin's citations, but none that requires the use of this particular work.[79]

Calvin four times cites Augustine's *De civitate dei* by name and it is the likely source of two further citations.[80] This is a work which Calvin regularly cited throughout his career[81] and with which he was clearly familiar. With one exception, the passages cited here have not previously been cited by Calvin. But rather than postulate that Calvin chose to read through the entire *De civitate dei* while expounding Genesis, it is most likely that he is citing it from memory, perhaps sometimes with the aid of an index to trace a particular passage. The exceptional passage is Augustine's comment on the discrepancy between Genesis 46:8 and Acts 7:14, which was also cited in Calvin's earlier (1552) Acts commentary.[82] Since 46:8 comes near the end of Genesis it is most likely that Calvin turned to this passage while preparing his Acts commentary and simply repeated the reference when he came to the Genesis passage.

This leaves nine further Augustinian citations. Two concern Augustine's trinitarian analogies in his *De trinitate*.[83] This is a work that Calvin cited throughout his career, though more especially in the late 1550s.[84] Augustine's analogies are well-known and Calvin's reference to them probably reflects memory of earlier reading, possibly brought to recollection by Luther's briefer mention of them.[85] Another citation is fully accounted for by Luther.[86] Augustine's famous prayer, 'Give what you

---

76 Peter and Gilmont, *Bibliotheca Calviniana*, 1:373.
77 E.g. #13; Heresies #3; Vague ##1, 3, 4, 21, 26, 28, 35, 36.
78 Smits, SAOJC vol. 2. The former work is a possible source for one 1539 citation (*Institutio* 2:1:11, OS 3:240) for which the alternative source is the *Opus imperfectum contra Julianum*. Since there are many other places where Calvin is likely to be referring to the latter work (Smits, SAOJC 2:209f.) and no other places where Calvin is likely to be referring to the former, the simplest explanation is that the latter is the source here too.
79 See the Appendixes for details.
80 ##3, 7, 20, 22; ##13, 44. #13 could come from a variety of sources. Smits, SAOJC 2:131 suggests *Enarrationes in Psalmos* 18:2:15. Another possibility is *De natura et gratia* 29:33. More likely is *De Genesi ad litteram* 11:5:7 and 11:15:19.
81 Smits, SAOJC 2:159–63.
82 #44.
83 ##5, 6.
84 Smits, SAOJC 2:254–56.
85 WA 42:45.
86 #23 and WA 42:310.

command and command what you will' is often quoted by Calvin prior to this time,[87] as is also the statement that God crowns his own gifts.[88] Three other citations are loose enough that they cannot be tied to any one passage.[89] Given this vagueness, and the fact that they can be attributed to works of Augustine that Calvin had at earlier stages cited,[90] there is no need to postulate fresh reading of Augustine nor indeed any intermediate source, unless a work which Calvin probably used should turn out to have the same citation. Finally, Calvin erroneously claims Augustine for the view that Adam and Eve fell after a mere six hours.[91] Calvin is either relying upon an inaccurate memory of Augustine or has been misled by an intermediate source.

This survey of the Augustine citations reveals one work which Calvin definitely seems to have been using while preparing his commentary, the *Quaestiones in Heptateuchum*. It is also highly likely that he made some use of the *De Genesi ad litteram*. He probably looked up in the *De Genesi contra Manichaeos* a passage that he had cited earlier. He may have checked some passages in the *De civitate dei*, being led to them either by memory or via the index.

(b) Jerome

References to Jerome fall into three groups. First, there are citations of the Vulgate, which have already been considered under translations. Secondly, there are citations of Jerome's *Hebraicae quaestiones in Genesim*. This Calvin never names, but three times that he refers to Jerome this work is in mind.[92] One of the translation citations also appears to refer to the *Hebraicae quaestiones*.[93] There are other passages where this work is a possible source, but only these four where it is the only source discovered. This evidence is limited, but given that Jerome is explicitly named, given Calvin's regular use of Jerome and given that no intermediate source has been found, it is safe to assume that he was working with the original.

This leaves just four citations of Jerome. With reference to Genesis 2:18 Calvin notes that this teaching refutes those with a negative view of marriage, as is found in Jerome's *Adversus Jovinianum*.[94] This is the first time that Calvin mentions Jerome's work against Jovinian in this context. But Calvin rebukes Jerome on this matter in the 1539 *Institutio* and repeatedly makes the same point in his commentaries.[95] It is very likely that it was Jerome's work against Jovinian that provoked those comments and that the only new feature of the present passage is that Calvin now actually mentions the work. With reference to Mount Ararat, Calvin cites

---

87 #17. E.g. in the 1536 *Institutio* (OS 1:55).
88 #25. E.g. in the 1539 *Institutio* 2:5:2.
89 #15, 29, 33. For suggested sources, cf. Smits, SAOJC 2:131.
90 As can be seen from Smits, SAOJC vol. 2.
91 #14. Cf. Smits, SAOJC 2:295.
92 ##39, 40, 45. ##39, 40 refer to the same passage in Jerome.
93 Translations #71. Four of the passages which have been treated as citations of the Vulgate might possibly refer to the *Hebraicae quaestiones*. See n. 49, above.
94 #12.
95 *Inst.* 4:12:28; *Comm.* 1 Corinthians 7:1, 7, 9, 33, 36 (1546); *Comm.* Hebrews 13:4 (1549).

a passage from Jerome's *Liber de situ et nominibus locorum hebraicorum*.[96] This he may have read from Jerome himself, but it is noteworthy that there is no indication that Calvin made any other use of this work.[97] It is more likely, therefore, that Calvin's source is Steuchus's *Recognitio*, where all that Calvin mentions is to be found. Finally, with reference to Melchizedek, there is a double citation of Jerome's 'ad Evagrium', in fact Jerome's *Epistola* 73 to Evangelus.[98] This letter would easily be found by looking up Melchizedek in the index of a contemporary collected edition of Jerome's works, where the recipient was called Evagrius. Calvin probably knew of the letter already and either cited it from memory or looked it up.[99]

This survey of the Jerome citations reveals only one work which Calvin is almost certain to have been using while preparing his commentary, the *Hebraicae quaestiones in Genesim*. Calvin may also have consulted Jerome's *Epistola* 73.

(c) The Remainder

There remain sixteen citations from other fathers. These fall into a number of distinct groups. Two are derived from other citations already considered.[100] Three are found in other works which we know Calvin to have been using.[101] One of these is, however, not straightforward. In the Argument Calvin cites (Cassiodore's) *Historia tripartita* on the question of what God was doing before he created the world.[102] Later, in the 1559 *Institutio* he attributes the same story to Augustine.[103] Luther in his Genesis commentary also cites it, attributing it to Augustine.[104] The most likely explanation is that Calvin read it in Luther, made a mistake in attributing it to the *Historia tripartita* in his Genesis commentary and corrected this in his 1559 *Institutio*.

A further seven citations are found in earlier works of Calvin and are presumably cited from memory.[105] Three of these are worthy of particular mention. First, on 14:18 Calvin attacks the ancient writers of the church, such as Tertullian, for seeing the parallel between Melchizedek and Christ in the fact that they offered bread and wine, a parallel which is never drawn in Hebrews.[106] The same point is made by Luther, who mentions Lyra but not the fathers.[107] Calvin's source for the *fathers* would seem to be the 1548 Augsburg *Interim*, which he printed in full in his attack on it. The

---

96 #27.
97 All the possible Hebrew names and places have been checked.
98 ##30, 31.
99 The reason for assuming prior knowledge is that he would have to have had some reason for looking for a letter by Jerome on Melchizedek.
100 #19 is found in the passages of Augustine cited immediately after (##20, 21); #26 is found in the passage of Jerome cited immediately after (#27). #26, like #27, is fully covered by Steuchus's *Recognitio*, which is the probable source.
101 ##1, 9, 18.
102 #1.
103 *Inst.* 1:14:1.
104 WA 42:8f.
105 ##4, 8, 11, 32, 35, 37, 42.
106 #32.
107 WA 42:536–38.

Interim cites passages from Cyprian, Arnobius and John of Damascus, then mentions Jerome, Augustine, Ambrose, Chrysostom and Theophylact.[108] But what of Tertullian? Not only is he not mentioned in the *Interim* but he does not seem even to have made the point concerned. The simplest explanation is that Calvin was working from memory. In his reply to the *Interim* he adds Athanasius to the above list.[109] But in fact the reference to Athanasius in the *Interim* does not relate to Melchizedek.[110] Thus even when answering a document which he is publishing in full in his own reply, Calvin can make mistakes of detail, almost certainly because of the time pressure under which he worked. It is not surprising then that he should, a few years later, draw on his (inaccurate) memory of that work without taking time to check the details.

Secondly, Calvin approves Ambrose's allegory of 27:27,[111] presumably because his approval of its message of justification by faith outweighed his disapproval of allegory! This passage was not new to Calvin, having been cited already in the 1539 *Institutio*. Significantly, one of the very few additions that Calvin made in the 1553 edition of that work comes at this point, where he adds a quotation of Ambrose's own words.[112] The picture is clear. When preparing his Genesis commentary Calvin remembered and looked up the passage cited in 1539. He decided not only to cite it in the commentary but also to add a further quotation to the next edition of the *Institutio*. Both of Calvin's explicit Ambrose citations are recycled from the *Institutio*.[113] A brief examination of Ambrose's exegetical works on Genesis will show why this should be so. Ambrose's homiletic and allegorical approach makes his works of theological interest (hence the citations in the *Institutio*) but of little value for a careful exegete like Calvin. Any other Ambrose influence is likely to reflect past reading, not fresh study for the exegesis of Genesis.

Thirdly, there appears to be incontrovertible evidence that Calvin used Chrysostom's homilies while preparing his commentary. Chrysostom was, together with Augustine and Jerome, one of the three fathers whom Calvin most often cited in his commentaries.[114] He cites Chrysostom's understanding of the image of God in terms of dominion.[115] This comment has not been found elsewhere, except in Steuchus's *Cosmopoeia*, which Calvin does not appear to have been using.[116] Furthermore, Calvin's copy of Chrysostom's works survives, together with his extensive underlinings, which include the homilies from which this comment is drawn.[117]

---

108 CO 7:579f.
109 CO 7:644.
110 CO 7:579.
111 #42.
112 *Inst.* 3:11:23 (OS 4:207).
113 ##37, 42.
114 Mooi, KDE 371, 377, 380f., 393f.
115 #8.
116 *Cosmopoeia* 106. This is one of the very few citations that have been found in the *Cosmopoeia*. The evidence suggests that Calvin is very unlikely to have been using it.
117 A. Ganoczy and K. Müller, *Calvins Handschriftliche Annotationen zu Chrysostomus* (Wiesbaden: Franz Steiner, 1981) esp. 58–66.

But despite this apparently impressive evidence, it seems that Calvin almost certainly did *not* use Chrysostom's homilies while preparing his Genesis commentary. It is noteworthy that Chrysostom is mentioned only once in this commentary and it is almost exclusively in his *New* Testament commentaries that Calvin cites him.[118] In his *Preface to Chrysostom's Homilies* Calvin states that his praise of Chrysostom's exegesis applies especially to his New Testament homilies.[119] A check has revealed that very few of Calvin's citations are found in Chrysostom's homilies.[120] A look at the nature of Chrysostom's Genesis homilies, which are more moralistic and homiletic than exegetical, will indicate why Calvin may not have bothered to consult them. But what of the one citation and the underlining? The question is *when* Calvin read and underlined the volume. The answer appears to be clear. The volume was published in 1536 and Calvin cites the Genesis homilies seven times in the 1539 *Institutio*, explicitly naming them five times.[121] Calvin also in that edition refers to Chrysostom's inter-pretation of the image of God, though without naming him.[122] Lest there be any doubt that Chrysostom is in mind, he is explicitly named for this same point in the *Psychopannychia*.[123] Thus Calvin's citation of him here reflects his memory of his reading of the homilies in the late 1530s and of his two earlier citations of this particular point. The paucity of citations that it is even possible to trace to Chrysostom's homilies suggests that Calvin is most unlikely to have used them for the preparation of his commentary. Calvin *did* read Chrysostom's Genesis homilies, but in the late 1530s, not in the early 1550s.

It has been alleged, however, that Calvin at one point 'simply para-phrases Chrysostom's teaching' on the clothing that God made for Adam and Eve, 'omitting all reference [in Chrysostom] to God's mercy'. This is argued on the basis that Calvin had carefully underlined the entire passage in his edition of Chrysostom.[124] Does this indicate that Calvin did after all use Chrysostom when preparing this commentary? Not necesarily. He could have drawn upon memory of his earlier reading, by no means impossible for someone with Calvin's prodigious power of memory. But there is a simpler explanation. The two basic points that Calvin makes are found also in Luther, whose commentary we know Calvin to have been

---

118 Mooi's figures (cf. n. 114, above) are three citations in the Old Testament commentaries; 126 citations in the New Testament commentaries.
119 CO 9:834: 'For the lack of Hebrew prevented him from showing so much expertise in the Old Testament' (W. I. P. Hazlett, 'Calvin's Latin Preface to his Proposed French Edition of Chrysostom's Homilies: Translation and Commentary' in J. Kirk (ed.), *Humanism and Reform: The Church in Europe, England and Scotland, 1400–1643* (Oxford: Blackwell, 1991) 144).
120 A careful, but not exhaustive, check revealed just three parallels apart from the explicit citation: Chrysostom is, together with other more likely sources, a possible source for two statements about the views of the ancients (Specific References, ##10, 11); one vague reference is found in Chrysostom (#46).
121 *Inst.* 2:2:4 (3x), 2:5:3, 3:4:38, 3:15:2, 3:16:3.
122 *Inst.* 1:15:4 (OS 3:181, n. a).
123 CO 5:181.
124 I. Backus, in an as yet unpublished paper on 'Calvin and the Greek Fathers' given at the Seventh International Congress on Calvin Research (Seoul, 1998), relates Calvin's comment on 3:21 to the passage in Chrysostom's homilies which Calvin had highlighted (Ganoczy and Müller, *Calvins Handschriftliche Annotationen*, 70f.).

using.[125] There is no need, therefore, to invoke Chrysostom and no need to talk of Calvin 'omitting all reference to God's mercy'. Here is a good example of the pitfall, mentioned above, of drawing hasty conclusions from what appear to be impressive parallels between two commentators.

This leaves four remaining citations. On 3:6 Calvin cites Bernard's warning about the potential for sin in fallen human nature.[126] A previous study has shown that this is probably evidence of Calvin's renewed reading of Bernard following his acquisition of the 1552 Basel edition of the *Opera omnia*.[127] This is not reading for the Genesis commentary in particular but general reading of Bernard which gives rise to a number of new citations from 1554.

Calvin cites Origen four times in his Genesis commentary. Three of these are already accounted for, Calvin's sources being Luther, Augustine and the earlier Galatians commentary.[128] That leaves just one citation, to the effect that (with reference to the Ark) Origen boldly sports with allegories.[129] This general knowledge of Origen requires no new reading of him, beyond the knowledge earlier shown. Given the allegorical character of Origen's *Homiliae in Genesim*, there would be little incentive for Calvin to devote his precious time to rereading them while preparing his own exposition.

On 9:4 Calvin criticized Tertullian for banning Christians from tasting the blood of cattle.[130] Calvin had not previously mentioned Tertullian's teaching on this point. The reference is to Tertullian's *Apology*, which Calvin had already cited in 1543 and 1548.[131] Unless one of the works used by Calvin also mentions Tertullian, we should assume that Calvin remembered this detail from his earlier reading of Tertullian and chose to mention it at the appropriate point.

On 23:11 Calvin cites Josephus for the judgment that a sanctuary shekel was worth four Attic drachmas.[132] Here he will either have been working from memory or will have checked up the relevant passage from Josephus.

The study of Calvin's sixteen citations from the 'remaining fathers' has produced very little evidence of direct reading of them by Calvin. There appears to be contemporary reading of Bernard (but not for the preparation of this commentary) and probably memory of earlier reading of Tertullian and Origen. There is a reference to Josephus which may have required Calvin to check the passage concerned. None of this suggests that Calvin read any of the fathers in his preparation for this commentary, other than Augustine and Jerome. It may be that some other father was a source for the commentary, but evidence for this is not be found in Calvin's citations.

---

125 WA 42:165f.

126 #16.

127 See chapter 5, above, at nn. 83–86.

128 ##9, 19, 35.

129 #24.

130 #28.

131 *Apologeticum* 9:13. Calvin cited this work four times previously to this commentary (CO 9:811 (1535), 6:531 (1543), 49:482 (1546) and 52:11 (1548). Cf. my forthcoming 'Tertullianus totus noster? Calvin's Use of Tertullian', which is likely to appear in *Auctoritas Patrum III*.

132 #38.

Of Calvin's forty-five named patristic citations we have found that thirteen are drawn from his earlier works and a further fourteen probably draw on his memory of earlier reading, even if he may have needed to refer back to the original in some instances.[133] Seven are derived from intermediate sources and one, which is inaccurate, is of uncertain origin.[134] Of the remaining ten, nine were probably read during the preparation of the commentary and one was drawn from Calvin's current reading.[135] Three of the forty-five are inaccurately attributed.[136]

Of the forty-five patristic citations, twenty are approving, twenty-two disapproving and three neutral.[137] The exegetical citations are significantly more disapproving than approving (17 against 11), while the theological citations are more approving (9 against 5). Interestingly, the fathers are six times criticized for allegorizing, but Ambrose is once praised for his allegory, when it leads him to teach about justification.[138]

V. CITATIONS OF ANCIENT HERESIES[139]

There are seven explicit references to ancient heresies in Calvin's Genesis commentary. On the first verse, Calvin notes how some in seeking to oppose Arianism have fallen into Sabellianism.[140] This is a citation not so much of the ancient heresy as of those who are accused of it, whose identity is discussed below.[141] In his comment on 1:26 Calvin refers to the Anthropomorphites who locate the likeness to God in the human body.[142] In the 1539 *Institutio* Calvin already refers to them in general terms[143] and in the *Psychopannychia* he mentions their belief with reference to Genesis 1:26.[144] The Anthropomorphites are mentioned in Augustine's *De haeresibus*,[145] with which Calvin was familiar by 1543 even if he had not known it in 1539.[146] In commenting on 3:6 Calvin notes that Pelagius denied original sin and again that he taught that Adam's sin is passed on by

---

133   Earlier works: ##2, 4, 8, 10, 11, 12, 17, 25, 32, 35, 37, 42, 44; memory: ##3, 5, 6, 7, 15, 20, 22, 24, 28, 29, 30, 31, 33, 38.
134   Intermediate sources: ##1, 9, 18, 19, 23, 26, 27; uncertain: #14.
135   Preparation: ##13, 21, 34, 36, 39, 40, 41, 43, 45; current reading: #16. Of the first group, one (#34) is also found in an intermediate source and another (#41) is also found in an earlier work, but as the evidence suggests that Calvin was reading Augustine's *Quaestiones in Heptateuchum* for himself we can assume that he found the citations there.
136   ##1, 14, 32.
137   This supports the claim that in his commentaries Calvin cites the fathers not so much as authorities (as in the *Institutio* and the polemical treatises) but more as debating partners.
138   #42.
139   Citations of ancient heresies are listed in Appendix 4. #n = citation n in that list.
140   #1.
141   #2 under Vague References.
142   #2.
143   *Inst.* 1:13:1.
144   CO 5:180.
145   *De haeresibus* 50 (PL 42:39).
146   Cf. chapter 6, above, at nn. 41f.

imitation.[147] Apart from the fact that such information was well-known, Calvin already states as much in the 1539 *Institutio*.[148]

There are two references to the Manichees. First, Calvin states that they deduced the existence of two principles or Gods from the fact of Adam's temptation.[149] This much could be deduced from Augustine's account of Manicheism in his *De haeresibus*,[150] a work which Calvin seems to have read (especially the chapter on the Manichees) in order to respond to Pighius in 1543.[151] The present comment is, therefore, no evidence of further reading on Manicheism. The other reference is simply the accusation that a certain Jewish opinion smacks of Manicheism.[152] Calvin learned about the Jewish opinion from Luther, who immediately before mentions the Manichees in connection with another Jewish view.[153] Luther may have given Calvin the idea of mentioning the Manichees and his existing knowledge of their teaching (through Augustine's *De haeresibus* among other works) would have sufficed.

Towards the end of the commentary Calvin states that Reuben's forgiveness in Genesis 35:22–27 refutes the error of Novatus and the Novatianists.[154] Calvin was already aware of their teaching by the time of the 1539 *Institutio*[155] and betrays no further knowledge here.

Calvin's citations of ancient heresies betray no new knowledge of them. Calvin simply inserts references to them where he deems it appropriate, making use of his earlier reading.

VI. JEWISH CITATIONS[156]

Tracing Calvin's Jewish citations is no easy task. He rarely names sources, referring instead to 'rabbini', 'Hebraei' and 'Iudaei'. Also, this topic has until very recently received almost no attention.[157]

Many of Calvin's Jewish citations can be accounted for on the basis of works which we already know Calvin to be using: Luther's commentary,

---

147 ##4, 5.
148 *Inst.* 2:1:5f. In the 1539 edition this is a statement about the 'Pelagiani', but it suffices to show what will come as no surprise: that Calvin by this time was familiar with the teaching of Pelagius. The same is shown by the many references to Pelagius in the 1543 response to Pighius (e.g. CO 6:293, 299, 301, 331, 360). Calvin refers in his Romans commentary to the Pelagian view that sin is transmitted from Adam by imitation, but this comment is not added until the 1556 edition (T. H. L. Parker (ed.), *Iohannis Calvini Commentarius in Epistolam Pauli ad Romanos* (Leiden: E. J. Brill, 1981) 110).
149 #3.
150 *De haeresibus* 46. Another possible source is Augustine's *De Genesi ad litteram* 11:13:17 (a work cited by Calvin).
151 Cf. n. 146, above.
152 #6.
153 WA 42:271f.
154 #7. Calvin calls Novatian 'Novatus' following Eusebius, *Historia ecclesiastica* 6:43.
155 *Inst.* 4:1:23.
156 Jewish citations are listed in Appendix 5. #n = citation n in that list.
157 D. L. Puckett, *John Calvin's Exegesis of the Old Testament* (Louisville: Westminster John Knox, 1995) 78, n. 64, which surveys the question, reveals how little is known. W. McKane, *A Late Harvest. Reflections on the Old Testament* (Edinburgh: T&T Clark, 1995) 45–47, presents a similar picture. Since the first edition of this chapter studies by Engammare and Phillips (cf. n. 51, above) have appeared.

Steuchus's *Recognitio*, Münster's *Hebraica Biblia Latina* and Vatable's notes. Of the seventy Jewish citations, at least forty-eight are covered by these works.[158] Where a citation is accounted for by works which we already know Calvin to be using there is no need to postulate further sources. This has one interesting implication. At least twelve of Calvin's citations are found in Lyra's *Postilla*. Most of these are also found in Luther,[159] and the remainder are all found in other works used by Calvin. This would suggest that Calvin was not himself using the *Postilla*, a conclusion that is strengthened by the fact that hardly any of Calvin's citations are found in the *Glossa ordinaria*.

What of the twenty-two citations not covered by works which we already know Calvin to be using? Five of these are observations about the Jews rather than references to specific Jewish exegesis.[160] A further seven can be accounted for by the use of two other works. Three of these citations are found in Fagius's *Exegesis*, which also accounts for one translation citation.[161] Four others are found in another work of Fagius, his *Thargum*.[162] Calvin four times refers to the 'Chaldaeus paraphrastes' and while two of these citations are found in another source (such as Vatable's notes) the other two are not.[163] In addition to accounting for these two citations, Fagius's work also accounts for some others in other categories. It is likely, therefore, that Calvin used these two works of Fagius, a judgment that would be reversed only by the discovery of some other source that covers the same citations.

This leaves ten citations unaccounted for. Two of these are found in other works, but not specifically with reference to the Jews.[164] Three others are found partly, but not wholly, in other works.[165] With one other it is possible that, while the sources do not contain all that Calvin reports, he deduced the rest.[166] Finally, four citations have not been traced at all.[167]

---

158 See Appendix 5 for details. For Münster's sources, cf. E. I. J. Rosenthal, 'Sebastian Muenster's Knowledge and Use of Jewish Exegesis' in I. Epstein, E. Levine and C. Roth (eds), *Essays in Honour of the Very Rev. Dr. J. H. Hertz* (London: Edward Goldstein, [1945]) 351–69.

159 For further information about ##4, 11, 14, 15, 17, 23, 24, 27, 32, 33, 35, 39, 44–47, 49, cf. [C.] Siegfried, 'Raschi's Einfluss auf Nicolaus von Lira und Luther in der Auslegung der Genesis', *Archiv für wissenschaftliche Erforschung des Alten Testamentes* 1 (1867–69) 435f., 438–40, 442, 444, 448, 450f., 455f. and 2 (1871–72) 44–47. This list was compiled by checking *all* of Calvin's Jewish citations against Siegfried, not just those which have been found in Luther or Lyra. The fact that the parallels run out at chapter 24 reinforces the conclusion that Calvin used only the first two volumes of Luther and that his access to Lyra was not direct but via Luther.

160 ##41, 52, 54, 55, 59. The only one that requires any *specific* knowledge of Jewish claims is #41 and this is unlikely to refer to this passage in particular.

161 ##7, 10, 13. Cf. Translation #28.

162 ##25, 43, 50, 51.

163 ##9, 18, 25, 51. Max Engammare has pointed out that Pagninus, *Thesaurus Linguae Sanctae*, often quotes the Targum. My examination of that work has not revealed any of the passages cited by Calvin.

164 ##21, 29. See the notes on these citations in Appendix 5.

165 ##23, 24, 35. See the notes on these citations in Appendix 5.

166 #47. See the note on this citation in Appendix 5.

167 ##40, 53, 60, 67. For the last three of these, cf. n. 177, below.

What conclusions may be drawn? A high proportion of Calvin's Jewish citations, including all of those which name specific Jewish authors, have been traced in works which we have reason to believe Calvin to be using. What of the recalcitrant ten? There are various possibilities. In his lectures on Daniel Calvin twice refers to the teaching of his colleague Antoine Chevallier, once acknowledging the latter as his source for a Jewish citation.[168] Chevallier was not in Geneva while Calvin was preparing his Genesis commentary, but the possibility that Calvin derived some of his citations from oral tradition cannot be discounted. Also possible is that Calvin derived the missing citations from intermediate sources that I have not traced: either that I have failed to discover them in works that I have examined or that they are in other works that I have not examined. Hebrew lexicons or grammars, which contain rabbinic material and citations would be a strong possibility.[169]

One other possibility has not yet been considered. Did Calvin read Rabbinic sources for himself: either the writings of individual rabbis or one of the editions of the Rabbinic Bible? Some have made bold claims for Calvin:

> We know today that Calvin was not content, as for instance Luther had been, to study the great Jewish commentators . . . in the compendia of Nicholas of Lyra (1270–1340), but read them in the original and referred to them constantly.[170]

The present chapter has shown clearly that one should not be fooled in this way by Calvin's occasional (and certainly not 'constant') name-dropping. Since the preparation of first edition of this chapter two studies have appeared which point in similar directions. Max Engammare, in an important article, accuses Baumgartner's standard work on Calvin's Hebrew of being insufficiently critical. 'Baumgartner s'extasie devant la science de Calvin, sans avoir jamais ouvert ni Münster ni les commentaires rabbiniques.'[171] He claims that 'la science rabbinique de Calvin est uniquement de seconde main'. 'Il a pu ouvrir un jour ou l'autre un commentaire rabbinique et lire quelques lignes faciles; c'est n'est peut-être pas rien, mais c'est tout'.[172] Just appeared is a thesis by Darryl Phillips on Calvin's ability with Hebrew, which was completed independently of the Engammare article and where the question of Calvin's citation of rabbinic sources is considered in passing.[173] He comments that 'throughout

---

168   CO 40:557, 604 on Daniel 2:1, 44f.
169   As has been pointed out by Max Engammare and Darryl Phillips in private correspondence. I have made a limited examination of these, especially Pagninus, *Thesaurus Linguae Sanctae*. Further investigation might affect the conclusions regarding Calvin's Jewish citations but not the remaining sections of this study.
170   H.-J. Kraus, 'Israel in the Theology of Calvin – Towards a New Approach to the Old Testament and Judaism', *Christian Jewish Relations* 22:3/4 (1989) 75. Cf. Phillips, *Inquiry into Extent*, 7 for Kraus's attempt to justify this claim.
171   Engammare, *'Johannes Calvinus trium linguarum peritus?'*, 44. Cf. 51, n. 67: 'C'est toujours l'hagiographe au travail.'
172   Ibid., 47.
173   Phillips, *Inquiry into Extent*, 361–66. I am grateful to him for letting me see the material prior to his examination.

this study I have found that almost without exception where Calvin's views coincide with Jewish sources a parallel Latin or French source can also readily be found'.[174] These two studies are welcome contributions to the long-neglected question of Calvin's knowledge of Hebrew. They both discuss the question of Calvin's Jewish and rabbinic sources but since they both (like the present chapter) are based on part only of Calvin's corpus there remains considerable scope for further examination of this aspect of Calvin's sources.

These two recent studies both suggest that Calvin did not use a Rabbinic Bible or other editions of the rabbis. But Jean-François Gilmont points out that the one item that Calvin chose to keep from the library that he inherited from his cousin Olivétan was a Bomberg Hebrew Bible, i.e. a copy of either the first (1516–17) or second (1524–25) Rabbinic Bible.[175] Does that mean that Calvin did after all use a Rabbinic Bible? Not necessarily. His retention of the Bible should be understood as a declaration of intent to master rabbinic Hebrew, not as a proof of his success in doing so either then or in the future.[176] It is also possible that the copy of the Rabbinic Bible did not in the end reach Calvin.

Finally, in order to test whether Calvin used a Rabbinic Bible, Graham Davies has kindly checked for me the ten untraced Jewish citations in the first and second Rabbinic Bibles. This yielded a possible source for two of the citations.[177] If all ten had been found that could have been taken as strong evidence but as eight remain unaccounted for there are clearly other source(s) to be found, which may equally cover the citations found in the Rabbinic Bible. The provisional conclusion, therefore, is that Calvin probably did not derive his Jewish citations from a Rabbinic Bible. On the other hand, a higher proportion of Jewish citations remain untraced than any other category apart from vague references. This is an area where further research is needed.

VII. CITATIONS OF 'POPE' AND 'PAPISTS'[178]

There are thirty-seven places where Calvin refers to the pope or to the 'papists', but only in a minority of these does one need to seek a source. In most of the instances Calvin moves from the text to make a point against the papists, without implying any knowledge of their exegesis of the passage concerned. There are just eight, or maybe ten, instances where

---

174 Ibid., 363.
175 Gilmont, *Jean Calvin et le Livre Imprimé*, 195, citing CRF 6:30f.
176 I raised this issue with Max Engammare and Darryl Phillips, both of whom responded thus (in private letters both of 21 July 1998), a judgment with which I concur.
177 ##53, 60 in Ibn Ezra. In addition, Rashi provides material that partially covers ##35, 47, adding nothing to the material found in Münster and elsewhere. (Cf. Appendix 5 for details.) Rashi is in the first and second Rabbinic Bibles, Ibn Ezra in the latter only: *Biblia Rabbinica. A Reprint of the 1525 Venice Edition* (Jerusalem: Makor, 1972). The comments of Ramban (Nachmanides) (*Commentary on the Torah*, vol. 1: *Genesis*, tr. C. B. Chavel (New York: Shilo, 1971) 586–90) might be the ultimate source of #67.
178 Citations of 'Pope' and 'Papists' are listed in Appendix 6. #n = citation n in that list.

Calvin is actually commenting on the Roman Catholic exegesis of the passage.[179] With the remaining citations there is no need to trace a source in order to account for them, but where they are paralleled in an earlier work this strengthens the case for Calvin having used that work. In fact we find five such passages where Calvin is following Luther,[180] further confirmation for his use of the latter.

Of the ten citations, five are straightforwardly found in confirmed sources.[181] Of the others, one is found in Cajetan's commentary.[182] Another is found in Luther's commentary, but in a volume which Calvin was probably not using.[183] This is one of those citations where it is not certainly necessary for Calvin to have a knowledge of Roman Catholic exegesis. Finally there are three citations for which no source has been found, one of these being the other citation for which it is not certainly necessary for Calvin to have a knowledge of Roman Catholic exegesis.[184]

What can we conclude from this? Calvin's use of Luther is confirmed. Some of Calvin's citations can be traced to the 1548 Augsburg *Interim*, to which Calvin had earlier responded. This suggests that the as yet untraced sources for the other citations may be found not in Roman Catholic exegetical works but in dogmatic and polemical works. These have not been searched systematically as the present concern is to trace sources that Calvin used for the actual writing of the commentary. But a search of the critical edition of Eck's *Enchiridion* reveals it to be a potential source of no less than five of the ten citations, including three of those for which no definite source had been found.[185] It does not necessarily follow, of course, that Calvin used Eck's *Enchiridion*. There may be dozens of other polemical works appealing to the same passages of Genesis. But it does strongly suggest that the five problem citations originate not from sources like Cajetan's commentary but from Calvin's earlier reading of Roman Catholic polemical works. Another possible source is Calvin's experience of face-to-face discussion with Roman Catholics, as at the colloquies of Hagenau, Worms and Regensburg.

It should also be noted that Calvin's citation of 'papist' views goes beyond the explicit citations considered here. In one place he criticizes those who seek to justify idolatry by childishly differentiating between 'dulia' and 'latria', a clear reference to Roman Catholic thought.[186] To start considering non-explicit citations would make the task endless and also

---

179 ##1, 6, 9, 14, 18, 19, 26, 36 and, less certainly, ##27, 37.

180 ##2, 4, 10, 16, 21.

181 ##1, 9, 18, 19, 36.

182 #26.

183 #27.

184 ##6, 14, 37.

185 J. Eck, *Enchiridion locorum communium* (Münster: Aschendorffsche Verlags-buchhandlung, 1979) 149 (#6), 174 (#36), 206 (#9), 210 (#27), 354 (#26).

186 CO 23:325:6–9 on 23:7. It has been objected that this is a Greek, not a 'papist' distinction. Calvin was fully aware of the Greek words and the Greek origin of the distinction, but it is the Roman Catholic use of it that he primarily attacks (*Inst.* 1:11:11, 1:12:2 – both 1550). OS 3:100, n. 2 and 3:106, n. 1, suggests some Roman Catholic opponents that Calvin might have in mind, of which the most plausible is Cochlaeus's 1549 response to Calvin's *Treatise on Relics*.

introduce an element of subjectivity, but it should be remembered that there are unnamed as well as explicit citations of papists, Jews, etc.[187]

VIII. SPECIFIC UNNAMED REFERENCES[188]

There are twenty-three places where Calvin's citation is precise enough to specify a particular group but does not fit into the categories so far considered. These fall into a number of different categories. Five are found already in earlier writings of Calvin.[189] Another five are found in Luther, Steuchus's *Recognitio* or Jerome's *Hebraicae quaestiones*.[190] Of these, one is especially significant. Calvin, commenting on Genesis 35:22, refers to a painting of the sacrifice of Iphigenia.[191] This allusion is found in Luther – in his comment on 4:9. Here is a dependence that would never have been traced by searching commentaries under 35:22. It may well be that other citations whose sources have not been traced are also to be found in the known sources, but in unexpected places.

Most of the other citations reflect general knowledge rather than knowledge of the exegesis of Genesis. Calvin draws upon his knowledge of contemporary science[192] and contemporary theology.[193] He draws upon his knowledge of the Libertines and the Anabaptists, groups against which he had written.[194] He refers to a philosophical commonplace (possibly prompted by Luther)[195] and makes a general comment about the fathers.[196]

This leaves just four citations. One has been traced to Peter Lombard.[197] A reference to the canonists is found in the *Decretum Gratiani*, a work with which Calvin was certainly familiar.[198] Calvin states that some of the ancients say Adam and Eve were allured by intemperance of appetite.[199] This may originate from Calvin's reading about the Pelagian controversy rather than his reading for the Genesis commentary. Finally, his comment that almost all ancient authors agree the mountains of Armenia to be the highest could be a misreading of Luther.[200]

---

187 A glance at the sources traced in Appendix 8 will reveal some further Jewish influence.
188 Specific unnamed references are listed in Appendix 7. #n = citation n in that list.
189 ##6, 9, 15, 16, 21.
190 ##10, 11, 18, 20, 22. Other possible sources for #10 are Chrysostom, *Homily* 22 and Augustine, *Quaestiones in Heptateuchum* 1:3.
191 #22.
192 ##1–3.
193 ##13, 23.
194 ##7, 14.
195 #4, later incorporated into the *Institutio* (1:5:3). Gamble, 'Sources of Calvin's Genesis Commentary', 209f. sees more of a parallel with Luther than exists as he mistakenly reads 'a vereribus' in place of 'a veteribus' (translating the non-existent 'vereribus' as 'rightly') thus eliminating Calvin's reference to the ancients which is not found in Luther.
196 #17.
197 #5.
198 #19. Mooi, KDE 306–12.
199 #8, later incorporated into the *Institutio* (2:1:4).
200 #12.

Examining Calvin's specific unnamed references has pointed to no new sources but has provided further evidence for sources already found.

IX. VAGUE REFERENCES[201]

In Calvin's Genesis commentary there are many hundreds of vague references to 'nonnulli', 'alii', etc. To attempt to trace these for the whole commentary would be a huge undertaking, yet such citations can provide useful confirmatory evidence. As a compromise, only citations from the first eleven chapters have been considered. Also, the aim has been not so much to trace every one as to check all potential sources against them. This limited study yields some interesting results.[202]

Of the one hundred and twenty-nine citations examined, no less than seventy are accounted for by Luther. With almost fifty of these Luther is the only source found. Here is overwhelming confirmation of Calvin's extensive use of Luther. Many others are accounted for by sources so far identified. These are listed below with, after each source, two numbers: the number of citations accounted for and the number of these not accounted for by any other established source. Steuchus, *Recognitio* (10, 5); Augustine, *De Genesi ad litteram* (9, 2); Fagius, *Exegesis* (9, 2); Vatable's notes (5, 2); Münster, *Hebraica Biblia Latina* (4, 1); Fagius, *Thargum* (3, 2); Augustine, *De civitate dei* (2, 2); Augustine, *Quaestiones in Heptateuchum* (1, 1).

This leaves thirty-one so far unaccounted for. Two of these are comments general enough not to require a specific source. A further five are comments about sceptical views that are unlikely to be part of the exegetical tradition.[203] Of the remaining twenty-four, six have been traced to other sources: two to Cajetan's commentary and one each to Josephus's *Contra Apionem*, Chrysostom's homilies, Augustine's *De Genesi contra Manichaeos* and Eck's *Enchiridion*. None of these should be regarded as conclusive as the citations themselves could well have other sources. It is possible that a more thorough search could trace some more to Luther, for example. This leaves just fourteen citations with no source and four with inadequate sources suggested.

The study of the vague references confirms the sources already traced, especially Luther. There is insufficient evidence to propose any new sources.

X. CONCLUSIONS

This study has traced sources for the overwhelming majority of Calvin's citations. A fairly clear picture has emerged. Calvin reused material from earlier works (especially the *Institutio*, also polemical works and

---

201 Vague references from chapters 1–11 are listed in Appendix 8. #n = citation n in that list.

202 All of the figures given below can be verified from Appendix 8.

203 Engammare (ed.), *Jean Calvin, Sermons sur la Genèse*, in his introduction (XLVIII-XLIX in the page proofs) notes similar references in the sermons and has identified some of these adversaries with specific Genevans who appeared before the Consistory. Unfortunately the five passages from chapters 1–11 in the commentary are not covered. Since our present concern is with Calvin's use of the exegetical tradition it is not too important to trace these citations.

commentaries) and also cited works that he had earlier read (such as Augustine's *De civitate dei* and the *Decretum Gratiani*). He also consulted works for specific questions, such as Budé's *De asse* and Ambrose's *De Jacob et vita beata*. He was reading Bernard's works at the time and reveals this by inserting an apt saying when it suits him.

But which works did Calvin actually use in the preparation of the commentary? Which works were on his desk and guiding Calvin in his exegesis? This study has revealed a small number of such works. Calvin clearly made extensive use of the first two volumes of Luther, for the first twenty-four and a half chapters. He also relied heavily upon Steuchus's *Recognitio* throughout his commentary,[204] which might have gone undetected were it not for the one solitary reference in the first chapter. This disparaging remark gives a totally false impression of the actual nature of Calvin's relationship to Steuchus. These two works have pride of place. Also important are three translations with notes that Calvin used throughout: the 1545 Stephanus Bible with the Vulgate and Zurich translations and the Vatable notes, Münster's 1534–35 *Hebraica Biblia Latina* and Fagius's *Thargum*. Calvin most likely read the Servetus marginal notes together perhaps with some or all of the Pagninus translation. For the opening chapters he used Augustine's *De Genesi ad litteram* (chs 1–3) and Fagius's *Exegesis* (chs 1–4). From chapter 4 he used Augustine's *Quaestiones in Heptateuchum* and for the whole commentary he consulted Jerome's *Hebraicae quaestiones*.

These are the works needed to account for Calvin's *citations*. What of his reading for the commentary as a whole? Did Calvin read much more than the items listed here? To answer this confidently is no easy task.[205] My instinctive opinion is that he probably did not (which is not to say that he never glanced at any other works), but it will take a thorough and soundly based study to check this. What we have here a modest bibliography and that makes it plausible. Calvin did not have the leisure to read dozens of commentaries. These works he could have used in the odd hours that he had to prepare the lectures and then write up the commentary. But does this accord with what we know from elsewhere of the breadth of Calvin's reading? In the dedication to the Romans commentary he discusses the commentaries of Melanchthon, Bullinger and Bucer and at least suggests that he has used others as well.[206] In his *Preface to Chrysostom's Homilies* he discusses the merits and demerits of a wide range of patristic commentators.[207] How is this breadth of learning consistent with the claims of the current chapter?

Three considerations need to be borne in mind. First, Calvin's commentary on Romans and his Chrysostom preface were written at an earlier stage in his career before the pressures on his time were so great. The

---

204 In the first edition of this chapter I referred to this as a 'surprising reliance' for which I was rightly chided by David Steinmetz, in a private letter of 31 October 1997. Cf. his 'Divided by a Common Past: The Reshaping of the Christian Exegetical Tradition in the Sixteenth Century', *Journal of Medieval and Early Modern Studies* 27 (1997) 245f.

205 Cf. n. 11, above.

206 Parker (ed.), *Commentarius*, 1–3.

207 CO 9:834f.

remarks about preparing lectures in an hour or so[208] relate to the 1550s, not to the period around 1540. The Romans commentary appeared in splendid isolation; the Genesis commentary appeared as a part of a production line of commentaries. This massively increased productivity was not achieved without a reduction in the time spent on each commentary. Secondly, we must not be misled by the comments that Calvin makes in the earlier works. A thinker of his calibre was capable of making insightful comments on a Romans commentary without necessarily having read all (or even most) of it. The remarks about 'other commentators' *need* not imply more than a passing acquaintance with them. Thirdly, the discussion of patristic commentators relates more to Calvin's knowledge of the fathers than to the preparation of his commentaries.[209] We must distinguish clearly between the question of Calvin's general reading (which was undoubtedly broad) and his specific reading while preparing a commentary, which is the topic of this chapter.[210]

Calvin is rightly regarded as one of the great commentators of all time. This is all the more remarkable when we consider how little time he had and how little he read. Not the least of his skills was the ability to read little and then to make the maximum use of this material in producing a commentary of lucid brevity.[211]

XI. WORKS CHECKED[212]

Where a work is found in the 1572 library catalogue of the Genevan Academy, its reference there is given. Gn = item n in Ganoczy, *La Bibliothèque de l'Academie de Calvin.*

(a) Bible editions

Biblia Rabbinica. A Reprint of the 1525 Venice Edition (Jerusalem: Makor, 1972)

Hebraica Biblia Latina planeque Nova Sebast. Munsteri Tralatione, vol. 1 (Basel: M. Isengrinus and H. Petrus, 1534) [G3]

---

208 Cf. n. 7, above.
209 Also, chapter 3, above, section III, questions how much Calvin actually knew of some of the fathers that he discusses in his *Preface to Chrysostom.*
210 Calvin's use of Chrysostom illustrates this well. Almost half of Calvin's underlinings in his Chrysostom edition appear in the Genesis homilies and yet, as Ganoczy and Müller have noted, almost none of them is taken up in the commentary (*Calvins Handschriftliche Annotationen,* 18f., 23). It appears that the underlinings reflect moral/ascetic rather than exegetical interests and correlate more to the *Institutio* than to the commentaries (ibid., 18f., 22–24). We should distinguish between the reading and underlining of the Chrysostom edition by the young Calvin and a later distinct use of it (without underlining) in the preparation of his New Testament commentaries. There is no need where Calvin cites a Chrysostom passage which has not been underlined to suggest any other source (*contra* ibid., 24–27). In the light of his usage elsewhere, what needs explaining is not why he didn't underline some Chrysostom passages but rather why any of them were underlined.
211 Cf. Parker (ed.), *Commentarius,* 1: 'praecipuam interpretis virtutem in perspicua brevitate esse positam'. Cf. R. C. Gamble, 'Brevitas et Facilitas: Toward an Understanding of Calvin's Hermeneutic', *Westminster Theological Journal* 47 (1985) 1–17.
212 In addition to the works listed here, most of the medieval commentaries on Genesis in PL have been glanced at to see what sort of material they provide.

La Bible Qui est toute la Saincte escripture [Neuchâtel: P. de Wingle, 1535]

La Bible en laquelle sont tous les livres canoniques ([Geneva: J Girard], 1540)

Biblia (Paris: R. Stephanus, 1540)

Libri Moysi quinque (Paris: R. Stephanus, 1541)

La saincte Bible en francois translatee (Antwerp: A. de la Haye, 1541)

Biblia ... Interprete Xante Pagnino Lucense (Cologne: M. Novesian, 1541)

Biblia Sacra ex Santis Pagnini Tralatione (Lyons: Hugues de La Port, 1542) [G42] [Servetus's revision]

Biblia Sacrosancta Testamenti Veteris & Noui (Zurich: C. Froschouer, 1543)

Biblia Sacra cum Glossis, Interlineari & Ordinaria, Nicolai Lyrani Postilla & Moralitatibus, Burgensis Additionibus, & Thoringi Replicis, vol. 1 (Lyons: G. Treschel, 1545) [G73]

Biblia (Paris: R. Stephanus, 1545) [G50]

La Bible Qui est toute la saincte escripture (Geneva: J. Girard, 1546)

Hebraica Biblia Latina planeque Nova Sebast. Munsteri Tralatione, vol. 1 (Basel: M. Isengrinus and H. Petrus, 1546)

Moses Latinus ex Hebraeo factus ... per Sebastianum Castalionem (Basel: J. Oporinus, 1546) [G43 = 1554 edition]

La Saincte Bible Nouuellement translatée de Latin (Louvain: B. de Grave, A. M. Bergagne and J. de Waen, 1550)

La Sainte Bible (Lyons: J. de Tournes, 1551)

Biblia, Interprete Sebastiano Castalione (Basel: J. Oporinus, 1551) [G43 = 1554 edition]

Hebraicus Pentateuchus ... [Sebastian Münster] (Venice: Justinianea, 1551)

La Bible, qui est toute la Saincte Escriture ([Geneva]: J. Crespin, 1554)

(b) Other Works

Alcuin, *In Genesim Quaestiones* (Hagenau: J. Secerius, 1529) (PL 100:515–66)

Ambrose, *Hexaemeron* (PL 14:133–288) [G69 = 1555 edition]

Ambrose, *De Paradiso* (PL 14:291–332) [G69 = 1555 edition]

Ambrose, *De Cain et Abel* (PL 14:333–80) [G69 = 1555 edition]

Ambrose, *De Noe et Arca* (PL 14:381–438) [G69 = 1555 edition]

Ambrose, *De Abraham* (PL 14:441–524) [G69 = 1555 edition]

Ambrose, *De Isaac et Anima* (PL 14:527–60) [G69 = 1555 edition]

Ambrose, *De Jacob et Vita Beata* (PL 14:627–70) [G69 = 1555 edition]

Ambrose, *De Joseph Patriarcha* (PL 14:673–704) [G69 = 1555 edition]

Ambrose, *De Benedictionibus Patriarcharum* (PL 14:707–28) [G69 = 1555 edition]

P. Artopoeus, *ΑΦΟΡΙΣΜΟΙ. De Prima Rerum Origine . . . breves Aphorismi* (Basel: H. Petrus, 1546)

Augustine, *De Genesi ad litteram* (PL 34:245–486) (in vol. 3 of Erasmus edition) [G72]

Augustine, *De Genesi ad litteram imperfectus liber* (PL 34:219–46) (in vol. 3 of Erasmus edition) [G72]

Augustine, *De Genesi contra Manichaeos* (PL 34:173–220) (in vol. 3 of Erasmus edition) [G72]

Augustine, *Locutiones in Heptateuchum* (PL 34:485–546; CCSL 33:381–465) (in vol. 3 of Erasmus edition) [G72]

Augustine, *Quaestiones in Heptateuchum* (PL 34:547–824; CCSL 33:1–377) (in vol. 4 of Erasmus edition) [G72]

Basil, *Omnia . . . Opera* (Basel: H. Froben and N. Episcopius, 1540) (PG 29:93–208) [G28, 65]

Bede, *Commentaria in quinque libros Moysis* (Antwerp: G. Montanus, 1542) (PL 91:189–394)

Cajetan, *Commentarii . . . in quinque Mosaicos libros* (Paris: J. Parvus, 1539) [G77.I]

W. Capito, *Hexemeron Dei Opus* (Strassburg: W. Rihel, 1539) [G97.I]

Ambrosius Catharinus, *Enarrationes in Quinque Priora Capita Libri Geneseos* (Rome: A. Bladus, 1552) [G76.I]

Chrysostom, *Homiliae in Genesim* (PG 53f.:21–580) [G70]

Dionysius the Carthusian, *Enarratio in Genesim* (*Opera Omnia*, vol. 1 (Monstrolii: S. M. de Pratis, 1896)) [cf. G88]

J. Eck, *Enchiridion locorum communium adversus Lutherum et alios hostes ecclesiae (1525–1543)*, ed. P. Fraenkel (Münster: Aschendorffsche Verlagsbuchhandlung, 1979)

(Pseudo-)Eucherius, *Lucubrationes in Genesim* (Basel: Froben, 1531) (PL 50:893–1048) [G63.I]

P. Fagius, *Exegesis sive Expositio Dictionum Hebraicarum Literalis & Simplex in Quatuor Capita Geneseos* (Isen, 1542)

P. Fagius, *Prima quatuor capita Geneseos hebraice, cum versione germanica . . . cum succinctis in fine adiectis scholiis* (Constance, 1543)

P. Fagius, *Thargum, hoc est, Paraphrasis Onkeli Chaldaica in Sacra Biblia* (Strassburg: G. Machaeropoeus, 1546) [G20.I]

Gregory of Nyssa, *De opificio hominis* (PG 44: 125–256)

Gregory of Nyssa, *Explicatio apologetica in Hexaemeron* (PG 44:61–124)

Hugh of St Cher, *Textus biblie cum postilla*, vol. 1 (Basel: J. Amerbach, 1504)

Isidore of Seville, *Enarrationes doctissimae breuissimaeque in Genesim . . .* (Cologne: J. Soter/P. Quentel, 1530) (PL 83:207–88)

Jerome, *Hebraicae quaestiones in libro Geneseos* (PL 23:935–1010; CCSL 72:1–56) [G61]

Jerome, *Liber de situ et nominibus locorum hebraicorum* (PL 23:859–928) [G61]

Jerome, *Liber interpretationis hebraicorum nominum* (PL 23:771–858; CCSL 72:59–161) [G61]

A. Lippoman, *Catena in Genesim* (Paris: C. Guillard, 1546)

M. Luther, *In Primum Librum Mose Enarrationes* (Wittenberg: P. Seitz, 1544) [chs 1–11:26] (WA 42) [cf. G93]

M. Luther, *In Genesin Enarrationum ... Tomus Secundus* (Nuremberg: J. Montanus and U. Neuber, 1550) [chs 11:27–25:10] (WA 42–43) [cf. G93]

M. Luther, *In Genesin Enarrationum ... Tomus Tertius* (Nuremberg: J. Montanus and U. Neuber, 1552) [chs 25:11–36] (WA 43–44) [cf. G93]

M. Luther, *In Genesin Enarrationum ... Tomus Quartus* (Nuremberg: J. Montanus and U. Neuber, 1554) [chs 37–50] (WA 44) [cf. G93]

P. Melanchthon, *In obscuriora aliquot capita Geneseos annotationes* (Hagenau: J. Secerius, 1523) (CR 13:761–92) [cf. G92]

J. Oecolampadius, *In Genesim Enarratio* (Basel: J. Bebel, 1536)

Origen, *Homiliae in Genesim* (PG 12:45–262) [G47]

S. Pagninus, *Thesaurus Linguae Sanctae* ([Paris]: R. Stephanus, 1548)

C. Pellican, *Commentaria Bibliorum, id est XXIII. Canonicorum Veteris Testamenti Librorum*, vol. 1 (Zurich: C. Froschauer, 1536) [G105]

G. Pepin, *Expositio in Genesim* (Paris: J. Parvus, 1528)

A. Placus, *Lexicon Biblicon Sacrae Philosophiae Candidatis Elaboratum* (Cologne: P. Quentel, 1543): ff. 8b-27b = *Expositio Vocularum Quarundam Difficilium super Genesim*

Rabanus Maurus, *Commentarius in Genesim* (PL 107:439–670)

M. Servetus, *Christianismi Restitutio* (Frankfurt: Minerva, 1966)[213]

A. E. Steuchus, *Recognitio Veteris Testamenti ad Hebraicam Veritatem* (Lyons: S. Gryphius, 1531) [G210]

A. E. Steuchus, *Cosmopoeia ... Expositio trium capitum Genesis* (Lyons: S. Gryphius, 1535)

Thomas Aquinas, *Postilla seu Expositio Aurea ... in Librum Geneseos* (Antwerp: J. Stelsius, 1563)

Peter Martyr Vermigli, *In Primum Librum Mosis ... Commentarii* (Zurich: C. Froschouer, 1569).[214]

F. Zephyrus, *Cathena, seu explicatio locorum qui in Pentateucho subobscuriores occurrunt ...* (Cologne: J. Birckmann, 1572)[215]

---

213 Facsimile reprint of 1790 Nuremberg edition which itself retained the same pagination as the 1553 original.
214 This work was first published in 1569 but is based on lectures that he gave while at Strassburg from 1542–47 (J. P. Donnelly and R. M. Kingdon, *A Bibliography of the Works of Peter Martyr Vermigli* (Kirksville (MO): Sixteenth Century Journal Publishers, 1990) 92). The possibility of this material having reached Calvin by one means or another needed to be considered.
215 A 1547 Florence edition is alleged to exist (M. Geerard, *Clavis Patrum Graecorum*, vol. 4 (Turnhout: Brepols, 1980) 187) but I have never seen it despite over a decade of searching in many European libraries. The dedicatory epistle is dated May 1546.

J. Ziegler, *In Genesim Mundi ... Commentarii* (Basel: J. Oporinus, 1548)

U. Zwingli, *Farrago annotationum in Genesim* (Zurich: C. Froschouer, 1527)
[cf. G107]

Appendixes

ABBREVIATIONS USED FOR SOURCES

Cajetan	Cajetan, *Commentarii . . . in quinque Mosaicos libros*
Cast	Castellio, *Moses Latina* and *Biblia*
CD	Augustine, *De civitate dei*
Comm.	Calvin's commentary on
Eck	J. Eck, *Enchiridion locorum communium* (Münster: Aschendorff, 1979)
Fag	Paul Fagius, *Exegesis*
Gen Lit	Augustine, *De Genesi ad litteram*
Heb Qu	Jerome, *Hebraicae quaestiones in Genesim*
Inst(39/50) x:y:z	Calvin, Institutio (1539/1550) at x:y:z in 1559 edition
LXX	Septuagint
Mün	Sebastien Münster, *Hebraica Biblia Latina* (1534)
Origen	Origen, *Homiliae in Genesim*
Pagn	Pagninus, *Biblia*
Post	Nicholas of Lyra, *Postilla*
Qu Hept	Augustine, *Quaestiones in Heptateuchum*
RB2	Second *Rabbinic Bible* (1524–25)
Rec	Augustinus Eugubinus Steuchus, *Recognitio* (1531)
Tharg	Paul Fagius, *Thargum*
Serv	Servetus's 1542 revision of the Pagninus Bible
Vat	Vatable notes in 1545 Stephanus *Biblia*
WA	*D. Martin Luthers Werke* (Weimar: Böhlau, 1883ff.)
Zur	Zurich Latin Bible

It is Calvin's practice in commenting on a passage to give the number of the first verse only rather than the extent of the passage (e.g. 1:16 rather than 1:16–19) and this has been followed here. To claim a work as a source for an opinion is, of course, only to state that the opinion is there *described*, not that it is necessarily approved.

For many citations more details on sources will be found above in the main body of text and notes. Where a source is relevant, but not sufficient to account for Calvin's citation, the source is listed in brackets and a footnote explains the situation.

Appendix 1: Named Contemporary Citations

Listed below are all named citations of contemporary authors in Calvin's Genesis commentary which indicate some knowledge of their writings.

#	CO 23	Gen.	Author	Content	Source
1	15:3–13	1:1	Steuchus	eternity of unformed matter	Rec 25–28
2	16:39–49	1:3	Servetus	Word not eternal	Inst(39) 1:13:8; CO 8:572f.
3	113:30–36	6:3	Luther	Hebrew דון refers to external ministry	WA 42:273
4	113:50–53	6:3	Luther	ditto	ditto
5	169:12–13	11:10	Luther	patriarchs' suffering like martyrdom	WA 42:428
6	170:4–7	11:27	Luther	Terah's missing sixty years	WA 42:431f.
7	193:40–42	13:14	Luther	God spoke through a prophet	WA 42:518
8	325:52–326:1	23:11	Budaeus	value of Attic drachma in French pounds	De asse lib.2

Appendix 2: Citations of Translations

Listed below are all explicit citations of translations of the Book of Genesis found in Calvin's Genesis commentary. Where there is a question mark after a source it means that the translation is not quite what Calvin says and may or may not be in Calvin's mind. Calvin's word for 'translate' is given.

Where the reading is found in a translation, no further information is given beyond the name of the translator/translation; where the reading is found in the notes the page or folio number is also given; where the reading concerned is a variant reading found in the margin, this is signified by 'v.l.'.

#	CO 23	Gen.	Citation[1]	Source
1	18:27–29	1:6	Greeks placuerit vertere: στερέωμα	Rec 46; LXX
2	18:27–29	1:6	Latins follow Greeks with 'firmamentum'	Vulg; Mün; Pagn; Fag 14; Rec 46
3	24:7–10	1:21	vulgo legunt 'cetos'	Mün; Pagn; Zur
4	24:7–10	1:21	vulgo legunt 'cete'	Vulg; Cast
5	34:44	2:5	alii transferunt 'virgultum'	Vulg; Pagn; Zur; Rec 77
6	36:32–33	2:8	vetus interpres transtulit 'paradisum'	Vulg
7	36:39–40	2:8	Hieronymus verterit 'a principio'	Vulg; Heb Qu 2:8
8	37:49–50	2:8	vetus interpres fecit 'voluptatem'	Vulg
9	39:49	2:10	no one doubts חידקל = Tigris (14)	e.g. Vulg; Cast; Mün 3a; Rec 100; Vat 2b
10	43:53–55	2:10	omnes interpretes vertunt 'Aethiopiam' (13)	Vulg; Cast; Mün; Pagn; Tharg; Vat 2b
11	47:52–53	2:18	Graeci interpretes reddiderunt: Κατ' αὐτὸν	Rec 110; LXX

1 Numbers in brackets are those of the verse being translated, where this is different.

#	CO 23	Gen.	Citation	Source
12	47:53–54	2:18	Hieronymus: 'Quod sit illi simile'	Vulg[2]
13	50:28–29	2:23	interpres forced reddere 'viraginem'	Vulg; Heb Qu 2:23; Mün; Tharg; Zur; Fag 68
14	50:55–56	2:24	vetus interpres transtulerit 'in carne una'	Vulg
15	50:56–51:2	2:24	Graeci interpretes habent 'erunt duo in carnem unam'	Rec 114; LXX
16	57:39–40	3:1	vetus interpres transtulit '*Cur dixit deus?*'	Vulg[3]
17	59:25	3:5	quidam vertunt 'similes *angelis*'	Fag 76; Rec 117; Tharg a5a;Vat 3a
18	60:1–3	3:6	להשכיל exponi potest 'ad videndum'	Vulg; Vat 3a[4]
19	60:1–3	3:6	להשכיל exponi potest 'ad prudentiam'	Mün; Tharg; WA 42:121; Vat 3a
20	65:16–17	3:8	Hieronymus vertit 'ad auram post meridiem'	Vulg
21	65:18–19	3:8	Graeci, omitting word 'wind,' posuerunt 'ad vesperam'	Rec 120; LXX
22	67:6–8	3:11	vulgaris translatio habet 'nisi quod de arbore'	Vulg[5]
23	67:53–54	3:13	vertunt interpretes 'Quare hoc fecisti?'	Vulg
24	70:13–16	3:15	Hieronymus vertit 'conteres caput' + 'insidiaberis calcaneo'	Vulg
25	71:12–21	3:15	Papists translate 'she' shall bruise	Vulg; WA143; Rec 123
26	72:50	3:17	vetus interpres transtulit 'in opere tuo'	Vulg
27	73:31–35	3:17	עצבון vertunt 'dolorem'	Mün; Zur; Fag 98; Rec 127
28	74:26–27	3:19	alii vertunt 'laborem' in place of 'sudorem'	Fag 100
29	82:42–46	4:1	quidam exponunt 'cum Domino'	Zur; Fag 118
30	82:46–47	4:1	altera interpretatio 'possedi *a Domino*'	Mün; Pagn; Tharg; Fag 118; Rec 131[6]
31	82:47–48	4:1	Hieronymus vertit 'per Dominum'	Vulg (v.l.);[7] Fag 118
32	82:52	4:1	alii subtilius 'possedi virum Dei'	WA 42:179f.[8]
33	88:22–32	4:7	Graeci interpretes miss Moses' sense	Rec 134; LXX
34	89:1–3	4:7	Hieronymus vertit 'recipies'	Vulg
35	91:4–5	4:8	Hieronymus expressit 'Veni, egrediamur foras'	Vulg[9]

2 Vulg readings are 'similem sui' and 'similem sibi', the latter in the 1545 Stephanus Bible.
3 Vulg reads 'Cur praecepit ... Deus?'
4 Vulg reads 'aspectuque delectabile'; Vat 3a reads 'ad contemplandum'.
5 Vulg reads 'Nisi quod ex ligno'.
6 Rec 131 reads 'possedi a Deo'. Mün, Tharg and Pagn read 'acquisivi ... a domino'.
7 In the Stephanus Bibles the text reads 'per Deum' with 'per Dominum' as a variant reading. In Heb Qu the reading is 'per Deum'. Fag cites Vulg as 'per Dominum'.
8 Luther gives the text as 'Aquisivi virum Domini' and proceeds to cite it as 'Aquisivi virum Dei'.
9 Vulg reads 'egrediamur foras', without the 'Veni'.

#	CO 23	Gen.	Citation	Source
36	114:4–7	6:3	Graeci legerunt wrongly 'Non permanebit'	Rec 157; LXX
37	115:40–44	6:4	Hieronymus reddidit badly	Heb Qu 6:4; Vulg
38	119:46–47	6:9	vetus interpres solet reddere תמים as 'perfectum'	Vulg
39	137:18–21	8:6	negative has crept into Graecam versionem (7)	Rec 181; LXX
40	137:18–21	8:6	negative has crept into Latinam versionem (7)	Vulg;[10] Heb Qu 8:6f.; Rec 181
41	137:35–36	8:6	Hieronymi versio habet 'ramum [fuisse] virentibus foliis' (11)	Vulg
42	140:21–23	8:21	adulterina illa versio: 'cogitatio *prona* ad malum'	Vulg
43	146:11–12	9:5	Hieronymus reddidit אך as 'enim'	Vulg
44	146:11–15	9:5	others legunt particle אך 'adversative' as '*alioqui* sanguinem vestrum'	Mün
45	146:11–15	9:5	optime sic vertere licet 'et *sane* sanguinem vestrum'	Vat 6b
46	154:52–53	9:27	most interpretes accipiunt יפת as 'dilatare'	Vulg; Mün; Pagn; Tharg; Zur; Rec 193
47	159:34–36	10:8	Hieronymi versio placet: paraphrase follows (9)	Vulg
48	165:31–32	11:4	quidam interpretes vertunt: '*Antequam* dispergamur'	Vulg; Cast; Rec 209[11]
49	180:3–8	12:6	'Elon' quidam vertunt 'quercetum'	Zur
50	180:3–8	12:6	'Elon' alii vertunt 'convallem'	Vulg
51	180:3–8	12:6	'Elon' alii vertunt as place name	Rec 218f.; Vat 8a
52	197:16–17	14:1	vetus interpres Arioch ex 'Ponto' accersit	Vulg
53	199:35–37	14:14	cur vetus interpres verterit 'numeravit Abram expeditos suos vernaculos'	Vulg
54	216:1–3	15:9	alii pro 'trienni' [heifers, etc.] vertunt: 'triplicatam'	Mün 13a; Serv (v.l.)
55	220:52–54	15:16	quidam accipiunt עון pro 'poena'	Pagn[12]
56	229:48–50	16:12	quidam exponunt פרא to mean 'sylvestrem'	Mün; Pagn; Tharg c2b; Vat 10a[13]
57	230:49–50	16:13	quidam vertunt 'Annon vidi post visionem meam?'	Zur[14]
58	231:1–3	16:13	alii sic accipiunt 'An ego vidi post visionem meam?', i.e. so late	Mün 14a

10 'non revertebatur' is a variant Vulgate reading which is found in the text of the Stephanus Bibles.

11 Vulg reads 'antequam dividamur'; Rec 209 has the Vulgate reading but also mentions the Zurich reading 'ne forte dispergamur'; Cast reads 'antequam … dispergerentur'.

12 Pagn reads 'punitio'. Pagninus, *Thesaurus Linguae Sanctae*, 888 suggests the meaning 'poena & punitio' for this word, citing Genesis 15:16.

13 Calvin adds 'et venandis feris addictum', which is not found in the translations and may indicate his use of a Hebrew dictionary.

14 Zur reads 'Annon etiam hic vidi post videntem me?'

#	CO 23	Gen.	Citation	Source
59	231:10–11	16:13	Hieronymus vertit 'posteriora videntis me'	Vulg
60	236:4–7	17:4	some transferunt 'Ecce, ego ferio tecum foedus'	Zur
61	236:4–7	17:4	others transferunt 'Ecce, ego et foedus meum tecum'	Mün
62	246:9–11	17:19	quidam accipiunt אבל pro 'vere'	Mün; Pagn; Tharg
63	253:19–21	18:10	Hieronymus vertit 'vita comite revertar'	Vulg
64	255:4–5	18:13	quidam vertunt פלא as 'occultum' (14)	Tharg; Vat 11a
65	261:10–11	18:21	Hieronymus vertit 'si opere compleverint'	Vulg
66	261:20–22	18:21	alii vertunt 'si ita fecerint, iam adest ultimus . . .'	Vat 11a[15]
67	268:47–48	19:5	Graeci interpretes verterunt 'cognoscere' in sense of 'rem habere'	Rec 259; LXX
68	309:1–2	21:32	alii vertunt 'puteum *septem*'	Serv (v.l.); Vat 13a
69	315:11–12	22:2	Hieronymus exposuit 'terram *visionis*'	Vulg; Heb Qu 22:2
70	315:14–15	22:2	quidam interpretantur 'myrrham Dei'	Serv (v.l.); Vat 13a
71	318:26–30	22:14	some activum verbum 'videbit' in passivum transtulerunt	Heb Qu 22:14[16]
72	334:40–41	24:12	Hieronymus vertit 'occurre' instead of 'occurrere'	Vulg
73	336:40–41	24:22	Hieronymus pro 'dimidio' posuit: 'duos siclos'	Vulg
74	340:18–20	24:63	שוח exponi potest 'egressum esse *meditandi*'	Vulg; Serv (v.l.); Zur; Mün 22b
75	340:18–20	24:63	שוח exponi potest 'egressum esse *orandi*	Mün; Pagn; Tharg; Rec 281; Vat 5b
76	347:45–46	25:21	some vertunt 'praesente uxore'	Tharg d4b; Vat 15b
77	391:45–46	28:12	some vertunt particulam על 'prope' (13)	Mün; Pagn[17]
78	410:1–4	30:8	alii vertunt 'coniunctionibus Dei coniuncta sum'	Mün 29a; Vat 18b[18]
79	410:4–5	30:8	alii vertunt 'duplicata sum duplicationibus Dei'	Pagninus?[19]
80	410:11–13	30:8	ab aliis affertur 'luctata sit divinis aut praeclaris luctationibus'	Mün 29a; Vat 18b[20]

15 This citation has been retained because Calvin uses the word 'vertunt', but here he is paraphrasing rather than giving a verbal translation.
16 Rec 272 makes the point of passive versus active, but it is only Heb Qu that draws from the translation the moral mentioned by Calvin.
17 These both read 'iuxta eam'.
18 These both read 'coniuncta sum per Deum'.
19 Cf. Pagninus, *Thesaurus Linguae Sanctae*, 1065f.
20 Neither of these gives the text precisely as Calvin has it. With Mün, the text is 'luctationibus divinis luctata sum' and the notes give the alternative meaning 'magnificis'.

#	CO 23	Gen.	Citation	Source
81	411:49–50	30:14	omnes vertunt 'mandragoras'	e.g. Vulg; Cast; Mün; Pagn; Tharg; Zur; Rec 295
82	415:12–13	30:29	Hieronymus transtulit 'antequam venirem' (30)	Vulg
83	416:7–8	30:33	quidam legunt 'quando *tu venies* ad mercedem meam'	Vat 19a
84	416:8–10	30:33	alii vertentes in tertia persona 'ad mercedem *ventura sit*'	Mün; Tharg; Zur[21]
85	428:1–2	31:29	quidam exponunt 'manus mea est ad Deum'	Mün 31a
86	445:31–32	32:28	Hieronymus faithfully renders sense	Vulg; Heb Qu 32:28f.
87	458:25–26	34:7	communiter vertunt interpretes 'non sic fieri decet'	Tharg[22]
88	491:28–30	37:38[23]	Graeci exponunt 'lanionum praefectum'	Tharg f.6a; Vat 24a; Rec 333; LXX[24]
89	493:43	38:2	quidam vertunt 'negotiator rem'	Zur; Vat 24a
90	511:33–34	40:1	quidam intelligunt 'annum integrum' (4)	Pagn;[25] Mün 40a; Tharg g2b; Vat 25a
91	524:47–48	41:40	alii legere malunt 'armabitur'	Mün; Pagn; Vat 26a
92	524:48–49	41:40	alii [legere malunt] 'cibabitur ad nutum vel mandatum'	Tharg; Zur; Mün 42a[26]
93	525:5–9	41:40	אברך some exponunt 'patrem tenerum' (43)	Heb Qu 41:43; Pagn; Mün 42a; Vat 26a
94	525:9–11	41:40	אברך some vertunt 'patrem regis' (43)	Tharg; Mün 42a; Vat 26a
95	525:11–13	41:40	אברך alii afferunt 'genu flecte' (43)	Vulg; Heb Qu 41:43; Cast; Mün; Vat 26a
96	525:16–19	41:40	by some vertitur 'mundi redemptor' (45)	Vulg; Heb Qu 41:45; Rec 349[27]
97	525:16–19	41:40	by others [vertitur] 'mysterio-expositor' (45)	Heb Qu 41:45; Cast; Pagn; Tharg; Mün 42a; Rec 350; Vat 26a[28]
98	525:19–21	41:40	Graeci leave words untranslated (45)	Rec 349; LXX
99	525:23–24	41:40	quum כוהן significet 'principem' (45)	Pagn; Tharg; Mün 42a; Vat 26a
100	548:33–34	44:5	alii vertunt 'in quo tentando tentavit vos, vel rimando rimatur'	Vat 28a
101	550:51–52	44:18	quidam vertunt 'peccavero in patrem meum' (32)	Mün; Zur

21 These versions bring out Calvin's point without having the exact wording.
22 Tharg reads 'sic enim non decebat fieri'; the other translations all have the same sense in different words.
23 The 1554 edition and CO both have v. 38, in error for v. 36.
24 Tharg f.6a and Rec 333 read 'coquorum principem', Vat 24a reads 'magistro coquorum'.
25 Pagn reads 'per annum'; the other works all have the word 'integrum' as well.
26 These all give the sense mentioned by Calvin, not the exact words.
27 These all read 'salvator mundi'.
28 These all give the sense of 'mysterio-expositor', but not the exact wording.

#	CO 23	Gen.	Citation	Source
102	550:51–52	44:18	[quidam vertunt] 'reus ero peccati' (32)	Vulg; Tharg
103	550:52–54	44:18	alii [vertunt] 'obnoxius ero: propterea . . .' (32)	Pagn; Vat 28b
104	556:41–43	45:22	Hieronymus transtulit 'binas stolas'	Vulg
105	556:41–44	45:22	alii interpretes eum sequuti exponunt 'dissimiles vestes'	Vat 29a
106	562:3–6	46:8	numerical error once only apud graecos interpretes	Heb Qu 46:26f.; Rec 356f.; LXX
107	570:28	47:12	alii vertunt 'pubem'	Zur
108	577:48–49	47:31	Graeci verterunt 'ad summitatem virgae'	Rec 359; LXX
109	581:30–32	48:3	עולם accipitur by some as 'diuturno tempore' (4)	Mün 49a; Tharg h5b; Vat 30b[29]
110	581:30–32	48:3	accipitur by others as 'aeternitate' (4)	Vulg; Cast; Pagn; Zur; Mün 49a; Tharg h5b[30]
111	592:44–46	49:3	quidam vertunt 'tu virtus mea et principium *seminis*'	Serv (v.l.)[31]
112	592:44–46	49:3	alii vertunt 'tu virtus mea et principium *doloris*'	Vulg; Zur; Mün 50a[32]
113	595:20–21	49:5	מכרות quidam accipiunt pro 'gladiis'	Zur; Mün 50a[33]
114	595:23	49:5	מכרות others vertunt 'habitationes'	Rec 363f.
115	595:35	49:5	שור quidam vertunt 'taurum' (6)	Heb Qu 49:5f.; Mün 50a; Rec 365; Vat 31a
116	599:5–6	49:10	Hieronymus vertit 'qui mittendus est'	Vulg
117	599:18–19	49:10	alii interpretes exponunt 'filium eius'	Tharg; Mün 50a; Vat 31a
118	602:37–43	49:10	scio 'aggregatio' exponi by some interpretibus 'debilitatio'	Mün 50a
119	602:37–43	49:10	by other interpretibus 'obedientia'	Mün 50a; Rec 370; Vat 31a[34]
120	606:33–34	49:22	alii vertunt 'filium decoris'	Mün 50b
121	607:31–34	49:22	quidam vertunt 'inde pastor lapis Israel' (24)	Vulg; Mün
122	607:34–36	49:22	alii legunt 'pastor lapidis,' in genitivo casu (24)	Mün 50b

29 These all give the sense mentioned by Calvin, not the exact words.
30 These all give the sense mentioned by Calvin, not the exact words.
31 The Servetus variant reading is 'tu fortitudo mea et principium seminis'.
32 These all give the sense mentioned by Calvin, not the exact words.
33 Mün and Zur read 'machaerae eorum'.
34 Mün has the noun 'obedientia'; the others use the verb.

Appendix 3: Named Patristic Citations

Listed below are all named citations of the Fathers and of Josephus in Calvin's Genesis commentary, excluding instances where 'Jerome' means 'the Vulgate'. As CO is not fully reliable for Calvin's marginal references these have all been checked in the 1554 original.

#	CO 23	Gen.	Author & Source {Text + (margin) +[actual]}: Content	Source
1	7f.:38–40	Argum't	[Cassiodore] *Historia tripartita*	WA 42:9; Augustine, *Confessiones* 11:12:14
2	9f.:2–4	Argum't	Augustinus (*De Genesi contra Manich.*) [1:2:4]	Inst(39) 3:23:2
3	9f.:2–4	Argum't	(Lib. II *de Civit. Dei*)	CD 2:11:5, 2:12:12
4	18:45–48	1:6	Gregorius [*Epp.* 9:105, 11:13]: books of unlearned	CO 7:26 (1544); Inst(50) 1:11:5
5	25:55–26:7	1:26	Augustinus, Librum 10 *de Trinit.* [10:11:17–12:19]	(WA 42:45)[35]
6	25:55–26:7	1:26	et 14	(WA 42:45)
7	25:55–26:7	1:26	item *de Civit. Dei* libro 11	CD 11:24–28
8	26:35–38	1:26	Chrysostomus [*Homiliae in Genesim* 8:3f.,9:2–4,10:3f.]	*Psychopannychia* (CO 5:181)
9	37:9–13	2:8	Origenes: allegorizes Garden of Eden	WA 42:68,74; Rec 91f.
10	38:51–54	2:9	Augustinus: tree of life figure of Christ	Gen Lit 8:4:8; Inst(50) 2:2:9
11	38:51–54	2:9	Eucherius: ditto [*Commentarius in Genesim* lib.1 in c.2 , v. 9]	Inst(39) 2:2:9
12	46:30–34	2:18	Hieronymus, *Contra Iovinianum* prior liber	Inst(39) 4:12:28 & Comm. various
13	60:35–38	3:6	Augustinus: pride = beginning of all evils	Gen Lit 11:5:7, 11:15:19; CD 14:13:1
14	63:1–2	3:6	Augustinus: Adam and Eve stood for 6 hours only	not Augustine
15	63:15–17	3:6	Augustinus: wretched freewill which so unstable	*Enchiridion* 106:28?
16	63:18–21	3:6	Bernardus: potential for evil since fall	*Epistola* 1:3
17	90:53–54	4:7	Augustinus: give what you command ...	e.g. Inst(36) (OS 1:55)
18	114:44–47	6:3	Lactantius [*Divinae institutiones* 2:14]: 120 years = limit of human life	Rec 160
19	123:8–10	6:14	Origenes [*Homiliae in Genesim* 2:2]: geometrical cubits	##20, 21
20	123:10–12	6:14	Augustinus lib. *de Civitate Dei* 15: agrees with Origen	CD 15:27:3
21	123:10–12	6:14	et lib. 1 *Quaestionum in Genesin*: ditto	Qu Hept 1:4
22	123:44–48	6:14	Augustinus, lib. 15 *de Civitate Dei*: allegorizes Ark	CD 15:26

---

35 Luther refers to Augustine's *De trinitate*, but without specifying which books.

#	CO 23	Gen.	Author & Source {Text + (margin) +[actual]}: Content	Source
23	123:44–48	6:14	[lib.] 12 *adversus Faustum* [12:14,16]: ditto	WA 42:310
24	123:48f.	6:14	Origenes: allegorizes Ark	Origen 2:3–6
25	129:13–14	7:1	Augustinus: God crowns his own gifts	e.g. Inst(39) 2:5:2
26	136:55–137:1	8:3	Josephus [*Antiquitates* 1:93–95]: fragments of Ark remain	#27; Rec 179
27	137:1–2	8:3	Hieronymus [*Liber de situ et nominibus locorum hebraicorum* (PL 23.859)]	Rec 179
28	145:55–146:1	9:4	Tertullianus: Christians not to taste blood [*Apologeticum* 9:13]	memory
29	189:12–15	13:1	Augustinus: rich and poor together heirs of life	*Enarrationes in Psalmos* 85:3?
30	201:20–22	14:18	Hieronymus *ad Evagrium*: heaps together absurdities	*Ep. 73:2–10 ad Evangelum*
31	201:26–29	14:18	Hieronymus: vestiges of Melchizedek's palace	*Ep. 73:7*
32	202:41–45	14:18	Tertullianus et similes: type of Eucharist	*Interim* (CO 7:579f.,644)
33	241:56–242:2	17:12	Augustinus: 8th day signifies resurrection	CD 16:26?
34	299:42–45	21:8	Augustinus: significance of Isaac's weaning	Qu Hept 1:50; WA 43:145
35	302:25–29	21:10[36]	Origenes [*Homiliae in Genesim* 7:2–6, esp. 7:2]: allegorizes	Comm. Gal. 4:22f.
36	317:41–42	22:12	Augustinus: forced exegesis	Qu Hept 1:58
37	322:46–49	23:2	Ambrosius: too much mourning wrong	*De Abraham* 1:9:80; Inst(36) (OS 3:19)
38	325:52–53	23:11	Josephus: shekel worth 4 Attic drachmas	[*Antiquitates* 3:195] memory/checked
39	326:10–15	23:16	Hieronymus: letter removed from Ephron's name	Heb Qu 23:16
40	326:26–29	23:16	Hieronymus: ditto	Heb Qu 23:16
41	343:35–38	25:1	Augustinus: source of Abraham's vigour	Qu Hept 1:35,70 ; Comm. Rom. 4:19
42	378:4–13	27:27	Ambrosius: allegorizes	*De Jacob et vita beata* 2:2:9; Inst(39) 3:11:23
43	470:43–46	35:10	Augustinus: Jacob/Israel w.r.t. present/future life	Qu Hept 1:114
44	561:47–49	46:8	Augustinus: Stephen adds three born in Egypt	CD 16:40 ; Comm. Acts 7:14
45	588:32–34	48:22	Hieronymus: allegorizes money	Heb Qu 48:22

36 In CO 23:302 the verse number (12) is given; in the 1554 edition no such number is given so this comment is listed under 21:10.

Appendix 4: Citations of Ancient Heresies

Listed below are all explicit references to ancient heresies in Calvin's Genesis commentary.

#	CO 23	Gen.	Heresy	Content	Source
1	15:25–30	1:1	Arriani; Sabellius	others' relation to them	general
2	26:28–30	1:26	Anthropomorphitae	likeness in body	*Psychopannychia* (CO 5:180); Inst(39) 1:13:1
3	55:15–23	3:1	Manichaei	temptation implies two Gods	Gen Lit 11:13:17, *De haeresibus* 46
4	61:53–56	3:6	Pelagius	denied original sin	Inst(39) 2:1:5f.
5	62:15–17	3:6	Pelagius	sin transmitted by imitation	Inst(39) 2:1:5f.
6	113:19–22	6:3	Manichaei	some Jews accused of	Augustine, *De haeresibus* 46
7	474:35–44	35:22	Novatus; Novatiani	refuted by this passage	Inst(39) 4:1:23

Appendix 5: Jewish Citations

Listed below are references to post-biblical Jews in Calvin's Genesis commentary. Excluded are Calvin's references to 'Hebraei' where he is thinking of the Hebrew language rather than views of Jewish exegetes or theologians.

#	CO 23	Gen.	Content	Source
1	17:50–53	1:5	Jews condemn others' reckoning	WA 42.16
2	21:36–37	1:14	Rabbis say מועדים refers to Jewish festivals	Fag 20; Rec 52
3	24:47–50	1:24	Some Hebrews distinguish iumentum and bestias	WA 42:41; Fag 25; Mün 2a
4	25:28–30	1:26	Jews say 'us' = earth or angels	Inst(39) (OS 3:144f., n. c); WA 42:43; Fag 26; Mün 2a
5	34:3–7	2:3	Jews say fauns, etc. = imperfect animals	Mün 3a
6	34:35–37	2:4	Some Hebrews: Yahweh first used when world complete	Fag 37; Mün 3a; Rec 78f.
7	47:46–47	2:18	Some of rabbis say כנגדו here is affirmative	Fag 60f.
8	57:15–21	3:1	Kimhi: אף כי means quanto magis	Fag 74f.; Mün 4a
9	57:23–25	3:1	better Chaldaeus paraphrastes: verumne	Tharg; Vat 3a
10	86:32–35	4:5	Jews say Cain defrauded God	Fag 122f.
11	86:43–48	4:5	Hebrews: Abel's sacrifice consumed by fire	Fag 125; Post 45a; Heb Qu 4:4f.; Rec 132[37]
12	88:39–42	4:7	some Hebrew doctors refer נשא to Cain's countenance	WA 42:199; Fag 127f.

---

37 Heb Qu and Post quote the Theodotian translation; Rec and Fag cite other sources.

#	CO 23	Gen.	Content	Source
13	88:42–44	4:7	other Hebrews apply it to remission of sins	Fag 127; Tharg
14	96:56–97:8	4:15	Jewish interpretation of this verse	WA 42:223; Post 46a
15	100:49–55	4:23	Jewish fable about Lamech	WA 42:235 & 223
16	105:49–51	5:2	Jewish writers say only married people called Adam	WA 42:248
17	108:52–56	5:29	Jews on Lamech's prophecy	WA 42:259; Post 49a
18	111:50–53	6:1	Chaldean paraphrast: promiscuous marriages condemned	Rec 156; Tharg b2b; Vat 4b
19	113:14–19	6:3	some Hebrews derive word from נדן	WA 42:272
20	113:22–24	6:3	other Jews derive word from דון	Rec 158
21	115:2–3	6:3	Jews say years cut off because human wickedness	(Heb Qu 6:3)[38]
22	122:39–42	6:14	Jews not agreed about type of wood: cedar, fir-tree or pine	Mün 6b; Rec 169f.[39]
23	122:42–48	6:14	Jews not agreed about number of stories	(WA 42:309; Post 51a-b)[40]
24	122:48–54	6:14	Jews not agreed about window: number and purpose	(WA 42:310f.; Post 51a)[41]
25	136:53–55	8:3	Chaldaeus paraphrastes designat quod montes Cardu	Tharg b3b[42]
26	136:53–55	8:3	quos alii Carduenos vocant	Rec 180; Tharg b3b
27	141:32	8:22	Jews divide year into six parts	WA 42:353; Post 55a
28	146:22–23	9:5	Jews distinguish four types of homicide	WA 42:359; Tharg b4b
29	153:16–19	9:25	Jews say Ham not cursed because special favour	(WA 42:384)[43]
30	163:20–24	11:1	Jews commonly reckon 340 years between Flood and Babel	Mün 10b
31	163:46–47	11:1	common opinion of Jews [= previous item]	Mün 10b
32	166:54–56	11:7	Jews say God addressing angels	WA 42:422; Rec 210
33	170:38–44	11:28	Jews say Haran burnt because shunned idolatry	Post 59b; Heb Qu 11:28; Rec 214f.
34	176:30–32	12:1	noun גוי detestable to Jews but here term of honour	WA 42:445
35	177:55–178:3	12:3	Jews say bless/curse in s.o. means after their pattern	(Mün 11a; Post 60b; Vat 8a)[44]
36	192:18–19	13:10	Hebrews call anything excellent 'divine'	WA 42:506f.

38 Heb Qu has it, but without mentioning the Jews. It is cited by WA 42:279, Rec 162, Post 50b.
39 Mün and Rec between them have the necessary information.
40 Post is not clearly about the Jews; Luther has some of the information, but mostly not explicitly referring to the Jews.
41 Post contains most, but not all, of what Calvin says of the Jewish view; Luther has most of it, but some not explicitly referring to the Jews.
42 The text of Tharg has 'super montes [Cordu]' and the notes give this as 'Cardu' (b3b).
43 Luther has the information, but without mentioning the Jews.
44 Mün, Post and Vat all have the same material, which refers to blessing only, not to cursing, and which doesn't mention any biblical proofs. Cf. Tharg e1b (on 28:4) and h5b-6a (on 48:20, about Ephraim and Manasseh) which bring in other passages, but still make no mention of cursing.

#	CO 23	Gen.	Content	Source
37	193:44–50	13:14	Jews contend over word עולם (v. 15)	WA 42:520
38	211:27–28	15:6	Jews, whose blindness is well known, miss the point of the verse	WA 42:563
39	230:52–54	16:13	Hebrews: why Hagar surprised	WA 42:599; Mün 14a; Post 67b; Tharg c2b[45]
40	232:18–22	16:14	some Hebrews say name of well is testimony to double favour	?
41	242:49–50	17:13	Jews object that Christ violates circumcision law	general
42	243:15–24	17:13	wrong to say that circumcision is still in force for Jews	WA 42:651
43	267:3–6	19:1	Jews say one angel to destroy Sodom, other to preserve Lot	Tharg c4a
44	298:56–299:4	21:7	Jews say Sarah suckled local infants to prove motherhood	WA 43:144; Post 75b
45	318:4–6	22:13	Jews say ram created on sixth day	WA 43:233; Post 78a
46	321:18–22	23:1	Jews say why word 'years' repeated	WA 43:270; Post 79b
47	330:44–48	24:2	most Jews say implies circumcision and Abraham author of such a way of swearing	WA 43:300f.?; Mün 22a?; Rec 277?; Tharg d3b?[46]
48	330:51–53	24:2	some Jews say it was token of subjection	Mün 22a; Rec 277; Tharg d3b
49	333:30–34	24:10	some Hebrews: servant took document	WA 43:321; Mün 22a; Post 80b; Tharg d3b
50	338:29–31	24:33	some Hebrews say right/left hand = Lot/Ishmael (v. 49)	Tharg d3b
51	346:42–45	25:18	Chaldean paraphrast supplies word 'lot'	Tharg d4b
52	353:14–18	25:28	Jews wrong to glory in flesh in light of Isaac's behaviour	general
53	391:1–5	28:12	Hebrews say Jacob's ladder is figure of Providence	RB2; (Tharg e1b; Vat 17b)[47]
54	411:36–46	30:14	Jews wrong to glory in their origins	general
55	461:36–40	34:25	Jews wrong to glory in their origins	general
56	483:38–41	37:9	certain Hebrews interpret it of Bilhah	Mün 37b
57	491:27–29	37:38[48]	some Hebrews say Potiphar was lanionum praefectum	Mün 37b; Tharg f.6a

45 Luther and Post both say thought *angels* seen only in A's house; while Calvin says *God*. Mün has 'dei nuncium', while Tharg has 'per angelos suos se conspiciendum praebuit dominus', which best explains Calvin's reference to 'God' rather than to 'angels'.

46 Mün, Rec and Tharg note that the Jews relate this method of swearing to circumcision as the sign of the covenant. Luther (following Lyra) mentions circumcision only. He also, unlike the others, discusses whether the practice originated with Abraham, but without stating the Jewish view. It might be that Calvin would have deduced from the reference to circumcision and the covenant that the Jews thought the practice originated with Abraham.

47 Tharg and Vat say that for Hebrews Jacob's ladder means that inferiors depend upon superiors.

48 The 1554 edition and CO both have v. 38, in error for v. 36.

#	CO 23	Gen.	Content	Source
58	491:30–31	37:38	other Hebrews say Potiphar was praefectum militum	Mün 37b; Tharg f.6a; Vat 24a
59	493:31–33	38:1	Moses does not glorify Jewish ancestors	general
60	495:48–49	38:10	The Jews prate insufficiently modestly about this shameful matter	RB2
61	511:20–22	40:1	Gerundensis: Pharaoh made them eunuchs because enraged	Mün 40a
62	562:41–43	46:8	Hebrews say Jochebed, mother of Moses, also included	Mün 47a
63	598:13–599:2	49:10	Jews obscure interpretation of this verse	Mün 50a-b; Rec 368–70; Tharg i2a-4a
64	599:9–12	49:10	some Jews say שילוה denotes place Shiloh	Mün 50a; Rec 368f.; Tharg i2b
65	599:22–23	49:10	Jews refer this to David	Mün 50a; Tharg a2a-3b
66	599:41–600:4	49:10	Jews haughtily object that events convicts us of error	Mün 50a-b
67	601:52–602:3	49:10	some Jews say Judah given *right* (vs. glory) of government	?[49]
68	604:33–36	49:16	Jews restrict this verse to Samson	Mün 50b
69	608:48–52	49:27	Some Jews say Benjamites condemned	Mün 51a
70	608:52–54	49:27	Others say honourable praise	Mün 51a

Appendix 6: *Citations of 'Pope' and 'Papists'*

Listed below are the explicit references to the pope or to 'papists' in Calvin's Genesis commentary.

#	CO 23	Gen.	Content	Source
1	71:12–21	3:15	papists translate 'she' shall bruise	Vulg; WA 42:143; Rec 123
2	120:45–48	6:9	shows papists foolish to urge following fathers	WA 42:300
3	124:8–10	6:18	papists foolish to say doctrine of faith distracts from good works	general
4	134:2f.	7:17	papists ridiculous to fabricate ark without word	WA 42:334
5	148:54–56	9:11	papists enchant bread, etc. with magical whisperings	general
6	152:18–20	9:23	papists seek cover from cloak of Shem and Japeth	Eck 149
7	154:28–33	9:25	pope claims to prophesy, but he is servant of servants as Canaan was	general
8	181:51–55	12:7	papists claim to worship God but trifle with foolish pageantry	general
9	203:5–15	14:18	papists find sacrifice of mass here	*Interim* (CO 7:579f., 644); WA 42:537–40; Eck 206
10	236:20–22	17:4	religion of papists is fictions of men	WA 42:625f.

[49] Cf. Ramban (Nachmanides), *Commentary on the Torah*, vol. 1: Genesis, tr. C. B. Chavel (New York: Shilo, 1971) 586–90.

#	CO 23	Gen.	Content	Source
11	240:19–27	17:9	papists have abolished sacraments because word of God missing	ditto
12	255:33–35	18:13	papists plunge into labyrinth with talk of absolute power of God	Comm. Is 23:9
13	270:54–271:3	19:9	papists criticize us for paucity of numbers and novelty	general
14	290:10f.	20:7	papists base patronage of dead intercessors on this	?
15	298:19–27	21:4	papists boast of seven sacraments	general; cf. WA 43:141
16	303:26–30	21:10[50]	papists boast of their succession	WA 43:155
17	306:14–18	21:20	pope denies rights of parents in marriage	*Interim* (CO 7:574,640)
18	318:49–51	22:15	papists find merits of works here	WA 43:256
19	319:16–20	22:15	what God meant as encouragement papists interpret as merit	ditto
20	326:29–33	23:16	papal sacrificers sell burial rights	general
21	331:50–52	24:3	pope denies rights of parents in marriage	*Interim* (CO 7:574,640); WA 43:296–8
22	377:12–15	27:21	papists make force of sacrament depend on intention of priest	general
23	384:23–26	27:41	papists commend confession as deterrent against sin	*De scandalis* (OS 2:226)
24	389:19–34	28:6	corruptions of popery make thorough reformation necessary	general
25	392:17–20	28:13	sacraments of papacy frivolous because no word	general
26	394:45–47	28:17	papists misapply this to their temples	Cajetan 120; Eck 354
27	396:45–397:1	28:20	papists take this as precedent for their vows[51]	WA 43:606; Eck 210
28	404:44–49	29:30	papists make practices of fathers laws and have unworthy fathers	general
29	428:50–55	31:30	papists think to escape idolatry because don't call idols gods	general
30	457:19–22	34:4	pope breaks bond of nature: parental rights re marriage	*Interim* (CO 7:574,640)
31	467:15–19	35:2	papacy full of superstitions because earlier generations tolerated it	general
32	468:19–22	35:4	impious superstitions in the papacy	general
33	469:9–11	35:7	papists have an affected humility which is degrading	general
34	469:31–34	35:7	in papacy ceremonies are empty because word missing	general
35	559:54–560:5	46:2	without the word, sacraments of papacy are lifeless	general
36	585:31–40	48:16	papists find prayers to dead here	Inst(39) 3:20:25; *Interim* (CO 7:583,653); Eck 174
37	594:14–19	49:5	papists say punishment remains while guilt remitted	general?

50 In CO 23:302 the verse number (12) is given; in the 1554 edition no such number is given so this comment is listed under 21:10.
51 CO 23:396:45 erroneously reads 'iustitia' where p. 206 of the 1554 edition has 'stultitia'.

Appendix 7: *Specific Unnamed References*

Listed below are those references in Calvin's Genesis commentary, where he is explicitly citing the views of a particular group, without naming individuals.

#	CO 23	Gen.	Content	Source
1	22:10–12	1:15	'astrologi' rightly say moon opaque	general
2	22:22–25	1:16	'astrologi' distinguish between spheres	general
3	22:26–28	1:16	'astrologi' prove Saturn larger than moon	general
4	25:25–26	1:26	man called μιϰϱόϰοσμος by ancients	commonplace; cf. WA 42:51
5	27:20–23	1:26	some fathers say Christ alone is God's image	Lombard, *Sententiae* 2, dist. 16:3, 5
6	35:38–42	2:7	'animali vita' meant, against most ancients	*Psychopannychia* (CO 5:181); Tharg a3b
7	39:32–35	2:9	libertines say pure lust is innocency	general
8	60:32–33	3:6	some of the ancients say Adam and Eve allured by intemperance of appetite	?
9	62:45–47	3:6	ancient figment of traducianism	Inst(39) 2:1:7
10	111:47–50	6:1	ancient figment of intercourse of angels and women	Heb Qu 6:2; Rec 153; Tharg b2b
11	114:44–47	6:3	some ancient writers say 120 year lifespan	Heb Qu 6:3; Rec 160
12	136:51–53	8:3	Armenia's mountains highest claimed by ancient writers	WA 42:338?[52]
13	141:6–8	8:21	philosophers transfer [original sin] from nature to habit	general
14	148:33–35	9:9	ignorant Anabaptists exclude infants from covenant	general
15	202:29–45	14:18	ancient church writers say bread & wine typical	*Interim* (CO 7:579f., 644)
16	202:52–53	14:18	falsehood of the ancients thus refuted	ditto
17	228:52–55	16:10	most of ancients say that Christ present in all the oracles	general
18	251:30–35	18:2	some of ancient writers say Abraham perceived Trinity	WA 43:11–14; Rec 252
19	326:26–29	23:16	canonists say sacrilege to sell sepulchre	*Decretum Gratiani* II, c.13, q.2, c.13
20	330:48–51	24:2	Christian writers say it is in honour of seed	WA 43:301; Heb Qu 24:9; Rec 277
21	428:56–429:2	31:30	metonymy is ancient idolaters' excuse	Inst(36–43) 1:11:9
22	474:6–9	35:22	Moses acts like painter of sacrifice of Iphigenia	WA 42:206f.
23	522:11–20	41:17	philosophers prefer Plato to God's word	general

---

52 If Calvin is dependent upon Luther, he has misread him.

Appendix 8: Vague References

Listed below are vaguer references in Calvin's Genesis commentary, as far as chapter 11, where he is explicitly citing someone's views, without being precise about whose. The following list is not totally exhaustive. A reference, for example, to the view held by the great majority of commentators (CO 23:25, lines 49f., on 1:26) is of little interest in seeking to trace Calvin's sources. Where the point concerned is found in a wide range of sources only those are listed that we know Calvin to be using.

#	CO 23	Gen.	Content	Source
1	14:34–35	1:1	frivolous to expound 'beginning' as Christ	WA 42:8f.; Heb Qu 1:1; Gen Lit 1.4.9–6:12
2	15:20–33	1:1	inferred from plural Elohim that Trinity implied	WA 42:10; Rec 28–32
3	17:54–56	1:5	error that world was made in one moment	WA 42:4,52,91; Gen Lit 4:33
4	18:11–16	1:5	this falsehood supported from Ecclus. 18:1	Gen Lit 4:33:52
5	18:39–41	1:6	some allegorize waters as angels	CD 11:34
6	21:19–21	1:14	abused to justify astrological predictions	WA 42:33f.
7	22:2–5	1:15	some dishonestly reproach Moses for inexactitude	sceptics
8	23:27–30	1:20	birds could not come from water	Augustine, *De Genesi contra Manichaeos* 1:15:24
9	23:50–52	1:21	some say fishes created because waters insufficient	?
10	25:36–38	1:26	others say plural is royal we	WA 42:43
11	27:12–15	1:26	some say particles indicate image eschatological	?
12	29:34–36	1:28	some infer that people were then vegetarian	WA 42:54f.; Origen 1:17 (69)
13	29:49–51	1:28	prudent judgment that earth marred by Flood	WA 42:74f.
14	31:35–37	2:1	error that world formed in a moment	as #3
15	34:10–13	2:3	some say 'creavit ut faceret' means God didn't withhold preservation	Tharg a3a
16	34:14–17	2:3	others say 'faceret' refers to *man* making works by his industry	?
17	34:24–27	2:4	'ingrati' and 'maligni' say world eternal or remove memory of creation	sceptics
18	36:47–49	2:8	some say Eden covered whole world	WA 42:55,74
19	37:44–47	2:8	some locate Eden in region of Mesopotamia	Rec 84f.
20	39:12–14	2:9	some restrict tree of life to corporeal life	WA 42:70f.

#	CO 23	Gen.	Content	Source
21	39:50–51	2:10	many say Pison/Gihon are Ganges/Nile	WA 42:74; Mün 3a; Rec 100–3; Gen Lit 8:7:13
22	39:53	2:10	others say Danube	Rec 103
23	39:55–40:2	2:10	others say names of two of the rivers now obsolete	Rec 105
24	40:6–11	2:10	some get round this by saying surface of globe changed by Flood	WA 42:74f.
25	46:40–42	2:18	some say singular 'faciam' because woman inferior	?
26	47:55–48:2	2:18	some say woman made/'good' only for procreation	WA 42:87–89; Gen Lit 9:5:9
27	48:8–10	2:18	others say means woman ready for obedience	Vat 2b
28	48:43–45 + 49:2–10	2:21	profane and perverse are sceptical about method of making woman	WA 42:92,97; Gen Lit 9:16:30
29	50:5–6	2:23	it is demanded how Adam knew this	sceptics
30	50:32–35	2:24	it is doubted whether God, Adam or Moses is speaking	WA 42:101
31	53:14–16	3:1	some say more acuteness found in other animals	Cajetan 27
32	53:33–37	3:1	opinion that Spirit purposely used obscure figures	WA 42:109
33	54:19–21	3:1	some foolishly allegorize snake	i.e. = Satan: Fag 72; Cajetan 27
34	54:21–25	3:1	many surprised no mention of tempter's own fall	Inst(43) 1:14:16
35	54:25–27	3:1	'fanatici' say Satan created evil	Gen Lit 11:20:27; cf. Inst(43) 1:14:16
36	55:3–6	3:1	some ask why God allowed temptation	Inst(39) 3:23:2–9; Gen Lit 11:4:6
37	55:30–35	3:1	many suppose God not cause of sin but left Adam to freewill	Inst(39) 3:23:6
38	55:44–45	3:1	some offended to hear that God willed the Fall	Inst(39) 3:23:7,8
39	55:56–56:2	3:1	unskilled infer from this that fall not free	Inst(39) 3:23:6
40	56:7–12	3:1	impious doubt whether snake could speak	Cajetan 27
41	56:46–49	3:1	curious sophists say Satan tempted because jealous of incarnation	?
42	57:25–26	3:1	some say snake's question is *simple* interrogation	?
43	57:25–26	3:1	others say *ironical* interrogation	WA 42:112
44	57:35–37	3:1	some say Satan openly denying God's word	cf. WA 42:112
45	57:37–39	3:1	others say weakening confidence by inquiring about cause	WA 42:115

#	CO 23	Gen.	Content	Source
46	58:1–4	3:1	some say Satan implies all trees forbidden	Chrysostom, *Homiliae in Genesim* 16:3
47	58:4–5	3:1	others that he implies that all trees are permitted	WA 42:115
48	58:30–33	3:1	some suppose added 'touch' charges God with excessive severity	?
49	59:8–13	3:5	some say Satan craftily praises God	WA 42:119
50	59:13–15	3:5	others say Satan charges God with envy	WA 42:119
51	60:6–8	3:6	some deduce Adam present when Eve fell	Fag 78; Rec 119
52	60:13	3:6	some refer particle עמה to conjugal bond	?
53	61:31–33	3:6	'perversi rhetores' excuse Eve/ Adam because allured by beauty/Eve	?[53]
54	63:2–4	3:6	others say Satan delayed temptation till sabbath	WA 42:62,108
55	65:29–30	3:8	others understand [word] as 'plaga vel regione australi'	WA 42:127
56	65:31–37	3:8	others say means time of clear daylight	WA 42:127
57	68:40–42	3:14	many interpret this passage allegorically and subtly	WA 42:138
58	69:24–27	3:14	some learned and able say serpent previously walked upright	WA 42:140
59	72:22–25	3:15	others say 'seed' refers to Christ	WA 42:144f.; Rec 123
60	73:55–74:1	3:18	some say earth is exhausted by long time	cf. WA 42:155f.
61	74:2–4	3:18	others that God's blessing impaired by increasing wickedness	WA 42:161
62	74:6–10	3:18	some say Adam deprived of all former fruits	WA 42:156f.
63	74:31–33	3:19	some ignorant persons say all to do manual labour	WA 42:157f.
64	75:53–76:4	3:19	some say God remits guilt (v. 15) but retains punishment (v. 19)	Eck 125
65	77:5–8	3:19	some understand 'you shall die' (2:17) in spiritual sense: physical death anyway	?
66	77:34–37	3:20	Some say Adam called Eve mother of living because of future hope	WA 42:164f.
67	78:51–54	3:22	some say plural 'us' refers to angels	WA 42:166
68	78:56–79:6	3:22	some Christians read Trinity in here	WA 42:167

53 For similar discussions of what tempted Adam and Eve, cf. *Comm.* 1 Timothy 2:14 and, for patristic material, Lombard, *Sententiae* Lib. 2, dist. 22, cc. 4–8.

#	CO 23	Gen.	Content	Source
69	79:12–15	3:22	those who think it is ironical are mistaken	WA 42:166
70	80:12–18	3:23	some say turning sword points to chance for repentance	WA 42:172
71	82:52–83:4	4:1	others say Eve thought Cain = deliverer	WA 42:144; Fag 118f.
72	83:16–18	4:2	some think Abel so called out of contempt	WA 42:180f; Fag 120
73	83:31–34	4:2	some censure Eve's judgment about sons	WA 42:182; Fag 120
74	85:54–86:2	4:4	vain philosophy that talks of faith, ignoring God's grace	general
75	86:2–4	4:4	faith purifies only because of gift of regeneration	Inst(39) 3:11:15
76	87:41–49	4:6	good men, pious and learned, say Adam speaking	WA 42:194
77	88:46–51	4:7	third exposition: exaltation refers to honour	Mün 4b; Vat 3b
78	88:52–55	4:7	others say Cain needed purity of heart through faith	Tharg a6b; cf. WA 42:196–8
79	90:13–21	4:7	nearly all commentators refer this to sin . . .	WA 42:199; Fag 129
80	90:45–46	4:7	childish trifle to say this proves free choice	Inst(39) 2:5:16; WA 42:199; Eck 313
81	91:2–4	4:8	some think Cain hid anger	WA 42:200; Fag 131
82	91:35–37	4:9	some say Adam speaking here	WA 42:202
83	94:3–6	4:11	some say cruelty ascribed to earth – like wild beast	Fag 136
84	94:16–20	4:11	some say Adam cursed less than Cain to spare human race	WA 42:214
85	94:22–27	4:11	others say Cain receives temporal punishment only	WA 42:215
86	94:55–95:3	4:12	some distinguish נע = no settled abode & נד = know not where to turn	WA 42:216f.
87	96:52–56	4:15	some say Cain wanted one immediate death	WA 42:222
88	97:38–40	4:15	commentators say Cain's body became tremulous	WA 42:226; Fag 143
89	99:10–13	4:17	mockers ask where Cain found builders and citizens	Qu Hept 1:1; cf. CD 15:8
90	102:27–30	4:24	some infer Adam and Eve left childless by loss of Abel and Cain	WA 42:239
91	106:12–13	5:3	some object that Seth and family unfallen because elected by grace	Inst(39) 2:1:7
92	109:23–24	5:29	some suppose Lamech thought Noah was the Christ	WA 42:259
93	109:44–47	5:32	they err who say Noah chaste because remained single 500 years	WA 42:261

#	CO 23	Gen.	Content	Source
94	113:26–30	6:3	some interpret it: God will no longer govern by his Spirit	Rec 158
95	114:20–21	6:3	those wrong who restrict 'flesh' to lower part of soul	general
96	115:40–44	6:4	other interpreters blunder after Jerome	WA 42:285; Mün 6b; Qu Hept 1:3; Vat 5a
97	116:5–7	6:4	some expound עולם ('a saeculo') as 'coram mundo'	WA 42:288
98	116:7–9	6:4	some think this spoken proverbially	Mün 6b
99	117:31–33	6:5	some expound particle 'continuously' to mean from infancy	?
100	119:25–28	6:8	some unlearned deduce subtly that we merit grace	general
101	127:54–128:4	7:1	year begins at autumnal equinox OR in March	WA 42:327
102	131:23–29	7:8	ditto for Hebrews: political versus sacred year	ditto
103	136:24–28	8:3	some think 150 days = whole time since beginning of Flood	WA 42:337
104	136:51–53	8:3	some deny view of ancient authors that Ararat is Armenia	WA 42:338
105	137:21–25	8:6	textual error → fable about raven → futile allegories	WA 42:339, 372–5
106	137:28–30	8:6	some philosophize about olive branch	WA 42:376
107	137:35–38	8:6	some say Vulg confirms idea Flood began in September	WA 42:327
108	137:46–49	8:15	profane say that Noah stayed in because timid	sceptics
109	145:32–34	9:4	some say not eat member cut off from living animal	WA 42:359; Rec 187
110	146:40	9:6	some say 'in man' means before witnesses	Tharg; Vat 6b
111	146:40–42	9:6	others say 'in man' means by man blood to be shed	WA 42:360
112	146:46–48	9:6	some say merely political law for punishment of homicide	WA 42:360f.
113	149:21–23	9:13	certain eminent theologians say no rainbow before Flood	WA 42:365f.
114	157:39–158:1	10:1	mockers doubt rapidity of population growth	sceptics
115	159:51–53	10:10	Semiramis built Babylon OR she only adorned it	Josephus, *Contra Apionem* 1.142
116	160:3–7	10:10	some say not in chronological order: 10:10 after 11:1ff.	WA 42:403
117	160:33–39	10:11	opinion that Asshur here is a country not a person	Vat 7a

#	CO 23	Gen.	Content	Source
118	162:45–49	11:1	some conjecture tower built against further flood	WA 42:410; Josephus, *Antiquitates* 1.114
119	163:16–24	11:1	some prefer Berosus (130 years) to Jews	(WA 42:414; Cajetan 64)[54]
120	163:24–29	11:1	others say Babel built because population already dispersing	?
121	165:39–46	11:4	some say Noah warned of future dispersion	WA 42:416f.
122	165:46–48	11:4	others say they prophesied against themselves	WA 42:415
123	166:19–27	11:6	some interpret v. 6 as God vigilant against wickedness (Ps 34:16)	WA 42:420?
124	166:27–31	11:6	others say comparison between less and greater size of population	?
125	168:4–6	11:9	error of those deriving Babylon from Jupiter Belus	Rec 211
126	169:38–40	11:10	others say not absurd that third son born after two years	WA 42:426
127	170:8–10	11:27	others say lived with father 60 years in Charran	CD 16:14f.
128	170:33–35	11:27	some object that Sarah step-daughter of or adopted by Nahor	WA 42:431
129	170:51–53	11:28	others say Ur so called because in valley (Hebrew אורים)	?

---

54 Luther does not mention Berosus and says about 100 years; Cajetan mentions Berosus but has 151 years.

10

❧

Bibliography of Modern Works
on Calvin and the Fathers/Medievals

This bibliography aims to be an exhaustive list of all works on the subject since 1800 although here, as elsewhere, perfection remains an eschatological goal. The many sixteenth- and seventeenth-century polemical works refuting Calvin from the writings of the fathers have been excluded. Also excluded are works which simply juxtapose material on Calvin and his predecessors, without significantly relating them to one another. This applies chiefly to works on the history of doctrine.

I have personally examined all of the works listed and all of the individual editions mentioned, except where noted. A brief guide to the contents of each work is given.

In addition to those totally devoted to the subject, works are also included which devote a section to it or which contain significant relevant material. Completeness here is impossible, short of consulting every work relating to Calvin, and inevitably the decision as to what constitutes 'significant' material is subjective. But the drawbacks of subjectivity are outweighed by the loss that would be incurred by the exclusion of these works, many of which have greatly contributed to the study of the subject. Such works, devoted only partly to the subject, are marked with an asterisk (*). A few works are also included which are not as relevant to the topic as their titles might suggest, the comment warning the reader of this.

The word 'reprinted' is used only for photographic reproductions. Where an article is published again with a different layout, and most likely with revisions, the word 'also' is used.

This chapter is an updated version of Appendix I of 'Calvin's Use of the Fathers and the Medievals' in *Calvin Theological Journal* 16 (1981) 191–200. Errors have been corrected, unseen items have been seen and gaps have been filled. The bibliography has also been brought up to date and is now arranged alphabetically rather than chronologically.

A considerable debt of gratitude is owed to the staff at the Meeter Center, Calvin College, Grand Rapids both for their hospitality and assistance on the three occasions that I have visited and also for material that has been posted to me. Thanks are due especially to the late Peter de Klerk, to Rick Gamble and to Paul Fields.

*ANDERSON, A. L. *Calvin's Conception of Sin and Guilt* (New York: Union Theological Seminary MTh thesis, 1947). [Ch. 8 on Calvin's sources, with mention of Augustine, Gottschalk, Aquinas, Scotus and Occam.]

ANDERSON, L. 'The *Imago Dei* Theme in John Calvin and Bernard of Clairvaux' in W. H. Neuser (ed.), *Calvinus Sacrae Scripturae Professor. Calvin as Confessor of Holy Scripture* (Grand Rapids: Eerdmans, 1994) 178–98. [Comparison of Calvin and Bernard.]

ANDREWS, M. C. *Doctrine of Grace in St. Augustine and John Calvin* (Dubuque (IA): Dubuque Theological Seminary STM thesis, 1963). [Ch. 6 includes elements of comparison.]

ANON. 'St. Augustine and Calvinism', *Brownson's Quarterly Review* 15 (1863) 289–312. [Sharply contrasts Augustine and Calvin on sin.]

*ARMOUR, M. C. *Calvin's Hermeneutic and the History of Christian Exegesis* (Los Angeles: University of California PhD thesis, 1992) [Chs 4–6 relate Calvin to patristic exegesis; ch. 6 also to medieval exegesis.]

AYERS, R. H. 'The View of Medieval Biblical Exegesis in Calvin's *Institutes*', *Perspectives in Religious Studies* 7 (1980) 188–93. Reprinted in R. C. Gamble (ed.), *Articles on Calvin and Calvinism*, 14 vols. (New York and London: Garland, 1992) 6:410–15. [Claims Calvin's exegetical methods influenced by Augustine's.]

*BABELOTZKY, G. *Platonische Bilder und Gedankengänge in Calvins Lehre vom Menschen* (Wiesbaden: Franz Steiner, 1977). [I:1:243 on Augustine's influence upon young Calvin; II:1:25 and II:2:6 compare them.]

*BACKUS, I. '"Aristotelianism" in Some of Calvin's and Beza's Expository and Exegetical Writings on the Doctrine of the Trinity with Parti-cular Reference to the Terms οὐσια and ὑπόστασις' in O. Fatio and P. Fraenkel (eds), *Histoire de l'exégèse au XVIe siècle* (Geneva: Droz 1978) 351–60. [Includes comparison of Calvin with Augustine and Aquinas.]

*—— 'L'Exode 20,3–4 et l'interdiction des images. L'emploi de la tradition patristique par Zwingli et par Calvin', *Nos monuments d'art et d'histoire* 35 (1984) 319–22. [Calvin's and Zwingli's commentaries on Ex. 20:3f. break with exegetical tradition but draw on patristic polemic against images.]

—— 'Calvin's Judgment of Eusebius of Caesarea: An Analysis', *Sixteenth Century Journal* 22 (1991) 419–37. Shorter version, 'Calvin's Judgment of Eusebius of Caesarea' in Neuser (ed.), *Calvinus Sacrae Scripturae Professor*, 233–36. [Examines Calvin's use of Eusebius with its sensitive historical insights and cavalier judgments.]

*—— 'Irenaeus, Calvin and Calvinistic Orthodoxy. The Patristic Manual of Abraham Scultetus (1598)', *Reformation and Renaissance Review* 1 (1999) 41–53. [41–44 on Calvin's reception of Irenaeus.]

*BAKER, G. C. *The Doctrine of the Church in Calvin with some Comparisons to the Doctrine of the Church in Saint Augustine* (Atlanta (GA): Emory University, Candler School of Divinity BD thesis, 1937). [Includes comparison of Calvin and Augustine.]

*BARCLAY, A. *The Protestant Doctrine of the Lord's Supper. A Study in the Eucharistic Teaching of Luther, Zwingli and Calvin* (Glasgow: Jackson, Wylie & Co., 1927). [Ch. 19 on Ratramnus and the Reformers, including Calvin.]

*BARNIKOL, H. 'Die Lehre Calvins vom unfreien Willen und ihr Verhältnis zur Lehre der übrigen Reformatoren und Augustins', *Theologische Arbeiten aus dem Wissenschaftlichen Prediger-Verein der Rhein-provinz* NF 22 (Neuwied a. Rhein, 1926) 49–193. Also, *Die Lehre Calvins vom unfreien Willen und ihr Verhältnis zur Lehre der übrigen Reformatoren und Augustins* (Neuwied a. Rhein: Heusersche Buchdruckerei (J. Meincke), 1927). [Calvin's use of Augustine and doctrinal comparison.]

*BARTH, K. *Die Theologie Calvins 1922. Vorlesungen Göttingen Sommersemester 1922*, ed. H. Scholl (Zurich: Theologischer Verlag, 1993). English translation: *The Theology of John Calvin* (Grand Rapids and Cambridge: Eerdmans, 1995). [15–92/13–68 on Reformation (especially Calvin) and Middle Ages; 440–52/323–31 on Caroli affair.]

*BATTLES, F. L. 'The Sources of Calvin's Seneca Commentary' in G. E. Duffield (ed.), *John Calvin* (Appleford, Abingdon: Sutton Courtenay and Grand Rapids: Eerdmans, 1966 + 1968 reprint) 38–66. Also in his *Interpreting John Calvin*, ed. R. Benedetto (Grand Rapids: Baker, 1996) 65–89. [Sources of classical and patristic citations.]

*—— 'God Was Accommodating Himself to Human Capacity', *Interpretation* 31 (1977) 19–38. Reprinted in Gamble (ed.), *Articles*, 6:13–32. Also in D. K. McKim (ed.), *Readings in Calvin's Theology* (Grand Rapids: Baker, 1984) 21–42. Also in his *Interpreting John Calvin*, 117–37. [22–26/16–20/25–29/120–24 look at patristic background.]

*—— *Calculus Fidei: Some Ruminations on the Structure of the Theology of John Calvin* (Grand Rapids: Calvin Theological Seminary, 1978). Also in *Interpreting John Calvin*, 139–246. [Appendix F (134–36/245f.) argues that Basil was source of concepts of *duplex cognitio* and *theatrum mundi*.]

*BAVAUD, G. 'La doctrine de la justification d'après saint Augustin et la Réforme', *Revue des études augustiniennes* 5 (1959) 21–32. [Comparison of Augustine with Luther and Calvin.]

—— 'La doctrine de la prédestination et de la réprobation d'après S. Augustin et Calvin', *Revue des études augustiniennes* 5 (1959) 431–38. [Comparison, showing differences.]

—— 'Les rapports de la grâce et du libre arbitre. Un dialogue entre saint Bernard, saint Thomas d'Aquin et Calvin', *Verbum Caro* 14 (1960) 328–38. [Comparison, drawing out similarities and differences.]

*BEACH, J. M. *Is There Injustice with God? The Doctrine of Predestination in Augustine, Calvin, and Berkouwer, with an Analysis of Key Questions* (Grand Rapids: Calvin Theological Seminary MTh thesis, 1994) [Ch. 3 contains elements of comparison of Calvin and Augustine.]

*BECK, G. 'Ueber die Prädestination. Die augustinische, calvinische und lutherische Lehre aus den Quellen dargestellt und mit besonderer Rücksicht auf Schleiermachers Erwählungslehre comparativ beurtheilt', *Theologische Studien und Kritiken* 20 (1847) 70–128, 331–68. [Includes some comparison of Calvin and Augustine.]

BECKMANN, J. *Vom Sakrament bei Calvin. Die Sakramentslehre Calvins in ihren Beziehungen zu Augustin* (Tübingen: J. C. B. Mohr (Paul Siebeck), 1926). [Calvin's use of Augustine, faithful interpretation of him and probable dependence upon him.]

*BENDISCIOLI, M. 'L'agostinismo dei riformatori protestanti', *Revue des études augustiniennes* 1 (1955) 203–24. [Claims Reformers, including Calvin, have a one-sided Augustinianism.]

*BERGER, H. *Calvins Geschichtsauffassung* (Zurich: Zwingli-Verlag, 1955). [Chs 2, 15a on Calvin's attitude to Middle Ages.]

*BERKOUWER, G. C. *Conflict met Rome* (Kampen: J. H. Kok, 1948). English translation: *The Conflict with Rome* (Philadelphia: Presbyterian & Reformed, 1958). [332–50/247–62 on the appeal to the fathers, especially in Calvin.]

BESSE, G. 'Saint Augustin dans les oeuvres exégétiques de Jean Calvin', *Revue des études augustiniennes* 6 (1960) 161–72. [Authority accorded to Augustine in Calvin's exegetical works.]

*BOISSET, J. *Sagesse et sainteté dans la pensée de Jean Calvin. Essai sur l'humanisme du réformateur français* (Paris: Presses Universitaires de France, 1959). [Part IV, ch. 1 on sources of Calvin's thought; ch. 4 on Platonism in Calvin and Augustine.]

—— 'La réforme et les pères de l'église. Les références patristiques dans l'*Institution de la Religion Chrétienne* de Jean Calvin' in A. Mandouze and J. Fouilheron (eds), *Migne et le renouveau des études patristiques* (Paris: Beauchesne, 1988) 39–51. [Use of fathers in *Institutio*.]

*BONNER, G. *St. Augustine of Hippo. Life and Controversies* (London: SCM Press, 1963 – revised edition Norwich: Canterbury Press, 1986). [386–89 compare Calvin and Augustine on predestination.]

*BOOT, I. *De allegorische Uitlegging van het Hooglied voornamelijk in Nederland* (Woerden: Zuijderduijn, 1971). [Ch. IV:2 on Calvin's use of Bernard.]

BOYER, C. 'Jean Calvin et saint Augustin', *Augustinian Studies* 3 (1972) 15–34. [Broad doctrinal comparison.]

*BOYLE, R. M. *The Doctrine of the Witness of the Holy Spirit in John Calvin's Theology considered against an Historical Background* (Abilene (TX): Abilene Christian College MA thesis, 1967). [Ch. 2 on historical roots of the Reformation.]

BRAEKMAN, E. M. 'Calvin et les conciles', *Le Flambeau* 53 (1970) 263–82. [Calvin's attitude to ecumenical councils and their decisions.]

BREEN, Q. 'St. Thomas and Calvin as Theologians: A Comparison' in J. H. Bratt (ed.), *The Heritage of John Calvin* (Grand Rapids: Eerdmans, 1973) 23–39. [Broad comparison of their theological methods.]

BRINK, L. 'Thomas en Calvijn tezamen ter Communie', *Tijdschrift voor Theologie* 29 (1989) 232–49. [Areas of agreement between Aquinas and Calvin over the Eucharist.]

BROPHY, L. 'Calvin — Cold Opposite of Saint Francis', *Friar* 22 (July-August 1964) 58–61. [Caricaturing contrast of Calvin and Francis.]

BROWN, E. 'Wat Leer Calvyn in Verband met die Bestudering van die Kerkgeskiedenis?' in E. Brown (ed.), *Calvyn Aktueel?* (Kaapstad: NG Kerk-Uitgewers, 1983) 52–71. [Calvin's attitude to church history traced chronologically through his works.]

BRÜMMER, V. 'Calvin, Bernard and the Freedom of the Will', *Religious Studies* 30 (1994) 437–55. [Comparison of Calvin and Bernard.]

BUEHRER, R. L. *John Calvin's Humanistic Approach to Church History* (Seattle: University of Washington PhD thesis, 1974). [Calvin's approach to and use of church history.]

BUJARD, J.-P. A. *Calvin's Use of Patristic Sources in his Doctrine of the Trinity: Two Case Studies* (Princeton: Princeton Theological Seminary MTh thesis, 1983). [Examines Caroli affair and Servetus controversy.]

BÜSSER, F. 'Die Rolle der Kirchenväter in Calvins Exegetica' in W. H. Neuser (hrsg.), *Calvinus Ecclesiae Genevensis Custos* (Frankfurt, etc.: Peter Lang, 1984) 163f. [Report of seminar discussion about Calvin's use of Chrysostom especially.]

*BUTIN, P. W. 'John Calvin's Humanist Image of Popular Late-Medieval Piety and its Contribution to Reformed Worship', *Calvin Theological Journal* 29 (1994) 419–31. [Despite the title, this is about popular Roman Catholic piety of Calvin's own time.]

CADIER, J. 'Calvin et Saint Augustin' in *Augustinus Magister. (Congrès International Augustinien, Paris, 21–24 septembre 1954. Communications)*, vol. 2 (Paris: Études Augustiniennes, 1954) 1039–56. [Calvin's appeal to Augustine and similarity between them. Vol. 3, 272f., contain subsequent discussion with L. Smits and M. Reulos.]

*—— 'Saint Augustin et la Réforme', *Recherches augustiniennes* 1 (1958) 357–71. [365–71 on use of Augustine by Luther and Calvin.]

*CALVIN, J. *Opera Selecta*, vols 3–5 (*Institutio Christianae Religionis* 1559), ed. P. Barth and G. Niesel (Munich: Chr. Kaiser, 1928, 1931 and 1936 and further editions). [Footnotes invaluable for tracing sources.]

*—— *Institutes of the Christian Religion*, 2 vols., ed. J. T. McNeill, tr. F. L. Battles, Library of Christian Classics vols. 20–21 (London: SCM Press and Philadelphia: Westminster, 1961 and reprints). [Footnotes, heavily dependent on *Opera Selecta*, contain a mine of information; useful indexes.]

—— 'Preface to the Homilies of Chrysostom', tr. J. H. McIndoe, *Hartford Quarterly* 5 (1965) 19–26. [Calvin's attitude to Chrysostom and Greek fathers.]

*—— *The Bondage and Liberation of the Will: A Defense of the Orthodox Doctrine of Human Choice against Pighius*, ed. A. N. S. Lane, tr. G. I. Davies (Grand Rapids: Baker Book House and Carlisle: Paternoster, 1996) [xxi-xxiv, 257–63 and footnotes *passim* on patristic material.]

*CAUGHEY, F. M. *The Sources of the Thought and Teaching of John Calvin* (Pittsburgh: Pittsburgh University PhD thesis, 1937). [Part II:III relates Calvin's thought to earlier Christian theology.]

CHAVANNES, H. 'La présence réelle chez saint Thomas et chez Calvin', *Verbum Caro* 13 (1959) 151–70. [Aims to show their substantial agreement.]

COOPER, D. J. C. 'The Theology of Image in Eastern Orthodoxy and John Calvin', *Scottish Journal of Theology* 35 (1982) 219–41. [Comparison of Calvin and Eastern Orthodoxy (including Nicea II) with attempt to mediate.]

*CRAWFORD, D. J. *God in Human History: A Study of Calvin's Understanding of History with Special Reference to the Institutes* (Toronto: Knox College MTh thesis, 1967) [Ch. 3 compares Calvin with Augustine; ch. 4 with medieval views.]

*DANKBAAR, W. F. *De Sacramentsleer van Calvijn* (Amsterdam: H. J. Paris, 1941). [References to fathers and medievals throughout; ch. 5 specifically on Calvin's relation to Augustine.]

*——— 'Augustinus en de Reformatie' in *Augustinus. Voordrachten gehouden bij de Viering van de Zestienhonderdste Geboortedag van Augustinus in de Aula van de Rijksuniversiteit te Groningen* (Groningen and Jakarta: J. B. Wolters, 1954) 33–42. [Includes Calvin's use of Augustine.]

*DAVIES, H. *The Vigilant God: Providence in the Thought of Augustine, Aquinas, Calvin and Barth* (New York, etc.: Peter Lang, 1992). [Ch. 4 on Calvin includes comparison with Augustine especially.]

*DEAN, E. T. *Calvin and Barth on Scripture and Tradition* (Chicago: Chicago University PhD thesis, 1959). [Ch. 3 on Calvin's approach to tradition; Appendixes B & D on Calvin's patristic citations.]

*DEAN, E. 'The Relation between Scripture and Tradition. Theoretical Statements by Calvin and Barth', *Encounter* 23 (1962) 277–91. [Ch. 3 of preceding item: Calvin's approach to tradition.]

*DOBIÁS, F. M. 'Calvin, Luther a Hus', *Husuv Sborník*, vol. 1 (V. Proze: Komenského evangelická fakulta bohaslovecká, 1966) 132–39; German translation: 'Calvin-Luther-Hus', *Communio Viatorum* 10 (1967) 259–67. [Discusses Calvin's sole reference to Hus.]

*DOUGLASS, J. D. 'Calvin's Historical Consciousness in the Sermons on Micah, with a Study of Miriam' in P. De Klerk (ed.), *Calvin as Exegete* (Grand Rapids: Calvin Studies Society, 1995) 119–44. [Calvin's exegesis set against patristic and medieval background.]

*DURHAM, D. W. *The Function of the Conception of the Judgment to Come in the Thought of: Thomas Aquinas, John Calvin and John Wesley* (Durham (NC): Duke University BD thesis, 1947). [Conclusion includes comparison.]

*ELDERS, L. J. 'De Reformatoren en Thomas' in L. J. Elders and C. A. Tukker, *Thomas van Aquino. Zijn Leven, Werk en Invloed* (Leiden: J. J. Groen en Zoon and Bruges: Tabor, 1992) 184–214. [200–13 on Calvin's use of Aquinas and comparison.]

*EMMEN, E. *De Christologie van Calvijn* (Amsterdam: H. J. Paris, 1935). [Scattered material relating Calvin to fathers and medievals.]

*EVANS, G. R., 'Calvin on Signs: An Augustinian Dilemma', *Renaissance Studies* 3 (1989) 35–45. Reprinted in Gamble (ed.), *Articles*, 10:153–63. [Calvin's teaching set in the context of medieval debates.]

EXALTO, K. 'Bernard en Calvijn over de Herders te Bethlehem', *De Waarheidsvriend* 75 (1987) 806–808. [Comparison of Bernard's and Calvin's sermons on Luke 2:15–20.]

FABER, J. 'Nominalisme in Calvijns Preken over Job?' in R. ter Beek, E. Brink, C. van Dam and G. Kwakkel (eds), *Een Sprekend Begin. Opstellen aangeboden aan Heinrich Marinus Ohmann* (Kampen: van den Berg, 1993) 68–85. [Denies influence of Nominalism on Calvin.]

*FARMER, C. S. 'Changing Images of the Samaritan Woman in Early Reformed Commentaries on John', *Church History* 65 (1996) 365–75. [How Calvin and others portray her differently from patristic and medieval exegetes.]

FICKETT, H. L. *A Comparative Study of the Christology of Origen and Calvin based on the* ΠΕΡΙ ᾽ΑΡΧΩΝ *and the Institutes of the Christian Religion* (Philadelphia: Eastern Baptist Theological Seminary ThD thesis, 1949). [Ch. 6 brings out similarities and differences.]

*FIJAN, D. W. 'Bernard van Clairvaux en zijn Invloed op de Reformatie' in C. T. Boerke and C. M. Désirée de Vries-Hofland (eds), *Studia Studiosorum. Kerkhistorische Opstellen aangeboden aan Willem van't Spijker* (Apeldoorn: Kerkhistorisch Werkgezelschap, 1991) 9–24. [21–24 discuss Calvin, drawn mainly from W. S. Reid's 1978–79 article.]

*FISCHER, D. *La polemique anti-Romaine dans l'Institution de la Religion Chrestienne de Jean Calvin*, 2 vols. (Strasbourg: Strasbourg University thesis, 1975). [I:ii:3A, III:ii, V:iii:2D on Calvin's use of fathers.]

*—— *Jean Calvin, historien de l'église. Sources et aspects de la pensée historique, et de l'historiographie du réformateur*, 3 vols. (Strasbourg: Strasbourg University Doctorat d'Etat en Théologie thesis, 1980). [Much on Calvin's use of fathers.]

*—— 'L'élément historique dans la prédication de Calvin. Un aspect original de l'homilétique du réformateur', *Revue d'histoire et de philosophie religieuses* 64 (1984) 365–86. [Claims importance of historical material in sermons.]

*—— 'L'histoire de l'église dans la pensée de Calvin', *Archiv für Reformationsgeschichte* 77 (1986) 79–125. [Calvin's approach to history and his activity as a historian; II:4 especially on fathers.]

FITZER, J. 'The Augustinian Roots of Calvin's Eucharistic Thought', *Augustinian Studies* 7 (1976) 69–98. Reprinted in Gamble (ed.), *Articles*, 10:165–94. [Argues that Calvin's teaching is substantially the same as Augustine's.]

FOSHEE, C. N. *The Doctrine of the Knowledge of God in the Writings of John Calvin and Thomas Aquinas* (Decatur (GA): Columbia Theological Seminary MTh thesis, 1953–54). [Conclusion compares them.]

FRIETHOFF, C. *De Predestinatie-Leer van Thomas en Calvijn* (Zwolle: Fa. J. M. W. Waanders, 1925). German translation: *Die Prädestinationslehre bei Thomas von Aquin und Calvin* (Freiburg: St. Paulus, 1926). Also 'Die Prädestinationslehre bei Thomas von Aquin und Calvin', *Divus Thomas* 4 (1926) 71–91, 195–206, 280–302, 445–66. Also, more popular version: *De Goddelijke Predestinatie naar de Leer van Thomas Aquinas en Calvijn* (Hilversum: Paul Brand, 1936). [Comparison of Calvin and Aquinas on predestination, showing similarities and differences.]

*GAMBLE, R. C. '*Brevitas et Facilitas:* Toward an Understanding of Calvin's Hermeneutic', *Westminster Theological Journal* 47 (1985) 1–17. [8f. on Chrysostom as a possible source of Calvin's methodology.]

*———. 'The Sources of Calvin's Genesis Commentary: A Preliminary Report', *Archiv für Reformationsgeshichte* 84 (1993) 206–21. [211–13, 216, 218, 219f. discuss possible patristic sources.]

*GANOCZY, A. *Le jeune Calvin, genèse et évolution de sa vocation réformatrice* (Wiesbaden: Franz Steiner, 1966). English translation: *The Young Calvin* (Philadelphia: Westminster, 1987). [Ch. 2:I:5 (ch. 16 in ET) explores the sources of Calvin's 1536 *Institutio* in scholastic theology, especially Gratian and Lombard.]

*——— *La Bibliothèque de l'Académie de Calvin. Le catalogue de 1572 et ses enseignements* (Geneva: Droz, 1969). [Ch. III:2:B / III:2:C:b:II on fathers / medievals in catalogue and in Calvin; some items in catalogue were Calvin's own.]

——— and MÜLLER, K. *Calvins handschriftliche Annotationen zu Chrysostomus. Ein Beitrag zur Hermeneutik Calvins* (Wiesbaden: Franz Steiner, 1981). [Includes text of Chrysostom passages highlighted by Calvin.]

*GILKEY, L. B. *Reaping the Whirlwind. A Christian Interpretation of History* (New York: Seabury, 1976). [Ch. 7 on Augustine's and Calvin's views of providence, with comparison.]

*GILMONT, J.-F. *Jean Calvin et le livre imprimé* (Geneva: Droz, 1997). [Ch. IV:3 on Calvin's patristic and classical reading.]

*GODFREY, W. R. '"Beyond the Sphere of our Judgment": Calvin and the Confirmation of Scripture', *Westminster Theological Journal* 58 (1966) 29–39. [Section II on sources of Calvin's teaching.]

GOETERS, J. F. G. 'Thomas von Kempen und Johannes Calvin' in Stadt Kempen (hrsg.), *Thomas von Kempen* (Kempen-Niederrhein: Thomas, 1971) 87–92. [Influence of *devotio moderna* upon Calvin.]

*GOSSELIN, E. A. *The King's Progress to Jerusalem. Some Interpretations of David during the Reformation Period and their Patristic and Medieval Background* (Malibu (CA): Undena, 1976). [Occasional comparison of Calvin's approach to Psalms with that of fathers and medievals.]

*GREENE-MCCREIGHT, K. E. *Ad Litteram: Understandings of the Plain Sense of Scripture in the Exegesis of Augustine, Calvin and Barth of Genesis 1–3* (New Haven: Yale University PhD thesis, 1994). [Traces 'trajectory' of understandings in Augustine, Calvin and Barth.]

*——— *Ad Litteram. How Augustine, Calvin, and Barth Read the 'Plain Sense' of Genesis 1–3* (New York, etc.: Peter Lang, 1999).[1]

---

1   I have seen only the announcement in the publisher's catalogue, which suggests that this is simply the publication of the previous item.

*HAAS, G. H. *The Concept of Equity in Calvin's Ethics* (Carlisle: Paternoster, 1997). [Relates Calvin's thought to earlier tradition, especially Aristotle, Augustine and Aquinas.]

HARMAN, A. M. 'Speech about the Trinity: with special reference to Novatian, Hilary and Calvin', *Scottish Journal of Theology* 26 (1973) 385–400. [Similarities drawn out.]

HAZLETT, W. I. P. 'Calvin's Latin Preface to his Proposed French Edition of Chrysostom's Homilies: Translation and Commentary' in J. Kirk (ed.), *Humanism and Reform: The Church in Europe, England and Scotland, 1400–1643* (Oxford: Basil Blackwell, 1991) 129–50. [Full introduction, translation and commentary.]

HEIM, S. M. 'The Powers of God: Calvin and Late Medieval Thought', *Andover Newton Quarterly* NS 19 (1978–79) 156–66. Reprinted in Gamble (ed.), *Articles*, 4:2–12. [Calvin's doctrine portrayed as a reaction to late medieval thought.]

*HELM, P. 'Reformation and Medieval Views on Justification', *Banner of Truth* 326 (November 1990) 9–14. [Contrasts Reformers (including Calvin) with Augustine and later Catholic tradition.]

—— 'Calvin and Bernard on Freedom and Necessity: A Reply to Brümmer', *Religious Studies* 30 (1994) 457–65. [Response to Brümmer article above.]

*HEMAN, R. *Mysterium Sanctum Magnum. Um die Auslegung des Abendmahls. Zwingli? Calvin? Luther? Rom?* (Lucerne and Leipzig: Räber, 1937). [Reformers' views related to patristic and medieval teaching.]

*HENDRIKX, E. 'Augustinus en de Reformatie. Is de Bisschop van Hippo tegelijk Katholiek en Protestant geweest?', *De Bazuin* 38:7 (13 November 1954) 4f. [Admission that Augustine has some Protestant elements.]

*HODGSON, L. *The Doctrine of the Trinity* (London: James Nisbet, 1943 and reprints). [VI.4 compares Calvin with Augustine and Aquinas; Appendix I compares Calvin's *Institutes* and Aquinas' *Summa theologiae* on reason and revelation.]

*HOFFECKER, W. A. 'Augustine, Aquinas, and the Reformers' in W. A. Hoffecker and G. S. Smith (eds), *Building a Christian World View*, vol. 1 (Phillipsburg (NJ): Presbyterian and Reformed, 1986) 235–58. [Claims that Luther and Calvin, in their epistemology, theology and anthropology, revived Augustinianism.]

*HOITENGA, D. J. *John Calvin and the Will. A Critique and Corrective* (Grand Rapids: Baker, 1997). [Calvin's teaching in light of Augustine, Aquinas and Scotus especially.]

*HUNTER, A. M. *The Teaching of Calvin* (Glasgow: Jackson, 1943 + 2nd edition, London: J. Clarke, 1950). [Ch. 3 on 'Sources of his theology, especially the fathers'.]

*Hunter, A. M. 'The Erudition of John Calvin', *Evangelical Quarterly* 18 (1946) 199–208. [Includes his knowledge of the fathers.]

*HWANG, J.-U. *Der junge Calvin und seine Psychopannychia* (Frankfurt, etc.: Peter Lang, 1991). [297–311 discuss Calvin's patristic citations.]

IZARD, C., 'Jean Calvin à l'écoute de saint Bernard', *Études théologiques et religieuses* 67 (1992) 19–41. [Reviews Bernardine citations in the *Institutio*.]

JONES, J. W. *The Doctrine of the Holy Spirit in Thomas Aquinas and John Calvin: a historical-theological investigation* (Cambridge (MA): Episcopal Theological School BD thesis, 1967.) [Chs 3:I, 4 compare Calvin and Aquinas, with critique]

*KATTENBUSCH, F. 'Arbitrium und Voluntas dasselbe? Bemerkungen zu H. Barnikols Calvin Dissertation', *Theologische Studien und Kritiken* 103 (1931) 129–35. [Critical review of Barnikol's 1926 thesis.]

*KIM, C. K. *The Doctrine of the Lord's Supper in John Calvin's Writings* (Abilene (TX): Abilene Christian College MA thesis, 1970). [76–87 on Calvin's use of fathers and medievals and their influence.]

KINGDON, R. M. 'Augustine and Calvin' in F. LeMoine and C. Kleinhenz (eds), *Saint Augustine the Bishop: A Book of Essays* (New York and London: Garland, 1994) 177f. [Calvin's fidelity to Augustine over predestination.]

*KINZEL, K. 'Darstellung der biblischen Erwählungslehre unter Vergleichung der Lehren Augustin's, Luther's und Calvin's', *Zeitschrift für die gesammte Lutherische Theologie und Kirche* 37 (1876) 66–113. [109–13 compare Calvin and Augustine.]

*KOOPMANS, J. *Het oudkerkelijk Dogma in de Reformatie, bepaaldelijk bij Calvijn* (Wageningen: H. Veenman, 1938; Amsterdam: ton Bolland, 1983 reprint). German translation: *Das altkirchliche Dogma in der Reformation* (Munich: Chr. Kaiser, 1955). [Calvin's attitude to Early Church.]

*KRAUS, G. *Vorherbestimmung. Traditionelle Prädestinationslehre im Licht gegenwärtiger Theologie* (Freiburg, Basel and Vienna: Herder, 1977). [Ch. 4 on Calvin includes comparison of his teaching with Augustine and Aquinas.]

LANE, A. N. S. 'Calvin's Sources of St. Bernard', *Archiv für Reformationsgeschichte* 67 (1976) 253–83. [Revised as ch. 5 of this volume.]

—— 'Calvin's Use of the Fathers and the Medievals', *Calvin Theological Journal* 16 (1981) 149–205. [Revised as ch. 2 of this volume.]

*—— 'Did Calvin Believe in Freewill?', *Vox Evangelica* 12 (1981) 72–90. [Includes discussion of Calvin's use of and fidelity to Augustine.]

—— *Calvin's Use of Bernard of Clairvaux* (Oxford: Oxford University BD thesis, 1982). [Calvin's use of Bernard, the fidelity of his interpretation and the extent of any influence.]

—— 'Bernard of Clairvaux: A Forerunner of John Calvin?' in J. R. Sommerfeldt (ed.), *Bernardus Magister* (Kalamazoo (MI): Cistercian Publications, 1992) 533–45. [Extent to which Bernard's doctrine of justification anticipated Calvin's.]

—— 'Saint Bernard et Calvin' in J. Leclercq, R. Genton and A. N. S. Lane, *Saint Bernard de Clairvaux* (Écublens: Église et Liturgie, 1994) 25–38. [More popular version of previous item.]

LANE, A. N. S. 'Calvin's Use of Bernard of Clairvaux' in K. Elm (hrsg.), *Bernhard von Clairvaux: Rezeption und Wirkung im Mittelalter und in der Neuzeit* (Wiesbaden: Harrassowitz, 1994) 303–32. [Revised as ch. 4 of this volume.]

—— 'Did Calvin Use Lippoman's *Catena in Genesim?*', *Calvin Theological Journal* 31 (1996) 404–19. [Revised as ch. 8 of this volume.]

—— *Calvin and Bernard of Clairvaux* (Studies in Reformed Theology and History New Series no. 1) (Princeton: Princeton Theological Seminary, 1996). [Revised version of 1982 thesis.]

—— 'Calvin and the Fathers in *Bondage and Liberation of the Will*' in W. H. Neuser and B. G. Armstrong (eds), *Calvinus Sincerioris Religionis Vindex. Calvin as Protector of the Purer Religion* (Kirksville (MO): Sixteenth Century Journal Publishers, 1997) 67–96. [Revised as ch. 6 of this volume.]

—— 'The Sources of Calvin's Citations in his Genesis Commentary' in A. N. S. Lane (ed.), *Interpreting the Bible. Historical and Theological Studies in Honour of David F. Wright* (Leicester: Apollos, 1997) 47–97. [Revised as ch. 9 of this volume.]

—— 'The Influence upon Calvin of his Debate with Pighius' in L. Grane, A. Schindler, M. Wriedt (eds), *Auctoritas Patrum II. New Contributions on the Reception of the Church Fathers in the 15th and 16th Centuries* (Mainz: Philipp von Zabern, 1998) 125–39. [Revised as ch. 7 of this volume.]

*—— 'Bondage and Liberation in Calvin's Treatise against Pighius' in J. H. Leith and R. A. Johnson (eds), *Calvin Studies IX* (Davidson (NC): Davidson College and Davidson College Presbyterian Church, 1998) 16–45. [Includes discussion of Calvin's use of and fidelity to Augustine.]

*LANG, A. 'Die ältesten theologischen Arbeiten Calvins', *Neue Jahrbücher für Deutsche Theologie* 2 (1893) 273–300. [297–300 discuss Calvin's preface to Chrysostom's homilies.]

LANGE VAN RAVENSWAAY, J. M. J. *Augustinus totus noster. Das Augustinverständnis bei Johannes Calvin* (Tübingen: Tübingen University doctoral thesis, 1985). Also (Göttingen: Vandenhoeck & Ruprecht, 1990). [The role of Augustine in Calvin's thought.]

—— 'Initia Augustiniana Calvini. Neues zur Genese von Calvins Augustinverständnis' in *Congresso Internazionale su S. Agostino nel XVI Centenario della Conversione* vol. 3 (Rome: Institutum Patristicum 'Augustinianum', 1987) 257–74. [Substantially ch. 6:2, 3 of previous item, on Calvin's student years.]

LAVALLEE, A. A. *Calvin's Criticism of Scholastic Theology* (Cambridge (MA): Harvard University PhD thesis, 1967). [Detailed study of Calvin's handling of scholastics.]

*LAVAUD, M.-B. 'Précurseur de Calvin ou témoin de l'Augustinisme? Le cas de Gotescalc', *Revue thomiste* 15 (1932) 71–101. [Explicit comparison with Calvin limited to title of article!]

LEDERLE, H. I. *Die Leer van die 'Extra Calvinisticum' vóór Calvyn. Die Weerlegging van 'n dogmahistoriese Legende* (Stellenbosch: Stellenbosch University Lisensiaat in Teologie thesis, 1975). [Calvin's relationship to earlier tradition.]

LEWIS, E. R. 'Calvin and Tradition', *Theology* 45 (1942) 220–22. [Calvin's attitude to tradition, supporting G. L. Prestige against J. S. Whale.]

*LIES, L. *Origenes' Eucharistielehre im Streit der Konfessionen. Die Auslegungsgeschichte seit der Reformation* (Innsbruck and Vienna: Tyrolia Verlag, 1985). [67–73 give critical account of Calvin's use of Origen.]

LITTLE, L. K. 'Calvin's Appreciation of Gregory the Great', *Harvard Theological Review* 56 (1963) 145–57. [Calvin's use of Gregory.]

*LONCKE, J. 'S. Augustinus patronus reformatorum in doctrina de peccato originali?' *Collationes Brugenses et Gandavenses* 44 (1948) 288–93. [Claims Reformers, Baius and Jansenists misinterpret Augustine.]

*LYON, O. H., *The Element of Subjectivity in Calvin* (New York: Columbia Theological Seminary MTh thesis, 1967–68). [Ch. 2 on Nominalist influence on Luther and Calvin, who always belonged to the 'Occamist faction'.]

*McDONNELL, K. *John Calvin, the Church, and the Eucharist* (Princeton: Princeton University Press, 1967). [Chs 1 and 2 discuss influences on Calvin.]

*McGINN, B. 'Introduction' in Bernard of Clairvaux, *Treatises III: On Grace and Free Choice; In Praise of the New Knighthood* (Kalamazoo (MI): Cistercian Publications, 1977 and reprints). [48f. examine Calvin's use of the former treatise.]

*McGRATH, A. E. 'Forerunners of the Reformation? A Critical Examination of the Evidence for Precursors of the Reformation Doctrines of Justification', *Harvard Theological Review* 75 (1982) 219–42. [Argues against patristic or medieval precedents for Reformation doctrines.]

—— 'John Calvin and Late Mediaeval Thought. A Study in Late Mediaeval Influences upon Calvin's Theological Development', *Archiv für Reformationsgeschichte* 77 (1986) 58–78. Reprinted in Gamble (ed.), *Articles*, 4:14–34. [Influence upon Calvin of *schola Augustiniana moderna* and Gregory of Rimini.]

*—— *The Intellectual Origins of the European Reformation* (Oxford: Basil Blackwell, 1987). [94–106 argue for influence upon Calvin of late-medieval *schola Augustiniana moderna*.]

*—— *A Life of John Calvin* (Oxford: Basil Blackwell, 1990). [36–47 argue for influence upon Calvin of late-medieval *schola Augustiniana moderna*.]

*McKEE, E. A. *John Calvin on the Diaconate and Liturgical Almsgiving* (Geneva: Droz, 1984). [Calvin's exegesis of key passages set against background of patristic and medieval exegesis.]

*—— *Elders and the Plural Ministry. The Role of Exegetical History in Illuminating John Calvin's Theology* (Geneva: Droz, 1988). [Calvin's exegesis of key passages set against background of patristic and medieval exegesis.]

*Márquez-André, G. *A Biblical, Theological, and Historical Study of the Paraclete in the Gospel of John* (Virginia Beach (VA): Regent University MA thesis, 1992). [61–74 expound Calvin's teaching, comparing it with Tertullian's and Augustine's.]

*Martin, J. *Ratramne. Une conception de la Cène au IXe siècle* (Montaubon: J. Granié, 1891). [Ch. 4 compares Ratramnus with later Reformers, including Calvin.]

Meijering, E. P. *Calvin wider die Neugierde. Ein Beitrag zum Vergleich zwischen reformatorischem und patristischem Denken* (Nieuwkoop: de Graaf, 1980). [Comparison of Calvin with Irenaeus, Tertullian and Augustine.]

*Meinhold, P. *Geschichte der kirchlichen Historiographie*, Band 1 (Munich and Freiburg: Karl Alber, 1967). [323–35, 511 on Calvin's attitude to the different phases of church history.]

*Michel, A. 'Prédestination et prédestinatianisme [*sic*]', *L'ami du clergé* 70 (1960) 615–19. [Calvinist and Jansenist doctrine contrasted with the Catholic doctrine of Paul and Augustine.]

*Millet, O. *Calvin et la dynamique de la parole. Étude de rhétorique réformée* (Paris: Honoré Champion and Geneva: Slatkine, 1992). [168–81 discuss Chrysostom as a model for Calvin; many other references to fathers.]

Mooi, R. J. *Het Kerk- en Dogmahistorisch Element in de Werken van Johannes Calvijn* (Wageningen: H. Veenman, 1962). [Major work summarizing Calvin's citations, surveying the authors cited and giving exhaustive tables of citations.]

*Moore, M.[2] *The Doctrine of the Dominical Sacraments in St. Thomas Aquinas, John Calvin and the early Scottish Reformers* (Grahamstown: Rhodes University thesis, 1957.)

*Morgan, E. L. *The Concept of Conscience by Representative Theologians. (According to Aquinas, Calvin and Arminius)* (Kansas City (MO): Nazarene Theological Seminary BD thesis, 1950). [Conclusion compares the three theologians.]

*Mozley, J. B. *A Treatise on the Augustinian Doctrine of Predestination* (London: J. Murray, 1855; 2nd edition, 1878). [Note XXI compares Calvin with Augustine and Aquinas.]

*Muller, R. A. '*Fides* and *Cognitio* in Relation to the Problem of Intellect and Will in the Theology of John Calvin', *Calvin Theological Journal* 25 (1990) 207–24. [Calvin's teaching related to that of Augustine, Aquinas and Scotus.]

*—— 'Calvin, Beza, and the Exegetical History of Romans 13:1–7' in P. de Klerk (ed.), *Calvin and the State* (Grand Rapids: Calvin Studies Society, 1993) 139–70. [Calvin's exegesis set against patristic and medieval background.]

—— 'Scholasticism in Calvin: A Question of Relation and Disjunction' in Neuser and Armstrong (eds), *Calvinus Sincerioris Religionis Vindex*, 247–65. [Calvin's knowledge and use of medieval scholasticism.]

---

2 This has not been consulted. Details are from D. Kempff, *A Bibliography of Calviniana 1959–1974* (Leiden: E. J. Brill, 1975) 116.

*NAUTA, D. 'Augustinus en de Reformatie' in *Augustinus. Redevoeringen in de Zitting van den Senaat der Vrije Universiteit* (Kampen: J. H. Kok, 1954) 25–44. English translation: 'Augustine and the Reformation,' *Free University Quarterly* 3 (1954–55) 237–47. [Use of Augustine by the Reformers, including Calvin.]

NEEFJES, G. *De Genadeleer volgens S. Thomas en Calvijn* (Rome, 1937). [Comparison.]

NIJENHUIS, W. 'Calvijns houding ten aanzien van de oudkerkelijke symbolen tijdens het conflict met Caroli', *Nederlands Theologisch Tijdschrift* 15 (1960–61) 24–47. English translation: 'Calvin's attitude towards the symbols of the Early Church during the conflict with Caroli' in his *Ecclesia Reformata. Studies on the Reformation* (Leiden: E. J. Brill, 1972) 73–96. [Historical account of the controversy.]

*NOORDMANS, O. *Augustinus* (Haarlem: De Erven F. Bohn, 1933). [210–19 compare Calvin and Augustine on the two cities.]

*NÖSGEN, D. 'Calvins Lehre von Gott und ihr Verhältnis zur Gotteslehre anderer Reformatoren', *Neue Kirchliche Zeitschrift* 23 (1912) 690–747. [713–19, 742 contain comparison with Augustine.]

*OBERMAN, H. A. 'Die "Extra"-Dimension in der Theologie Calvins' in H. Liebing and K. Scholder (eds), *Geist und Geschichte der Reformation. Festgabe Hanns Rückert zum 65 Geburtstag* (Berlin: Walter de Gruyter, 1966) 323–56. Also in his *Die Reformation. Von Wittenberg nach Genf* (Göttingen: Vandenhoeck & Ruprecht, 1986) 253–82. English translation: 'The "Extra" Dimension in the Theology of Calvin', *Journal of Ecclesiastical History* 21 (1970) 43–64. Also in his *The Dawn of the Reformation* (Edinburgh: T & T Clark, 1986) 234–58. Reprinted in Gamble (ed.), *Articles*, 8:160–84. [Includes material on Calvin's relation to scholasticism.]

*—— *Initia Calvini: The Matrix of Calvin's Reformation* (Amsterdam, etc.: Noord-Hollandsche, 1991). Also 'Initia Calvini: The Matrix of Calvin's Reformation' in Neuser (ed.), *Calvinus Sacrae Scripturae Professor*, 113–54. Afrikaans translation: 'Initia Calvini: die Matrix van Calvyn se Hervorming', *Studia Historiae Ecclesiasticae* 17 (1991) 123–52.[3] [10–19/117–27 on the pitfalls of pursuing Calvin's medieval pedigree.]

*OLD, H. O. *The Patristic Roots of Reformed Worship* (Zurich: Theologischer Verlag, 1975). [141–55 on Calvin's use of the fathers; 310–18 on his use of canon law.]

*OPITZ, P. *Calvins theologische Hermeneutik* (Neukirchen-Vluyn: Neukirchener Verlag, 1994). [9–15 compare Calvin's exegesis of Ps. 19 with Augustine's.]

*OSMAN, J. *The Sources of Thought in John Calvin. Calvin and Cosmology* (Richmond (VA): Union Theological Seminary MTh thesis, 1942). [Relates Calvin to classical thought, fathers and medievals.]

PARTEE, C. B. 'Predestination in Aquinas and Calvin', *Reformed Review* 32 (1978–79) 14–22. [Comparison.]

---

3 I have not seen the Afrikaans version. Details are from P. De Klerk, 'Calvin Bibliography 1995', *Calvin Theological Journal* 30 (1995) 425.

*PAULSELL, W. O. 'The Use of Bernard of Clairvaux in Reformation Preaching' in J. R. Sommerfeldt (ed.), *Erudition at God's Service* (Kalamazoo (MI): Cistercian Publications, 1987) 327–38. [330–33 summarize some of Calvin's citations.]

PAYNE, G. R. 'Augustinianism in Calvin and Bonaventure', *Westminster Theological Journal* 44 (1982) 1–30. [Calvin's and Bonaventure's conceptions of theology compared.]

*PAYTON, J. R. 'History as Rhetorical Weapon: Christian Humanism in Calvin's Reply to Sadoleto, 1539' in E. J. Furcha (ed.), *In Honor of John Calvin, 1509–64* (Montreal: Faculty of Religious Studies McGill University, 1987) 96–132. Reprinted in Gamble (ed.), *Articles*, 2:208–44. [Calvin's humanist approach to fathers and medievals.]

—— 'Calvin and the Legitimation of Icons: His Treatment of the Seventh Ecumenical Council', *Archiv für Reformationsgeschichte* 84 (1993) 222–41. [Argues Calvin misrepresents Nicea II.]

PAYTON, J. R. 'Calvin and the *Libri Carolini*', *Sixteenth Century Journal* 28 (1997) 467–80. [How Calvin gained access to this work before its publication.]

PETER, J. F. 'The Ministry in the Early Church as seen by John Calvin', *Evangelical Quarterly* 35 (1963) 68–78, 133–43. [Calvin's interpretation of and attitude to the fathers.]

—— 'The Place of Tradition in Reformed Theology', *Scottish Journal of Theology* 18 (1965) 294–307. [Calvin's attitude to tradition.]

*PIERSON, A. *Studien over Johannes Kalvijn (1527–1536)* (Amsterdam: P. N. van Kampen, 1881). [Ch. 4 compares the *Institutio* with Aquinas' *Summa theologiae*.]

PIJPER, F. 'De Invloed van de Broeders des Gemeenen Levens op de Schoolstichting van Calvijn' in *Kerkhistorische Opstellen, van het gezelschap S.S.S. Nieuwe bundel* (The Hague: Nijhoff, 1914) 115–29. [Influence of Brethren on Genevan Academy via Erasmus and Sturm.]

PINTARD, J. 'Au sujet du culte des saints et de la vierge. Calvin est-il fidèle disciple de saint Augustin?' *Esprit et vie* 90 (1980) 425–32. [Draws out differences between Calvin and Augustine.]

*PLANTINGA, T. *Learning to Live with Evil* (Grand Rapids: Eerdmans, 1982). [Ch. 7 on Augustine and Calvin, with comparison.]

POLMAN, A. D. R. *De Praedestinatieleer van Augustinus, Thomas van Aquino en Calvijn. Een dogmahistorische studie* (Franeker: T. Wever, 1936). [History of the doctrine of predestination with a certain amount of comparison.]

—— 'Calvijn en de Oude Kerk', *Vox Theologica* 30 (1959–60) 72–79. [Calvin's use of the fathers.]

*POLMAN, P. *L'élément historique dans la controverse religieuse du XVIe siècle* (Gembloux: J. Duculot, 1932). [65–94 on Calvin's use of fathers.]

*POWELL, J. H. *Determinism in Calvin* (Edinburgh: Edinburgh University PhD thesis, 1928). [Ch. 9 on Calvin's sources, especially Augustine — similarities and differences.]

PRANGER, M. B. 'Masters of Suspense: Argumentation and Imagination in Anselm, Bernard, and Calvin' in P. A. Knapp and M. A. Stugrin (eds), *Assays: Critical Approaches to Medieval and Renaissance Texts*, vol. 1 (Pittsburgh: University of Pittsburgh Press, 1981) 15–32. [Comparison of method of theological argumentation of Anselm, Bernard and Calvin.]

*RAINBOW, J. H. *Redemptor Ecclesiae, Redemptor Mundi: An Historical and Theological Study of John Calvin's Doctrine of the Extent of Redemption* (Santa Barbara: University of California PhD thesis, 1986).[4]

*—— *The Will of God and the Cross. An Historical and Theological Study of John Calvin's Doctrine of Limited Redemption* (Allison Park (PA): Pickwick, 1990). [Chs 2–4 give patristic and medieval background.]

RAITT, J. 'Calvin's Use of Bernard of Clairvaux', *Archiv für Reformationsgeschichte* 72 (1981) 98–121. [Fidelity of Calvin's interpretation of Bernard in *Institutio*.]

*RAMM, B. L. 'The Exegesis of Matt. 16:13–20 in the Patristic and Reformation Period', *Foundations* 5 (1962) 206–16. [Calvin's exegesis in context of fathers and Luther.]

*RANKIN, W. D. *Carnal Union with Christ in the Theology of T. F. Torrance* (Edinburgh: Edinburgh University PhD thesis, 1997). [Chs 2f. on Athanasius and Calvin, in light of Torrance's claim that former influenced latter.]

REID, W. S. 'Calvinism in Sixteenth Century Historiography', *Philosophia Reformata* 30 (1965) 178–97. [Calvin's attitude to church history.]

—— *The Present Significance of Calvin's View of Tradition* (Redhill: Sovereign Grace Union, 1966). [Calvin's attitude to tradition, against some recent interpretations.]

—— 'Bernard of Clairvaux in the Thought of John Calvin', *Westminster Theological Journal* 41 (1978–79) 127–45. Reprinted in Gamble (ed.), *Articles*, 4:35–53. [Comparison of their thought.]

*REULOS, M. 'Le Décret de Gratien chez les humanistes, les gallicans et les réformés français du XVIème siècle', *Studia Gratiana* 2 (1954) 679–96. [692–96 on Calvin's use of Gratian.]

*REUTER, K. *Das Grundverständnis der Theologie Calvins* (Neukirchen-Vluyn: Neukirchener Verlag, 1963). [Much on influence of Bernard, *devotio moderna*, Scotus, Bradwardine and Gregory of Rimini on Calvin.]

*—— *Vom Scholaren bis zum jungen Reformator. Studien zum Werdegang Johannes Calvins* (Neukirchen-Vluyn: Neukirchener Verlag, 1981). [Thesis of previous book refined and developed.]

REUVER, A. DE *Calvin, Breuk of Brug? Over de spiritualiteit van Thomas a Kempis en Johannes Calvijn* (Utrecht: Faculteit der Godleerdheid, 1995). [Compares Thomas' *devotio* with Calvin's *pietas*.]

---

4 I have not seen this thesis, but cf. the next item.

RÉVEILLAUD, M. 'L'autorité de la tradition chez Calvin', *La revue réformée* 9 (1958) 25–45. [Status of fathers for Calvin.]

REYNOLDS, S. M. 'Calvin's View of the Athanasian and Nicene Creeds', *Westminster Theological Journal* 23 (1960–61) 33–37. Reprinted in Gamble (ed.), *Articles*, 9:125–29. [Considers whether Calvin changed his view between 1537 and 1559.]

*RICHARD, L. J. *The Spirituality of John Calvin: its Sources and Originality* (Cambridge (MA): Harvard University PhD thesis, 1971). Also *The Spirituality of John Calvin* (Atlanta: John Knox, 1974). [Much on Calvin's sources, especially his relation to *devotio moderna*.]

*RIST, G. *Objet et méthode de la théologie d'après saint Anselme, Abélard, saint Bernard, saint Thomas, Calvin et Karl Barth* (Geneva: Faculté autonome de théologie protestante thesis, 1964). [Includes a limited element of comparison.]

*RU, G. de *De Rechtvaardiging bij Augustinus, vergeleken met de leer der iustificatio bij Luther en Calvijn* (Wageningen: H. Veenman, 1966). [Chs 6f. compare Augustine and Calvin, drawing out similarities.]

RUSSELL, S. H. *A Study in Augustine and Calvin of the Church Regarded as the Number of the Elect and as the Body of the Faithful* (Oxford: Oxford University DPhil thesis, 1958). [Includes comparison on predestination, baptism and eschatology.]

*SCHÄR, M. *Das Nachleben des Origenes im Zeitalter des Humanismus* (Basel and Stuttgart: Helbing und Lichtenhahn, 1979). [226–28 on Calvin's use of Origen.]

*SCHELLONG, D. *Calvins Auslegung der Synoptischen Evangelien* (Munich: Chr. Kaiser, 1969). [46–52 on Augustine's commentary; later references relate this to Calvin.]

*SCHEPERS, B. M. *The Interior Testimony of the Holy Ghost: A Critique of John Calvin's Doctrine Establishing the Divine Authority of the Sacred Scripture* (Washington (DC): Dominican House of Studies Lector of Sacred Theology thesis, 1957). [63–71 on Calvin's use of Augustine quotation on authority of gospel/church.]

*SCHINDLER, A. 'Augustins Werk *De Civitate Dei* bei den Reformatoren, vor allem bei Luther und Zwingli' in J. van Oort (ed.), *De Kerkvaders in Reformatie en Nadere Reformatie* (Zoetermeer: Uitgeverij Boekencentrum, 1997) 35–44. Italian translation: 'Il *De civitate Dei* nelle biblioteche e nel pensiero dei Riformatori, soprattutto di Lutero e Zwingli' in E. Cavalcanti (ed.), *Il* De civitate Dei: *L'opera, le interpretazioni, l'influsso* (Rome: Herder, 1996) 435–46. [40f./444f. argue Calvin's use parallels Luther's and Zwingli's.]

SCHNEUWLY, J. 'La prédestination d'après Saint Thomas d'Aquin et Calvin', *Nova et Vetera* 6 (1931) 84–93. [Summary of Friethoff's book.]

*SCHREINER, S. E. *The Theater of his Glory: Nature and the Natural Order in the Thought of John Calvin* (Durham (NC): Duke University PhD thesis, 1983). Also (Durham (NC): Labyrinth Press, 1991). Also (Grand

Rapids: Baker, 1995) reprint.[5] [Includes comparison of Calvin with patristic and medieval thought.]

*SCHREINER, S. E. '"Through a Mirror Dimly": Calvin's Sermons on Job', *Calvin Theological Journal* 21 (1986) 175–93. Reprinted in Gamble (ed.), *Articles*, 6:231–49. [Calvin's sermons stand within tradition of Aquinas rather than Gregory the Great.]

*—— 'Exegesis and Double Justice in Calvin's Sermons on Job', *Church History* 58 (1989) 322–38. [Calvin's knowledge of and relation to medieval exegetical tradition.]

*—— *Where Shall Wisdom Be Found? Calvin's Exegesis of Job from Medieval and Modern Perspectives* (Chicago and London: University of Chicago Press, 1994). [Calvin's exposition read against the medieval background, especially Gregory, Aquinas and Maimonides.]

*SCHROTEN, H. *Christus, de Middelaar, bij Calvijn. Bijdrage tot de Leer van de Zekerheid des Geloofs* (Utrecht: P. den Boer, 1948). [207–27 draw parallels between Calvin and Irenaeus's doctrine of recapitulation.]

*SCHÜTZEICHEL, H. *Die Glaubenstheologie Calvins* (Munich: Max Hueber, 1971). [42–56, 68–121 on Calvin's sources and his attitude to scholasticism.]

*—— 'Calvins Protest gegen das Fegfeuer', *Catholica* 36 (1982) 130–49. Also in his *Katholische Beiträge zur Calvinforschung* (Trier: Paulinus-Verlag, 1988) 25–44. [144–47/39–42 on Calvin's approach to patristic material.]

—— 'Das altkirchliche Papsttum in der Sicht Calvins', *Catholica* 43 (1989) 31–53. Fuller version, 'Calvins Darstellung der Geschichte des Papsttums' in his *In der Schule Calvins* (Trier: Paulinus-Verlag, 1996) 150–97. [Calvin's approach to patristic material down to Gregory the Great / Bernard of Clairvaux.]

*SCOTT, T. *Remarks on the Refutation of Calvinism, by George Tomline, D.D. F.R.S.*, 2 vols (London: L. B. Seeley, 1811). Also, 1 vol. (London: L. B. Seeley, 1817 – 2nd edition). [Vol. 2, 223–556/557–591 respond to chs 5/6 of Tomline's 1811 volume; in the 2nd edition this reduced to pp. 690–710/711 only.]

*SELINGER, S. *Calvin Against Himself. An Inquiry into Intellectual History* (Hamden (CT): Archon Books, 1984). [Contains comparison of Calvin with fathers and medievals.]

SHARP, L. D. 'The Doctrines of Grace in Calvin and Augustine', *Evangelical Quarterly* 52 (1980) 84–96. [Comparison.]

SIBMACHER ZIJNEN, F. P. J. *Specimen Historico-Dogmaticum, quo Anselmi et Calvini placita de Hominum per Christum a Peccato Redemptione inter se conferuntur* (Delft: G. N. C. Roldanum and Schoonhoven: S. E. van Nooten, 1852). [Contrasts *Cur Deus Homo* and *Institutio*.]

*SIKTBERG, W. R. *The Mystical Element in the Theology of John Calvin* (New York: Union Theological Seminary thesis, 1951). [15–19 on Augustine and Bernard as sources for Calvin's thought.]

---

5 I have not seen the Baker reprint.

*SIMPSON, H. W. 'Wat Calvyn onder Reformasie Verstaan het in Vergely-king met Laat-Middeleeuse Idees in Verband Daarmee' in B. J. van der Walt (ed.), *Die Idee van Reformasie, Gister en Vandag* (Potchefstroom: Potchefstroomse Universiteit vir Christelike Hoër Onderwys, 1991) 47–82. [Despite the title, almost entirely on Roman Catholic environment of Reformation rather than Middle Ages.]

SMITS, L. 'L'autorité de saint Augustin dans "L'Institution Chrétienne" de Jean Calvin', *Revue d'histoire ecclésiastique* 45 (1950) 670–87. Also *L'autorité de saint Augustin dans "L'Institution Chrétienne" de Jean Calvin* (Louvain: Publications Universitaires de Louvain, 1950). [Calvin's attitude to fathers in general and Augustine in particular.]

—— *Saint Augustin dans l'oeuvre de Jean Calvin*, 2 vols. (Assen: van Gorcum, 1956/57 and 1958). [Vol. 1 is a magisterial study of Calvin's use of Augustine; vol. 2 contains exhaustive tables of Augustinian citations and allusions.]

—— 'Calvijn en de Oude Kerk', *Jaarboek der Rijksuniversiteit te Utrecht* (1958–59) 55–62. [Calvin's use of the fathers.]

SNELL, F. W. *The Place of Augustine in Calvin's Concept of Righteousness* (New York: Union Theological Seminary ThD thesis, 1968). [Augustine's relation to and possible influence upon Calvin.]

*SOUTHGATE, W. M. *John Jewel and the Problem of Doctrinal Authority* (Cambridge (MA): Harvard University Press, 1962). [165–72 on Calvin's attitude to the fathers.]

*STADTLAND, T. *Rechtfertigung und Heiligung bei Calvin* (Neukirchen-Vluyn: Neukirchener Verlag, 1972). [Ch. II:2–3 on Calvin's patristic and medieval sources.]

*STADTLAND-NEUMANN, H. *Evangelische Radikalismus in der Sicht Calvins. Sein Verständnis der Bergpredigt und der Aussendungsrede (Matth. 10)* (Neukirchen: Neukirchener Verlag, 1966). [B.I.1 on Calvin's sources, patristic (56–64) and medieval (64–70). Aquinas especially important.]

*STAUFFER, R. *Dieu, la création et la providence dans la prédication de Calvin* (Bern, etc.: Peter Lang, 1978). [151–58 on attitude to early tradition and dogma.]

STEINMETZ, D. C. 'John Calvin on Isaiah 6: A Problem in the History of Exegesis', *Interpretation* 36 (1982) 156–70. Reprinted in Gamble (ed.), *Articles*, 6:174–88. Also in J. L. Mays and P. J. A. Achtemeier (eds), *Interpreting the Prophets* (Philadelphia: Fortress, 1987) 86–99. Also as 'Calvin and Isaiah' in his *Calvin in Context* (New York and Oxford: OUP, 1995) 95–109. [Calvin compared with earlier tradition.]

*—— 'Luther and Calvin on Church and Tradition', *Michigan Germanic Studies* 10 (1984) 98–111. Reprinted in Gamble (ed.), *Articles*, 10:2–15. Also in G. Dünnhaupt (ed.), *The Martin Luther Quincentennial* (Detroit: Wayne University Press for Michigan Germanic Studies, 1985) 98–111. Also in *Luther in Context* (Bloomington: Indiana University Press, 1986; 2nd edition Grand Rapids: Baker, 1995) 85–97, 138. [Compares approach of Luther's *On the Councils and the Church* and Calvin's *Reply to Sadoleto*.]

STEINMETZ, D. C. 'Calvin and the Absolute Power of God', *Journal of Medieval and Renaissance Studies* 18 (1988) 65–79. Reprinted in Gamble (ed.), *Articles*, 9:1–15. Also in *Calvin in Context*, 40–52. [Calvin's approach set in medieval context.]

—— 'Calvin and the Patristic Exegesis of Paul' in D. C. Steinmetz (ed.), *The Bible in the Sixteenth Century* (Durham (NC) and London: Duke University Press, 1990) 100–118, 231–35. Also as 'Calvin and Patristic Exegesis' in *Calvin in Context*, 122–40. [Calvin's exegesis of Rom. 8:1–11 compared with Chrysostom and Ambrosiaster especially.]

*—— 'Calvin and the Natural Knowledge of God' in H. A. Oberman and F. A. James (eds), *Via Augustini: Augustine in the Later Middle Ages, Renaissance and Reformation* (Leiden: E. J. Brill, 1991) 142–56. Also in *Calvin in Context*, 23–39. [Calvin's exegesis of Rom. 1:18–32 compared with Augustine and Dionysius the Carthusian.]

—— 'Calvin among the Thomists' in M. S. Burrows and P. Rorem (eds), *Biblical Hermeneutics in Historical Perspective* (Grand Rapids: Eerdmans, 1991) 198–214. Also in *Calvin in Context*, 141–56. [Bucer and Calvin compared with Aquinas on Rom. 9.]

—— 'Calvin and the Monastic Ideal' in P. A. Dykema and H. A. Oberman (eds), *Anticlericalism in Late Medieval and Early Modern Europe* (Leiden: E. J. Brill, 1993) 605–16. Also in *Calvin in Context*, 187–98. [Calvin's attitude compared with that of Aquinas, Gerson and John Pupper of Goch.]

*—— 'Calvin and Tamar' in P. De Klerk (ed.), *Calvin as Exegete* (Grand Rapids: Calvin Studies Society, 1995) 145–61, followed by 'Response' by D. A. Weir (163–69). Also in *Calvin in Context*, 79–94. [Calvin's exegesis of Gen. 38 compared with that of Luther, Nicholas of Lyra, Hugh of St. Cher and Dionysius the Carthusian.]

*—— 'Calvin and the Baptism of John' in *Calvin in Context*, 157–71.[6] [Calvin's view compared with Zwingli and Hubmaier, in the light of Biel's account of medieval views.]

—— 'Calvin and the Irrepressible Spirit', *Ex Auditu* 12 (1996) 94–107. [Calvin's approach to II Cor. 3:6 in the light of Origen, Augustine and medieval exegetes.]

*—— 'Calvin as an Interpreter of Genesis' in Neuser and Armstrong (eds), *Calvinus Sincerioris Religionis Vindex*, 53–66. German translation: 'Luther und Calvin am Jabbokufer', *Evangelische Theologie* 57 (1997) 522–36. [Calvin's exegesis of Gen. 32:24–32 compared with that of Luther and Dionysius the Carthusian.]

—— 'The Scholastic Calvin' in C. R. Trueman and R. S. Clark (eds), *Protestant Scholasticism: Essays in Reassessment* (Carlisle: Paternoster, 1999) 16–30 [Assesses Calvin's relationship to scholasticism.]

---

6 An earlier version, 'The Baptism of John and the Baptism of Jesus in Huldrych Zwingli, Balthasar Hubmaier, and Late Medieval Theology' in F. F. Church and T. George (eds), *Continuity and Discontinuity in Church History* (Leiden: E. J. Brill, 1979) 169–81, does not contain the material on Calvin.

*Steinmetz, D. C. 'The Judaizing Calvin' in D. C. Steinmetz (hrsg.), *Die Patristik in der Bibelexegese des 16. Jahrhunderts* (Wiesbaden: Harrassowitz, 1999) 135–45. [Includes Calvin's attitude to patristic anti-Arian Exegesis.]

Stinson, C. H. *Reason and Sin according to Calvin and Aquinas – the Noetic effects of the Fall of Man* (Washington (DC): Catholic University of America MA thesis, 1966). [Ch. 3 compares Calvin and Aquinas.]

Stob, H. 'Calvin and Aquinas', *Reformed Journal* 24:5 (May–June 1974) 17–20. Also in his *Theological Reflections. Essays on Related Themes* (Grand Rapids: Eerdmans, 1981) 126–30. [Contrasting attitudes to nature, sin and grace.]

Strand, K. A. 'John Calvin and the Brethren of the Common Life', *Andrews University Seminary Studies* 13 (1975) 67–78. Reprinted in Gamble (ed.), *Articles*, 5:133–44. [Discusses influence of *devotio moderna* upon Calvin.]

—— 'John Calvin and the Brethren of the Common Life: The Role of Strassburg', *Andrews University Seminary Studies* 15 (1977) 43–56. Reprinted in Gamble (ed.), *Articles*, 2:193–206. [Continuation of previous item.]

*Strehle, S. *The Extent of the Atonement within the Theological Systems of the Sixteenth and Seventeenth Centuries* (Dallas: Dallas Theological seminary ThD thesis, 1980). [Ch. 2 on patristic and medieval background; 84–95 on Calvin.]

*—— *Calvinism, Federalism, and Scholasticism. A Study of the Reformed Doctrine of Covenant* (Bern, etc.: Peter Lang, 1988). [Reformed ideas against medieval scholastic background (ch. 1); 149–56 on Calvin.]

*—— 'Calvinism, Augustinianism and the Will of God', *Theologische Zeitschrift* 47 (1992) 221–37 [Mostly on Calvin*ism* and Augustinian*ism*; limited amount on Calvin and Augustine]

*—— *The Catholic Roots of the Protestant Gospel: Encounter between the Middle Ages and the Reformation* (Leiden, etc.: E. J. Brill, 1995). [On medieval roots of Reformation, including Calvin; ch. 5 substantially repeats previous item.]

Strimple, R. B. 'St. Anselm's *Cur deus homo* and John Calvin's Doctrine of the Atonement' in D. E. Luscombe and G. R. Evans (eds), *Anselm: Aosta, Bec, and Canterbury: Papers in Commemoration of the Nine-Hundredth Anniversary of Anselm's Enthronement as Archbishop* (Sheffield: Sheffield Academic Press, 1996) 248–60. [Comparison.]

Sturkenboom, A. J. M. *Het Traktaat 'Over de Sakramenten' bij Thomas Aquinas en Johannes Calvijn* (Nijmegen: University of Nijmegen doctoral thesis, 1968). [Ch. 4 compares Calvin and Aquinas, arguing differences not so great.]

TAMBURELLO, D. E. *Christ and Mystical Union: A Comparative Study of the Theologies of Bernard of Clairvaux and John Calvin* (Chicago: University of Chicago PhD thesis, 1990). Also *Union with Christ. John Calvin and the Mysticism of St. Bernard* (Louisville (KT): Westminster John Knox Press, 1994). [Primarily comparison of Calvin and Bernard, with discussion of Calvin's use of Bernard.]

*THOMAS, I. B. *John Calvin's Rejection of Roman Catholic Christianity* (New York: Union Theological Seminary ThD thesis, 1966). [Ch. 1 on Calvin's attitude to different phases of church history; chs 2–6 include medieval scholastic elements rejected by Calvin; ch. 7 on Calvin's acceptance of teachings of fathers and Anselm.]

*THOMPSON, J. L. 'The Immoralities of the Patriarchs in the History of Exegesis: A Reappraisal of Calvin's Position', *Calvin Theological Journal* 26 (1991) 9–46. [Calvin's exegesis in context of patristic and medieval exegesis.]

*—— *John Calvin and the Daughters of Sarah. Women in Regular and Exceptional Roles in the Exegesis of Calvin, his Predecessors and his Contemporaries* (Geneva: Droz, 1992). [Calvin's exegesis in context of patristic and medieval exegesis.]

TODD, W. N. *The Function of the Patristic Writings in the Thought of John Calvin* (New York: Union Theological Seminary ThD thesis, 1964). [Comprehensive study of Calvin's use of the fathers.]

*TOMLINE, G. *A Refutation of Calvinism: In which the Doctrines of Original Sin, Grace, Regeneration, Justification and Universal Redemption are Explained, and the Peculiar Tenets Maintained by Calvin upon these Points are Proved to be contrary to Scripture, to the Writings of the Ancient Fathers of the Christian Church and to the Public Formularies of the Church of England* (London: Cadell & Davies, 1811 and many reprints). [Ch. 5 has quotations from fathers opposed to Calvinism; ch. 6 has quotations from fathers showing similarities between Calvinism and early heresies.][7]

*TORRANCE, T. F. 'Knowledge of God and Speech about him according to John Calvin' in *Regards contemporains sur Jean Calvin. Actes du Colloque Calvin, Strasbourg, 1964* (Paris: Presses Universitaires de France, 1965) 140–60. Also in *Revue d'histoire et de philosophie religieuses* 44 (1964) 402–22. Reprinted in Gamble (ed.), *Articles*, 9:86–106. Also in his *Theology in Reconstruction* (London: SCM Press, 1965) 76–98. [Much on Calvin's relation to scholasticism.]

—— 'Intuitive and Abstractive Knowledge: from Duns Scotus to Calvin' in C. Balic (ed.), *De Doctrina Ioannis Duns Scoti*, vol. 4 (Rome: Congressus Scotisticus Internationalis, 1968) 291–305. [Historical development traced from Scotus to Calvin.]

---

7 See responses by Scott and Williams, above and below. There were many other reponses to Tomline which did not pick up the patristic element.

*Torrance, T. F. *The Hermeneutics of John Calvin* (Edinburgh: Scottish Academic Press, 1988). [73–79 on the influence on Calvin of the *Devotio moderna*; 80–95 on Major's mediation to Calvin of patristic and medieval scholastic tradition.]

—— 'The Doctrine of the Holy Trinity: Gregory of [*sic*.] Nazianzen and Calvin' in J. H. Leith (ed.), *Calvin Studies V* (Davidson (NC): Davidson: Davidson College, 1990) 7–19. Also as 'The Doctrine of the Holy Trinity in Gregory Nazianzen and John Calvin' in *Sobornost* 12 (1990) 7–24. Also as 'The Doctrine of the Holy Trinity in Gregory Nazianzen and Calvin' in his *Trinitarian Perspectives. Toward Doctrinal Agreement* (Edinburgh: T&T Clark, 1994) 21–40. [Comparison of Calvin and Gregory.]

*—— 'Calvin's Doctrine of the Trinity', *Calvin Theological Journal* 25 (1990) 165–93. Also in his *Trinitarian Perspectives*, 41–76. [Exposition of Calvin's doctrine, related to patristic teaching.]

Tylenda, J. N. 'Calvin and the Avignon Sermons of John XXII', *Irish Theological Quarterly* 41 (1974) 37–52. Reprinted in Gamble (ed.), *Articles*, 5:145–60. [Examination of Calvin's references to John XXII and the role of Gerson.]

*Ugolnik, A. 'The *Libri Carolini*: Antecedents of Reformation Iconoclasm' in C. Davidson and A. E. Nichols (eds), *Iconoclasm vs. Art and Drama* (Kalamazoo (MI): Medieval Institute Publications, 1989) 1–32. [Repeated reference to Calvin.]

*Urban, P. L. *The Will of God: a Study of the Origin and Development of Nominalism and its Influence upon the Reformation* (New York: General Theological Seminary STD thesis, 1959). [Ch. 6 relates Calvin to Late Middle Ages, arguing his indebtedness to and difference from Occam.]

*van Buren, P. *Christ in our Place. The Substitutionary Character of Calvin's Doctrine of Reconciliation* (Edinburgh and London: Oliver & Boyd, 1957). [Part II compares Calvin with Anselm, Lombard and Aquinas.]

*van de Merwe, N. T. 'Calvin, Augustine and Platonism. A Few Aspects of Calvin's Philosophical Background' in B. J. van der Walt (ed.), *Calvinus Reformator. His Contribution to Theology, Church and Society* (Potchefstroom: Potchefstroom University for Christian Higher Education, 1982) 69–84. Reprinted in Gamble (ed.), *Articles*, 4:117–32. [Augustine and Plato were important influences upon Calvin.]

van der Linde, S. 'Gereformeerde Scholastiek IV: Calvijn', *Theologia Reformata* 29 (1986), 244–66. [Calvin's use of and attitude towards medieval scholasticism.]

*van der Walt, B. J. *Die Natuurlike Teologie met besondere aandag aan die visie daarop by Thomas van Aquino, Johannes Calvyn en die Synopsis Purioris Theologiae – 'n wysgerige ondersoek* (Potchefstroom: Universiteit vir Christelike Hoër Onderwys PhD thesis, 1974). [Ch. 2:1:2 on pastristic and medieval influences on Calvin; ch. 6 compares *Institutio* with Aquinas' *Summa contra Gentiles* and the *Synopsis Purioris Theologiae*.]

*van der Walt, B. J. *Heartbeat. Taking the Pulse of our Christian Theological and Philosophical Heritage* (Potchefstroom: Potchefstroom University for Christian Higher Education, 1978 and reprints). [Ch. 14 is summary of previous item.]

*van der Woude, C. *Op de Grens van Reformatie en Scholastiek* (Kampen: J. H. Kok, 1964). French translation: 'Réforme et scolastique', *Études évangéliques* 25 (1965) 77–97. [8–10/82–84 on Calvin's attitude to scholasticism.]

Vanderschaaf, M. E. 'Predestination and Certainty of Salvation in Augustine and Calvin', *Reformed Review* 30 (1976–77) 1–8. [Comparison.]

van Oort, J. 'John Calvin and the Church Fathers' in I. Backus (ed.), *The Reception of the Church Fathers in the West*, vol. 2 (Leiden, etc.: E. J. Brill, 1997) 661–700. [Patristic elements in Calvin's writings and Calvin's knowledge and use of the fathers.]

—— 'Calvinus patristicus: Calvijns Kennis, Gebruik en Misbruik van de Patres' in van Oort (ed.), *Kerkvaders in Reformatie en Nadere Reformatie*, 67–81. [Abridgement of previous item with some new material.]

*van 't Spijker, W. 'Reformatie tussen Patristiek en Scholastiek: Bucers theologische Positie' in van Oort (ed.), *Kerkvaders in Reformatie en Nadere Reformatie*, 45–66. [45–47 discuss a letter of Calvin's on the authority of the fathers.]

Verhey, A. D. 'Natural Law in Aquinas and Calvin' in C. Orlebeke and L. Smedes (eds), *God and the Good* (Grand Rapids: Eerdmans, 1975) 80–92. [Comparison.]

*Vinay, V. 'La Riforma del XVI secolo e l'autorità dei concili', *Vita Monastica* 32 (1978) 59–68. [63–67 on Calvin's attitude to councils.]

*Vincent, G. *Exigence éthique et interprétation dans l'oeuvre de Calvin* (Geneva: Labor et Fides, 1984). [18–33/33–50 compare Calvin with Aquinas / Augustine.]

*Vos, A. *Aquinas, Calvin, and Contemporary Protestant Thought. A Critique of Protestant Views on the Thought of Thomas Aquinas* (Grand Rapids: Christian University Press, 1985). [Chs 1f. compare Calvin and Aquinas on the nature of faith.]

—— 'Calvin and Aquinas', *Theology Digest* 34 (1987) 337–41. [Calvin's attitude to Aquinas and extent of his knowledge of him.]

Walchenbach, J. R. *John Calvin as Biblical Commentator: An Investigation into Calvin's Use of John Chrysostom as an Exegetical Tutor* (Pittsburgh: University of Pittsburgh PhD thesis, 1974). [Calvin's exegetical use of Chrysostom.]

*Walker, D. A. *Creation, Salvation and the Triune God: A Study based on the Theology of St. Thomas Aquinas, John Calvin and Karl Barth* (Nottingham: Nottingham University PhD thesis, 1982. [Pt. II, on Calvin, contains small element of comparison with Aquinas.]

Walzer, M. 'Exodus 32 and the Theory of Holy War: The History of a Citation', *Harvard Theological Review* 61 (1968) 1–14. [Comparison of use of this passage by Augustine, Aquinas and Calvin.]

*WARFIELD, B. B. 'Calvin's Doctrine of God', *Princeton Theological Review* 7 (1909) 381–436. Reprinted in Gamble (ed.), *Articles*, 9:17–72. Also in his *Calvin and Calvinism* (New York, etc.: OUP, 1931) 133–85. Also in his *Calvin and Augustine* (Philadelphia: Presbyterian & Reformed, 1956) 133–85. [403–12/154–62 deny that Calvin was a Scotist.]

*WAWRYKOW, J. 'John Calvin and Condign Merit', *Archiv für Reformationsgeschichte* 83 (1992) 73–90. [Calvin not as unequivocally opposed to medieval concepts of merit as at first sight appears.]

*WENDEL, F. *Calvin, sources et évolution de sa pensée religieuse* (Paris: Presses Universitaires de France, 1950; 2nd edition, 'revue et complétée' Geneva: Labor et Fides, 1985). English translation: *Calvin, The Origins and Development of his Religious Thought* (London: Collins and New York: Harper & Row, 1963 and later reprints; Durham (NC): Labyrinth, 1987; Grand Rapids: Baker, 1997). German translation: *Calvin, Ursprung und Entwicklung seiner Theologie* (Neukirchen-Vluyn: Neukirchener Verlag, 1968). [Much in general and Part 2, ch. 1:II in particular on Calvin's sources.]

*WETTER, P. *Die Federstreit zwischen Sadolet und Calvin. Anlaß, Analyse beider Briefe (mit Beurteilung beider Argumente), Auswirkung* (Kampen: Theologische Hogeschool doctoral thesis, 1975). [27–32 on the issue of consensus with the Early Church.]

*WILLIAMS, E. *A Defence of Modern Calvinism: Containing an Examination of the Bishop of Lincoln's Work, Entitled A Refutation of Calvinism* (London: J. Black, 1812). [Chs 5f. respond to chs 5f. of Tomline's work.]

*WILLIS, E. D. *Calvin's Catholic Christology. The Function of the So-called 'Extra Calvinisticum' in Calvin's Theology* (Leiden: E. J. Brill, 1966). [Ch. 2 is on Calvin's traditional sources, patristic and medieval.]

*WITTE, J. L. 'Die Christologie Calvins' in A. Grillmeier and H. Bacht (hrsg.), *Das Konzil von Chalkedon, Geschichte und Gegenwart*, vol. 3 (Würzburg: Echter-Verlag, 1954) 487–529. [Calvin compared with Chalcedon.]

WOOD, G. D. *Clothed in his Righteousness: Calvin's Doctrine of Justification against the late medieval theological Background* (Cambridge (MA): Episcopal Theological School BD thesis, 1967). [Ch. 1 compares Thomas and Calvin; ch. 4 sets Calvin against the scholastic background.]

*WRIGHT, D. F. 'Basil the Great in the Protestant Reformers' in E. A. Livingstone (ed.), *Studia Patristica* 18 (Oxford and New York: Pergamon, 1982) 1149–55. [1149f. on Calvin's attitude to Basil.]

*—— 'Calvin's "Accommodation" Revisited' in De Klerk (ed.), *Calvin as Exegete*, 171–90. [172–75 + 184–87 discuss possible patristic sources.]

*—— '1 Corinthians 7:14 in Fathers and Reformers' in Steinmetz (hrsg.), *Die Patristik in der Bibelexegese*, 93–113. [105–107 compare Calvin and Augustine.]

YOU, H. Y. *Bonaventure and John Calvin: The Restoration of the Image of God as a Mode of Spiritual Consummation* (New York: Fordham University PhD thesis, 1992). [Comparison of Calvin and Bonaventure.]

ZILLENBILLER, A. *Die Einheit der Katholischen Kirche: Calvins Cyprianrezeption in seinen ekklesiologischen Schriften* (Mainz: Philipp von Zabern, 1993). [Calvin's ecclesiological use of Cyprian and comparison of them.]

—— 'Calvins Uminterpretation Cyprians bei der Beantwortung der Fragen: Auf wen ist die Kirche gegründet und Von wem wird der Bischof gewählt?' in Neuser and Armstrong (eds), *Calvinus Sincerioris Religionis Vindex*, 323–33. [Calvin's use of Cyprian and comparison.]

INDEX

For coverage of the indivuals and movements below, turn especially to the authors listed.

---

8 For works with a broader coverage which should not be ignored for information on individual figures.

Eusebius of Caesarea	Backus
Francis of Assisi	Brophy
Jean Gerson	Steinmetz; Tylenda
Gottschalk	Anderson; Lavaud
Gratian	Ganoczy; Reulos
Gregory Nazianzen	Torrance
Gregory I (pope)	Little; Schreiner
Gregory of Rimini	McGrath; Reuter
Hilary	Harman
Hugh of St Cher	Steinmetz
Jan Hus	Dobiás
Irenaeus	Backus; Meijering; Schroten
John XXII (pope)	Tylenda
Libri Carolini	Payton; Ugolnik
Nicholas of Lyra	Steinmetz
Novatian	Harman
William of Occam	Anderson; Lyon; Urban
Origen	Fickett; Lies; Schär; Steinmetz
Peter Lombard	Ganoczy; van Buren
Ratramnus	Barclay; Martin
Scotus/Scotism	Anderson; Hoitenga; Muller; Reuter; Torrance; Warfield
Tertullian	Márquez-André; Meijering
Thomas à Kempis	Goeters; Reuver

Index of Ancients (to 500)

Index of Medievals (500–1500)

Index of Early Moderns (1500–1700)

Index of Modern Authors